W9-BMV-364

THE OFFICIAL PRICE GUIDE TO

MOVIE

Autographs and Memorabilia

By Daniel Cohen

House of Collectibles
New York

Important Notice: All the information, including valuations, in this book has been compiled from the most reliable sources, and every effort has been made to eliminate errors and questionable data. Nevertheless, the possibility of error, in a work of such immense scope, always exists. The publisher will not be held responsible for losses that may occur in the purchase, sale, or other transaction of items because of information contained herein. Readers who feel they have discovered errors are invited to *write* and inform us, so they may be corrected in subsequent editions. Those seeking further information on the topics covered in this book are advised to refer to the complete line of *Official Price Guides* published by the House of Collectibles.

Copyright © 2003 by Daniel Cohen

All rights reserved under International and Pan-American Copyright Conventions. No part of this book may be reproduced or transmitted in any form or by any means, electronic or mechanical, including photocopying, recording, or by any information storage and retrieval system, without permission in writing from the publisher.

Published by House of Collectibles, 1745 Broadway, New York, New York 10019. Distributed by the Random House Information Group, a division of Random House, Inc., New York, and simultaneously in Canada by Random House of Canada, Limited, Toronto.

House of Collectibles and colophon are registered trademarks of Random House, Inc.

Random House is a registered trademark of Random House, Inc.

www.houseofcollectibles.com

Author photograph by Gus Sarino

Text design by Geraldine Sarmiento

Text composition by North Market Street Graphics

Printed in the United States of America

ISBN 1-4000-4731-5

ISSN 1547-0040

10 9 8 7 6 5 4 3 2 1

First Edition

For Rose

ACKNOWLEDGMENTS

I would like to thank Dorothy Harris, my editor, for her support and guidance throughout the process of writing this book. I would also like to thank Beth Levy, assistant managing editor, and Lisa Montebello, production manager, at House of Collectibles. I would also like to thank Roger Generazzo and Lindsey Glass for their guidance and assistance.

Thank you to the multitude of dealers and auction houses who extended their sales results, images, and expertise. I would personally like to thank Bob Eaton and Bill White (R&R Enterprises), John Kisch (PosterPrice.com), Fong Sam and Joseph Maddalena (Profiles in History), Debbie Weiss (Wonderful World of Animation), Laura Harden (MastroNet, Inc.), Lennard Billin (Reel Clothes), and Al Wittnebert (UACC).

Thank you to my customers, whose e-mails, telephone calls, and letters make collecting movie memorabilia both fun and inspiring and made the writing of this book truly enjoyable.

Thank you to my family and friends, who lent me their ears, eyes, and ideas.

Last, but not least, thank you to my wife and children, who unselfishly gave me up for the year and a half that this project needed.

CONTENTS

6 Collecting Oscar Statuettes   473

INTRODUCTION

Did you hear about the young couple who recently found over $1 million worth of rare movie posters insulating the walls of a home they were renovating? Did you know that the 1953 calendar of a nude Marilyn Monroe that your mother made your dad put away instead of hanging up in the kitchen could be worth up to $1,500 today? How about the *Star Wars* drinking cups you collected for twenty-nine cents at McDonald's—how does ten dollars apiece sound?

Movie memorabilia maintains one of the highest profiles of any genre of collectibles. Prestigious auction houses catalog rare vintage posters and celebrity autographs next to the works of Picasso and Tiffany. Celebrity-owned and -themed restaurants display movie props and costumes as their main attractions. Every new Hollywood blockbuster is unleashed with an onslaught of "instant collectibles" for the masses. The universal appeal of cinema and its stars has made nearly everyone a possessor of some form of movie memorabilia at some point in their lifetime.

Movie memorabilia items have evolved from promotional products designed strictly to sell theater tickets into revenue-generating mass-marketed commodities. This evolution directly follows the transformation of the moving picture technology of Thomas Edison into the commercial movie industry of Hollywood. The public hysteria created by the initial phenomenon of cinema was unparalleled in the early twentieth century in America. Thousands of patrons would wait hours to watch a movie about *anything*. This caused a huge explosion in the number of would-be film moguls and indirectly flooded the market with substandard and repetitive films.

The public quickly grew tired of watching moving pictures of circus animals doing tricks and the same sleight-of-hand gags from second-rate vaudeville acts. To claim the largest share of the public's interest and their money, forward-thinking moviemaking visionaries decided they had to come up with a formula to distinguish their films from others'. Their recipe called for the two main ingredients that have been the Hollywood standard ever since. First, they began making pictures of higher quality—molding their films around the finest works of fiction and nonfiction. The second ingredient, and arguably the most potent, was the creation of movie stars—men and women who would be idolized by the adoring fans as more beautiful, graceful, dashing, and funny than anyone they would ever meet in their daily lives. The public responded by rewarding the studios with huge grosses for their films and by elevating movie stars to a new form of American royalty.

Until the creation of secondary viewing markets for films, namely television and the VCR, the movie industry focused all its energy on promoting the latest and greatest new release. Promotional display products such as movie posters, lobby cards, and promotional stills were designed to sell a currently released film from a studio. Since this was their only form of promotion to a competitive marketplace, the studios spent lavishly on producing very high quality products. Once a film was replaced at the local theater with the studio's latest release, those promotional items were supposed to be thrown out and replaced by the new sets. Many theater owners and employees responded to these gorgeous works of art by personally keeping them or storing them in a back room. This act signaled the birth of collecting movie-related promotional items not designed for the consumer market.

As the drawing power of movie stars became more evident, the studios began to create promotional products tied in to a specific film or star as an attempt to recoup the increasing costs of producing the more extravagant and star-studded films. Studios licensed the images and characters from their films to a plethora of companies, including toy manufacturers, book publishers, and clothing companies.

As the Hollywood movie industry matured, it began to be widely viewed as a celebrated art form. The studios devised an award system in 1927, dubbed the Academy Awards, for rewarding the finest achievements in the areas of writing, producing, directing, and performing. Distinguishing specific films and performances as "the best" created the desire by audiences to revisit these films. The studios responded by re-releasing new prints of older films to a series of repertory theaters along with promotional materials related to these films—a new generation of posters and lobby cards, as well as selected merchandise such as toys and books. Starting in the late 1940s, films also began to find an extended life on the new medium of television.

Up until the late 1970s, studios looked at the secondary viewing markets and at the merchandising industries as nothing more than a minor revenue source. Two key elements changed their perceptions sharply.

The incredible popularity of the home videocassette recorder (VCR) created an entirely new offshoot industry for the movie studios, allowing them to rent and sell their films directly to the public. This also allowed the promotion of a film to be extended to what has now become a nearly endless life cycle—the original release in a theater, pay-per-view and satellite viewing, home video, and television replays. Studios were now able to carry over the promotion of a film to an endless array of merchandise that was no longer restricted to a limited lifetime.

Secondly, the *Star Wars* phenomenon saw a promotional merchandising mayhem ensue that was previously unthinkable, creating a wealth of revenue that continues to flood in more than twenty-five years after the release of the first film. Since *Star Wars,* merchandising now crosses over into almost every conceivable industry and product. The latest Hollywood blockbuster is welcomed with an assortment of fast-food restaurant collectibles, limited edition books, soundtracks on compact disc, plush toys, clothing, trading cards, action figures, multiple-image posters, and video games. The list goes on and on into a mind-numbing array of products that may bear little or no resemblance to the actual film or its characters. A popular film is now viewed as a merchandising franchise that can be more profitable over time than the actual box-office receipts generated by the film itself.

The saturation of memorabilia merchandise in the collecting marketplace has required a distinction to be drawn between the original vintage Hollywood collectibles, the reissued items, and the current collectibles dating from the early 1980s to the present. The terminology and methodology applied to vintage and modern collectibles is very different. What is termed rare in vintage items is not the same when applied to modern collectibles: vintage collectibles are rare because they were not intended to survive the journey of time, while modern collectibles are rare because they are marketed as rare by their manufacturers and are preserved by modern collectors in a pristine state.

The movie memorabilia collecting hobby has evolved over the last ninety years into an industry of multinational dealers and millions of collectors around the world. The most significant changes to the collecting landscape have occurred over the last decade. Television programs such as *Antiques Road Show* and *The Incurable Collector* have enlightened the average person about the incredible value that the long-forgotten and discarded treasures from our past have in today's collectibles markets. Highly publicized auctions for vintage movie memorabilia in all collecting areas have seen prices skyrocket above their estimated values. The Internet, and especially the eBay auction marketplace, has aided the massive expansion of collectors and caused a shift in the traditional relationship between buyers and sellers.

The negative impact of these events has also been felt. The sheer number and range of movie memorabilia available to the collector is staggering, leaving novice collectors overwhelmed and without a proper understanding of what determines value. The strain on supply and demand for quality authentic material has indirectly caused a flooding of the marketplace with illegal reproductions and forgeries by those trying to cash in on the popularity of the hobby.

The purpose of this collectors' guide is to serve as an illustrated journey through the history and diversity of film collectibles. Its aim is to become a valuable reference for the seasoned collector, and a much-needed introduction and explanation of the intricacies of collecting for the new collector. For each type of movie memorabilia covered in this book you will be presented with the prices these items are currently realizing at auction and through reputable dealers. The book will also extensively address the factors that will determine the future value of these collectibles—supply and demand, condition and preservation, authenticity, and future trends.

The complexities of movie memorabilia collecting have never been so dramatic, and the need for informative insight never greater. This guide will be an essential tool for anyone who is serious about starting or continuing a movie memorabilia collection in the twenty-first century.

THE OFFICIAL PRICE GUIDE TO

MOVIE

Autographs and Memorabilia

1 Autographs

THE HISTORY OF COLLECTING MOVIE STAR AUTOGRAPHS

The collecting of autographs of the famous predates the creation of the cinema by more than one hundred years. Before there were movie stars, requests for autographs were reserved for the elite newsmakers of society—namely politicians, explorers, authors, and composers. The requests for autographs of the players of cinema announced the arrival of a new celebrity: the movie star.

In the early days of Golden Hollywood during the 1920s and 1930s, gala movie premieres at Hollywood's grandest theaters provided the opportunity for stars to meet their adoring fans and to sign autographs. Fans would carry with them a small book with colored pages bound inside called an *autograph book*. When they met a celebrity, they would ask him or her to sign a page in the book. In modern times, when these loose-leaf pages are offered for sale, they are referred to as a signature on an *album page. See illustrations #1 and #2.*

Many times, the studios would produce photographs of the stars with a printed tag line on the bottom of the photo ("See Cary Grant now starring in Paramount's _____"). These photos would be handed out at the premieres, and the respective stars would meet their fans and sign the photos. In autograph terminology, this is referred to as an *SP (signed photograph). See illustration #3.*

The majority of filmgoers did not live in the major cities where the film premieres were held. The only method of communication they had was through letters of adoration sent to the Hollywood studios ("fan mail"). To solidify their fan base and to take advantage of the crossover marketing potential of these letters, the studios instructed their stars to respond with a return letter of thanks. They also made sure to promote their new film to be released shortly, and to comply with a simple autograph request at the bottom of the letter. In autograph terminology, these are referred to as *TLS (typed letter signed), ANS (autograph note signed),* and *ALS (autograph letter signed). See illustration #4.*

As the stars became more popular, more letters and autograph requests began to pour in to the studio mailrooms. Studios soon assigned secretaries to the stars to type personally addressed but routine content replies. The stars would then sit down and sign stacks of these pretyped letters at one time. In autograph terminology, these are referred to as *LS (letter signed)*. Requests for autographed photographs of the stars began to come in by mail, and the studios obliged by hiring the finest portrait photographers in the world (George Hurrell, Clarence Sinclair Bull). Stars would sign their gorgeous eight-by-ten-inch sepia-toned portraits in magnificent fountain pen inks with personalized sentiments ('To Jane Kennedy, Thank you for your kind letter. With Best Wishes"). In autograph terminology, these are referred to as *ISP (inscribed signed photograph).*

As a measure to reduce the now-multiplying overhead costs associated with fulfilling these requests, the studios reduced the overall size of the photographs that they would send out to smaller (and less expensive to reproduce and mail) five-by-seven and three-by-five formats. They also instructed their stars to sign stacks of these photographs in one sitting with a simple "Sincerely Yours" or "Best Wishes." The secretaries then filled autograph requests at their own pace with these presigned and unpersonalized photos.

1 A selection of vintage autograph albums

2 An autograph album page signed by Marilyn Monroe

3 Audie Murphy signed promotional photograph

4 Stan Laurel TLS on Laurel and Hardy letterhead

As the volume of requests became unmanageable, the studios and stars began to look at other methods to satisfy their fans' requests.

The Facsimiles

Hollywood historians would probably name Mary Pickford and Rudolph Valentino as the first true movie stars of Hollywood. It is also interesting to note, from an autograph collecting perspective, that both Pickford and Valentino were among the first stars to employ a mechanically produced version of their signature for autograph requests. The *rubber stamp,* as it is referred to in autographic terms, is a piece of rubber that has been carved out in the impression of a hand-drawn signature. When dipped in a pad of ink, the stamp is then applied to any flat surface (paper, photograph), leaving an ink impression that reproduces an original signature. *See illustration #5.*

Studio secretaries, and not the stars themselves, would now be the ones responding with "signed" letters, photographs, slips of paper, etc., bearing the rubber stamp–produced signatures of Valentino, Pickford, and soon many others. This would mark the first time that a movie star would have no direct contact with autograph request replies.

A very large percentage of "signed" photographs of Rudolph Valentino that surface in the autograph market today are in fact these rubber-stamped examples. Many of these fooled the original recipients and their heirs into believing they were authentic signatures, mostly due to the fact that they were used on dark photographs where the ink is difficult to see. On a surface allowing better contrast between the signature and paper, a rubber stamp signature is much easier to detect.

The rubber stamp proved to be a very impersonal response, so the studios and stars began employing studio secretaries to personally sign photographs, letters, and pages on behalf of the celebrity. In autograph terminology, this is referred to as a *secretarial.* Many times, a letter writ-

ten and signed by a secretary in his or her own name would accompany a secretarially signed photograph, stating "Mr. Gable enjoyed your letter very much and was more than happy to sign the enclosed photograph for your collection" (even though the photo was actually signed by the secretary). The intent was not to deceive, but merely to comply with the great number of requests using the most personal-looking response. Fortunately for the modern collector, secretaries were not forgers, and their signature patterns have become quite distinguishable from authentic examples upon comparison by an experienced collector or dealer. *See Illustrations #6 and #6A.*

Advancements in photographic reproduction technology in the 1940s allowed a generically signed photograph to be rephotographed and reproduced by the thousands, creating what is termed a preprinted signed photograph, or *pre-print* for short. *See illustration #7.*

For the several decades to follow, movie fans requesting an autograph through the mail for the most part received facsimile "signed" photos and applications to join various fan clubs. In the late 1960s and early 1970s a new development indirectly took movie star autograph collecting to the next level: Television stations began to replay classic films from Hollywood's Golden Age. This rekindled long-lost memories in the now middle-aged fans from this era and introduced the next generation (their children) to these classic films.

Autograph Redux

Out came the long-forgotten autograph albums and scrapbooks with pasted-in signed photographs collected thirty to forty years prior. Many of these now-older collectors wanted to continue their autograph collections, adding the signatures of the many stars they never met or wrote to. Many of these former stars, now in their sixties and seventies and long since retired, were overjoyed at the newfound interest in their careers. They happily spent their days writing back wonderful and spirited letters to all those who wrote with praise and requests for

5 Charlie Chaplin rubber stamp signature

6 Spencer Tracy Secretarial

6A Spencer Tracy Authentic Signed
Photo

their autographs. Collectors began to dig up vintage unsigned photographs at local flea markets and used bookstores and sent them off to be signed as well. In autograph terms, these
later-signed vintage photographs are termed *signed later in life*.

James Stewart spent a great many of his later years responding to all who wrote, personally
sketching and signing hundreds of drawings of Harvey the Rabbit from his beloved film
Harvey. Stan Laurel and Moe Howard wrote many replies commenting on their favorite
Laurel and Hardy and Three Stooges films. Urged on by the sheer volume of requests for autographed photos, many stars sat for their first new publicity photo sessions in over thirty
years. The collecting bug soon passed to the next generation, with autographed photos arriv-
ing in the mail in pairs—one for the parent and one for the child. Many collectors began to
seek out other collectors, forming autograph collecting clubs to trade duplicates and exchange
successful mailing addresses. A whole industry of selling home addresses of movie stars
began to emerge, filling the needs of the next generation of through-the-mail autograph collectors.

The desire to acquire vintage signed material from deceased movie stars was the catalyst for
many collectors to seek out and purchase long-forgotten and inherited autograph collections.
The economic rules of supply and demand then began to apply, with the finest and rarest
signed items beginning to trade hands to whoever was willing to pay or trade the most for
them. Factors determining value such as condition, content, and authenticity were established. Experienced collectors with extensive collections became dealers, publishing autograph catalogs and setting up tables at collectibles shows.

Autograph collecting through the mail continued to swell until the end of the 1980s. At that
time movie stars began to notice multiple requests from the same collector. Actors such as
Alan Alda began to keep a computer log of all those who wrote, limiting an autograph request
to one per collector for life. Many new collectors did not adhere to the courtesy rule of enclos-

7

7 Lana Turner Pre-Print

ing a self-addressed stamped envelope with their autograph request. Many movie stars, especially those who were retired and on fixed pensions, began to feel the pinch of having to spend thousands of dollars in return postage costs per year.

After the 1980s, nearly all through-the-mail autograph requests were answered with a preprint and/or secretarial-signed photo. Many studios and stars directly employed fan mail services that read, sorted, and replied to all autograph requests with mass-produced reproductions. In what may be an attempt to return to the days of trying to reply with an honest-looking authentic autograph, the use of a robotic signing machine called the *Autopen* was also employed. Autopens have been used by political figures since Presidents Eisenhower and Kennedy, but they found their way into the world of movie stars in just the last ten years. To the untrained eye, this is the most authentic-looking facsimile autograph one can receive. Tracing a pre-etched signature pattern, the machine can mechanically "sign" any type of flat surface from photograph to baseball hat rim. Autopen signature patterns appear to be authentic and cannot be determined as such without comparison to another Autopen signature from the same pattern. When held up to one another, the two signatures will match up almost perfectly. This is where the key to detection lies, as it is physically impossible for a human to sign his or her name exactly the same way twice. When two "signatures" match up, an Autopen pattern has been discovered.

Because it is exceedingly difficult today to receive an authentically signed autograph from your favorite Hollywood star through the mail, a new industry has evolved—the *in-person* autograph collector/dealer. In-person collectors live mostly in New York and Los Angeles, have contacts at all the major restaurants, nightclubs, hotels, and airports, and are on the scene within minutes when a call comes through that a movie star is on the premises. They wait for hours for the star to emerge and, if they are lucky, are rewarded with the star signing one or possibly a few photographs provided by the collector. To document this meeting, many in-person collectors will have photos taken of themselves with the star, or of the star signing the photos. These collectors then sell these signed photos to professional autograph dealers specializing in in-person signed photos, or sell them directly through on-line auctions.

The Current and Future State of the Hobby

The explosion of the Internet during the second half of the 1990s and into the new millennium has caused an incredible surge in both the number of autograph collectors and the global expansion of the hobby. The chances of receiving an authentic autograph by writing to your favorite star are very slim. Movie stars' personal security issues have sharply limited their public accessibility, making it increasingly difficult to obtain an in-person signature. The strain on supply and demand for quality authentic material has indirectly caused a flooding of forgeries into the marketplace by those trying to cash in on this burgeoning industry.

These factors are contributing to a swell in prices for authentic material, especially vintage and rare items. One can only assume that prices will continue to rise as new collectors look to add these rare items to their own collections.

As for the current stars of modern cinema, many have begun to set up their own avenues to sell their signed photographs directly to their fans via authorized personal signing sessions with approved dealers or retailers directly linked with the studios. Many retired stars have set up their own Internet Web sites to sell various signed photographs and other memorabilia. Disney, Universal Studios, and MGM have already begun to sell and auction off memorabilia from their own stars and films.

As long as there are movie stars, and the fans who want to collect their autographs, the mechanics of this hobby will surely continue to evolve.

FACTORS DETERMINING VALUE

Collecting autographs is a very exciting and challenging hobby that can bring you hours of enjoyment. It also reward you with amazing treasures of both emotional and monetary value. Whether you are a novice or experienced collector, whether your collection is for personal fulfillment or a serious investment tool (or a little of both), there are some crucial factors that *must* be considered when adding any autographed item to your collection. The more familiar a collector is with these factors, the better suited he or she will be to make educated and valuable additions to a collection.

The three most important variables are *Authenticity, Condition,* and *Content.* The combination of all three components determines the current value of an autographed item and the potential it has to attain a higher value in the future.

Authenticity

Authenticity is the most important factor when looking at autographs. If an item is not authentically signed by the celebrity in question, there is little or no value to the item. The only exception to this is a secretarial, Autopen, or rubber stamp–signed letter that contains exceptional and historical content, which would then have an overall value that is not being determined by the signature. Forgeries have absolutely no value whatsoever, except as an educational tool for the collector/dealer in understanding and identifying chronic forgeries entering the marketplace. A vintage unsigned photograph that has a $50 value becomes absolutely worthless when signed with a forged signature.

Types of Nonauthentic Signatures

Forgery
A signature created by an individual other than the celebrity with the intent to deceive.

Secretarial
An authorized signature created by an individual on behalf of the celebrity.

Autopen
An authorized signature created by a robotic machine on behalf of the celebrity.

Pre-Print
A photograph bearing a reproduction of an original signature.

Rubber Stamp
A reproduction of an original signature by a rubber stamp and inkpad.

Condition

After an item has been determined to be authentically signed, it is brought under the looking glass for an assessment of its condition. The condition of an item can severely affect the overall value, and can play an integral role in determining future value. The condition of an authentic autographed item can become one of the most important factors for the experienced collector when making a decision to purchase one of several signed items from the same celebrity. In basic terms, the better the condition of an item, the more valuable it is in comparison to other autographed items from the same celebrity in the same format.

Dealers and auction houses use a grading system and basic terminology to classify the condition of an item. Every dealer has his or her own methods and scales; some use a number scale from one to ten, but most use terms such as Excellent, Fine, Good, all the way down the scale to Poor. Dealers also use specific terminology such as "four pinholes in each corner," "moderate age toning," "mounting traces on the reverse side," "moderate contrast to the signature," "expected age wear," "slight creasing," etc.

The extent to which the condition of an item determines the overall value is directly linked to the rarity of that item or celebrity. The rarer an item is the more forgiving a collector will be on the condition factors. If a collector has the ability to choose among three or four similar signed items of the same celebrity, then the condition of the item becomes one of the more important factors.

In the different autograph formats, the following factors can determine overall condition:

Signatures

Signature prices in the general listings of this guide reflect a clean ink signature, on a sheet of paper or cut from a document or letter, with enough room around the signature to allow it to be properly matted for display. Variables that can lessen the value of a signature include ink smears or fading, paper wrinkles or tears, gluing of the signature page to another sheet underneath, or an irregularly cut sheet that is not mattable or able to be displayed. Pencil signatures of the more common name celebrities have a 50 percent value of ink signatures due to lesser presentability of the signature. The rarer the signature, the less the ink/pencil ratio becomes a factor.

Signed Letters and Documents

Signed letter and document prices in the general listings of this guide reflect a clean ink signature on a sheet of paper that appears the same as the day it was signed. Variables that can lessen the value of a signed letter include ink fading and page yellowing due to excessive exposure to daylight, tears, repairs with nonarchival tape, nonarchival mounting to another page or board, and laminating or varnishing of the letter. Expected age wear and toning to vintage items is overlooked with rare or one-of-a-kind items.

Signed Photographs

Signed photograph prices in the general listings of this guide reflect a clean ink signature with good signature contrast in relation to the image. Variables that can lessen the value of a signed photograph include ink fading and photo yellowing from excessive daylight exposure, tears, repairs with nonarchival tape, nonarchival mounting to another page or board, laminating or varnishing of the photo, and silvering of the image due to chemical deterioration in the print. Expected age wear and toning to vintage items are overlooked with rare or one-of-a-kind items. Inscriptions on photographs do not generally lessen the value of rare items. For common celebrities, inscriptions reduce the overall value of a signed photograph by up to 50 percent.

Content

After an item has been determined to be authentic, and the condition has been classified, the next important factor that distinguishes an autographed item from all others in the marketplace is the *content* of the item.

Content refers to the significance of the item in relation to the celebrity in reference. For example, a signed photograph of Clark Gable as Rhett Butler or a historically significant signed contract is considered better content than a signed portrait or routine document. All autograph items with exceptional content are regarded as the Holy Grail pieces of autograph collecting. Historically, pieces with the best content appreciate the most in value. When seeking to purchase an autographed item in any format, look for the best possible content available in your price range.

Content can vary so significantly across all autograph formats that it has made it virtually impossible to accurately price autographed items in this guide according to content. All listings in this guide refer to routine content, meaning nothing greater than average for that format. The selected Celebrity Autograph Feature of this guide illustrate how exceptional content for certain celebrities and items can vastly increase the overall appeal and value of an item. What follows is an explanation of the relationship between content and value for each autograph format.

Signatures

Content applies to signatures when the document also includes an inscription to a significant recipient. For example, a signature by Marilyn Monroe inscribed to John F. Kennedy would have a tremendous increase in value over an example inscribed to an unknown "To John." Another type of signature content would be an added character name or film reference—a signature of Judy Garland with an added "Dorothy, *The Wizard of Oz*" would be worth many times more than just a simple signature. As content in signatures is unique, *all signature prices in the general listings in this guide are reflective of no content.*

Signed Letters

Content in signed letters is very important in determining the overall value. A letter written by a celebrity to a secret love, or one that refers directly to a famous role, can have significantly more value than a routine thank-you letter to a fan. The more historic the content of the letter, the greater the appeal and overall value. *All prices for signed letters in the general listings in this guide reflect routine content.*

Signed Photographs

Content in signed photographs can refer to several areas. The size of a photograph can determine value. Traditionally eight-by-ten-inch and smaller photographs are most common; larger formats like ten-by-thirteen, eleven-by-fourteen, and larger are much rarer, and therefore a larger format can indicate better content. A photograph of the star in the prime of his or her life is considered better content than a later-in-life pose. Second, a photograph that depicts the star in a famous role is considered better content than a lesser-known role. Prices for signed photographs with exceptional content can far exceed routine poses. *All prices for signed photographs in the general listings in this guide reflect routine content:* the most common signed portrait for that star (black-and-white poses for vintage stars, color poses for modern stars) and a common size of eight-by-ten.

Signed Documents

Content in signed documents is very important in determining overall value. A signed contract that refers to a famous or Academy Award–winning role is much more valuable than a routine employment contract signed with a management agency. A signed check made payable to another celebrity is worth more than one endorsed to the local supermarket. *All prices for signed documents in the general listings in this guide reflect routine content.*

Long-Term and Future Values

The *emotional value* a collector places on an item is based on his or her own personal connection with a celebrity or a film. Someone who has a treasured memory linked to a particular film may place more value on a signed poster from that film than another collector who did not care as much for it. When emotions dictate how much a collector pays for an autographed item, the emotional value of the item becomes more important than the physical factors detailed previously.

When many collectors share the emotional value of an item or celebrity, the economic rules of supply and demand take over. The rarer an item is, and the greater the number of collectors wanting that item, the more valuable it becomes to the marketplace as a whole. Today's hot star may be a very difficult autograph to obtain. The demand from the many collectors wanting to add that autograph to their collections right now will cause the price for that celebrity's autograph to rise. A few years later, that celebrity's fame may fade, and in turn, he or she may become more accessible and willing to sign. As the quantity of available autographs from a celebrity increases in the marketplace and the demand fades, the prices subsequently fall.

As stars pass away, the new supply of autograph material ends, causing collectors to do battle for the existing pieces. As long as the demand for a particular celebrity's autograph material remains strong, the prices remain solid. There have been cases where the quantity of available material of a deceased celebrity sometimes increases because of previously unforeseen forces other than lack of demand. Descendants of a deceased celebrity may unleash hundreds or even thousands of signed canceled checks or other signed, posthumous material to the marketplace. An otherwise rare and expensive autograph can suddenly become common beyond demand. This flooding of the market can cause the prices for all signed material from that particular celebrity to significantly drop, sometimes for many years.

What Makes One Celebrity More Valuable than Another?

Ever-shifting population demographics alter and shape the autograph collecting landscape on a daily basis. As the prevailing population that dictates the hot trends shifts, prices adjust accordingly. Currently, the most powerful generation of collectors in the marketplace is in the forty- to fifty-year-old range. They grew up with the stars of Golden Hollywood, the Golden Age of Television, and the explosion of rock and roll, and this is where their collecting interests lie. The prices for the autograph material of Marilyn Monroe, James Dean, the Beatles, and the classic television shows *I Love Lucy* and *The Honeymooners* have hit a fever pitch, as the supply of quality material from these names far underweighs the demand from these collectors. Collectors in this age bracket have large discretionary incomes to spend on these gems, so the market prices for the items on their collecting palettes are increasing far more than others.

What Autographs Will Be Worth the Most in the Future?

Historically, the autographs of Hollywood legends such as Marilyn Monroe, James Dean, and Humphrey Bogart have fared the best over time. The main reasons for this are a very limited supply of autograph material to a very large and continually expanding population of collectors looking to add these pieces to their collections. Will these stars mean as much to the collectors of twenty or thirty years from now? Will modern stars such as Arnold Schwarzenegger, Julia Roberts, Russell Crowe, and Tom Cruise become the autograph treasures of the future, and will the next generation care about the earlier legends?

One could argue that a limited supply of maybe one thousand Marilyn Monroe signatures is available to about two million current collectors. Twenty years from now, a community of twenty million collectors may be able to choose from a supply of possibly ten thousand Julia Roberts autographs. How many of those twenty million collectors will also want Marilyn Monroe's autograph? What percentage of those original one thousand pieces will be held by collectors who do not want to sell their treasures for any price? How many will be available for sale, and at what price?

It is impossible to accurately predict what celebrities will be most in demand in the future, and it is financial suicide to purchase everything and anything that is valuable today in hope of striking it rich with your collection years from now. An autograph collector should always be comfortable with the price he or she pays for any item. If and when a collector makes a decision to sell that autographed item in the future, the current generation of market-driving collectors will determine the value.

STARTING AND BUILDING AN AUTOGRAPH COLLECTION

The building of an autograph collection quickly becomes a passion for many collectors. The number of movie stars to collect, and the methods and formats of obtaining autographed items available to you, are almost endless. Only your patience, persistence, and financial resources limit the extent to which you can collect autographs.

Whether you collect autographs by writing away to your favorite stars, by trading with other collectors, or by purchasing them through dealers and on-line auction houses, it is important to understand the risks and rewards associated with each. The following details the pros and cons of collecting autographs through each method.

Collecting Autographs Through the Mail

If you do not live in a major city, like Los Angeles or New York, the chances of meeting your favorite movie stars can be remote. Even if you are fortunate enough to meet them, they are becoming harder and harder to approach because of personal security issues. One of the most creative and cost-effective ways to collect autographs of your favorite current stars is to write them a letter requesting an autograph.

Whom Should I Write To?

The choice is up to you. First, you have to decide if you are going to be writing to specific celebrities, or if you are going to try to write to as many stars as possible. If you choose the latter, you will quickly realize that not only will you be spending every waking moment of your life writing letters, but you will quickly become disappointed with a very poor rate of success.

Movie stars of all levels of fame receive *thousands* of letters weekly, all requesting autographs, charitable donations, etc. Try writing to actors and actresses who are not yet feature stars. Many of Hollywood's legends spent years as bit players in many films before finding fame as leading men and starlets. Many of the most prized signed photos and letters from vintage Hollywood stars came from when they were on the rise and were honestly touched by receiving a fan letter, responding with wonderful letters and gorgeous signed photos.

Many retired and aging stars spend their days replying to fan mail. Many are grateful that they are still in the public conscience and are thankful for sincere and respectful requests for their autographs.

What Should I Say?

Write a sincere, honest, and unique letter that will get the attention of the star, and hopefully he or she will reward you with an autograph for your hard work.

Handwrite your letter. Handwritten letters are perceived as much more personal than a typed letter. Typed letters appear cold and may get mistaken for junk mail. If you have poor penmanship, improve your handwriting.

Letters should be no longer than one page in length, preferably less. You may think your letter is important, but to the star it is just one in the pile, and no one has time to read an essay from a stranger.

Be complimentary and to the point. Mention a favorite performance or film of theirs and why you liked it. Do not go into too much detail, as stars are very sensitive to letters that may sound threatening or harmful in any way.

Ask them for their autograph. Mention that you are starting to collect autographs, and that their autograph would make a valuable addition to your collection. If you are collecting Oscar winners, mention that you need their autograph to add to your collection, even if they haven't won one yet (make sure you tell them that you think they will one day be a winner).

Thank them. Just because you have taken the time and expense to write and send this letter off does not obligate the star to read or reply to your request. Thank them for taking the time to read your letter and for complying with your autograph request.

What Do I Ask to Be Signed?

When you request an autograph through the mail, it is generally good form to send the item to be autographed with your letter. Sending a letter requesting that the celebrity send you a signed photograph puts the cost of the photograph on the celebrity, and this severely reduces your chances of receiving a reply. If you want a signed photograph, purchase an unsigned photograph and send it to be signed.

Request no more than one autograph. Collectors have sent various items, from three-by-five index cards and a favorite photograph to movie posters and video boxes. An important thing to consider when sending an item to be signed is that there is a very good chance you may never get your item back. Never send a rare or cherished item to be signed without sending a prior letter mentioning the item and requesting it to be signed. If you get a positive response, then proceed. Another consideration is that the larger the item you send, the more expensive your mailing costs will be for your request.

Addresses

There are many places where movie stars receive fan mail. You can send your letters to the movie studio that produced their latest film or to the address of their management or production companies, or you can purchase address lists from some companies advertising home addresses of movie stars. Many stars resent receiving fan mail at their homes and will flatly return all letters sent to their home address.

One of the best resources for star addresses is available at your local library. *Who's Who in America* lists thousands of celebrities in all fields and in most cases lists a contact address. This resource is especially good for many of the retired stars who do not have current studios to forward their mail.

Always Enclose a SASE

A self-addressed stamped envelope (SASE) is essential for improving your chances of getting a reply. You are already taking the valuable time of the stars to read and reply to your request; asking them to pay for your return letter is not only selfish but unreasonable. Many retired stars live very modestly, and the added expenses of return postage can be a struggle for them, even if they truly do value your request. Always consider what the postage costs will be for your return letter and include the SASE with all requests.

If you are writing to a star in another country, enclose in your letter an International Reply Coupon (available at the post office) to cover return postage. The coupon is exchangeable by the star for postage costs in their country. He or she will appreciate the extra effort and the consideration on your part.

If You Receive a Reply

Congratulations! The fun has just begun. A successful autograph reply *does not* require a thank-you follow-up. If you do decide to send a thank-you, make it very brief, in the form of a thank-you card, mention how grateful you are for the reply, and leave it at that. *Do not request more autographs* or expect another reply. Many collectors believe a successful reply is an invitation to send another request, this time for countless signed photos and other items. You just may lose those photos, and indirectly turn the celebrity off from replying to other collectors.

The Downside: *Rate of Success*

Before you run off to pick up hundreds of stamps, envelopes, and sheets of lined paper, there are certain facts you must understand as reality before you get your expectations up too high.

Depending upon the celebrities, addresses, and content of your letters, your *reply ratio* will be probably a lot lower than you may have hoped. The most successful through-the-mail autograph collectors have a reply ratio of around 5 to 10 percent.

In addition to this low response rate, and again depending on the factors above, the *success ratio* of receiving an authentic autograph may be very small. What could you find inside your return envelope other than the autograph material you requested?

- You may receive your material returned unsigned, but enclosed with it an authentically signed photo supplied by the celebrity. In this case, a star has sat down and signed a stack of these photos for the staff to return to fans requesting autographs.

- Some may include a pre-print photo with a facsimile autograph.

- Some celebrities will reply with a facsimile-signed form letter thanking you for your letter but stating that they are unable to fill your request due to any number of reasons (they will most likely return your material unsigned as well).

- Some may include information on joining their fan club, which may offer authentically signed photos and a monthly newsletter in exchange for a yearly membership fee.

- Other celebrities may return your material unsigned with an enclosed letter asking for a fee (which can range from $10 to $50 per item depending on the celebrity). Many say that this has been instituted due to the volume of mail they receive from resellers presenting themselves as collectors who then turn around and sell the autographs that the celebrity has taken the time to sign.

- There is also the chance that you will receive your return envelope without your material returned back to you.

If you receive what appears to be an autograph on the item you sent in, you will have one of a few things (listed in the most common form, based on experience):

1) *Secretarial.* Get out the reference guides (catalogs, Web sites) of autograph dealers who are *known to sell authentic material* and compare your example to in-person signed examples, as well as signed documents that date from as recent as possible. Through-the-mail signatures may not match up 100 percent to the rushed in-person examples, but the characteristics and flow should be there. Try to look at as many authentic reference examples as possible. Use the reproduced signatures in this book as a guide. Correspond with other through-the-mail collectors in on-line newsgroups and find out who else has had success with these stars and what their replies looked like. If a celebrity has been known to use secretaries for many years, that does not mean that your example is guaranteed to be a secretarial. Some stars personally sign some requests when they have time off, and some revert to secretaries when they are flooded with mail (after the release of a hit movie, for example).

2) *Autopen.* If your item is not inscribed to your name, and the signature appears to be shaky and jerked in certain places, your item may have been signed using the robotic signing machine called the Autopen. The only way to determine this is to compare your signature with those received by other collectors. If they match up, you have an Autopen example.

3) *An authentic autograph!* Congratulations and happy collecting!

Trading Autographs with Other Collectors

Once you have begun collecting autographs, you may want to connect with other collectors to share successful addresses, learn which stars do not respond to autograph requests by mail, and possibly trade some of the autographs in your collection for some that may not be obtainable anymore.

Start locally in your own city or state. Check the Yellow Pages for collectibles stores in your area. Pay them a visit and find out if there are any collectibles clubs that get together. If not, talk to the store owners and see if they think there would be enough collectors in your area to start one. Post a newsletter in the store, and you may be surprised how many calls you get.

Subscribe to collectibles publications. The publications listed in this book offer classified ads that collectors use to advertise items they are buying or selling and items they are willing to trade.

Use on-line newsgroups. On-line newsgroups are another electronic classified ad venue to meet and correspond with other collectors.

Join national and international autograph collectors' clubs. The autograph clubs listed in this book offer quarterly publications that publish addresses of collectors you can contact, as well as classified ads for buying, selling, and trading autographs.

Whatever means you use to connect with other collectors, you should always proceed with trades cautiously and never assume that every trade will go off without any hitches. Use these tips to make your trades more successful for both parties:

- If you cannot meet in person to make a trade, always request an electronic scan of the item by e-mail or a color photocopy by mail so you can check the authenticity of the item before making the trade. Remember, your trading partner may not be experienced in authenticating, and may mistake a forgery, pre-print, Autopen, or secretarial for an authentic example. It is much harder trying to exchange your item after a trade has been done. If the item is in fact one of these facsimiles, inform the other party.

- Always describe the condition of your item with as much detail as possible. Condition is a very personal issue for collectors, and every person has a different opinion of what defines "mint" and "poor."

- If both parties come to an agreement over the items to be traded, an agreement to ship the respective items to each other must be made that satisfies both sides. As you build up a relationship with other collectors, and a reputation as a solid trade partner, experienced traders will be more trusting to send you items. Try to come up with a complementary method of shipment. Sending each parcel by registered mail, which requires both parties to sign at both ends of shipment and arrival, at an agreed-upon ship date, and following up with the tracking numbers to each other is a good method.

- Ask for trading references. Ask for the names and contact telephone numbers of other collectors who have traded with this partner before. *Do not trust e-mail.* E-mail is anonymous, and you have no idea with whom you are corresponding. Make brief calls to the references, state that you are considering doing a trade with this collector, and ask for their advice and how their trade experience went.

Trading autographs with other collectors will allow you to expand your collection in a way that doesn't cost you much more than postage. You will also make friendships with collectors who have similar interests to your own—including autographs. It will also prepare you for the next big step in expanding your autograph collection, making an autograph purchase.

Buying Autographs

As your autograph collection grows, you will want to add the autographs of stars that are either unobtainable by mail or too costly to trade for based on the current roster of your collection. You may also want to begin adding rare and one-of-a-kind items to your collection.

There are many venues and types of sellers from whom you can purchase autographed items. You can find autographed items for sale at local garage sales, flea markets, collectibles stores and shows, on-line auction venues like eBay and Yahoo, professional autograph dealers, and high-profile live auction houses like Sotheby's and Christie's. Each has its own distinct benefits and possible drawbacks, and depending on your level of expertise in terms of authenticity and the amount of trust you are willing to put in a seller, many great authentic items await you. As you work down the following list of different seller types, the degree of responsibility shifts from the buyer to the seller. The following will assist you in making purchases from each and all.

Flea Markets and Garage Sales

These are the least authoritative sources for finding autograph material, meaning they are not experts, nor do they profess to be, and they make absolutely no guarantees regarding authenticity or refunds. At garage sales, you will be looking at the collections of one of the children, or possibly the parents or grandparents (if you are lucky). At flea markets, sellers are trying to sell off either part of their own collections, or autographed items they acquired as part of bulk purchase of material from an estate or garage sale. In exchange for purchasing the more desirable items for resale (furniture, appliances, etc.), the seller has purchased the other contents as part of a package deal. Many times, sellers have already made back their profits on the larger items and are basically looking to get whatever they can for what remains.

At these types of venues the process of authenticating autographed items is purely up to you. Most prices will be set very reasonably, and there are many opportunities to pick up great deals at this level if you are sharp and a good negotiator. Many times, a seller may only want to sell a stack of the autographed items as a whole. There may be some good pieces, and some facsimiles, and you will have to figure out how much you are willing to pay for the good items, and write off the rest of the lot.

Collectibles Stores and Shows

This category references retail stores and collectibles shows *that do not specialize in autographs*. These can include your local comic book or sports card store, a used-book or movie poster store, a stamp collectors' store, or even an antiques store. Again, many of these sellers may have acquired autographed items as part of a collection they purchased, or they may be private collectors themselves. Many times, they will not display these items, as they do not fit in with the format of the store, but it never hurts to ask the shop owner if he or she has any autographed items for sale. The authenticity factor will rely upon you, the buyer, and you should not expect a guarantee from the seller in terms of authenticity.

Specialty shops selling rare books, stamps, or posters have a different method of pricing from that of an autograph dealer. A book dealer selling an autographed book will price the item according to the book value, and add a nominal price in for the autograph component. Many times, this pricing structure can benefit you as an autograph collector, as you will be placing more value in the autograph than the book itself.

High-profile tourist stops such as Walt Disney World or Universal Studios sell autographed items in their gift shops. The store managers and corporate buyers have purchased autographed items from various sources and have had them professionally framed in an elaborate presentation. There are many things to consider when purchasing autographed items from these sources. The fact that the retailer is a well-known and respected enterprise does not automatically mean that all items for sale will be authentic. Their authenticity will be only as reliable as the sources they were acquired from. As resellers, these retailers are not obligated to disclose their original sources. Approaching these sellers after the sale with a dispute over authenticity can be tricky, and many will not warrant returns based on this factor. Finally, the price you will be paying to this seller incorporates the original purchase price, the cost of the framing, the overhead costs of running a high-profile retail establishment, and the healthy markup that has made these businesses so successful. I have personally seen what are $50 valued autographs with $200 framing jobs sell for over $800 in these stores. If you are looking for a wonderful autograph display for your home, they do a great job. But you may be disappointed when you are offered a fraction of your purchase price down the road if you decide to sell that item.

eBay and Other On-line Auction Sites

These venues are quickly becoming a very popular choice for novice and experienced collectors to buy their autographed items. Refer to the Auction Houses and Retailers reference in this guide for contact information for these venues.

Some on-line auction houses are known as a person-to-person marketplace, where transactions take place between an individual buyer and seller. Registered sellers include professional autograph dealers or auctioneers, nonautograph collectible retailers, on-line flea market bulk sellers, and everyday people who have a family heirloom or personal collectible to sell.

There are many benefits to using eBay and other person-to-person auction marketplaces to purchase autographed items. The sheer volume of autograph merchandise available on eBay is overwhelming, even to experienced autograph dealers. There are hundreds of categories and subcategories where autograph items are listed. I personally scour an average of about ten thousand autographed items *a day*. The range of material available covers all celebrities and their respective price ranges. Best of all, because these items are being sold in an auction venue, you get to determine your price. Many times, I have purchased items for far less than I would have paid in conventional buyer-seller transactions.

There are also some serious risks and concerns one has to understand about these venues. EBay and other person-to-person auction houses act strictly as the marketplace—they will not take any responsibility for guaranteeing the authenticity of any autographed item bought or sold through their sites. Their aim is to remain neutral, and allow the buyer and seller to agree upon a displayed set of rules that have been preset by the seller. These include policies regarding authenticity, returns, guarantees, payment terms, shipping terms, geographical locations they will ship to, and t he like. By bidding on a seller's item you are agreeing to the seller's terms.

Partly because of this neutrality, these venues have inadvertently become the homes of many fraudulent sellers offering pre-prints, secretarials, Autopens, and blatant forgeries misrepresented as authentic autographs to an unsuspecting mass of millions of potential bidders. Educating yourself as an autograph collector about the forces working both for and against you is imperative when dealing in these venues. The following tips will help make your experiences more enjoyable and successful.

Make use of feedback. Each registered buyer and seller (or user) is assigned a feedback profile, which allows the buyer and seller of a successful transaction to leave a three-tiered rating (positive, neutral, and negative) and brief comment for each other. The accumulated rating and profile of a buyer or seller will help you gauge whom you should purchase items from (and whom you should sell to as well).

Many users confuse a high feedback rating number with a quality authentic merchandise seller. Quite simply, *feedback represents customer satisfaction with the overall transaction, NOT AUTHENTICITY.* Many buyers are inexperienced collectors, and some are not even autograph collectors, but purchase an item as a onetime gift for a family member or business associate. If they receive their item in a timely manner and in good condition, they are happy with the transaction and leave a glowing feedback rating. They never question or challenge the authenticity. There are sellers with incredible feedback profiles who offer quality merchandise, and there are sellers with even greater feedback profiles who sell complete garbage.

You must also consider that if you are purchasing an item from a seller who has never sold anything in the marketplace before. If so, the seller will have a zero feedback profile. This seller could be a hit-and-run scam artist, or a family member selling his or her inherited treasures for the first time. Review feedback comments and use them as a guideline only.

Review the seller's credentials. Most sellers will list professional credentials (if they have them) in their listings. If they are professional autograph dealers, many will have their own Web sites that sell their merchandise directly. For more information, refer to the Professional Autograph Dealers section later on in this chapter.

Review the seller's other offerings. Go into the current listings for this seller and review the other items they are selling, as well as their past auctions that have already closed. Gauge if the seller is an autograph dealer, or someone who offers a range of collectibles in many different collecting categories. If they are primarily an autograph seller, try to determine their area of specialty based on the items they offer. If the majority of items are sports related, they may not specialize in the entertainment fields, and the authentication process may fall more into your hands.

Review the seller's terms. Review payment methods and terms, shipping rates and methods, geographical limits set for bidders, and the claims and guarantees offered on authenticity and return policies.

Contact the seller BEFORE the auction ends, and BEFORE you place a bid. E-mail the seller with any and all questions you may have about the item or any of the seller's terms. Try to contact the seller at least two to three days before the end of the auction. If you contact them hours before the close of the auction, you may not get your questions answered in time.

Do not bid on any item unless you are willing to pay for it. Retracting bids is frowned upon by all auction users, as it causes confusion among other bidders in the auction and can cause the listing of an item to be canceled outright. Any bid retractions you make will be listed in your feedback profile, and some sellers may not allow you to bid in their auctions if you have a habit of making bid retractions.

Set your limits. "Auction fever" is a term that describes how the sheer excitement of an auction can cause bidders to sometimes bid more than they may be willing to pay for an item. This phenomenon can reach a fever pitch with on-line auctions. Unlike conventional auction houses where auctions take place less frequently, and where you have to establish credit before you are allowed to bid on any item, on-line auctions take place every second of every day. It is very easy to overwhelm yourself with purchases very quickly. Also working against you is the fact that the amount that you bid is just a few keystrokes and a click of the mouse away. Competitively bidding with other users can easily force you to spend much more on an item than you would ever plan to.

Always determine the absolute highest amount you are willing to spend on an item *before* placing a bid on it, and bid up to that amount only. Use the proxy bidding (also referred to as maximum bidding) feature to allow the auction house to bid for you against competing bids up to your preset maximum bid. This will take the emotion out of the auction bidding, and win or lose, you will always come away satisfied that you bid effectively.

Auction Houses Specializing in Autographs

There are several high-profile auction houses such as Sotheby's and Christie's that occasionally have autograph-related auctions. These are generally termed "live auctions," where a collection of material has been accepted on consignment from collectors and other dealers, and a catalog has been printed and sent out to a list of clientele. The auction takes place live at a selected venue where qualified bidders are allowed to make bids in several ways:

1) *In person* at the live event. You can also view the lots in person, termed a "preview," a day or two before the event.

2) *By telephone* either live as the auction is going on or with "absentee bids," which the auction houses place on your behalf.

3) *By mail or fax* submitted before a specified closing date.

4) *On-line.* Many auctions are linked to respective Web sites, and the articles are available to be previewed and the auction participated in through the sites and by e-mail.

There are also specific autograph-only autograph dealers/auction houses that hold regular autograph auctions permitting bidding by some or all of the methods listed above. A listing of autograph auction houses can be referenced in the directory of this book.

The benefits of purchasing autographs through these types of venues are similar to those of the on-line auction venues, namely that you set your own price and can select from a wide variety of material. The increased benefits are that you are dealing with autograph specialists, and the question of authenticity becomes less of a concern to you. These sellers all offer guarantees on the authenticity of their items. Many of these items are consigned by experienced collectors and dealers looking to sell their cherished items so they can add newer items to their collections, or possibly realize a profit on an item that they held for a period of time. Because these auction houses have a very strong clientele of specialized collectors and dealers, the final realized prices for items can far exceed what they would get by selling their items directly to a dealer or on-line themselves.

There can also be several downsides to purchasing autographs through these sellers. Although these are autograph-specialized sellers, they are not always 100 percent accurate when authenticating their items. You can put nearly all of your trust in these sellers, but you should always do your own assessment before assuming any item is authentic. If an auction house specializes in a certain genre of autographed collectibles (sports, animation, etc.), they may not be as well informed in other categories. Always make your decision regarding authenticity before bidding.

You will be bidding against many experienced collectors and dealers, so the chances of winning an item for a price much lower than book value are minimal. The auction houses have instituted reserve prices to protect their consigning clientele's investments. A reserve price is the minimum price the auction house will accept for an item.

You will be charged a commission called a buyer's premium *in addition* to your final winning bid. These rates are usually 15 to 20 percent of the final winning bid price and are not negotiable. This, as well as the premium they charge the seller, is how the auction houses pay for their lovely catalogs, Web sites, and their staff. Always factor the premium into your budget before bidding.

Professional Autograph Dealers

A professional autograph dealer is a person or a company of people who, operating on either a full- or part-time basis, buy and sell select autograph material according to their areas of interest and specialty. Some may offer a specific category of autographs (entertainment, sports, in-person only) or a generalized combination of many categories. Most issue printed catalogs on a regular basis and will send them to you upon request. Some may charge a catalog fee, or waive this fee with a purchase from their inventory. Many have developed their own Web sites with illustrated inventories.

The main benefit of purchasing material from a professional autograph dealer is that you are purchasing the experience, reputation, and integrity of that dealer with every autograph that is offered to customers. Over time, you can develop a close relationship with a dealer, and they will keep a list of autographs you may be looking to add to your collection. Many offer layaway payment plans to help you pay off larger purchases in installments.

What should you look for in an autograph dealer?

Length of time in business. Find out how long they have been a collector and a dealer.

Professional affiliations. A solid reputation is the most important criterion you should look for when purchasing autographs from dealers. They should have professional affiliations with autograph collectors' clubs like the Universal Autograph Collectors Club (UACC) and the International Autograph Collectors Club and Dealers Association (IACC/DA) and should be *registered dealers* beyond the more typical club memberships. Registered dealers must abide by the strict code of ethics of these organizations, and this should offer you some extra assurance of quality and service. Contact these organizations for listings of registered dealers in your area.

Certificate of authenticity. Known as a COA or LOA (letter of authenticity), it is simply that— a page that lists the item being sold and guarantees the authenticity of the autograph on the item. The one imperative rule to understand is that a COA is only as good as the dealer who issues it. Just because someone offers a COA does not automatically ensure that the item is authentic. The guarantee on authenticity should be without a time limit.

Return policy. Other than authenticity, most autograph dealers will offer a limited time return policy. This is usually limited to a few days after an item has been received. If you feel that a dealer did not advertise the item properly in regard to condition, size, or overall quality, contact the dealer as soon as possible to arrange a return.

Selling Autographs

At some point in time you may decide to sell selected pieces from your collection, or possibly your entire collection. Depending on how flexible you are with payment timelines, and how much risk you are willing to take in getting the greatest amount of money for your autographs, you can choose to sell your items via several routes, each with its own varying degrees of flexibility and risk.

Selling Directly to Other Collectors

If you are connected with other collectors in the autograph community, you can spread the word with your other collecting friends about the items you are looking to sell. Placing classified ads in autograph collecting magazines and collector club publications listing your various items can be another means of attracting buyers.

If you are selling a number of items, you should prepare a typed list detailing each item, a brief description of the item and its condition, as well as an asking price. The prices listed in this book can serve as a valuable guideline for establishing your price. Be prepared to receive offers based on your asking prices, and also be prepared to receive offers from professional dealers who will offer you a price based on a percentage of the book value.

The benefits of selling to other collectors are that you will be able to determine how much of a demand there is for your items, and you will be able to accept or refuse any offer you wish.

The negatives are that you will have to spend funds on classified ads and the printing and mailing of your lists. It may take you quite a while before you are able to sell any or all of your items. You will also be dealing with individuals, and you will be taking on all of the risks a dealer assumes when dealing with nonpaying individuals or those with unreasonable expectations.

Selling Through On-line Auctions

This is one step above selling directly to other collectors in that you will be essentially setting up a business to sell your autographs to potentially millions of bidders. If you are already a registered user of on-line auction services like eBay and Yahoo!, you are already 90 percent of the way there to selling your items. Review each venue's specific policies regarding sellers and make the appropriate registrations.

You will be able to list your items for a nominal *insertion fee* (between $0.30 and $3.30 per item) as well as a *final value fee* (seller's premium) based on the final selling price of the item (range 5.25 to 10 percent). You will be required to write the item descriptions, payment terms, the auction timeline (this can range from three days to two weeks), and an opening bid amount.

You will have the option of providing color digital photographs of the items, which you will also have to upload to an image-hosting server or provider. Scans are not essential but are *highly recommended*. The age-old expression "A picture is worth a thousand words" is absolutely the case when deciding on providing a scan. Since you are an unknown seller, a scan is the only way that your items will be seen by experienced collectors and dealers, and the only way that they will have the confidence to bid on your items. There are many, many items competing with yours in these venues, and clear scans and detailed descriptions will give a serious bidder little reason to look elsewhere. Review the listing and description format of some of your favorite sellers and reference their examples to make your listings as professional as possible.

Once your auction is live (running), be prepared to receive questions and comments from many potential bidders. You may receive offers asking you to end your auction early and sell the item directly outside the auction venue for an agreed-upon price. While an auction is live, you are not permitted to close an auction early for any reason. This is part of the agreement you make with the venue before the auction goes live, and breaking this rule could result in the suspension of your account.

The benefits of selling your autographs through on-line auctions are that your listing costs are minimal and your items have the potential to be seen and bid on by millions of collectors and dealers. If you have quality, authentic autographs that are in demand, the auction format could bring you prices that exceed a fixed price you would set based on book value.

There are also some drawbacks that could potentially affect your on-line auction experience. These include less-than-desired final high bids, bidder fraud, nonpaying customers, and the returning of your merchandise (and your sales) due to any number of reasons. Here are some useful tips to help protect yourself and make your on-line auction selling experience successful.

Set a Reserve Price. One way to protect yourself from your auction not meeting your price expectations is to set a reserve price for your item. This is the minimum price you are willing to sell your item for. If this reserve price is not reached in the auction, you are not obligated to sell your item to the high bidder. This reserve price is determined by you alone and is not listed on the auction listing page. The starting price of the auction can be set much lower than your reserve. As you receive bids, the current high bid will be displayed with a "Reserve Price Not Met" tag beside it. Once the reserve price has been met, and exceeded, you are now obligated to accept the final high bid. This is the best way to ensure that you get a minimum amount for your item. The only drawback to reserve auctions is that "auction fever" can sometimes be affected by a reserve price, as some bidders do not participate in reserve auctions if they feel the reserve price may be set too high.

Offer a "Buy It Now" fixed price. In addition to setting a reserve and opening bid amount, you can also add a fixed price amount to your item (called "Buy It Now" on eBay). This will allow bidders to purchase the item outright, for a set price predetermined by you, ending the auction at that point. Some bidders will opt to pay a fair fixed price for an item to avoid the risks of losing the item to another bidder in the auction, even if it means that they might be paying more than what they could have won the item for bidding at auction. The only drawback to setting a fixed price is that you could conceivably limit your final selling price by not allowing competitive bidding to take place beyond your set price.

Avoid nonpaying and fraudulent bidders. Check the bid status of your auctions as they are proceeding, especially in the last few hours. Specify in your auction terms that you will not permit bidders with negative or zero feedback ratings (unknown bidders) to participate. There are some devious individuals who will enter false bids (usually in the last minutes of an auction) with the intent of ruining the auction. As the seller, you are permitted to remove the bids of these types of bidders as soon as you can, and *before the end of the auction.* Legitimate bidders get very nervous when bidder fraud has affected the outcome of an auction, and you may lose some of your legitimate bids if this happens.

Selling to Other Auction Houses

Depending upon the quality of the autograph material you are selling, traditional auction houses will accept your items on consignment, or may offer to purchase them outright from you for an agreed-upon price. In most cases, the consignment route will be the preferred manner, and this process requires extra work and costs that exceed the on-line auction venues.

The first step is to contact the auction house and ask to speak with the person in charge of acquisitions for autograph material. You may have a quick conversation or e-mail exchange in which they will ask for the types of items that you have available. From this discussion they will be able to tell you if they are interested in your items. Every auction house has its own respective clientele with its own areas of specialty. An auction house may also be having a theme auction planned that your material may be suited for. If they do not wish to proceed, thank them for their time and look at other auction houses and other selling methods listed in this chapter as options.

If the auction house does wish to proceed, they will ask you to send them high-quality scans or photographs of your items so they can assess authenticity and condition. If the auction house is interested in listing your items, they will ask you to send the actual items to them (most often at your expense) for an in-person inspection. You will have to sign a contractual agreement with the auction house, permitting them to offer your items to their bidders. The terms of agreement will detail the following:

Date of auction. The date of the auction could range from one month to one year from the time of submission, depending on the cycles and schedules of the auction house. During this period, you will not have the items in your possession, and you will not be paid anything for the item.

Fees. In addition to the costs of shipping your items to the auction house, you will be charged fees for any and possibly all of the following:

- Catalog listing fee (rates vary from free to $50 per item)

- Web site listing fee (same as catalog, but may be packaged together for a set price)

- Photography fee (for the catalog and Web—can range from $10 to $50 per item)

- Seller's premium (similar to a buyer's premium) based on a percentage of the final realized price your item gets in the auction. This price does not include the buyer's premium.

Depending upon the quality and quantity of items you are consigning, some or all of these fees are negotiable.

Auction estimate and reserve price. The auction house will work with you to establish an auction estimate that is based on what they feel the item should bring in the auction and to set a reserve price to protect your investment in your item. The estimate is just that, an estimate, and it has no bearing on the final hammer price. Some items reach a fraction of their estimates while many surpass the estimates by multiples of ten. The reserve price is basically what you feel comfortable receiving as a minimum. Remember that the seller's premium will be deducted from the final price. The auction house will try to get you to set as small a reserve as possible since they want to have a successful sale on both ends, as they profit only when they can charge premiums to both the buyers and the sellers. They may argue that a high reserve will scare off many potential bidders, and this may be true. Set a reserve price that is acceptable to both you and the auction house.

When will you get paid? There is generally a forty-five- to ninety-day waiting period *after the auction ends* before you can expect the auction house to issue you a check.

What if your item does not sell? The auction house may suggest since your item received several bids that did not meet your reserve price that you consider relisting the item in their next auction with a lower reserve price. If there was little interest in your item, you may wish to try your luck with another auction house with a clientele better suited to your item. You may also ask to have the item sent back to you (once again at your expense), or the auction house may offer to purchase the item outright from you for an agreed-upon price.

The benefits of consigning your items to auction houses are that you benefit from their experience, advanced marketing skills, and a specialized clientele that could bring prices that far exceed any other competing venue. The downsides are what could be relatively high costs, slow payment turnaround, and no guarantees of a sale.

Selling to Professional Autograph Dealers

Another option for selling your autographed items is the professional autograph dealers from whom you may even have been buying some of your items. If you have a good relationship with a particular autograph dealer, or if the item you are selling was purchased originally from an autograph dealer, contact that dealer first before approaching other dealers. If they originally handled that item, they may be interested in acquiring the item again.

If you do not have any past dealings with particular dealers, search the listings of the autograph dealer organizations listed in this book. Decide upon *one* whose inventory best reflects your collection or one that is located geographically close to you for the convenience of a possible in-person appraisal.

Before contacting any dealers, do your own research about the book value of your items based on the prices in this guide. Search on-line completed auctions for realized prices for items similar to yours. Use the range of prices you find as an indication of the current prices these items are selling for.

These prices are considered *market value,* and are not what you should expect to be paid by a dealer. Most dealers will pay anywhere from 40 to 75 percent of market value, depending on the scarcity and condition of your items. They may pay more for the individual pieces of a collection, or less on a per-item basis overall if you sell your collection as a whole.

Make a detailed inventory of your items listing celebrity name, format (signed photo, signature, letter, etc.), sizes, and condition. Make color laser copies, digital photos, or scans of all the items.

Contact the first dealer of your choice. Mention that you have autographed items for sale and ask them if they are interested in purchasing your collection. If the dealer does purchase items privately, they will then ask you for some of the names and brief descriptions. If they are interested, they will make an arrangement to get more information from you. At this point, you can fax, e-mail, or mail the list of items and the photos/copies to them.

Tell the dealer that they are the only dealer you are contacting at this time, and that you selected them based on your research or experience with them. Tell them that you will not contact another dealer until you hear back from them, but give them a timeline. *They will greatly appreciate this.* If you are e-mailing or faxing the information to them, a period of three business days from the time of sending is sufficient. If you are mailing the information, a period of two to three weeks is appropriate.

If you have not heard back from the dealer at the end of the given time period, contact them again, ask if they have received the information yet, and ask them if they are interested in continuing with the transaction. If you do not seem to be progressing with this dealer, at this time you can proceed to contact another dealer.

It is common courtesy to contact one dealer at a time. Dealers are friends with many other dealers, and they do not like to compete directly with others when purchasing material privately. In an auction venue it is each bidder out for themselves, but private dealings are just that. If a dealer realizes that your solicitation was sent out to several others, he or she just may pull out of the negotiations completely.

A dealer will ask to inspect the items personally before agreeing to a price. They will never send payment for an item without viewing it in person. If they are located close to you, you can make an appointment to meet to review the collection. If a collection is a very valuable find for them, they may travel to meet with you at their expense (be prepared to make a deal at this meeting). If you are not located near each other, it is common practice for you to ship your items to the dealer for inspection. It is generally not good form to question the integrity or reputation of the dealer at this stage. Remember, you did your own research and selected this dealer yourself. Professional dealers have a business reputation and professional affiliations to back them up. They have no idea who you are, regardless of your personal integrity and honesty. You may be able to negotiate a price range for your items, depending upon condition and authenticity. If you agree to the prices, you will most likely be responsible for paying the shipping costs of getting your items to the dealer. *Send your items Insured for full replacement value and by Registered Mail or by Courier or any other method that requires a signature as proof of delivery.*

Upon inspection, a dealer will offer you a price. This may or may not be negotiable; it really depends on the dealer. If you are happy with the price, congratulations, you have just made a deal! If you are not happy, explain why to the dealer. If you were expecting a certain price, they may be understanding and explain why they offered you the price they did. Remember, a seller has to incur certain fixed costs to sell a piece, including overhead, marketing, catalog printing, sales commissions, etc. If you cannot reach an agreeable price with a dealer, thank them for their time, arrange to have your items returned to you, and approach the next dealer on your list.

Dealers may offer you the option of putting your items on consignment in their catalogs. With this arrangement, you both determine an agreed-upon selling price and a commission rate for the dealer upon a sale. You may also wish to give the dealer a certain price range that they may negotiate if they receive offers from potential buyers that are below your asking price. Determining this up front allows the dealer to finalize a sale without having to reach you for your acceptance. During the consignment period, a dealer must have the item in their possession. In the long run, you may end up realizing a better selling price for your item, but your sale is dependent upon the dealer making a sale, and the time frame for payment may be much longer than if you sold directly to the dealer.

PRESERVING AND DISPLAYING YOUR AUTOGRAPH COLLECTION

The condition of an autographed item is very important in determining present and future value, so it is critical to understand and adhere to the simple rules of autograph preservation.

As you acquire pieces for your collection, you must immediately assess each item's current state of condition. It is very difficult and can be very expensive to restore or improve the present condition of an item; therefore you should attempt to pinpoint the item's condition and avoid anything that may promote deterioration in the condition of the item.

Preservation

Experienced collectors and dealers expect a vintage item to have some age toning and signs of wear. What you should be trying to accomplish is to freeze the current state of condition of the item for the future. Do not do anything to change the current state of the autograph or item. Never cut out an autograph or glue an autograph to a larger page. Do not laminate or shellac an autograph or remove an inscription from an autographed page or photo.

The following preservation factors should be considered with all autographed items. If the preservation of the present condition of a vintage item requires more involvement, you may wish to consult a conservation specialist in your area (try contacting your local museum), although the relatively high cost of this should be reserved for museum-quality pieces only.

Paper items such as signed photographs, letters, documents, or album pages have built within themselves their most destructive force: the *acid* content in the paper. The acid that exists in the wood content of the paper (termed pulp) causes the paper to yellow and become more brittle, eventually crumbling into pieces. The acid content of other paper products coming into contact with your autographed page (a file folder, other pages on top or below the page) will also react with the autograph page. Acid can be physically extracted from a page, but this should be entrusted only to a professional conservator and can be a very expensive process.

The easiest way to lessen the effects of the acid in paper is to store the item in an acid-free environment. Your local comic book and sports card collectibles stores offer acetate comic bags and acid-free cardboard backers that allow you to store your signed paper items in an acid-free environment. You can also purchase acetate sheets that have been three-hole punched for storage in a binder (these are also referred to as sheet protectors or print protectors). These are offered by a variety of manufacturers in different quality grades. Before using any of these products, contact the customer service department of the manufacturer and ask them to specify which of their products are guaranteed as acid-free or archival. Use only these products to store your collectibles.

Photographs are printed with a variety of chemicals. If the chemicals were not completely removed from the photograph at the time of printing (termed wash), they will slowly eat away at the print over time, causing a deterioration of the image called silvering. An unsigned photograph can be put through another wash to attempt to remove chemicals, but treating a signed photograph as such would ruin the signature. There is really nothing that can be done to prevent the future deterioration of the image, other than slowing down the process by storage in an acid-free environment and out of direct sunlight.

Never store a paper item folded, as a fold will in time deteriorate into a tear. If a page has been torn, you may be able to repair the tear by using archival tape (acid-free tape) on the reverse side of the item. This should be attempted only by an experienced conservator. Many experts suggest leaving the tear as it is, storing the item in a manner in which no undue stress will cause the tear to extend further along the page.

Remove all staples and paper clips from any multipage documents. These will rust in time and cause discoloration and stain the pages. Store each page individually in acetate sheets.

The *humidity* (amount of water vapor in the air) surrounding your autograph items is a very important factor to consider as well. Excessive humidity can cause paper items to mold and severely affect the overall appearance and condition. Avoid storing paper items in the basement or garage of a home.

Framing

One of the greatest rewards of autograph collecting is displaying your most treasured items on your desk or on the walls of your home or office. A creatively presented autograph can also increase the desirability for resale dramatically. The biggest problem with displaying autographs is that contact with light causes ink to fade over time. The more direct the light is, the quicker that deterioration takes place. If you still desire to display your autographs, *always hang them out of direct sunlight*. Remember that indirect or reflected daylight also causes fading over time.

Always have your autographs framed by a professional who is familiar with museum-grade framing techniques. Use nonreflective glass with UV (ultraviolet) protection to reduce the penetration of light to the item. All items should be adhered to a matte board that is composed of acid-free material (also called museum board) and is thick enough to keep the item from touching the glass. Any tape that is used to attach the item to the matte board must be archival tape. Never have your item dry-mounted or glued to a backing board to avoid wrinkling. Ask that your item be able to be returned to its original unframed state if it was to be removed from the frame.

Insurance and Record Keeping

It is very important to keep good records of the information surrounding your autograph acquisitions. Detailing the date of acquisition, source, price, and any background provenance offered by the seller is very important for insurance and future resale purposes. If you purchased an item from a catalog, make a copy of the catalog page and include it with the dealer's certificate of authenticity and sales receipt in a file folder. If you have a personal computer and a scanner, make a scan of the item, print out a copy of the image for your files (a photocopy will also do), and keep a collection of scans on computer disks or CDs. Keep a detailed database of all your autographs in a computer spreadsheet program.

The cost of insuring your collectibles is very minor in comparison with the value of your collection. Insurance gives you peace of mind that the time, effort, and money you have invested in your collection, although not replaceable, will be at least not lost for good in the event of theft or damage. Most homeowner insurance policies will not cover you beyond basic household goods; therefore you should speak to your insurance agent about adding a rider to your policy to cover your collectibles. If your agent cannot cover you, he or she will most likely be able to recommend an agent who specializes in these policies. They will require a detailed list of your items, as well as photographs and current replacement values. You will want to update this file with your agent as you add to or sell items from your collection, or if the value of your items goes up beyond your specified replacement value.

AUTHENTICATION

As an autograph dealer, I am inundated on a daily basis by telephone calls, mail, and e-mail with requests to purchase the rarest and most incredible autographs of all time. The sad reality is that a large percentage of what is offered to me ends up not being authentic. The most common scenarios are as follows:

"My grandmother wrote a letter to James Dean, and she received this wonderful signed photograph back in the mail." The photo was in fact signed by a studio secretary (secretarial), or is a photographically reproduced print from an original signed photo (pre-print).

"My aunt saw the Beatles in a London restaurant and the Fab Four signed this restaurant menu for her personally." The menu was actually handed to Neil Aspinall, the band's road manager, who took it to the back room to be signed (with the band's full permission) by him for all four members (authorized forgery).

But the worst of the bunch is a flat-out forgery administered by one of the evildoers looking to prey on the trusting collector who thinks he has been offered the bargain of his life (forgery). The unfortunate aspect of the rise in popularity and in the prices of vintage-signed material is that this latter example is becoming more and more common.

One of the most crucial components in the authenticating of autographs is research. I have personally studied the signatures of thousands of stars for over twenty years, and I maintain an extensive library of reference material to assist me on a daily basis. You never know when that signature reference you put aside a few years ago will come in handy. Even with all of this experience, I still have moments of excitement at the thought of possibly finding another rare gem, only to be let down after an extensive comparison to my reference material. I cannot stress enough how important doing one's research is. The list of variables that go into authenticating is almost endless, and is probably impossible to detail completely, but with experience and patience, one develops over time the authenticator's instinct.

The Unmasking of a Marilyn Monroe Treasure

Once (or hopefully a few times) in a lifetime, we do find those rare authentic gems. Here is the story of one of those wonderful moments in my collecting lifetime, and the processes I employed to authenticate an extremely rare signed photograph of Marilyn Monroe.

I received an e-mail from a woman in Michigan detailing how her grandmother met Marilyn Monroe in the early 1950s in Detroit. The autographed photograph she received at the time had been kept locked in a bank vault for over fifty years, and the family now wished to sell it.

Marilyn was notorious for signing photographs only for personal friends or associates (her makeup artist, her chauffeur, etc.). Nearly every "signed" photograph of Marilyn Monroe that is offered to the public is either a studio-issued secretarial (the most common), or a forgery (becoming the most common).

Secretarially signed Marilyn photographs are very distinctively signed in a manner that, to the trained eye, is very different from Marilyn's autograph style. Even though an experienced authenticator can spot a Marilyn secretarial in about three seconds, many prestigious auction houses have been fooled over the years by these secretarials and by forgeries. Even one of the most popular antiques television programs incorrectly identified a secretarially signed Marilyn Monroe photograph as authentic and gave out some very incorrect information about her choice of inks (red ink signatures are mostly secretarials, not authentic signatures by Marilyn). Please refer to the conclusion of this story for some illustrations of common Marilyn Monroe secretarial signatures.

Authentically signed Marilyn Monroe photographs are, in my estimation, in the 1 to 2 percent range of all pieces offered in the marketplace. It wasn't that Marilyn disliked signing autographs—in fact, if you were fortunate enough to run into her on the street, she would gladly sign a slip of paper you had in your pocket, or a theater program, or whatever. It is more the fact that the enormous amount of fan mail she generated would have been virtually impossible for her to personally respond to.

With this in mind, I practically wrote this case off as most likely a secretarial or a forgery (people will tell you *any* story, whether it is the truth or not), but I still wrote back and requested a photocopy or electronic scan of the image.

A few days later, the following scan arrived by e-mail: *See illustration #8.*

I was immediately surprised not only by Marilyn's beautiful pose, but by the fact that this was not a typical Marilyn image that you often see. It is a pose from her earliest days in Hollywood. This told me to take a closer look at the photo and scan.

The following is my brief assessment of the photographic image itself:

1. *This is not a classic Marilyn photograph*. A forger will usually select the most famous (and most marketable) pose of a celebrity. It makes the desirability and overall appeal that much easier to market. This is not a typical Marilyn image; in fact, many would not even recognize it as being Marilyn Monroe upon first glance.

2. *This is a vintage print*. Fortunately, most forgers are not smart enough (or just plain too lazy) to match a vintage signature with a vintage print. You would not believe the number of Marilyn Monroe forgeries I have seen over the years on recent resin-coated reprints and not vintage prints. I have also seen countless vintage prints signed with the current autograph pen of choice, the Sharpie (which was not in use until the 1970s).

3. *This is an official studio print*. The credit at the bottom of the photograph lists the copyright as belonging to United Artists Corporation. A quick scan of my Marilyn reference books confirmed that she was under contract mainly to Fox and then to MGM. What was the young Marilyn doing in a United Artists promotional photograph?

Looking at the signature and inscription on the photograph, it appeared to be much clearer and better defined than the authentic Marilyn Monroe samples I have handled in the past. My first instinct led me to believe that this might be a secretarial example, but something seemed unusual about it, and considering the above-listed quirks, I decided that I should take a closer look at the signature and inscription. Here is my assessment:

1. *Marilyn would not have had a studio secretary to sign for her at this stage in her career*. Studio staff were set up to handle the correspondence of the major stars. The young Marilyn in this photo would not have had a staff at this stage in her career, and she definitely would have not sent out this photo to her fans during the more glamorous stages of her career.

2. *Forgers* rarely *inscribe a photograph*. This is a general rule of thumb, but not always 100 percent foolproof. There are two main reasons for this; first, the forgers' point of view is that a photograph inscribed to a person's name ("To John," "To Mary," etc.) is less desirable to the marketplace. This is true for common celebrities whose supply of signed material far exceeds the demand. But I have never heard of a dealer or collector refusing to purchase an authentic signed photograph of such rare signers as James Dean and Marilyn Monroe because they were inscribed to a name other than their own. The truth is, most of these vintage photographs were signed *specifically* for someone, as it was much more personal and courteous to inscribe the photo to that particular person. Second, the more handwriting a forger adds to a signature, the greater the chance that they will be discovered. Most forgers will stick with just a signature, or a simple sentiment like "Best Wishes" or "Sincerely." I must specify that there are authentic signed photographs that are not inscribed, and there are forgeries with lengthy inscriptions, but a vintage signed photo with an inscription is *usually* an indication of authenticity, or at the very least, a secretarial.

3. *The signature was placed in a clear area on the photograph*. It is common for forgers to locate all or part of a signature in a darker portion of a photograph to hide any imperfections in their deception. Most vintage signed photographs were generally signed in the most visible and presentable area of the image. Rarely would movie stars sign on their face. These rules do not

8

Copyright 1949, United Artists Corporation.
Permission granted for Newspaper and
Magazine reproduction. (Made in U.S.A.)

LH-G-130

8 Marilyn Monroe signed picture

apply for current celebrities, who will sign the most rushed and poorly located signatures on a photograph for whatever reason imaginable.

4. *The signature and inscription flow very naturally*. We all have a tendency to sign our names in a very natural and uninterrupted manner. Try signing someone else's name, and see the subtle differences that take place in the ink pressure and overall consistency of ink flow. As well, we have characteristics to our handwriting, especially in the way we form certain letters, that remain surprisingly consistent throughout our lifetimes. In this example, the *T* in "To," the *F* in "Findlay," and the loopy *t* in "Best" are all characteristics that are very similar to the authentic handwriting samples I have in my Marilyn Monroe library (always back to the reference material!). The best forgers in the world pick up on certain handwriting specifics, but they don't usually catch them all, and that is where a letter-by-letter analysis or even a chemical analysis of the inks and paper can sometimes be necessary to determine authenticity. Please refer to the In-Person handwriting and signature examples at the conclusion of this story.

5. *Marilyn Monroe's signature did not change much during her career*. This is where having an extensive library of signatures and handwriting samples from different dates can be a very useful tool. As Marilyn's fame skyrocketed her signature did take on a sloppier and more rushed appearance. The distinction between individual letters began to blur, but some main features remained consistent. For this example to be authentic, I estimated it must have been signed in the late 1940s or very early 1950s (specifically 1948–1950) because the formation of each letter in her name is very clear. Therefore, her signature *must* match up with known authentic examples from that time period. *See illustrations #9 and 10.*

Here are my findings after one week of solid research into this amazing puzzle:

What was Marilyn doing on a United Artists promotional photograph?

In 1949, Marilyn Monroe (still an unknown in Hollywood) made her fifth film appearance, her third with billing, in a one-line, one-minute walk-on role in the Marx Brothers' last film, *Love Happy,* for United Artists (she was loaned out by Fox, who tried to get her exposure any way they could). United Artists tried everything to promote the film—a complete bomb by almost all accounts—so they hired young Marilyn (just twenty-three at the time) to tour the United States to promote the film (for just $100 a week!). She traveled to various U.S. cities (Los Angeles, New York, etc.) to attend the premieres and generate a little publicity for the film. United Artists printed some promotional photographs of the starlet to sign at these appearances (Marilyn was paid $300 for the photo session).

Was she ever in Detroit during this early period of her career?

On July 21, 1949, the film premiered at the Loew's Theater in Detroit, and the nearly unknown Marilyn was on hand to promote the opening.

Is it possible that this woman did meet Marilyn and get this photograph signed?

In further discussions with the family it was revealed that Miss Findlay was a housekeeper at the Book/Cadillac Hotel in Detroit and was assigned to Marilyn's room. In appreciation for her services, Marilyn signed and inscribed a gorgeous sepia-toned eight-by-ten head shot for her.

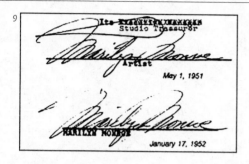

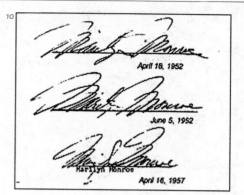

9 and 10 The following are examples of authentic signatures of Marilyn Monroe on contracts dating from 1951 to 1957. Note the subtle changes to her form, but the consistencies that remain, too.

Is the signature authentic?

After studying nearly forty authentic examples of her handwriting and signatures from all periods of her life, I was very pleased to positively authenticate the signature as that of a very young Marilyn Monroe.

Final Analysis

1. *This is a very rare photograph, even unsigned.* This photograph may very well be the first professional studio portrait ever used to promote Marilyn Monroe. It was used over a very short period of a few months to promote a very small picture to very few markets. A few dozen local fans probably greeted each promotional stop, and very few people would have asked an unknown bit player for an autograph. If they did receive a signed photograph, it would have probably been lost in the shuffle before Marilyn's star truly began to rise three or four years later, let alone over fifty years later. In fact, my research to date has yet to turn up another one of these original prints (signed or unsigned) ever hitting the open markets.

2. *This may be the earliest signed photograph of Marilyn Monroe in existence.* Other early 1950s-era signed prints have come to market, but not one from this very early period. This was signed as Norma Jean Baker was just starting to become Marilyn Monroe. There are very few signatures from this era that come to market (most are on early studio contracts), and a signed photograph is otherwise almost unheard of.

This is just one example of the processes a professional autograph dealer will undertake in authenticating a signature. Some cases are more analytical, some more scientific, but each one is definitely unique and very time-consuming. Professional autograph dealers take pride in their work, and every autographed item they offer for sale carries that seller's reputation with it.

Without taking the time to research the family's story, the background of this unique photograph, or a signature study with an archive of specifically dated reference material, this rare gem might have been passed off as one of the many secretarials or forgeries that exist today. *See illustrations #11, 12, 13, and 14.*

SPECIALIZATION

After years of accumulating the signatures or signed photos of your favorite movie stars and film notables into a collection, you may find yourself with a dilemma, namely: *What should I collect next?*

A simple answer is to *specialize* by creating unique and challenging themes for your collection. Depending on how far you take it, the results can be the culmination of years of tracking down rare and obscure names and/or items.

The following examples may help add some inspiration to your collection:

The Main Cast of a Film

Collecting cast signatures is a very popular theme for collectors. It can be a rewarding challenge on many levels. A complete cast collection of signatures can be worth many times the combined value of the individual signatures. One of the most desirable ways to present a collection of signatures of a favorite film is to collect the signatures in a similar size or format (e.g., signatures on white three-by-five index cards) and matte and frame them with an original poster, lobby card, or photograph from the film. The difference between looking at a few signatures on slips of paper, and the signatures of Clark Gable and Vivien Leigh matted under a gorgeous pose of the duo embracing in *Gone with the Wind* is without comparison. *See illustration #15.*

*11 and 12 Marilyn Monroe signatures
and handwriting samples*

*13 and 14 Common Marilyn Monroe
secretarial signatures*

*Special thanks to Bill White for his
assistance and select images.*

A more challenging (and expensive) form of a cast collection is seeking out signed photographs of the performers of a film *in character* from that particular film. This presents many challenges, because usually a popular role is the most desired format of a signed photograph of any particular actor or actress. At the same time, a signed photograph in character from a famed role can be substantially more expensive to purchase. For example, a handsome signed portrait photograph of Humphrey Bogart costs around $3,000, but a signed photograph of Bogie in character from *Casablanca* sold at auction for over $15,000!

The length to which you wish to go before considering your cast collection "complete" is up to your discretion and budget. I have seen *The Wizard of Oz* cast signature collections range from the most popular and obtainable (the four main cast members—Judy Garland [Dorothy], Ray Bolger [the Scarecrow], Jack Haley [the Tin Man], and Bert Lahr [the Cowardly Lion]) to the extended main cast to include Margaret Hamilton (the Wicked Witch of the West), Billie Burke (Glinda, the Good Witch), and Frank Morgan (the Wizard of Oz) and beyond that to include all main contributors such as director, producers, writers, composers, art directors, etc.

Because of the phenomenon of creating the ultimate cast collection, the signatures of some very obscure personalities can command astronomical prices, vastly outweighing their popularity and the depth of their achievements. Using the example of *The Wizard of Oz* again, did you know that the two most valuable signatures to a cast collector of this film are not Judy Garland or Ray Bolger, but Clara Blandick (Auntie Em) and Charley Grapewin (Uncle Henry). Both of these actors were character players who never realized movie star status, and therefore signed very few autographs in their lifetime. Many people looking through an old autograph album found in the attic may not even recognize these names, and would consider them worthless. For the collector who is looking for these two autographs to complete his or her cast collection, the very few examples that get offered to the marketplace go for very spirited bidding at auction.

15 Ghostbusters cast signatures matted with photos

Oscar Winners

This is another popular collection theme. Starting in 1927–1928, the Academy of Motion Picture Arts and Sciences has named its favorite selections yearly. The Oscar is the highest form of recognition and achievement in cinema. *See illustration #16.*

Many collectors pursue the signatures of all Oscar winners in certain categories (Best Actor/Actress), or collect and compile the signatures of all main winners from each year. As an interesting footnote, the price of Emil Jannings's signature is probably worth double due to the fact that he won the first Oscar for Best Actor in 1927–28 for *The Way of All Flesh* (how many of us remember that role!), and every Oscar autograph collector must have his autograph to lead off his or her collection.

Signed Quotes

This area of collecting can be unique and inspiring. Some enterprising autograph collectors who write to their favorite stars try to make their request stand out among the legions of letters a celebrity receives by typing a favorite line of dialogue or quote from that celebrity on a blank sheet of paper, requesting that the celebrity autograph the quote. When signed, these quotations can be much more presentable and desirable than just a plain signature.

Can you visualize how attractive the poster from *The Godfather* matted with a typescript "We'll make him an offer he can' t refuse" signed by Marlon Brando would be?

Another collectible and desired format for many collectors is handwritten quotations by famous authors and composers. I have seen several wonderful handwritten and signed quotations by Mario Puzo from his screenplay for *The Godfather,* as well as a few handwritten and signed music bars from the score for *West Side Story* by composer Leonard Bernstein. *See illustration # 17.*

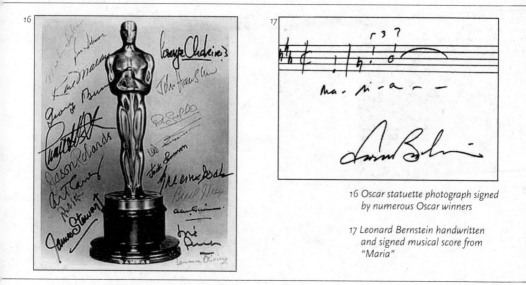

16 Oscar statuette photograph signed
by numerous Oscar winners

17 Leonard Bernstein handwritten
and signed musical score from
"Maria"

Movie Genres and Famous Roles

Fans of certain types or genres of films (horror, gangster, musicals, etc.) put together collections of autographs that represent these films. Horror fans sometimes collect autographs of all actors who portrayed Dracula and Frankenstein as well as the secondary players.

Hollywood Does Its Part: Collecting Naval Aid Auxiliary Autograph Cards

During World War II there were many fund drives set up to raise money for the war effort, from local bake sales to national war bonds campaigns. One organization, the Naval Aid Auxiliary, was responsible for what may very well be the first case of Hollywood stars selling their autographs to the public for a charitable cause.

In 1942–1943, the Naval Aid Auxiliary Autograph Department, located in Hollywood, created special autograph cards. The cards were off-white thick cardstock, three by seven inches in size (including a two-inch detachable certificate on the end) with red and blue bands running across the top and bottom borders and an NAA crest in the upper center of the card. *See illustrations #18 and 19.*

The NAA recruited 185 Hollywood movie stars, including screen legends Humphrey Bogart, Errol Flynn, Clark Gable, Cary Grant, and Ronald Reagan, to sign the cards (several hundred cards per star, it is speculated). In turn, the NAA then sold the cards for twenty-five cents each and the funds were then donated to the war effort.

There really is not too much information available about how successful the NAA autograph card drive was in helping to win the war, but for collectors of Golden Hollywood autographs, they offer a treasure trove of insight. The list of participating movie stars is quite diverse. *See illustration #20.*

18 Ad featuring Rita Hayworth in her Naval Aid Auxiliary uniform

19 Shirley Temple signed Naval Aid Auxiliary card with attached certificate

Factors Concerning Value

An advantage of collecting these NAA cards over basic signatures on album pages is that all the cards have the same design, making them very presentable when placed together in a photo album.

Authenticity

The cards offer certified authentic signatures—the stars wouldn't have had their secretaries sign something being sold for the war effort. The perfect example of this is Humphrey Bogart, who employed secretaries to sign nearly all autograph requests sent to him but whose autograph on the NAA card is absolutely authentic. *See illustration #21.*

Condition

Signed NAA cards are difficult to find—in any condition. It is rare to find a card in pristine condition, especially with the original certificate still attached. Most of these cards were glued into autograph albums or scrapbooks, and many examples will have the glue or paper remnants from previous mountings on the reverse of the card. In addition, many of the cards will show the signs of discoloration or signature fading due to years of contact with sunlight or acids in other papers coming into contact with the card.

Value

The NAA card itself does not add much to the overall value of the signature. For example, a Bogart-signed NAA card may be worth only 10 to 15 percent more than a clean authentic Bogart signature on an album page. However, it is important to note that the fact that the signature is on a World War II–related piece of memorabilia may interest a military-oriented collector who otherwise might not be interested in purchasing a Bogart signature on a blank page.

The more prominent movie stars of the day signed the autograph cards that were requested the most; consequently, most examples to hit the current marketplace tend to be the more A-

20

NAVAL AID AUXILIARY
Autograph Department

June Allyson	Ava Gardner	Dennis Morgan
Don Ameche	John Garfield	George Murphy
Mary Anderson	Judy Garland	
Dana Andrews	Peggy Ann Garner	Lloyd Nolan
Lois Andrews	Greer Garson	
Heather Angel	Gildersleeve (H.P.)	Jack Oakie
Jean Arthur	Paulette Goddard	Merle Oberon
	Betty Grable	Edmund O'Brien
Jane Ball	Farley Granger	Margaret O'Brien
Lynn Bari	Cary Grant	Virginia O'Brien
Lionel Barrymore	Bonita Granville	Donald O'Connor
Ann Baxter	Kathryn Grayson	Maureen O'Hara
William Bendix	Sydney Greenstreet	Dennis O'Keefe
Constance Bennett		Michael O'Shea
Joan Bennett	Alan Hale	
Ingrid Bergman	Jon Hall	John Payne
Turhan Bey	Dare Harris	Gregory Peck
Julie Bishop	John Harvey	Susan Peters
Charles Bickford	Signe Hasso	Walter Pidgeon
Vivian Blaine	June Haver	William Powell
Janet Blair	Dick Haymes	Tyrone Power
Joan Blondell	Susan Hayward	B. S. Pully
Humphrey Bogart	Rita Hayworth	
Charles Boyer	Paul Henreid	Francis Rafferty
Eddie Bracken	Katherine Hepburn	George Raft
Barbara Britton	John Hodiak	Martha Raye
Jim Brown	Bob Hope	Ronald Reagan
Joe E. Brown	Marsha Hunt	Donna Reed
	Walter Huston	Walter Reed
Eddie Cantor	Betty Hutton	George Reeves
Margaret Chapman	Bob Hutton	Ginger Rogers
Claudette Colbert		Roy Rogers
Nancy Coleman	Richard Jaeckel	Rosalind Russell
Ronald Colman	Harry James	Ann Rutherford
Richard Conte	Gloria Jean	Eddie Ryan
Gary Cooper	Van Johnson	Sheila Ryan
Joseph Cotten	Jennifer Jones	
James Craig	Brenda Joyce	Randolph Scott
Jeanne Crain	Arline Judge	Ann Sheridan
Richard Crane		Ransom Sherman
Stephen Crane	Danny Kaye	Dinah Shore
Laird Cregar	Gene Kelly	Phil Silvers
Bing Crosby	Kay Kyser	Ginny Simms
Xavier Cugat		Frank Sinatra
Alan Curtis	Alan Ladd	Eric Sinclair
	Hedy Lamarr	Red Skelton
Helmut Dantine	Dorothy Lamour	Alexis Smith
Linda Darnell	Carole Landis	Ann Sothern
Bette Davis	Priscilla Lane	
Laraine Day	Joan Leslie	Shirley Temple
Gloria De Haven	John Loder	Gene Tierney
Olivia De Havilland	Myrna Loy	Franchot Tone
Marlene Dietrich	Lum & Abner	Spencer Tracy
Tommy Dix	Ida Lupine	Sonny Tufts
Brian Donlevy		Lana Turner
Tom Drake	Lon McCallister	
Jimmy Durante	Roddy McDowall	Bob Walker
	Renny McEvoy	John Wayne
William Eythe	Dorothy McGuire	Cornel Wilde
	Fibber McGee & Molly	Esther Williams
Jinx Falkenberg	Irene Manning	Warren Williams
Alice Faye	Trudy Marshall	Monty Woolley
Gracie Fields	Marilyn Maxwell	Jane Wyman
Geraldine Fitzgerald	Doris Merrick	Keenan Wynn
Errol Flynn	Carmen Miranda	
Preston Foster	Thomas Mitchell	Loretta Young
Susanna Foster	Connie Moore	Robert Young
Kay Francis	George Montgomery	

21

20 *The following illustration is the original typed list of movie star signatures available to collectors in 1943.*

21 *Note the rare printed celebrity name in certificate.*

list names who were collected and preserved in private collections for the past sixty years. This being said, it can also be stated that signed NAA cards from *all* celebrities should be considered scarce. I have been collecting them for over five years, and I personally see only two or three examples hit the marketplace every year.

Collecting signed Naval Aid Auxiliary autograph cards is a unique example of an autograph format available to the Hollywood autograph collector. They also provide an insight into the link between Hollywood and movie stars and their fans in the war relief effort in the United States during World War II.

22 A rare, signed James Dean photograph

23 Inscription on a signed album
page

CELEBRITY AUTOGRAPH FEATURES

James Dean

James Dean (1931–1955) is considered one of the most influential Method actors of his generation, and the role model for every young Hollywood rebel actor to follow. *See Illustration 22.*

His autograph is rare in all formats, especially signed photographs. His tragic death at the pinnacle of his short career solidified his legendary status, and his popularity increases daily; it's
been fifty years since his last film.

The following is a breakdown of values for the different formats of James Dean's signature.

Signature

James Dean's star was just beginning to rise when he died. He completed only three films, so
he was not in the public eye long enough to sign hundreds of autographs at premieres and
other events. Dean was also very anti-studio, and he was hesitant to attend industry functions.
As such, very few examples of his in-person signatures are available. Some of the examples
that exist were signed at the Fairmont, Indiana, High School reunion dance that he attended
shortly before his death. Many of these were signed on the back of the actual dance ticket. Estimated value of his signature on a slip of paper: $2,000–$2,500. *See illustration #23.*

Signed Photographs

Mainly because of the reasons specified above, there are few examples of authentically signed
photographs of James Dean. To deal with the mounting requests for autographed photos that
the star began receiving, a James Dean Fan Club was instituted that offered members an authentically signed photograph as part of the membership dues. These photographs were generally one of two head and shoulders profile poses of Dean from *Rebel without a Cause* (see

Jim Dean, who made a fine showing on the second team last year and as guard this year on the first. Should be a regular next year.

24 James Dean signature on a high school yearbook

25 James Dean signature on a photograph

image above). Dean personally inscribed several of these poses, and some were sent uninscribed (probably bulk signed in one signing session). The majority of these were eight by ten inches in size, but some five-by-seven examples have also surfaced. Dean also personally signed photographs for studio associates, and most of these examples are inscribed as such. Estimated value of a signed photograph: $10,000–$15,000.

Signed Documents

Very few signed documents by Dean have surfaced over the years. I have personally seen two signed checks and one signed bank account agreement. I have never seen a signed contract or other acting-related document. As such, all routine signed documents should be considered scarce (est. $3,000–$5,000), with film-related documents having a substantially greater value (est. $8,000 and up).

Signed Letters

There is only one example of a handwritten signed letter by James Dean ever hitting the marketplace, and that example was a severely faded, torn, and laminated example that still sold in excess of $20,000! Due to the scarcity of this material, it is virtually impossible to put a range of values to these types of items from James Dean.

Miscellaneous Items

One of the more common of the few examples of James Dean's signatures to appear on the market are in the form of signed high school yearbooks from Dean's pre-film career in Fairmont, Indiana. Back in the 1940s, it was common for classmates to sign yearbooks for everyone in their school. These examples are still scarce, as there were limited students and very few copies have survived over fifty years. Occasionally these signed yearbooks do surface; many of them were signed simply "Jim Dean," but some include his high school nickname of "Rack." These have a value less than a Hollywood-era autograph, but still offer a unique collectible for

26

27

26 *A rare, signed Humphrey Bogart image from* Casablanca

27 *Humphrey Bogart signature*

Dean collectors. Estimated value of his signature on a high school yearbook: $5,000–$7,000. *See illustration #24.*

What to Look Out For

James Dean's autograph is forged in all formats, mostly on photographs and slips of paper. His signature remained very consistent, with most examples being very legible, with a distinct paraph (or flourish) underneath the signature. Please refer to the selection of authentic James Dean signature patterns illustrated above as a guide for what you should be looking for in an authentic James Dean signature. *See illustration #25.*

Humphrey Bogart

Humphrey Bogart (1899–1957) is one of the most loved and idolized actors from the Golden Age of Hollywood. *See illustration #26.*

His autograph is rare in all formats. It is one of the most requested autographs by collectors of Golden Hollywood and considered a very strong investment for future increases in value.

The following is a breakdown of values for the different formats of Bogie's signature. *See illustration #27.*

Signature

Bogart was most courteous as a signer if you were fortunate enough to meet him at a Hollywood premiere, at one of his favorite boxing matches, or strolling the streets with his love, Lauren Bacall. His signature is most common on slips of paper or signed album pages (pages from a fan's autograph book), but these examples are becoming quite scarce. The most treasured form of this format is a single page signed by both Humphrey Bogart and Lauren Bacall Bogart. Estimated value of a signature on a slip of paper: $800–$1,000.

Signed Photographs

This is the format that fools many new collectors, and even some auction houses. Please see the "What to Look Out For" section for more details. Photographs authentically signed by Bogart were generally given to a specific person close to him (friends, makeup artist, another actor) and are usually inscribed to that person. Authentically signed photographs are scarce. The most treasured form of this format is a signed photograph in character from *Casablanca* or *The Maltese Falcon*. A super-rare signed photo of Bogie in character from *Casablanca* sold at auction in 2001 for over $15,000! Estimated value of a signed photograph: $3,000–$4,000.

Signed Documents

Several signed Bogart documents have appeared on the market over the years. Collectors look to these as solid investments because they are a good indication of authenticity. But you must be forewarned: forgers have started to forge signatures on documents, therefore one must look at all signatures as suspect until proven authentic. Prices can range according to the subject matter—routine legal matters (bank account cards, power of attorney) have little more value than a routine signature (est. $1,000–$1,500), but signed documents relating to his film work can be worth substantially more (est. $2,000 and up).

Signed Letters

Bogart is not common in signed letters at all. Those that do exist are usually very brief. In the different formats, prices can vary significantly if the content of the letter relates to his career. Price ranges reflect routine content—Typed Letters Signed (TLS): est. $2,000, Autograph Letter Signed (ALS): $5,000+.

What to Look Out For

Humphrey Bogart had little patience to deal with the thousands of letters he received requesting his autograph. Thus he employed a personal secretary, Miss Verita Thompson, and a personal assistant, Kathryn Sloan, who were responsible for responding to all who wrote to him. They were authorized to sign all through-the-mail autograph requests on everything from sheets of paper to photographs. Nearly all signed Bogart photographs (that are not forgeries) were signed by them. Please refer to the secretarial signature patterns illustrated above that differentiate between an authentic and secretarial Bogie.

Bogart is also one of the most forged signatures of Golden Hollywood icons. His signature remained fairly constant throughout his career. Please refer to the selection of authentic Humphrey Bogart signature patterns illustrated on page 47.

Authentic Humphrey Bogart Signatures

See illustration #28.

Secretarial "Humphrey Bogart" Signatures

See illustration #29.

28

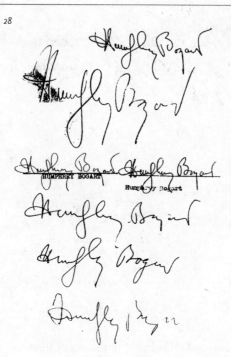

29

28 *Authentic Humphrey Bogart signature*

29 *Secretarial Humphrey Bogart signature*

(images courtesy of U.A.C.C.)

30

31

Thanks and best wishes
Charlie Chaplin
19.44.

30 *Charlie Chaplin signed photo as*
   The Tramp

31 *Charlie Chaplin Signature*

Charles Chaplin

Charles Chaplin (1889–1977) is considered one of the most influential filmmakers of all time, and his lovable Tramp character is enshrined in the annals of film history. *See illustration #30.*

His autograph is desired in all formats, especially signed photographs depicting him as the Tramp, which are considered extremely rare.

The following is a breakdown of values for the different formats of Charles Chaplin's signature. *See illustration #31.*

Signature

Because Chaplin lived a very long life, and had an extensive career lasting the majority of his life, his autograph material is available to the marketplace. Chaplin was a very social celebrity and was one of the most recognizable stars in the world. He was very pleasant to autograph seekers in person and readily signed autographs for his fans. Estimated value of his signature on a slip of paper: $350–$400. *See illustrations #34, 35, and 36.*

Signed Photographs

Chaplin received enormous amounts of fan mail, and most requests were fulfilled with a beautiful portrait photograph, usually five by seven or three by five in size, that bore a rubber stamp, pre-printed, or secretarially signed signature. Many of these were signed with the sentiment "Faithfully" or "Yours Truly." Chaplin did sign some photos personally, but most of them were reserved for friends or associates, and these examples are usually inscribed and are sometimes signed with a first name only. Estimated value of a signed photograph: $700–$1,200. *See illustration #32.* There are very few signed photographs of Chaplin in character as the Tramp. These are the most sought after by collectors and have an estimated value of $3,000–$5,000.

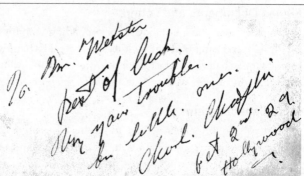

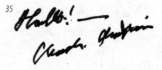

32 Formal Chaplin signed photograph

33 Rare Chaplin family signatures with rare Charlie Tramp sketch

34 Lengthy Chaplin inscription ca. 1929

35 and 36 Two late-in-life (ca. 1970s) Chaplin signatures

Signed Documents and Letters

In Chaplin's later years, he enjoyed corresponding with his fans and generally replied with a very brief typed letter of thanks with a signature. His handwritten material is very scarce. All routine signed letters and documents have an estimated value of $500–$800, with film-related letters and documents having a substantially greater value (est. $2,000 and up).

Miscellaneous Items

On rare occasions, Chaplin would add to his signature a hand-drawn sketch of his beloved Tramp, or sometimes just a pair of the Tramp's shoes and a cane. These are very uncommon, and greatly desired by collectors because of the direct relation to the Tramp character. Estimated value of a Chaplin-penned Tramp sketch: $2,000–$2,500. *See illustration #33.*

What to Look Out For

Chaplin is an often forged autograph in all formats, especially on Tramp poses and slips of paper.

Bruce Lee

Bruce Lee (1940–1973) is considered the most influential martial artist actor of all time, and his techniques set the precedent for every martial arts film to follow. *See illustration #37.*

His autograph is rare in all formats, especially signed photographs, which are the most desired by collectors. His tragic death at the pinnacle of his career has taken his legend to mythic levels with martial arts fans across the globe.

The following is a breakdown of values for the different formats of Bruce Lee's signature. *See illustration #38.*

Signature

As with James Dean, Bruce Lee's star was just beginning to rise with American audiences when he died. He was not in the American public eye long enough to sign hundreds of autographs at premieres and other events. As such, there are very few examples of his in-person signatures available. Estimated value of his signature on a slip of paper: $1,000–$1,400.

Signed Photographs

Mainly because of the reasons specified above, there are few examples of authentically signed photographs of Bruce Lee. Signed photographs of the star are considered extremely scarce, especially in martial arts poses or stills from his films. Value of a signed photograph: $3,000–$4,000.

Signed Documents

Because of the scarcity of his autograph material and the overwhelming demand by collectors, Bruce's widow, Linda Lee, released a very limited series of signed canceled bank checks and credit card slips in the early 1990s. *See illustration #39.* These have become very desirable to collectors because of the unparalleled authenticity factor, and have practically disappeared from the marketplace into the personal collections of fans and collectors. I have never seen a signed contract or other acting-related document from Bruce Lee become available to the marketplace. All signed documents should be considered scarce (est. $1,200–$1,800), with film-related documents having a substantially greater value (est. $5,000 and up).

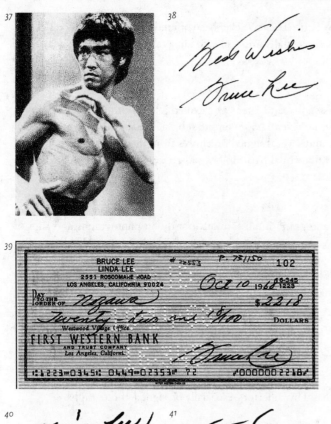

37 *Bruce Lee*

38 *Bruce Lee signature*

39 *Bruce Lee signed check*

40 and 41 *Bruce Lee English and
Chinese signatures*

Signed Letters

Very few handwritten letters by Bruce Lee have ever been offered to the marketplace. Because of the scarcity of this material, it is virtually impossible to put a range of value to these types of items from Bruce Lee.

Miscellaneous Items

Other than his film and television career, Bruce Lee devoted a lot of time and energy to his martial arts training, and he wrote several books on the subject. He also held several martial arts competitions at his studio, and several signed brochures from these events have surfaced over the years. These have a value equal to a Hollywood-related autograph, as both of his worlds were so closely linked.

What to Look Out For

Bruce Lee is an often forged autograph in all formats, mostly on photographs and slips of paper. His signature remained very consistent, with most examples being very legible, and this has indirectly led to forgeries appearing to closely resemble his authentic script. Bruce Lee on occasion did sign in both English and Chinese. Please refer to the selection of authentic Bruce Lee signature patterns illustrated above as a guideline. *See illustrations #40 and 41.*

John Wayne

John Wayne (1907–1979), the Duke, is regarded as the quintessential American hero of Hollywood. *See illustration #42.*

His autograph is always in demand by collectors, especially on signed photographs.

The following is a breakdown of values for the different formats of John Wayne's signature.

Signature

John Wayne was a very willing signer when he was approached in person. In his later years, he printed a business card that read "JOHN WAYNE" on the front, and on the reverse was a reproduction of his famous signature, plus a generic inscription "Good Luck" (his favorite sentiment) as well as a date. *See illustration #43.* These were printed in bulk and carried in his pockets. When approached in a large crowd, he would hand out these cards. There are some authentically signed examples (the first few he printed were hand-signed before he stepped out), but the demands on his time required him to go the route of the facsimile signature so as not to disappoint his fans. These pre-printed cards do carry a value strictly as a collectible (est. $75–$100), while the hand-signed examples are worth significantly more (est. $500–$700). Estimated value of his signature on a slip of paper: $350–$500.

Signed Photographs

John Wayne signed many photographs for personal friends and associates, and most of these examples are inscribed to those individuals. Most who wrote to him requesting a signed photograph in fact received a secretarially signed photograph. Wayne's secretarial signatures are quite good mimics of his authentic example, but in most cases, the handwriting in the inscription and sentiment are very feminine and discernible from Wayne's distinct script. The most

42 A rare, signed photograph with
added "Duke"

43 Pre-print John Wayne card

44 John Wayne signed western pose

45 Authentic John Wayne signature
(ca. 1962)

46 Secretarial John Wayne signature

desired signed photographs have him in western poses. Estimated value of a signed photograph in a non-western pose: $800–$1,000. Estimated value of a signed western photograph: $1,300–$1,700. *See illustration #44.*

Signed Letters and Documents

The majority of John Wayne signed letters are typewritten, signed, and have general content. A large percentage of these are secretarially signed as well. All routine signed letters or documents have a modest value (est. $500–$700), but film-related documents or letters have a substantially greater value (est. $1,000 and up).

What to Look Out For

John Wayne is a frequently forged autograph in all formats, mostly on photographs and slips of paper. There is also a significant amount of secretarially signed material being offered as authentic. *See illustrations #45 and 46.*

Walt Disney

Walt Disney (1901–1966) is considered one of the most influential innovators in the art of cinematic animation, and the Disney empire that bears his name and vision is one of the most loved and successful organizations around the globe. *See illustration #47.*

His autograph is rare in all formats, most notably in signed photographs and original signed sketches, which are the most desired by collectors.

The following is a breakdown of values for the different formats of Walt Disney's signature. *See illustration #48.*

Signature

Walt Disney was a very busy and somewhat reclusive executive throughout his career. He possessed one of the most ornate and distinguishable signatures, the printed variation of which became the logo of the Disney companies. He was very courteous to the patrons of his theme park, and would grant an autograph to all who asked for it. In fact, to accommodate autograph seekers, he would sit at his desk and sign a notepad of his personal stationery (with a printed Mickey Mouse sketch on it) before walking through the park, handing out the presigned sheets to allow him to continue on throughout his day without excessive delay. *See illustration #48.* These signed sheets, because of their direct Mickey Mouse link, have a higher value (est. $2,000–$2,500) than a signature on a plain piece of paper, while the estimated value of his signature on a slip of paper is $1,500–$2,000.

Signed Photographs

There are few examples of authentically signed photographs of Walt Disney available. To deal with the mounting requests for autographs that he began receiving, Disney had his animators sign the majority of fan mail requests. Most "signed" photos that were sent by mail were signed by the animators (many by Bob Moore). *See illustration #50.* Disney did personally sign (and almost always inscribed) photographs on occasion, but these were almost always reserved for personal friends and business associates. Estimated value of a signed photograph: $4,000–$6,000.

47 A rare, signed vintage Walt Disney photograph

48 Signed notepad page

49 Disney's Mickey Mouse sketch

50 Bob Moore "Disney" signature from a book

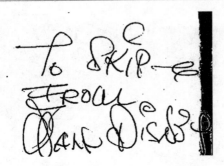

51

52

Sincerely,

51 Authentic early Disney book signature

52 Walt Disney later signature from a letter

53 Greta Garbo secretarial signed photo

54 Rare, vintage Greta Garbo signature

Signed Documents and Letters

Numerous signed documents by Walt Disney have surfaced over the years. Typed signed letters range from general content letters on personal stationery to amazing examples detailing his theme park plans and films. There have been several signed checks to surface as well. All routine signed documents should be considered scarce (est. $3,000–$4,000), with film or theme park–related documents having a substantially greater value (est. $6,000 and up).

Miscellaneous Items

One of the most sought after and *rare* Disney autograph formats are signed sketches and signed original animation cels and prints. Disney issued limited edition prints and original animation cels from some of the studio's most loved films. On rare occasions, Walt would sign and inscribe these, usually in a colorful artist's ink pen on the matte board surrounding the image. These were also signed by his animators on his behalf. The authentic examples are exceedingly rare, and depending on the image, can sell for huge sums (est. $8,000–$15,000). A small handful of original sketches by Walt Disney have surfaced, two examples being a Mickey Mouse and a Goofy sketch. Estimated value of a Walt Disney–signed sketch: $15,000–$25,000. *See illustration #49.*

What to Look Out For

The aforementioned "Walt Disney" autographs signed by Disney animators are plentiful, but fortunately are easily distinguishable from authentic examples signed by Walt himself. Disney is a highly forged autograph in all formats, mostly on Disney-related memorabilia like coloring books and song sheets, and especially slips of paper. Please refer to the selection of authentic Walt Disney signature patterns illustrated above as a guideline. *See illustrations #51 and 52.*

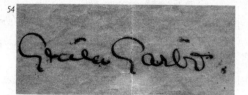

Greta Garbo

Greta Garbo (1905–1990) was one of the most mysterious and legendary Hollywood icons of the Golden Age of Hollywood. Her retirement at the peak of her career, and the subsequent reclusive lifestyle she led for the remaining forty-eight years of her life, made her a bigger legend than she had ever wished to be. *See illustration #53.*

Her autograph is extremely rare in all formats, especially signed photographs, which are the most desired by collectors. She is considered the rarest autograph of the Golden Hollywood age.

The following is a breakdown of values for the different formats of Greta Garbo's signature.

Signed Photographs

There are few examples of authentically signed photographs of Garbo. Studio secretaries signed all studio fan mail requests on her behalf. *See illustration #58.* The few authentic examples that have surfaced were signed specifically for very close friends, and are inscribed as such. Estimated value of a signed photograph: $15,000–$20,000.

Signature

Garbo disliked the Hollywood promotion machine from the very start of her career, and she was hesitant to attend industry functions. Thus there are very few examples of her in-person signatures available. In my research, I know of maybe three or four examples ever to surface in the marketplace. Estimated value of her signature on a slip of paper: $1,500–$2,000. *See illustration #54.*

Signed Documents

Very few documents signed by Garbo have surfaced over the years. *See illustrations #55 and 56.* I have personally seen several signed checks and a few signed bank account agreements. I have seen one or two signed contracts or other acting-related documents. All routine signed docu-

55 Rare 1942 Greta Garbo signed
check

56 1927 Garbo contractual signature

57 1950s Garbo postcard with initials

58 Greta Garbo secretarial signature
from a photo

59 Rare Garbo ALS—signed "H"
(Harry)

ments should be considered scarce (est. $2,500–$3,000), with film-related documents having a substantially greater value (est. $8,000 and up).

Signed Letters

In her secluded retirement, Garbo wrote many very personal letters to her close friends. Most of these were written in pencil, on onionskin paper, and most are signed with her secret pen names "Harry" or "Gilly" and some with initials "G.G." These examples are generally filled with her ramblings about the outside world, and some contain film-related content. All routine handwritten letters should be considered scarce (est. $4,000–$5,500), with film-related letters having a substantially greater value (est. $6,000 and up). *See illustrations #57 and 59.*

What to Look Out For

Due to the incredible prices realized for authentic examples, Greta Garbo's signature is often a forged autograph in all formats.

Jean Harlow

Jean Harlow (1911–1937) was the first of the tragic Hollywood platinum-blond bombshells. *See illustration #60.*

Her autograph is rare in all formats, especially signed photographs, which are the most desired by collectors. Her tragic death at the height of her young career has caused her legend to grow to mythic proportions.

The following is a breakdown of values for the different formats of Jean Harlow's signature.

Signature

Jean Harlow's mother (also named Jean Harlow, she is referred to as Mama Jean) was a failed actress, and she poured all her energy into the career of her daughter. In fact Mama Jean, on behalf of her daughter, signed nearly all correspondence and photographs. Therefore very few examples of the star's authentic autographs in all formats are available, the majority being in-person signatures. Estimated value of her signature on a slip of paper: $1,200–$1,800.

Signed Photographs

There are few examples of authentically signed photographs of Jean Harlow. Mama Jean took great pleasure in signing the photographs of her daughter, as most are wonderfully inscribed and very legibly signed. Jean herself did personally sign photographs, but these were reserved for close friends, and most of these examples are inscribed and signed with a first name only. Because of the rarity of finding an authentic Jean Harlow signed photo, the Mama Jean–signed poses are considered "official" signatures, and most are on gorgeous vintage original stills. These examples are very collectible and have a value (based on the image) in the range of $300–$800. Estimated value of a Jean Harlow authentically signed photograph: $3,500–$6,000. *See illustration #61.*

Signed Letters and Documents

The majority of Jean Harlow signed letters are typewritten and signed by Mama Jean, and have general content. As such, all Mama Jean signed letters and documents have a modest

60 Jean Harlow

61 Rare Jean Harlow authentic signature (photo 11 x 14)

62 Authentic Jean Harlow signed album page

63 Mama Jean Harlow signature

64 1937 Rose Bowl ticket signed in person by Jean Harlow and William Powell

value (est. $200–$300), with film-related documents or letters with an authentic Jean signature having a substantially greater value (est. $5,000 and up).

What to Look Out For

The Mama Jean and authentic Jean Harlow signatures are easily distinguishable. *See illustrations #62, 63, and 64.* Because of the high value of her items, Jean Harlow is a highly forged autograph in all formats, mostly on photographs and slips of paper.

Katharine Hepburn

Katharine Hepburn (1907–2003) was one of the most celebrated and revered actresses in the history of cinema. *See illustration #65.*

Hepburn's autograph has always been in high demand by collectors, and her unusual signing habits have made the supply of material scarce and rarely available for long.

The following is a breakdown of values for the different formats of Katharine Hepburn's signature.

Signature

During the early stages of her career, Kate was a ready signer if approached in public. As her career progressed, she began making fewer and fewer public appearances. Thus most of the star's in-person signatures are from the early to late 1930s. There are very few examples that date from later periods than this. In most cases, later period signatures offered are in fact signatures that have been clipped from a signed letter. Estimated value of her signature on a slip of paper: $200–$300. *See illustration #66.*

Signed Photographs

The majority of authentically signed photographs of Katharine Hepburn date from her early period, as noted above. She quickly drew up a policy of signing photographs on the reverse side of the image, and soon began refusing to sign photographs except for personal friends and associates. Because of this fact, any signed photograph that is not personally inscribed to an individual should be considered suspect, and all signed photographs are considered scarce. Estimated value of a photograph signed on the reverse side: $400–$600. Estimated value of a photograph signed on the image side: $1,000–$2,000.

Signed Documents

Very few Katharine Hepburn signed documents have surfaced over the years. Most have been personal checks filled out and signed by her. As such, all routine signed documents should be considered slightly above signature value (est. $300–$500), with film-related documents having a substantially greater value (est. $1,500 and up).

Signed Letters

This is the area of autograph material that is most plentiful for Katharine Hepburn. Kate stopped signing all letters about 1997, as her health deteriorated to the point where she could no longer correspond. Before 1997, those who wrote to her requesting an autograph were flatly refused. Those who wrote to her and sent her a small gift would receive a very brief

65

66

67

I - 5 - 1978

Dear Mr. Haber --

    I am sorry -- I have no idea whom it is from. Certainly his paper and writing. But so many Eddie's he knew --

68 Katharine Houghton Hepburn

69

65 A rare, signed vintage 11 x 14 Katharine Hepburn photograph

66 Kate Hepburn's full signature

67 Katharine Hepburn signed letter

68 Rare Katharine Hepburn ALS

69 Katharine Hepburn signed Broadway Playbill magazine

typed thank-you note on her personal stationery, with a bold signature on the bottom. If you wrote asking her to sign a photograph, she would reply with a similar note stating that she did not sign photographs, but would include a signature on the letter. *See illustration #67.*

To personal friends, Kate would sometimes reply with a handwritten and signed letter, in her amazingly unique and hard-to-decipher script. She would also sign her correspondence sometimes as "Katharine," "Kate," or "K. Hepburn." Most typed letters represent routine correspondence, and these examples are considered equal in value to a signature (est. $200–$300).

Handwritten material is scarce, and value is subject to content (est. $700–$1,200). *See illustration #68.*

Miscellaneous Items

Katharine Hepburn would sign Broadway *Playbill* magazine covers with her photograph on them (but not photographs!). These are becoming scarce, and are collected by Broadway and *Playbill* collectors as well. Estimated value of a signed *Playbill* magazine: $500–$800. *See illustration #69.*

What to Look Out For

Katharine Hepburn is a highly forged autograph, mostly on photographs, as this is where most of the demand from collectors lies. During the majority of her career her signature remained very consistent, with later-year examples dissolving into a near-scribble. Please refer to the selection of authentic Katharine Hepburn signature patterns illustrated above as a guide.

Marlon Brando

Marlon Brando (b. 1924) is considered one of the finest actors of modern cinema. His blistering breakout performances in the 1950s and throughout the 1960s and 1970s defined him as one of the leaders of the Method school of acting. *See illustration #70.*

Brando's autograph material is much rarer than most collectors realize, and the very limited supply of authentic material will surely be in high demand by future collectors.

The following is a breakdown of values for the different formats of Marlon Brando's signature.

Signature

During the early stages of Marlon Brando's Hollywood career, namely during the 1950s and early 1960s, Brando played by the Hollywood publicity game and was a ready signer if approached in public. As his disdain for all things Hollywood grew, so did his refusal to sign autographs. There are very few authentic examples of in-person signatures of Marlon Brando dating later than the early 1960s. Since the early 1980s, Brando has flatly refused to sign anything; therefore any modern-signed index cards or album pages should be questioned as suspect. Estimated value of his signature on a slip of paper: $300–$500. *See illustration #71.*

Signed Photographs

As noted above, the majority of authentically signed photographs of Marlon Brando date from his early career. Many of these examples were signed for associates and are in some cases signed with first name only, or sometimes "Mar." Many examples are on small photographs—Brando printed up a two-by-three-inch black-and-white close-up pose to send to fans that he signed in bulk in the early 1960s (see top image). I know of only three authentically signed *Godfather* poses, with one being signed on the set of *The Freshman* after a collector persisted with a request for four days before Brando finally signed. Brando is considered scarce in signed photographs. Estimated value of a signed photograph (depending upon size, image, etc.): $500–$2,000.

Signed Documents

Very few signed documents by Brando have surfaced over the years. Many signed contracts relate to his non-Hollywood investments, while some directly reference his less-regarded roles. As such, all routine signed documents should be considered slightly above signature value (est. $500–$1,000), with film-related documents having a substantially greater value (est. $1,500 and up).

Signed Letters

There are very few examples of signed letters by Marlon Brando. Most express routine correspondence, and these examples should be considered equal in value to routine signed documents (est. $500–$1,000). Handwritten material is scarce, and value would be subject to content.

What to Look Out For

Marlon Brando is a highly forged autograph in all formats, mostly on photographs from his most famous roles. During his younger days, his signature remained very consistent, with later-years' examples dissolving into a near-scribble. As such, collectors should concentrate on

70

71 *positively af... ing a rather manish young aryan. the book?* "Notes on Bicycle Seat Smelling in Wet Weather"

your loving pal Mar.

72 APPROVED AND ACCEPTED:

Marlon Brando

73 and initiation fees. (See reverse side.)
(7) I affirm that I have truthfully answered the questions on the reverse side hereof.
Dated 5/14/63 19
(Sign here) Marlon Brando
(Sign here) Marlon Brando

74 Receipt of the original hereof is hereby acknowledged:
by: Marlon Brando
Secretary or Assistant Secretary

70 *A rare, signed Marlon Brando photograph*

71 *Rare Marlon Brando handwritten note*

72 *1953 signed document*

73 *1963 signed document*

74 *1977 signed document*

75

75 *Rare Judy Garland 1930 Oz-era signed photograph*

76 *1939 Garland signature style*

77 *1967 Garland signature style*

vintage-signed material. Please refer to the selection of authentic Marlon Brando signature patterns illustrated above as a guide to what you should look for in an authentic Marlon Brando signature. *See illustration #72, 73, and 74.*

The Wizard of Oz

The signatures of the cast of this classic 1939 epic are some of the most beloved and desired of all Hollywood autographs. The following is a brief breakdown of the values for the different formats of autographs for the main cast of the film.

Judy Garland

Judy Garland (1922–1969) was catapulted into the annals of Hollywood lore for her incredible performance as Dorothy Gale, filmed when she was just fifteen years old. *See illustration #75.*

She was a very gracious signer for her adoring fans, and many autograph albums from the 1930s all the way up to the 1960s have an in-person signature of hers among them.

Signature

Early in her career she changed the formation of the *G* in her last name from a capital *G* to a lowercase *g*. Estimated value of Judy's signature on a slip of paper: $400–$500 *See illustrations #76 and 77.*

Signed Photographs

Most fan mail sent to the studio was responded to with a pre-print or a secretarial. She did sign photographs, mostly to close friends and associates, and these are almost always personally inscribed. I do not have a record of an authentic signed photo as "Dorothy" ever being sold.

Estimated value of a Judy Garland signed photograph: $1,000–$1,500.

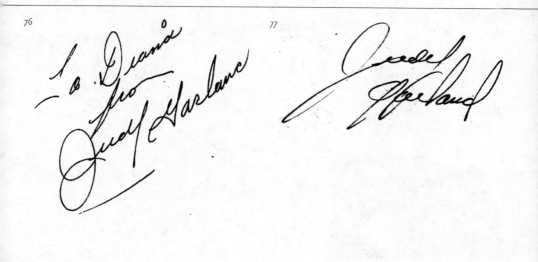

76   77

A signed photograph as Dorothy: $15,000 +.

Signed Documents

Numerous business and personal checks signed by Judy Garland have been offered for sale. Many collectors look to these as a sure sign of authenticity. Estimated value of a signed check: $400–$500. Very few film-related documents such as contracts have been offered, and these have a substantially greater value (est. $2,000 and up).

Frank Morgan

Frank Morgan (1890–1949) actually had *five roles* in the film (Professor Marvel/Emerald City Doorman/The Cabbie/The Wizard's Guard) but is best remembered as the Wizard of Oz. *See illustration #78.*

He was a notable character actor, but he was not recognized until years later for his roles in the film. He died just ten years after the release of the film, so there are very few of his autographs available.

Signature

Estimated value of Frank Morgan's signature on a slip of paper: $400–$500. *See illustration #79.*

Signed Photographs

Because of Morgan's character actor status during his career he is very seldom found in signed photographs. Most examples found bear lengthy inscriptions to friends. He is extremely rare on signed photos as the Wizard (I know of only one example ever being offered).

Estimated value of a Morgan signed photograph: $700–$900.

Estimated value of a signed photograph as the Wizard: $8,000–$10,000.

78

79

78 *Frank Morgan signed photograph*

79 *Frank Morgan signed album page*

Bert Lahr

Bert Lahr (1895–1967), who played the Cowardly Lion (and Zeke), was a seasoned vaudeville performer who maintained a character actor status like Frank Morgan. *See illustration #82.*

There is very limited autograph material of his available, many examples being on album pages and signed theater programs.

Signature

Estimated value of Bert Lahr's signature on a slip of paper: $400–$500. *See illustration #81.*

Signed Photographs

Signed photos of Bert Lahr are scarce, and many examples are personal portraits signed in white ink, which he sent out to autograph seekers. He is very rare in poses as the Lion, and only two or three have ever been offered on the market.

Estimated value of a signed photograph as the Lion: $10,000 +.

Estimated value of a signed photograph: $1,000–$1,300. *See illustration #80.*

Ray Bolger

Ray Bolger (1904–1987) played the Scarecrow (and Hunk). He was always a gracious autograph signer and replied to all fan mail during his later years with authentically signed photographs, many of which he inscribed "From the Scarecrow of Oz." *See illustration #83.*

Signature

Estimated value of Ray Bolger's signature on a slip of paper: $75–$100 (if inscribed as the Scarecrow: $150–$200).

80

81

82

83

80 *Rare Bert Lahr signed photo-graph as the Lion*

81 *Bert Lahr signed album page*

82 *Bert Lahr signed portrait*

83 *Ray Bolger signed photo as the scarecrow*

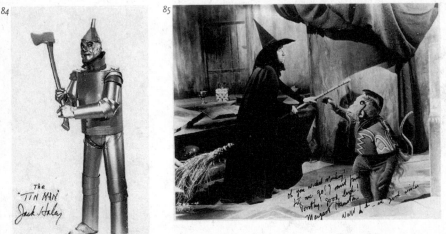

84 Jack Haley, the "Tin Man"

85 Margaret Hamilton as the
Wicked Witch of the West

Signed Photographs

Signed photos of Ray Bolger are available from all stages in his career; the most desired are in character as the Scarecrow. The Oz examples are becoming scarce. Estimated value of a signed photograph: $150–$200. Estimated value of a signed photograph as the Scarecrow: $300–$350.

Jack Haley

Jack Haley (1898–1979), played the Tin Man (and Hickory). He was always a gracious autograph signer and replied to all fan mail during his later years with authentically signed photographs, on many of which he inscribed "The Tin Man." *See illustration #84.*

Signature

Estimated value of Jack Haley's signature on a slip of paper: $75–$100 (if inscribed as the Tin Man: $150–$200).

Signed Photographs

Signed photos of Jack Haley are available from all stages in his career; the most desired are in character as the Tin Man. The Oz examples are becoming scarce. Estimated value of a signed photograph: $150–$200. Estimated value of a signed photograph as the Tin Man: $300–$350.

Margaret Hamilton

Margaret Hamilton (1902–1985) played the Wicked Witch of the West and Miss Almira Gulch. She was a generous autograph signer and replied to all fan mail, especially during her later years. Many signed photographs bear lengthy inscriptions and references to Oz. She was also known to use a secretary in later years, as well as signing photos as "M.H." and "W.W.W." (Wicked Witch of the West). *See illustration #85.*

86 *Billie Burke*

87 *Clara Blandick*

Signature

Estimated value of Margaret Hamilton's signature on a slip of paper: $100–$125 (if inscribed as the Wicked Witch: $150–$200).

Signed Photographs

Signed photos of Margaret Hamilton are available, but are most desired in character as the Witch. The Oz examples are becoming scarce. Estimated value of a signed photograph $150–$200. Estimated value of a signed photograph as Witch: $450–$600.

Billie Burke

Billie Burke (1885–1970) played Glinda, the Good Witch of the North. She was always a gracious autograph signer and replied to all fan mail during her life. *See illustration #86.*

Signature

Estimated value of Billie Burke's signature on a slip of paper: $150–$200.

Signed Photographs

Signed photos of Billie Burke are available as herself, but she is extremely rare on signed photos as Glinda (I know of only one example ever being offered). Estimated value of a signed photograph: $400–$600. Estimated value of a signed photograph as Glinda: $6,000 +.

Clara Blandick

Clara Blandick (1881–1962) played Auntie Em. She was a character actress in Hollywood and never became a big star. As such, her autograph is excessively rare in all formats. *See illustration #87.*

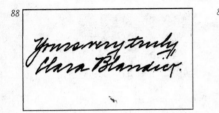

88

89

90

88 Clara Blandick signature

89 Charley Grapewin

90 Charley Grapewin signature

Signature

Estimated value of Clara Blandick's signature on a slip of paper: $700–$850. *See illustration #88.*

Signed Photographs

Signed photos of Clara Blandick are almost nonexistent. Estimated value of a signed photograph: $6000 +.

Charley Grapewin

Charley Grapewin (1869–1956) played Uncle Henry. He was a character actor in Hollywood and, as such, his autograph is excessively rare in all formats. *See illustration #89.*

Signature

Estimated value of Charley Grapewin's signature on a slip of paper: $500–$600. *See illustration #90.*

Signed Photographs

Signed photos of Charley Grapewin are almost nonexistent. Estimated value of a signed photograph: $2,000 +.

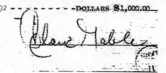

88 *Clara Blandick signature*

89 *Charley Grapewin*

90 *Charley Grapewin signature*

91 *Rare Clark Gable signed GWTW pose*

92 *Clark Gable business check signature*

Gone with the Wind

The signatures of the cast of this classic 1939 epic are some of the most sought-after and collectible of all Hollywood autographs. The following is a brief breakdown of the values for the different formats of autographs for the main cast of the film.

Clark Gable

Gable (1901–1960), who played Rhett Butler, was nominated for Best Actor for this role. He was an icon of Hollywood and is considered the quintessential leading man. *See illustration #91.*

He was a very gracious signer for his adoring fans, and many autograph albums from the 1930s and 1940s have an in-person signature of Gable's among them. *See illustration #92.*

Signature

Estimated value of Clark Gable's signature on a slip of paper: $350–$400.

Signed Photographs

Most fan mail sent to the studio was responded to with a secretarially signed photograph. Gable did sign photographs, mostly to close friends and associates, and these are almost always personally inscribed, and many are signed with just a first name. Signed photos of Gable as Rhett Butler are very rare, and only a small handful have ever been offered on the market. Estimated value of a signed photograph: $1,000–$1,500. Estimated value of a signed photograph as Rhett Butler: $5,000–$7,500.

Signed Documents

A number of business and personal checks signed by Clark Gable have been offered for sale. Many collectors look to these as a sure sign of authenticity. Estimated value of a signed check:

$400–$450. Very few film-related documents such as contracts have been offered, and these have a substantially greater value (est. $1,000 and up).

What to Look Out For

Very early in his career, Gable changed the formation of the *G* in his last name from a capital *G* to a lowercase *g*. This did not change on business documents, as these continued to be signed with the uppercase *G*.

Vivien Leigh

Leigh (1913–1967), who played Scarlett O'Hara, won an Academy Award as Best Actress for her role. *See illustration #93.*

She was another very gracious signer for her adoring fans, and many autograph albums from the 1930s and 1940s have an in-person signature of hers, sometimes on the same page as her leading man in real life, Laurence Olivier.

Signature

Estimated value of Vivien Leigh's signature on a slip of paper: $350–$400.

Signed Photographs

Vivien Leigh responded to fan mail on most occasions with an authentically signed photograph. Many of these are personally inscribed, and many are signed with just a first name. She is very rare on signed photos as Scarlett O'Hara, and only a small handful have ever been offered on the market. Estimated value of a signed photograph: $1,000–$1,400. Estimated value of a signed photograph as Scarlett: $5,000–$7,000. *See illustration #93.*

Signed Letters

Leigh corresponded with both typed and handwritten letters. On rare occasions these letters did include film content, with several directly referring to her *GWTW* role. Estimated value of a routine content letter: $500–$700. Film-related letters have a substantially greater value: (est. $1,500 and up).

What to Look Out For

Leigh is often forged on *GWTW* stills and on slips of paper, due to the popularity of the film.

Hattie McDaniel

Hattie McDaniel (1895–1952), who played Mammy, has the distinction of being the first African-American to win an Academy Award for Best Supporting Actress, winning for her role in this film (beating out costar Olivia de Havilland). *See illustration #95.*

Her autograph is very scarce and is considered one of the rarest of the *GWTW* cast.

Signature

Estimated value of Hattie McDaniel's signature on a slip of paper: $700–$800: *See illustration #96.*

93

94

95

96

93 *Rare Vivien Leigh signed GWTW pose*

94 *Vivien Leigh signed GWTW program*

95 *Rare Hattie McDaniel signed photograph*

96 *Hattie McDaniel signed album page ca. 1935*

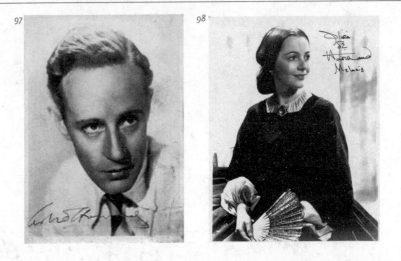

97 *Leslie Howard*

98 *Olivia de Havilland*

Signed Photographs

Signed photos of Hattie McDaniel are scarce, and the majority of examples are inscribed to a friend or associate. She is very rare in poses as Mammy, and only a small handful have ever been offered on the market. Estimated value of a signed photograph: $1,800–$2,000. Estimated value of a signed photograph as Mammy: $3,000–$4,000.

What to Look Out For

McDaniel is often forged on *GWTW* stills and on slips of paper, due to the popularity of the movie and the fact that her autograph is fairly easy to replicate.

Leslie Howard

Leslie Howard (1893–1943), who played Ashley Wilkes, is a rare autograph in all formats, and his signature is considered one of the rarest of the *GWTW* cast due to his death just four years after the release of the film. *See illustration #97.*

Signature

Estimated value of Leslie Howard's signature on a slip of paper: $300–$350.

Signed Photographs

Signed photos of Leslie Howard are scarce, especially in poses from *GWTW,* and only a small handful have ever been offered on the market. Estimated value of a signed photograph: $450–$500. Estimated value of a signed photograph as Ashley: $2,000–$3,000.

Olivia de Havilland

Olivia de Havilland (b.1916), who played Melanie Hamilton, was nominated for an Academy Award for Best Supporting Actress for her role in this film. *See illustration #98.*

99 *Butterfly McQueen*

100 *Ann Rutherford and Evelyn Keyes*

Her autograph is available in all formats but is becoming scarce in signed poses from the film.

Signature
Estimated value of Olivia de Havilland's signature on a slip of paper: $75–$100.

Signed Photographs
Signed photos of Olivia de Havilland are available on stills from *GWTW,* and she has from time to time included her character name underneath the signature. Estimated value of a signed photograph: $100–$150. Estimated value of a signed photograph as Melanie: $200–$300.

Butterfly McQueen—"Prissy" (1911–1995)
Signature: $75–$100. *See illustration #99.*

Signed photograph as Prissy: $200–$250.

Ann Rutherford—"Careen O'Hara" (b.1920)
Signature: $50. *See illustration #100.*

Signed photograph as Careen: $75–$100.

Evelyn Keyes—"Suellen O'Hara" (b. 1919)
Signature: $50.

Signed photograph as Suellen: $75–$100.

101 Rand Brooks

102 Cammie King

Rand Brooks—"Charles Hamilton" (1918–2003)

Signature: $50. *See illustration #101.*

Signed photograph as Charles: $50–$75.

Cammie King—"Bonnie Blue Butler" (b. 1934)

Signature: $50. *See illustration #102.*

Signed photograph as Bonnie: $50–$75.

GLOSSARY OF AUTOGRAPH TERMINOLOGY

The following abbreviations indicate formats of autographs. Each description details optimum features.

SIG (Signature)

A single signature in ink on a piece of paper, or cut from a document or letter (also referred to as a "cut"). For optimum value, the page should have enough room around the signature to allow it to be properly matted. Variables that can lessen the value of a signature include ink smears, paper wrinkles or tears, gluing of the page to another sheet underneath, or an irregularly cut sheet that is not mattable or displayable.

DS (Document Signed)

Any document containing a signature including checks, contracts, applications, etc. Greatest value pertains to subject matter of the document and its relation to the signer. Prices in this guide reflect routine subject matter.

TLS (Typed Letter Signed)

A typed letter signed by the celebrity. (Prices for TLS are equal to DS in this guide.)

LS (Letter Signed)

A letter handwritten by another person (often by a secretary) and signed by the celebrity. (Prices for LS are equal to DS in this guide.)

ALS (Autograph Letter Signed)

A handwritten letter signed and written entirely in the hand of the celebrity. Greatest value pertains to subject matter of the letter and its relation to the signer. Prices in this guide reflect routine subject matter.

SP (Signed Photograph)

For optimum value, a photograph should be signed clearly in ink with good signature contrast. Prices indicated are for an eight-by-ten portrait. The value of signed photographs increases with size, condition, and subject matter (a signed photo of an actor in his or her most famous role as opposed to an older age portrait).

Inscribed

A personalized signature (e.g., "To John").

ISP (Inscribed Signed Photograph)

For rare celebrities, inscriptions do not detract from overall value. For common celebrities, an inscription can reduce the overall value of a signed photograph by up to 50 percent.

AUTOGRAPH PRICE LISTINGS

A

NAME	SIG	DS	ALS	SP
A				
Aadland, Beverly	10	25		20
Aaker, Lee	10			25
Aaliyah	50	75	125	200
Aames, Willie	10			25
Abbott & Costello	500	1,000		1,500
Abbott, Bud	300	500	700	500
Abbott, George	40		80	100
Abbott, John	10			20
Abel, Walter	20			50
Abraham, F. Murray	20	40		40
Adams, Brooke	10			20
Adams, Don	10			30
Addy, Mark	15	25		25
Adler, Buddy	25			50
Adler, Stella	15			25
Affleck, Ben	25	35	40	75
Affleck, Casey	15			35
Agar, John	10	20		20
Agutter, Jenny	10			20
Aiello, Danny	20	25	25	35
Akins, Claude	10	20	20	40
Albert, Eddie	10	20	25	35
Albertson, Jack	30	40		40
Alda, Alan	25	35	40	60
Alda, Robert	15			40
Alexander, Ben	55			120
Alexander, Jane	10	20	20	20
Alexander, Jason	25	40	40	50
Alexis, Kim	15	20	30	40
Allen, Barbara Jo	40			50
Allen, Bob	25			60
Allen, Debbie	10			20
Allen, Gracie	100	150		200
Allen, Joan	15	25	50	35
Allen, Karen	15			40

NAME	SIG	DS	ALS	SP
Allen, Marty	10			20
Allen, Rex	10	20	20	20
Allen, Tim	20			50
Allen, Woody	40	75	80	70
Alley, Kirstie	20			35
Allison, May	25	35	45	45
Allyson, June	20		35	40
Alonso, Maria Conchita	15	20		30
Altman, Robert	20	35	50	75
Alyn, Kirk	25			50
Ameche, Don	30	35	35	50
Ames, Ed	15			25
Amis, Suzy	20			35
Amos & Andy	170	300	375	325
Amsterdam, Morey	25			40
Anderson, Anthony	15	25		30
Anderson, Bronco Billy	150	225	320	450
Anderson, Dame Judith	30			50
Anderson, Eddie	70	125	225	225
Anderson, Gillian	30	50	85	75
Anderson, Loni	10	15	25	35
Anderson, Pamela	30	50	80	75
Anderson, Paul Thomas	25	50		60
Andress, Ursula	30	35	45	60
Andrews, Dana	10			25
Andrews, Julie	35	70	90	100
Angeli, Pier	65	80	200	150
Aniston, Jennifer	25	40	60	65
Ankers, Evelyn	25			40
Ann-Margret	35	40	75	90
Annabella	20			40
Anton, Susan	10			35
Antonelli, Laura	20			60
Antonioni, Michelangelo	40	80	150	200
Anwar, Gabrielle	20			40
Applegate, Christina	20			40
Apted, Michael	20			35
Arbuckle, Roscoe "Fatty"	425	700	1,000	1,250

A

A

NAME	SIG	DS	ALS	SP
Archer, Anne	20			35
Arden, Eve	25	35	55	60
Arkin, Adam	10	15	25	25
Arkin, Alan	20	25	30	30
Arlen, Richard	30			80
Arliss, George	55	65	80	120
Armstrong, Robert	75			220
Arnaz, Desi	70	150	200	225
Arnaz, Desi, Jr.	10			20
Arnaz, Lucie	10			20
Arness, James	30	60	80	75
Arnold, Edward	30			70
Arnold, Tom	10			35
Arquette, David	20			35
Arquette, Patricia	20			50
Arquette, Rosanna	25			50
Arthur, Beatrice	10			30
Arthur, Jean	120	150	250	200
Arthur, Julia	20			40
Ashcroft, Peggy	30			70
Asner, Ed	15			35
Assante, Armand	25			45
Astaire & Rogers	250	350		650
Astaire, Adele	40			80
Astaire, Fred	80	125	250	200
Astin, John	20			40
Astin, Sean	20			40
Astor, Mary	55			150
Atkins, Christopher	20			45
Atkinson, Rowan	25	55		75
Attenborough, Richard	25	50	80	75
Atwill, Lionel	120	350	400	300
Auberjonois, Rene	20			40
Auer, Mishca	25			50
Auger, Claudine	25			40
Autry, Gene	45	125	200	125
Aykroyd, Dan	20	40	40	70
Ayres, Agnes	70			175

NAME	SIG	DS	ALS	SP
Ayres, Lew	25	40	40	45
Azaria, Hank	20	40	70	40
B				
Bacall, Lauren	25	40	85	75
Bach, Barbara	25			40
Bach, Catherine	20			40
Backus, Jim	40			65
Bacon, Kevin	35	40	65	60
Badalucco, Michael	15	25	40	30
Badham, John	20			45
Baer, Max, Jr.	25			60
Bain, Barbara	20			45
Bainter, Fay	60	80	120	120
Baio, Scott	15			35
Baker, Bob	60			120
Baker, Dylan	10	20	40	20
Baker, Kenny	20			45
Bakula, Scott	25			45
Balaban, Bob	15		35	30
Baldwin, Alec	35	45	60	70
Baldwin, Daniel	20			40
Baldwin, Stephen	20			40
Baldwin, William	20			45
Bale, Christian	20	40	60	35
Balk, Fairuza	20			40
Ball, Lucille	200	250	350	500
Ball, Lucille (signed as "Lucy")	75		150	200
Ballard, Kaye	20			50
Balsam, Martin	15			40
Bancroft, Anne	20			50
Bancroft, George	30			85
Banderas, Antonio	30	35	60	70
Bankhead, Tallulah	70	100	175	150
Bara, Theda	150	200	300	300
Barbeau, Adrienne	20			45
Bardot, Brigitte	40	60	120	90
Barishnikov, Mikhail	75			150
Barker, Lex	100	150	200	200

103

104

105

106

107

103 *Abbott and Costello and Frank Sinatra*

104 *Fred Astaire and Ginger Rogers*

105 *Lucille Ball*

106 *John Belushi*

107 *Ingrid Bergman*

NAME	SIG	DS	ALS	SP
Barkin, Ellen	25			45
Barr, Roseanne	25			45
Barrett, Majel	15			45
Barry, Raymond J.	15			25
Barrymore, Diana	40			60
Barrymore, Drew	25	50		75
Barrymore, Ethel	125	180		250
Barrymore, John	180	300	350	575
Barrymore, Lionel	75	180		175
Bartholomew, Freddie	25		50	85
Bartok, Eva	15			25
Barty, Billy	25			40
Basinger, Kim	30	60	80	75
Baskett, James	225			750
Bassett, Angela	25			45
Bateman, Jason	15			25
Bateman, Justine	20			30
Bates, Alan	20			50
Bates, Kathy	25			70
Bauer, Steven	15			30
Bavier, Frances	125			400
Baxter, Anne	25			50
Baxter, Warner	75	150		225
Baxter-Birney, Meredith	10			25
Bay, Michael	20	45	50	30
Beals, Jennifer	20			45
Bean, Sean	20		40	70
Beard, "Stymie"	125			300
Beatty, Ned	15			35
Beatty, Warren	35	80	150	100
Beaumont, Hugh	300	750		800
Beavers, Louise	125			300
Becker, Harold	15	25		25
Beckinsale, Kate	20	40	60	40
Bedelia, Bonnie	10			25
Beery, Noah	80			200
Beery, Wallace	125	200	300	300
Begley, Ed, Jr.	10			35

B

NAME	SIG	DS	ALS	SP
Begley, Ed, Sr.	30			85
Bel Geddes, Barbara	20			35
Bellamy, Madge	15			35
Bellamy, Ralph	20			50
Belmondo, Jean Paul	20			45
Belushi, James	15			35
Belushi, John	300	500	1,000	800
Belzer, Richard	15			35
Bendix, William	50	125	200	175
Bening, Annette	25			50
Benjamin, Richard	15	25		25
Bennett, Constance	35		150	85
Bennett, Joan	20		45	60
Benny, Jack	80			175
Benson, Robby	20			35
Benton, Barbi	10			25
Benton, Robert	15			20
Berenger, Tom	20			70
Berenson, Marisa	15			35
Bergen, Candice	20			50
Bergman, Ingmar	80	125	200	200
Bergman, Ingrid	150	300	400	350
Berkeley, Busby	125			350
Berkeley, Elizabeth	20			55
Berkeley, Xander	10			20
Berle, Milton	40			90
Bernhardt, Sandra	20			45
Bernhardt, Sarah	200	350	600	750
Berry, Halle	25	40	60	75
Berry, Noah, Jr.	25			50
Bertinelli, Valerie	15			35
Bertolucci, Bernardo	20			40
Besser, Joe	45			80
Biehn, Michael	15	25	40	25
Biel, Jessica	15			25
Biggs, Jason	20	25	40	30
Bikel, Theodore	15			45
Billingsley, Barbara	10			35

B

NAME	SIG	DS	ALS	SP
Binoche, Juliette	25			70
Birch, Thora	20	40	60	70
Bird, Antonia	15	25		20
Birney, David	10			25
Bishop, Joey	15			25
Bisset, Jacqueline	15			35
Bixby, Bill	35			55
Black, Jack	20	25		70
Black, Karen	15			35
Blackman, Honor	10			35
Blair, Linda	20		45	45
Blair, Selma	20	25	40	30
Blake, Amanda	50			100
Blake, Madge	125			300
Blake, Robert	20			80
Blanc, Mel	75	150	250	250
Blanchett, Cate	25	40	60	90
Blandick, Clara	750	RARE	RARE	6,000
Blocker, Dan	225	300		500
Blondell, Joan	40		85	75
Blue, Monte	40			100
Bluth, Don	10	25		15
Blyth, Ann	20			40
Blythe, Betty	40			200
Bogart, Humphrey	950	1,500	4,000	3,500
Bogdanovich, Peter	20			45
Boland, Mary	25			80
Boles, John	40			65
Bolger, Ray	100	200	400	250
Bologna, Joseph	15			30
Bond, Tommy Butch	20			35
Bond, Ward	100	175		275
Bonet, Lisa	15			50
Bonneville, Hugh	15	25	40	25
Boone, Richard	80			150
Boorman, John	15	25		25
Booth, Edwin	120			300
Booth, Shirley	35			55

B

NAME	SIG	DS	ALS	SP
Boothe, Powers	15			25
Borden, Olive	40			180
Borgnine, Ernest	20	25	40	45
Borzage, Frank	80			170
Bosco, Philip	15	25	40	20
Bostwick, Barry	15			40
Bottoms, Joseph	10			25
Bottoms, Timothy	10			25
Bow, Clara	225	400	500	650
Boxleitner, Bruce	15			35
Boyer, Charles	40	60		125
Boyle, Danny	25	40		40
Boyle, Lara Flynn	25			50
Boyle, Peter	20			45
Bracco, Lorraine	25			80
Bracken, Eddie	10			25
Brady, Alice	80		150	200
Brady, Pat	100			300
Braga, Sonia	20			60
Branagh, Kenneth	25	40	80	90
Brand, Neville	75			140
Brandauer, Klaus Maria	20	25	40	45
Brando, Marlon	400	600	900	850
Braugher, Andre	15	25		25
Brazzi, Rossano	20			40
Brennan, Eileen	15			35
Brennan, Walter	120	180	300	250
Brett, Jeremy	40			125
Brice, Fanny	120	220	350	325
Bridges, Beau	15	25		50
Bridges, Jeff	20	30		60
Bridges, Lloyd	35			55
Brimley, Wilford	20			35
Briscoe, Brent	15	25		25
Britt, May	20			35
Broadbent, Jim	25	40	60	40
Brocoli, Albert Cubby	25	45		50
Broderick, Helen	25			65

NAME	SIG	DS	ALS	SP
Broderick, Matthew	20			60
Brolin, James	15			40
Brolin, Josh	15	20		25
Bronson, Charles	25			80
Brook, Clive	60	70		100
Brooks, Albert	15	25	40	40
Brooks, Foster	15			25
Brooks, James L.	15			30
Brooks, Louise	200	450	600	800
Brooks, Mel	15	35	50	60
Brooks, Rand	15			40
Brooks, Richard	25	40		55
Brosnan, Pierce	35			90
Brown, Joe E.	40	50	70	85
Brown, Johnny Mack	55	120		200
Brown, Julie	15			35
Browning, Ricou	20	30	45	100
Browning, Tod	120			300
Bruce, Nigel	175	200	300	375
Bruce, Virginia	20			35
Brynner, Yul	65	75	85	175
Buchanan, Edgar	50	75		85
Buckley, Betty	20			45
Bujold, Genevieve	20			35
Bullock, Sandra	30	50	85	85
Bunny, John	100			200
Buono, Victor	80	100		125
Burke, Billie	180	250	400	400
Burnett, Carol	20	25	50	60
Burnette, Smiley	50	75		95
Burns & Allen	225	500	550	500
Burns, Edmund	35			75
Burns, Edward	20			55
Burns, George	40	60	75	125
Burns, Ken	10	20	40	25
Burr, Raymond	45	60	80	125
Burstyn, Ellen	15			40
Burton, LeVar	25	50		60

B

B

NAME	SIG	DS	ALS	SP
Burton, Richard	120	250	300	250
Burton, Tim	25	50	80	80
Buscemi, Steve	25	40		60
Busey, Gary	20	40	60	50
Bushman, Francis X.	50	80	150	125
Butler, Yancy	15		40	35
Buttons, Red	15			25
Buttram, Pat	40	50		75
Byrd, Ralph	120	150		400
Byrne, Gabriel	20			65
C				
Caan, James	20	35	60	70
Caan, Scott	15			35
Cabot, Bruce	75	125	150	175
Cabot, Sebastian	45			75
Caesar, Sid	10	25	40	45
Cage, Nicolas	20	45	65	70
Cagney, James	85	225	350	300
Cain, Dean	15			40
Caine, Michael	25	40	65	55
Calhern, Louis	35			55
Calhoun, Rory	15			30
Callas, Charlie	15			25
Calleia, Joseph	25			60
Callow, Simon	15	25	40	30
Campbell, Neve	15			40
Campbell, William	20			40
Candy, John	70	100	150	150
Cannon, Dyan	15	25	40	40
Canova, Judy	10			25
Cantinflas	40			100
Cantor, Eddie	100	175	200	175
Canutt, Yakima	25	40		85
Capra, Frank	40	75	125	150
Capshaw, Kate	20			40
Capucine	25	50		75
Cardinale, Claudia	20			85
Carrera, Barbara	15			40

NAME	SIG	DS	ALS	SP
Carerre, Tia	20			55
Carey, Harry, Jr.	15	25		40
Carey, Harry, Sr.	125	135	200	275
Carey, MacDonald	15			35
Carlisle, Mary	15	25		35
Carlson, Richard	20			45
Carlyle, Robert	15	20		35
Carney, Art	15	25	45	45
Caron, Leslie	25		50	50
Carpenter, John	20			60
Carr, Jane	10			20
Carradine, David	25			50
Carradine, John	85	120		150
Carradine, Keith	15			30
Carradine, Robert	15			30
Carrey, Jim	40	70	125	125
Carrillo, Leo	70	100		150
Carroll, Diahann	15			30
Carroll, Mickey	15			40
Carson, Jack	20			50
Carson, Sunset	35	40		65
Carter, Ben	120			200
Carter, Helena Bonham	25			80
Carter, Lynda	20	40	60	80
Caruso, Anthony	25			50
Caruso, David	10			35
Carvey, Dana	15			40
Caselotti, Adriana	25		75	60
Cassavetes, John	25	40		40
Cassel, Vincent	15	25	40	25
Cassidy, Jack	25			55
Cassidy, Joanna	10			25
Cassidy, Ted	200	350	500	500
Castle, Irene	50			75
Castle, Vernon	50			125
Castle, William	45			100
Cates, Phoebe	15			60
Cattrall, Kim	20	25	40	60

108 Clara Bow

109 Louise Brooks

110 Yul Brynner

111 Richard Burton

112 James Cagney

113 John Candy

NAME	SIG	DS	ALS	SP
Caviezel, James	15	25	40	30
Chabert, Lacey	15			40
Chakiris, George	20	30	30	35
Chamberlain, Richard	15	25	40	35
Chambers, Marilyn	20		50	45
Chan, Jackie	30	50	80	75
Chandler, Jeff	75	100	200	175
Chaney, Lon, Jr.	350	700	1,000	750
Chaney, Lon, Sr.	1,250	3,000	2,500	2,000
Channing, Carol	10			20
Channing, Stockard	20	25		40
Chaplin, Ben	10			35
Chaplin, Charles	400	750	1,500	850
Chaplin, Geraldine	15			35
Chaplin, Lita Grey	20			40
Chaplin, Sydney	35	55	75	75
Chapman, Graham	20	40	60	45
Charisse, Cyd	20	40	65	95
Chase, Charley	35			120
Chase, Chevy	30	40	60	70
Chatterton, Ruth	15			50
Chaykin, Maury	10	20		20
Cheadle, Don	20	25		45
Cheech and Chong	40	75	350	125
Chen, Joan	15			40
Chevalier, Maurice	40	65	200	150
Childress, Alvin	50			140
Chong, Rae Dawn	10			30
Christenson, Hayden	40			75
Christian, Claudia	10			35
Christie, Julie	15	25	60	60
Clark, Susan	10			15
Clarke, Mae	40	60		75
Clarkson, Patricia	20		40	35
Clayburgh, Jill	10			20
Cleese, John	20	40	60	80
Clift, Montgomery	250	400	700	850
Clive, Colin	300	400		700

C

NAME	SIG	DS	ALS	SP
Clive, E. E.	25			70
Clooney, George	20	50	75	70
Clooney, Rosemary	20			50
Close, Glenn	20	50	75	65
Clyde, Andy	75			200
Coates, Phyllis	15			30
Cobb, Lee J.	80	100		100
Coburn, Charles	50	100	120	150
Coburn, James	15	25	50	35
Coca, Imogene	15			35
Coco, James	15			35
Coen, Ethan	25	50		55
Coen, Joel	25	50		55
Coghlan, Frank, Jr.	15			25
Cohen, Rob	10	15		20
Colbert, Claudette	50	150	175	150
Coleman, Dabney	15			30
Coleman, Gary	15			35
Collette, Toni	25	50	50	45
Collins, Joan	10	25	40	45
Collins, Ray	50	75		180
Colman, Ronald	75	150		200
Coltrane, Robbie	20		40	35
Columbo, Russ	55	100		175
Columbus, Chris	25	40		60
Combs, Holly Marie	15	20		40
Conaway, Jeff	15			35
Conklin, Chester	120	150		250
Connelly, Jennifer	20			60
Connery, Sean	60	150	250	150
Connolly, Walter	60			75
Connors, Chuck	35	80		80
Connors, Mike	15			35
Conrad, Robert	25			50
Conrad, William	30			60
Conway, Kevin	15			20
Conway, Tim	10			25
Coogan, Jackie	35	55		80

NAME	SIG	DS	ALS	SP
Cook, Elisha, Jr.	75			100
Cook, Peter	75	125		175
Coolidge, Jennifer	15	20		30
Cooper, Gary	200	400	650	600
Cooper, Jackie	25	50	50	75
Cooper, Merian C.	200			300
Coppola, Francis Ford	40	100	150	90
Corey, Wendell	35			80
Corman, Roger	15			40
Cosby, Bill	20	40	75	65
Costello, Lou	200	250	450	500
Costner, Kevin	25	50	75	75
Cotten, Joseph	25	40		40
Cox, Brian	20			30
Cox, Courtney	20	40	75	65
Cox, Nikki	15			45
Cox, Ronny	15			20
Cox, Wally	30			50
Coyote, Peter	15			40
Crabbe, Buster	30	50		125
Craig, Yvonne	15			50
Crain, Jeanne	20	25		45
Crane, Bob	150	300	300	300
Crane, Fred	40			80
Crane, William H.	40	55	75	60
Craven, Matt	15			25
Craven, Wes	15			35
Crawford, Broderick	40	80		125
Crawford, Cindy	25			65
Crawford, Joan	85	250	275	250
Cregar, Laird	100	150		350
Crenna, Richard	15			35
Crews, Laura Hope	200			400
Crewson, Wendy	15			25
Crisp, Donald	50	75		200
Cromwell, James	15			45
Cronenberg, David	20	40		70
Cronin, Hume	20	25	40	45

C

C

NAME	SIG	DS	ALS	SP
Crosby, Bing	75	250	400	225
Crosby, Denise	15			40
Crosby, Norm	10			25
Crothers, Scatman	35	45		65
Crouse, Lindsay	15			25
Crowe, Cameron	20	50		70
Crowe, Russell	30	50	100	125
Cruise, Tom	40	150	300	150
Cruz, Penelope	30	50	80	85
Cryer, Jon	20			40
Crystal, Billy	20	40		50
Cukor, George	50	125		150
Culkin, Macaulay	20			50
Culp, Robert	15			35
Cumming, Alan	15	25		35
Cummings, Jim	15			20
Curry, Tim	15	25		55
Curtis, Alan	10			35
Curtis, Cliff	20			35
Curtis, Jamie Lee	20	60	80	70
Curtis, Tony	15			70
Curtis-Hall, Vondie	15			25
Curtiz, Michael	35	50		75
Cusack, Joan	15			40
Cusack, John	20			100
Cushing, Peter	70	80	100	175
D				
D'Abo, Miriam	10			35
D'Abo, Olivia	15			40
D'Angelo, Beverly	15			50
D'Onofrio, Vincent	15	25		30
Dafoe, Willem	20	40	60	75
Dagover, Lil	100			200
Dahl, Arlene	15			30
Dalton, Timothy	25			70
Damon, Matt	20			80
Danes, Claire	15			45
Dangerfield, Rodney	15			40

D

NAME	SIG	DS	ALS	SP
Daniels, Jeff	15			40
Darnell, Linda	60	175		250
Darwell, Jane	125	250		250
Dauphin, Claude	40			80
Davenport, Harry	150			250
Davidtz, Embeth	15			30
Davies, Jeremy	15			30
Davies, Marion	35	60	200	175
Davis, Bette	100	225	400	250
Davis, Geena	15			70
Davis, Joan	25			55
Davis, Judy	25	50	60	45
Davis, Ossie	15			35
Davis, Sammy, Jr.	50	80	150	175
Davison, Bruce	15			30
Day, Doris	15			40
Day, Laraine	15			45
Day-Lewis, Daniel	35			100
De Mornay, Rebecca	15			40
De Palma, Brian	20	40		50
De Rita, Curly Joe	30	70		80
De Rossi, Portia	20			40
De Wilde, Brandon	125			350
DeCarlo, Yvonne	15			60
DeGeneres, Ellen	15			50
DeHaven, Gloria	10			30
De Havilland, Olivia	50	75	80	100
DeLuise, Dom	15			30
DeMille, Cecil B.	125	300	500	375
DeNiro, Robert	65	100		150
DeVito, Danny	20	40		85
Dean, James	2,000	5,000	RARE	10,000
Decamp, Rosemary	15			45
Dee, Ruby	10			20
Dee, Sandra	15			40
Del Toro, Benicio	25	50		75
Delany, Dana	15			50
Deluise, Dom	10			25

D

NAME	SIG	DS	ALS	SP
Demarest, William	25			55
Demme, Jonathan	20			40
Demme, Ted	20			40
Dempsey, Patrick	10			30
Dench, Dame Judi	20			65
Deneuve, Catherine	15	25		45
Dennehy, Brian	15			35
Dennis, Sandy	30			85
Denny, Reginald	30			75
Depardieu, Gerard	15			40
Depp, Johnny	20	50	100	75
Derek, Bo	15			60
Derek, John	15			40
Dern, Bruce	15			35
Dern, Laura	15			40
Detmer, Amanda	20			45
Devine, Andy	65	125		150
Dewhurst, Colleen	20			55
DiCaprio, Leonardo	25	50		100
Diaz, Cameron	20	50		90
Dickinson, Angie	10			35
Diesel, Vin	20			65
Dietrich, Marlene	65	200	250	150
Diggs, Taye	15			35
Dillon, Kevin	10			35
Dillon, Matt	15			40
Divine	50			100
Dix, Richard	25	50		75
Dixon, Donna	10			30
Doherty, Shannen	20			45
Donahue, Elinor	10			25
Donat, Robert	60	80		225
Donner, Richard	10			25
Donohue, Amanda	10			35
Doohan, James	15			65
Dorff, Stephen	15			40
Dors, Diana	40			150
Douglas, Illeana	20			40

E

NAME	SIG	DS	ALS	SP
Douglas, Kirk	35	50	75	75
Douglas, Melvyn	30			65
Douglas, Michael	25	50		75
Dourif, Brad	15			25
Dove, Billie	15			60
Down, Lesley-Anne	10			25
Downey, Robert, Jr.	25	50	85	75
Dressler, Marie	150	200	300	300
Drew, John	65	80	200	125
Dreyfuss, Richard	20	50		65
Driver, Minnie	20			50
Duchovny, David	25	50		55
Dukakis, Olympia	15			40
Duke, Patty	20			35
Dunaway, Faye	20	45	70	70
Dunbar, Dixie	10			35
Duncan, Michael Clarke	20			40
Dunn, James	40			125
Dunn, Nora	15			25
Dunne, Griffin	15			30
Dunne, Irene	20	40		50
Dunst, Kirsten	20			65
Durante, Jimmy	40	85		125
Durbin, Deanna	20			55
Durning, Charles	10			25
Dushku, Eliza	20			35
Dutton, Charles S.	20			35
Duvall, Robert	20	35		75
Duvall, Shelley	10			25
E				
Eastwood, Clint	35	100	150	125
Eaton, Shirley	15			35
Eddy, Nelson	50	80	125	100
Edwards, Blake	10	50		40
Elliott, Denholm	20	35		35
Ekberg, Anita	10	25	40	35
Ekland, Britt	10	25	40	30
Elfman, Jenna	20	40	50	35

F

NAME	SIG	DS	ALS	SP
Elizabeth, Shannon	20			40
Elizondo, Hector	10	20		25
Elliott, Sam	15	40	65	40
Elvira	10			35
Elwes, Cary	10	25		30
Emmerich, Noah	15			25
Englund, Robert	10			25
Epps, Omar	20			35
Erickson, Leif	20			55
Esposito, Jennifer	20			40
Estevez, Emilio	10	30	50	30
Etting, Ruth	25	40	75	65
Evans, Dale	25	50	80	65
Evans, Lee	10			25
Evans, Linda	10	20	40	25
Evans, Madge	20	25		35
Everett, Chad	10			25
Everett, Rupert	20		50	40
Ewell, Tom	15	25	40	35
F				
Fabares, Shelley	10	20		20
Fabray, Nanette	10		15	20
Fahey, Jeff	10			20
Fairbanks, Douglas, Jr.	25	45	60	55
Fairbanks, Douglas, Sr.	150	200	300	300
Fairchild, Morgan	10			25
Falk, Peter	10	25		35
Farina, Dennis	10	25	40	25
Farley, Chris	75	100	200	150
Farmer, Frances	200	250	300	650
Farnsworth, Richard	10		40	25
Farnum, William	50			150
Farrelly, Bobby	15	25		35
Farrelly, Peter	15	25		35
Farrow, Mia	20	35		75
Faversham, William	20			50
Fawcett, Farrah	15	25		70
Faye, Alice	25			70

F

NAME	SIG	DS	ALS	SP
Fehr, Oded	20			45
Feldman, Marty	55	75	150	175
Fellini, Federico	70	225	300	150
Fenn, Sherilyn	10			35
Feore, Colm	15			30
Ferguson, William J.	200	250		500
Ferrell, Will	20			35
Ferrer, José	25	40	50	65
Fetchit, Stepin	50			165
Fichtner, William	20			40
Field, Sally	15	35	60	60
Fields, W. C.	250	500	650	1,750
Fiennes, Ralph	20	40	65	60
Finch, Peter	70			170
Fincher, David	25	50		50
Fine, Larry	125	175	250	400
Finney, Albert	15		25	30
Fiorentino, Linda	10			35
Fishburne, Lawrence	20	35		60
Fisher, Carrie	20	40		70
Fisher, Frances	10			35
Fitzgerald, Barry	125		175	250
Flanery, Sean Patrick	20			40
Fleming, Victor	550	1,000		1,200
Flemyng, Jason	15			30
Fletcher, Louise	10			35
Flynn, Errol	250	550	800	650
Flynn, Joe	50			125
Foch, Nina	10			25
Foley, Dave	20			40
Fonda, Bridget	15	25		60
Fonda, Henry	70	125	200	175
Fonda, Jane	15	40	60	65
Fonda, Peter	15	25		65
Fontaine, Joan	15	30	50	55
Ford, Glenn	30	50		80
Ford, Harrison	60	150		150
Ford, John	200	250		250

G

NAME	SIG	DS	ALS	SP
Forlani, Claire	20			60
Forman, Milos	25			55
Forrest, Frederic	15			30
Forster, Robert	10			25
Fosse, Bob	45			85
Foster, Jodie	40	75		125
Foster, Preston	25			75
Fox, Michael J.	25	50		70
Fox, Vivica A.	20			40
Foxx, Jamie	20			45
Frakes, Jonathan	15			40
Francis, Anne	10			25
Francis, Kay	25	35		120
Frankenheimer, John	15			35
Fraser, Brendan	20			50
Frawley, William	300	450	500	550
Frears, Stephen	25			50
Freeman, Morgan	20			65
French, Victor	10			45
Fricker, Brenda	15			75
Friedkin, William	15			45
Frobe, Gert	60			125
Frye, Dwight	1,250			2,500
Funicello, Annette	45			110
Furlong, Edward	20			55
G				
Gable, Clark	350	500		1,250
Gabor, Eva	20			40
Gabor, Zsa Zsa	10			15
Gabrielle, Monique	15			40
Galecki, Johnny	15			30
Gallagher, Peter	10			30
Gambon, Michael	20			35
Gance, Abel	150			400
Garber, Victor	15			35
Garbo, Greta	1,500	2,500	5,000	15,000
Garcia, Andy	20			50
Gardner, Ava	60	85	150	250

G

NAME	SIG	DS	ALS	SP
Garfield, John	80	120		450
Garland, Beverly	20			30
Garland, Judy	450	700	1,500	1,200
Garner, James	10			55
Garner, Jennifer	20			50
Garofalo, Janeane	20			45
Garr, Teri	10			25
Garson, Greer	40		120	90
Gavin, John	20			50
Gayheart, Rebecca	15			30
Gaynor, Janet	25	40		95
Gaynor, Mitzi	20			55
Gazzara, Ben	10			20
Gellar, Sarah Michelle	20	40	75	55
George, Susan	10			20
Gere, Richard	20	80		55
Gershon, Gina	20			45
Gertz, Jamie	10			30
Giamatti, Paul	15			30
Giannini, Giancarlo	20			40
Gibbons, Cedric	100	250		400
Gibson, Hoot	175	250		250
Gibson, Mel	50	80		125
Gielgud, John	25			50
Gilbert, John	150	200	200	275
Gilliam, Terry	20			50
Gish, Annabeth	15			40
Gish, Dorothy	60	75		150
Gish, Lillian	75	120		125
Givens, Robin	10			35
Glaser, Paul Michael	20			35
Gleason, Jackie	80	200	300	200
Gleeson, Brendan	15			30
Glenn, Scott	10			30
Glover, Crispin	20			65
Glover, Danny	10			40
Goddard, Paulette	40			150
Goldberg, Whoopi	20			60

NAME	SIG	DS	ALS	SP
Goldblum, Jeff	20			45
Goldwyn, Samuel	125	200		250
Goldwyn, Samuel, Jr.	10			25
Goldwyn, Tony	15			30
Golino, Valeria	15			35
Gooding, Cuba, Jr.	20			55
Goodman, John	15			35
Gorcey, Leo	150	200		200
Gordon, Ruth	25	40		55
Gossett, Louis, Jr.	10			35
Gould, Elliott	10			30
Grable, Betty	125	150	250	250
Graham, Heather	15	25		55
Grahame, Gloria	55	95		175
Granger, Farley	15			40
Granger, Stewart	20			55
Grant, Cary	225	400	500	550
Grant, Hugh	15	40		55
Grapewin, Charley	550	650		2,000
Green, Seth	20			40
Green, Tom	20			40
Greene, Graham	20			35
Greene, Lorne	50	75		200
Greenstreet, Sidney	250	375		650
Greenwood, Bruce	20			35
Greer, Jane	10			20
Gregory, Dick	20			35
Grey, Jennifer	15			40
Grey, Joel	15			35
Grier, Pam	10			30
Griffith, Andy	20	50		85
Griffith, D.W.	400	600		1,400
Griffith, Hugh	200			450
Griffith, Melanie	15	40		55
Griffiths, Rachel	20			50
Grodin, Charles	10			20
Gugino, Carla	20			35
Guilfoyle, Paul	15			30

G

G

NAME	SIG	DS	ALS	SP
Guinness, Alec	40	50	75	75
Gunton, Bob	15			30
Guttenberg, Steve	10			10
Guzman, Luis	20			40
Gwenn, Edmund	100	150		250
Gwynne, Fred	75	100		150
H				
Hackford, Taylor	15			40
Hackman, Gene	20	50	60	75
Hagerty, Julie	15			30
Hagman, Larry	10	25		35
Haim, Corey	10	20		30
Haines, William	15	25	40	50
Hale, Alan, Jr.	100	150		150
Hale, Alan, Sr.	50	80	100	125
Hale, Monte	10	25		40
Haley, Jack	125	175		225
Hall, Albert	15			35
Hall, Anthony Michael	15			40
Hall, Huntz	10	20	25	35
Hall, Jerry	10			30
Hall, Jon	40	50		65
Hall, Juanita	75			125
Hall, Philip Baker	20			40
Hallström, Lasse	20			45
Hamill, Mark	25	40		75
Hamilton, George	10	20		30
Hamilton, John	425			600
Hamilton, Linda	25			45
Hamilton, Margaret	125	200	300	200
Hamilton, Neil	50	75		125
Hamlin, Harry	10			25
Hanks, Tom	40	80	150	125
Hannah, Daryl	15	25	40	45
Hannigan, Alison	15			35
Harding, Ann	15		35	30
Hardwicke, Cedric	100			175
Hardy, Oliver	300	400	600	750

120

121

122

123

124

125

120 Russell Crowe

121 Tom Cruise

122 Bette Davis

123 Robert DeNiro

124 Marlene Dietrich

125 Clint Eastwood

H

NAME	SIG	DS	ALS	SP
Harlin, Renny	15	40		35
Harlow, Jean	1,500	5,000	3,000	5,000
Harmon, Mark	10	20	35	30
Harper, Tess	10			30
Harper, Valerie	10			20
Harrelson, Woody	20	35		45
Harris, Ed	15	25		45
Harris, Richard	25	40		85
Harrison, Linda	20			35
Harrison, Rex	40	75		85
Harryhausen, Ray	10			30
Hart, Ian	20			35
Hart, William S.	150	200	300	500
Hartman, Phil	100	100	200	200
Hartnett, Josh	20			55
Hatcher, Teri	20			45
Hauer, Rutger	15	25		45
Havoc, June	10			25
Hawke, Ethan	15			40
Hawks, Howard	125	225		300
Hawn, Goldie	20	50		65
Hawthorne, Nigel	20			60
Hayden, Sterling	25			55
Hayek, Salma	20	40		65
Hayes, George "Gabby"	175	300		525
Hayes, Helen	25	40		60
Hayes, Isaac	20			40
Haysbert, Dennis	15			30
Hayward, Susan	150	225	500	425
Hayworth, Rita	200	300		500
Head, Edith	50			150
Healy, Ted	100			500
Heatherton, Joey	20			35
Heche, Anne	15			35
Heckerling, Amy	10			25
Hedaya, Dan	10			25
Hedren, Tippi	20	25		45
Heflin, Van	35	75		120

H

NAME	SIG	DS	ALS	SP
Hemingway, Margaux	45			85
Hemingway, Mariel	15			35
Henie, Sonja	75	125		225
Henried, Paul	50	120		125
Henriksen, Lance	20			40
Henson, Jim	100	150		250
Henstridge, Natasha	20			45
Hepburn, Audrey	150	350	500	400
Hepburn, Katharine	250	500	900	1,500
Herman, Pee Wee	20			70
Herrmann, Edward	15			30
Hershey, Barbara	10			30
Hersholt, Jean	25	45		75
Heston, Charlton	15			55
Hewitt, Jennifer Love	20			45
Hexum, Jon-Erik	75			150
Hill, Walter	10			25
Hiller, Arthur	10			15
Hines, Gregory	10			25
Hingle, Pat	15			25
Hirsch, Judd	10			20
Hitchcock, Alfred	300	600	800	1,000
Hitchcock, Raymond	20			40
Hoffman, Dustin	30			75
Hoffman, Philip Seymour	20			50
Hogan, Paul	10			35
Holbrook, Hal	20			40
Holden, William	80			225
Holly, Lauren	15			35
Holm, Celeste	10			20
Holm, Ian	15			50
Holmes, Katie	20			40
Holt, Jack	50			120
Hong, James	20			45
Hope, Bob	75	150	250	175
Hopkins, Anthony	25	75		85
Hopkins, Miriam	40	55		85
Hopper, Dennis	15			40

H

NAME	SIG	DS	ALS	SP
Hopper, Hedda	20	40		35
Horne, Lena	15			40
Hoskins, Bob	15			40
Houseman, John	25			60
Howard, Clint	10			25
Howard, Jerry "Curly"	500	1,000		1,200
Howard, Leslie	300	300		500
Howard, Moe	200	300	650	500
Howard, Ron	25	50		70
Howard, Shemp	500	750		650
Howard, Trevor	15			35
Howell, C. Thomas	10			35
Hudson, Ernie	10			25
Hudson, Kate	20			55
Hudson, Rock	50	65		150
Hughes, Miko	10			25
Hulce, Tom	20			35
Hull, Josephine	200			325
Hunt, Bonnie	10			35
Hunt, Helen	25			65
Hunt, Linda	20			60
Hunter, Holly	20			55
Hunter, Kim	10			30
Hunter, Tab	25			50
Hurley, Elizabeth	15			55
Hurt, John	20			40
Hurt, Mary Beth	15			40
Hurt, William	15			45
Hussey, Olivia	10			25
Hussey, Ruth	10			25
Huston, Anjelica	15			55
Huston, John	40	125		125
Huston, Walter	100	150		200
Hutchins, Will	15			25
Hutton, Betty	15			30
Hutton, Lauren	15	25	40	30
Hutton, Robert	40	50		125
Hutton, Timothy	20			55

NAME	SIG	DS	ALS	SP
Hyde, Jonathan	20			40
I				
Ice Cube	15	25	40	35
Idle, Eric	20			50
Ifans, Rhys	15			30
Ingram, Rex	125			300
Ireland, Jill	20			65
Ireland, Kathy	15			35
Irons, Jeremy	20			50
Irving, Amy	10			30
Irwin, May	25			50
Isaacs, Jason	25			50
Ives, Burl	30	50		60
J				
Jackman, Hugh	20			50
Jackson, Glenda	15	25		40
Jackson, Joshua	20			40
Jackson, Peter	25			70
Jackson, Samuel L.	20			65
Jaffe, Sam	25			55
Jagger, Dean	20	35		45
Janney, Allison	20			45
Jannings, Emil	200			350
Janssen, David	100	125		175
Janssen, Famke	20			45
Jeffreys, Anne	15			25
Jenkins, Richard	15			35
Jessel, George	35	75		100
Jeter, Michael	10	25		40
Jewison, Norman	15			35
Johann, Zita	25			70
Johnson, Ben	35	70		75
Johnson, Don	15			45
Johnson, Van	15			40
Jolie, Angelina	20			65
Jolson, Al	150	250		325
Jones, Buck	200	250		450
Jones, Carolyn	100	225		350

J

J

NAME	SIG	DS	ALS	SP
Jones, James Earl	15			40
Jones, Janet	15			25
Jones, Jennifer	150	225		325
Jones, Orlando	15			30
Jones, Rashida	15			30
Jones, Tommy Lee	25	70		70
Jordan, Neil	20			55
Jory, Victor	50	75		125
Jourdan, Louis	15			35
Jovovich, Milla	20			45
Judd, Ashley	20			70
Julia, Raul	40			85
K				
Kahn, Madeline	25	40		90
Kamen, Milt	20			40
Kane, Carol	15			25
Karloff, Boris	300	500	800	650
Karras, Alex	10			20
Kasdan, Jake	15			20
Kasdan, Lawrence	20			40
Kattan, Chris	15			30
Kaufman, Andy	100	200		225
Kavner, Julie	20			35
Kaye, Danny	75	125		125
Kazan, Elia	25	65		70
Keach, Stacey	15			25
Keaton, Buster	300	500		1,000
Keaton, Diane	25	50		80
Keaton, Michael	15			65
Keel, Howard	10			20
Keeler, Ruby	40			65
Keener, Catherine	20			50
Keeslar, Matt	10			25
Keitel, Harvey	25			55
Keith, David	10			25
Kellerman, Sally	10			25
Kelley, DeForest	35			75
Kelly, David Patrick	15			30

NAME	SIG	DS	ALS	SP
Kelly, Gene	40	100	200	150
Kelly, Grace	350		800	650
Kelly, Moira	10			25
Kennedy, Edgar	125			325
Kennedy, George	15			40
Kennedy, Jamie	20			40
Kensit, Patsy	15			30
Kerr, Deborah	20			55
Keyes, Evelyn	20	40		50
Kidder, Margot	25	50		55
Kidman, Nicole	30	55		95
Kiel, Richard	15			35
Kier, Udo	15			30
Kilbride, Percy	200			400
Kilmer, Joanne Whalley	15			25
Kilmer, Val	25	50		75
King, Cammie	15			45
King, Perry	10			25
Kingsley, Ben	25	50		65
Kinnear, Greg	15			40
Kinney, Terry	15			25
Kinski, Klaus	25	40		50
Kinski, Nastassja	20	40		70
Kirkland, Sally	10			25
Kirshner, Mia	15			30
Klein, Chris	20			35
Kline, Kevin	20			55
Klugman, Jack	10			35
Knight, Wayne	15			30
Knotts, Don	15			45
Koening, Walter	20	40		55
Koteas, Elias	20			35
Kotto, Yaphet	15			25
Kovacs, Ernie	225	400		450
Kristofferson, Kris	15			40
Kruger, Otto	30			70
Kubrick, Stanley	200	350		300
Kudrow, Lisa	15			55

K

113

126 Douglas Fairbanks, Sr.

127 Federico Fellini

128 W. C. Fields

129 Errol Flynn

130 Harrison Ford

131 Jodie Foster

NAME	SIG	DS	ALS	SP
Kunis, Mila	15			30
Kurtz, Swoosie	10			30
L				
LaPaglia, Anthony	10			30
Ladd, Alan	55	120	200	200
Ladd, Cheryl	15		40	30
Laemmle, Carl	125	300		800
Lahr, Bert	350	700		1,000
Lahti, Christine	15	25		35
Laine, Frankie	15			35
Lake, Arthur	55			75
Lake, Ricki	10			25
Lake, Veronica	150	250		500
Lamarr, Hedy	50	120		150
Lamas, Fernando	25	35		50
Lamas, Lorenzo	10	20		25
Lambert, Christopher	20			45
Lamour, Dorothy	25	50		75
Lancaster, Burt	50	150		150
Lanchester, Elsa	75	100		150
Landau, Martin	20	40		70
Landers, Audrey	10			25
Landers, Judy	10			20
Landis, Carole	100			200
Landis, John	15			25
Landon, Michael	100	125		225
Lane, Diane	10	20		45
Lane, Nathan	20			45
Lang, Fritz	125	400		275
Langdon, Harry	125			275
Lange, Jessica	25			80
Langella, Frank	10			35
Langtry, Lillie	400			600
Lansbury, Angela	15	25		35
Larter, Ali	20			35
Lasky, Jesse L.	50	90		100
Lauder, Harry	60	100	125	85
Laughton, Charles	80	150		275

L

115

L

NAME	SIG	DS	ALS	SP
Laurel & Hardy	600	900		1,400
Laurel, Stan	200	500	550	450
Law, John Phillip	10			30
Law, Jude	20			55
Lawford, Peter	50	125	150	150
Lawless, Lucy	15			55
Lawrence, Gertrude	25	50		55
Lawrence, Martin	20			40
Lazenby, George	25	50		55
LeBlanc, Matt	20			45
LeBrock, Kelly	10			30
LeRoy, Mervyn	40	75		100
Leachman, Cloris	15	25	55	30
Lean, David	50	75	100	95
Leary, Denis	20			45
Leder, Mimi	20			40
Ledger, Heath	20			45
Ledoyen, Virginie	20			40
Lee, Ang	25			50
Lee, Bernard	70			125
Lee, Brandon	200	500		600
Lee, Bruce	1,200	1,500		4,000
Lee, Christopher	30			60
Lee, Gypsy Rose	80		200	350
Lee, Jason	15			45
Lee, Jason Scott	10			25
Lee, Spike	15			50
Leguizamo, John	15			35
Lehmann, Michael	15			30
Leigh, Janet	10	25	35	50
Leigh, Jennifer Jason	25			65
Leigh, Vivien	350	600	750	1,000
Lemmon, Jack	40	50	75	125
Leone, Sergio	125	250		500
Leoni, Téa	20			45
Leto, Jared	20	50		40
Levine, Ted	15			20
Levinson, Barry	20	40		45

NAME	SIG	DS	ALS	SP
Levy, Eugene	20			40
Lewis, Jerry	25	40		75
Lewis, Juliette	20			45
Li, Jet	25			70
Lillard, Matthew	15			30
Lindo, Delroy	15			30
Linklater, Richard	25			60
Linney, Laura	20			40
Liotta, Ray	20			65
Lithgow, John	20			45
Little, Cleavon	30			75
Liu, Lucy	15			50
Llewelyn, Desmond	20			45
Lloyd, Christopher	20		60	45
Lloyd, Emily	20			35
Lloyd, Frank	40	80		100
Lloyd, Harold	225	325	350	450
Lloyd, Jake	20			75
Loggia, Robert	10	20	35	20
Logue, Donal	15			35
Lombard, Carole	325	850		1,000
Lopez, Jennifer	25			85
Lords, Traci	20	50	75	45
Loren, Sophia	20	40	75	65
Lorre, Peter	225	350		450
Louis-Dreyfus, Julia	20			55
Love, Bessie	25			65
Love, Courtney	20			40
Lowe, Edmund	25	50	65	55
Lowe, Rob	20			45
Lowell, Carey	10			25
Loy, Myrna	25	50	75	60
Lubitsch, Ernst	60	100		125
Lucas, George	40	125	200	100
Lugosi, Bela	500	1,000		1,200
Lukas, Paul	55			125
Luke, Keye	25	50		65
Lundgren, Dolph	20			35

L

L

NAME	SIG	DS	ALS	SP
Lupino, Ida	35	75	120	100
Lynch, David	25	55		55
Lynch, Kelly	15	25		30
Lyonne, Natasha	20			45
Lytell, Bert	30	50	80	65
M				
Mac, Bernie	10			35
MacDonald, Jeanette	75	200	300	225
MacDonald, Norm	10			30
MacDowell, Andie	15	35	45	30
MacGraw, Ali	20	40	60	45
MacGregor, Ewan	30	50		75
MacLachlan, Kyle	10	25	40	20
MacLaine, Shirley	20	25	55	70
MacMurray, Fred	25	50	75	50
MacNee, Patrick	20	25		35
Macchio, Ralph	10	20	40	25
Mack, Marion	15	25	40	20
Macy, William H.	20			45
Madigan, Amy	15	25		40
Madsen, Michael	15	25		40
Madsen, Virginia	10	25	40	35
Magnani, Anna	300			550
Magnuson, Ann	10			35
Maguire, Tobey	25			75
Maharis, George	15	25		25
Mahoney, Jock	25	50	75	65
Mahoney, John	15			40
Main, Marjorie	120	150		300
Malden, Karl	15	25	40	40
Malkovich, John	25	50	75	70
Malle, Louis	25	50		45
Mamet, David	30	40		45
Mangold, James	20			50
Mankiewicz, Joseph	40	75	125	75
Mann, Michael	20			50
Mansfield, Jayne	250	350	450	500
Mantegna, Joe	10			30

M

NAME	SIG	DS	ALS	SP
March, Frederic	45	100	125	150
Maren, Jerry	10	25		35
Margret, Ann-	20	40	75	60
Marin, Cheech	20			45
Marshall, Gary	10	25		30
Marshall, Penny	20	25		35
Martin & Lewis	200	450		350
Martin, Andrea	10	20	40	25
Martin, Dean	35	125	200	150
Martin, Steve	20	55	75	75
Marvin, Lee	125	175	250	225
Marx Brothers (signed by 3)	1,200	2,000		4,000
Marx Brothers (signed by 4)	1,750	2,500		5,000
Marx, Chico	150	200	400	400
Marx, Groucho	300	450	500	450
Marx, Harpo	500			1,000
Marx, Zeppo	100	150		175
Mason, James	50	75	100	125
Mason, Marsha	10	25		30
Massey, Raymond	40	50		60
Masterson, Mary Stuart	15	25		40
Mastroantonio, Mary E.	10	20	40	35
Mastroianni, Marcello	25	40	75	60
Masur, Richard	15			30
Matarazzo, Heather	20			35
Matheson, Tim	15			30
Mathis, Samantha	10	25	40	30
Matlin, Marlee	15	25	40	30
Matthau, Walter	25	40	75	70
Mature, Victor	25	40		45
Mayer, Louis B.	100	200	300	275
Maynard, Ken	125	150	150	200
Mayo, Virginia	10	20		35
Mazar, Debi	15			30
Mazurski, Paul	20	45		35
McCarthy, Andrew	10	20	35	25
McCarthy, Jenny	20	25	50	30
McCarthy, Kevin	10	20		30

M

NAME	SIG	DS	ALS	SP
McConaughey, Matthew	20	40		50
McCormack, Catherine	15			30
McCormack, Mary	15			30
McCrea, Joel	15	40		50
McDaniel, Hattie	750	1,500		2,000
McDermott, Dylan	15	25	40	30
McDonald, Marie	50	70		100
McDormand, Frances	25			65
McDowell, Malcolm	20	40		55
McDowell, Roddy	25	45	70	65
McFadden, Gates	20	25		35
McFarland, Spanky	40	50		100
McGillis, Kelly	15	25		40
McGovern, Elizabeth	10	20	40	20
McGowan, Rose	15			35
McKean, Michael	15			35
McKellan, Ian	20	50		75
McLaglen, Victor	150	200		325
McNichol, Kristy	10	25	35	20
McQueen, Butterfly	75	100	125	125
McQueen, Steve	500	600	750	800
McTiernan, John	20			50
Meadows, Audrey	25	40		60
Meadows, Jayne	15			25
Meaney, Colm	15	25		40
Menjou, Adolphe	25	40		95
Meredith, Burgess	25	40	50	40
Merkel, Una	15	20		40
Mewes, Jason	15			35
Meyer, Breckin	15			30
Midler, Bette	30	50	80	70
Mifune, Toshiro	20	40	75	50
Milano, Alyssa	20			55
Milland, Ray	35	55		85
Miller, Ann	10	25		25
Miller, Larry	10			25
Miller, Marilyn	85	150		250
Miller, Penelope Ann	15	25		35

132 Ava Gardner

133 Mel Gibson

134 Cary Grant

135 Tom Hanks

136 Rita Hayworth

137 Audrey Hepburn

M

NAME	SIG	DS	ALS	SP
Mimieux, Yvette	10	25		20
Mineo, Sal	250	300	450	400
Minnelli, Liza	20	40	90	70
Minnelli, Vincente	35	55		90
Minter, Mary Miles	150	200	200	250
Miranda, Carmen	125	225	300	375
Mirren, Helen	10			25
Mitchell, Thomas	300	350		650
Mitchum, Robert	25	50	75	90
Mix, Tom	175	200		450
Modine, Matthew	10	20		30
Mohr, Jay	15			30
Molina, Alfred	15			30
Monroe, Marilyn	1,800	3,000	8,500	8,500
Montalban, Ricardo	20	25	30	40
Montand, Yves	20	30		40
Montez, Maria	55	70		125
Moore, Colleen	20	40		45
Moore, Demi	20	40	75	55
Moore, Dudley	20	40		85
Moore, Julianne	20	35	75	40
Moore, Mary Tyler	20	40	75	60
Moore, Roger	25	60		75
Moore, Terry	10	20		30
Moorehead, Agnes	60	75		125
Moranis, Rick	10	20		30
Moreno, Rita	10	20	40	30
Morgan, Frank	450	600	600	850
Morgan, Harry	10	20		30
Morgan, Helen	70	200	200	250
Moriarty, Cathy	20	30		40
Moriarty, Michael	20	25		35
Morita, Pat	10	20		20
Morrow, Vic	125	200		225
Morse, Barry	20			25
Morse, David	15			35
Mortensen, Viggo	20			75
Moss, Carrie-Anne	25			75

NAME	SIG	DS	ALS	SP
Mostel, Zero	60	125		200
Mueller-Stahl, Armin	15			40
Mulgrew, Kate	10	20		30
Mulroney, Dermot	15	25		35
Muni, Paul	100	125	150	175
Munson, Ona	150	200		250
Murphy, Brittany	15			35
Murphy, Eddie	25	40		65
Murray, Bill	25	40		65
Murray, Ken	20			25
Murray, Mae	35	40		65
Myers, Mike	20	40	60	55
N				
Nagel, Conrad	25	40		85
Neal, Patricia	10	20		35
Neal, Sam	15	25		35
Needham, Hal	15			35
Neeson, Liam	25	40		95
Negri, Pola	40	85	200	150
Nelligan, Kate	15			35
Neuwirth, Bebe	15			35
Newell, Mike	20			45
Newman, Paul	150	250	400	325
Newton, Thandie	15			35
Newton-John, Olivia	20	40		65
Nichols, Mike	35	50		85
Nichols, Nichelle	20	25		30
Nicholson, Jack	40	75	200	100
Nielsen, Brigitte	10	25		30
Nielson, Leslie	15	25		30
Nimoy, Leonard	40	60	150	90
Nior, Haing S.	50	75		125
Niven, David	50	80	150	125
Nolan, Lloyd	20	65		50
Nolte, Nick	20	40		50
Normand, Mabel	200	300		550
Norris, Chuck	20	30		40
Northam, Jeremy	20			40

N

N

NAME	SIG	DS	ALS	SP
Norton, Edward	25	40		80
Noseworthy, Jack	15			30
Novak, Kim	40	70	100	125
Novarro, Ramon	50	75		125
Noyce, Phillip	20			45
Nucci, Danny	15			25
O				
O'Brien, Edmond	25	50		55
O'Brien, Margaret	20			30
O'Connor, Carroll	20	40		40
O'Connor, Donald	20	25	40	40
O'Connor, Una	50	75		90
O'Donnell, Chris	15	25		35
O'Donnell, Rosie	20		60	40
O'Hara, Catherine	20			45
O'Hara, Maureen	25	35		75
O'Neal, Ryan	20	30	50	30
O'Neal, Tatum	15	25	40	30
O'Neil, Barbara	200			300
O'Sullivan, Maureen	25	40		65
O'Toole, Annette	20	25		30
O'Toole, Peter	25	75		85
Oakie, Jack	25	70		60
Oberon, Merle	45	60		100
Oland, Warner	200	225		275
Olin, Lena	20	40		40
Olivier, Laurence	100	150	250	200
Olmos, Edward James	10	25		30
Ormond, Julia	20	40		55
Ouspenskaya, Maria	300	450		500
Oz, Frank	20	35		75
P				
Pacino, Al	50	125	200	100
Page, Anita	20			20
Page, Geraldine	25	40		55
Paget, Debra	40	50		60
Paige, Janis	15	25		25
Palance, Jack	45	75		100

NAME	SIG	DS	ALS	SP
Palin, Michael	20			45
Palminteri, Chazz	15	25		30
Paltrow, Gwyneth	25	50		65
Pantoliano, Joe	10	20		45
Paquin, Anna	20	25		45
Park, Ray	10	20		35
Parker, Eleanor	10	25		25
Parker, Mary-Louise	15			30
Parker, Sarah Jessica	20	40	75	75
Patinkin, Mandy	20			30
Patric, Jason	20			30
Patrick, Robert	15			35
Patton, Will	15			35
Paxinou, Katina	200	300		300
Paxton, Bill	15			30
Paymer, David	15			30
Payne, John	25	40		75
Peck, Gregory	45	100	125	75
Peckinpah, Sam	150	250		250
Penn, Arthur	15			25
Penn, Sean	25	50		75
Peppard, George	45	75		75
Perabo, Piper	15			35
Perez, Rosie	20	40		35
Perez, Vincent	20			35
Perkins, Anthony	100	150		150
Perkins, Elizabeth	10	25		30
Perlman, Ron	15			30
Perry, Luke	10			25
Perry, Matthew	20			45
Pesci, Joe	25	40		70
Peters, Bernadette	10			35
Peters, Jean	55			100
Petersen, Wolfgang	15			40
Petrie, Donald	15			35
Petty, Lori	15			30
Pfeiffer, Michelle	40	100		80
Phifer, Mekhi	15			30

P

P

NAME	SIG	DS	ALS	SP
Phillippe, Ryan	20	40		40
Phillips, Lou Diamond	15	25		30
Phoenix, Joaquin	20	40		55
Phoenix, River	225	500	650	500
Pickens, Slim	125			225
Pickford, Jack	55			175
Pickford, Mary	65	200	250	200
Pidgeon, Walter	30	75		100
Pinkett-Smith, Jada	15	25		35
Piscopo, Joe	15	25	50	35
Pitt, Brad	30	60	100	75
Pitt, Ingrid	25	30		35
Pitts, Zazu	40	50		80
Piven, Jeremy	15			30
Place, Mary Kay	15			30
Platt, Oliver	15			30
Pleasence, Donald	40	50	65	55
Plimpton, Martha	15	25		25
Plowright, Joan	20	25		25
Plummer, Amanda	10	20		30
Plummer, Christopher	20	35		40
Poitier, Sidney	40	60	120	125
Polanski, Roman	35	55	120	95
Pollack, Sidney	20	25		40
Polley, Sarah	20			45
Pollock, Kevin	10	20		25
Portman, Natalie	25	40		75
Posey, Parker	10			25
Postlethwaite, Pete	15			35
Potente, Franka	20			40
Potter, Monica	15			35
Potts, Annie	10	25		25
Powell, Dick	40	55		75
Powell, Eleanor	25	40		75
Powell, William	50	75		125
Power, Tyrone	100	125		250
Preminger, Otto	55	75		100
Presley, Elvis	800	2,000	5,000	2,000

NAME	SIG	DS	ALS	SP
Pressly, Jaime	15			35
Preston, Kelly	15	25		30
Preston, Robert	50	75		100
Price, Vincent	75	125	150	125
Priestly, Jason	15	40		35
Principal, Victoria	20		40	40
Prinze, Freddie, Jr.	20	40		45
Prinze, Freddie, Sr.	125	200		300
Prowse, David	20	25		40
Prowse, Juliet	15			40
Pryce, Jonathan	15			35
Pryor, Richard	70	100		100
Pullman, Bill	15			35
Q				
Quaid, Dennis	20	25		30
Quaid, Randy	15	20		25
Quinlan, Kathleen	15			35
Quinn, Aidan	15	25		30
Quinn, Anthony	40	70	125	80
R				
Raabe, Meinhardt	20	40	40	40
Radner, Gilda	75	125	200	200
Raft, George	55	100	150	150
Raimi, Sam	25			60
Rainer, Luise	25	40		65
Rains, Claude	150	250	400	300
Ramis, Harold	20	40		40
Rand, Sally	25	40		75
Randall, Tony	20	25		30
Randolph, Joyce	20	25		40
Randolph, Lillian	125			300
Rapaport, Michael	15			35
Rathbone, Basil	225	400	500	600
Ratner, Brett	15	40		35
Raye, Martha	20	45		60
Rea, Stephen	20			40
Redford, Robert	80	150	250	125
Redgrave, Lynn	20	40		40

R

138

139

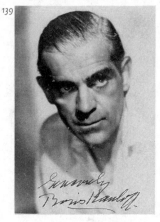

140

141

142

143

138 Alfred Hitchcock

139 Boris Karloff

140 Grace Kelly

141 Elsa Lanchester

142 Laurel and Hardy

143 Carole Lombard

R

NAME	SIG	DS	ALS	SP
Redgrave, Vanessa	20	30		45
Reed, Donna	100	150	250	250
Reed, Oliver	20	25		50
Reed, Pamela	15			30
Reeve, Christopher	75	150	250	175
Reeves, George	1,000	2,000		1,800
Reeves, Keanu	25	40	80	65
Reeves, Steve	15	25		30
Reid, Tara	15			35
Reid, Wallace	225			600
Reilly, John C.	20			35
Reiner, Carl	15	30	40	30
Reiner, Rob	15	25	40	35
Reinhardt, Max	125	200	450	350
Reinhold, Judge	15	20		30
Reiser, Paul	10	15		30
Reitman, Ivan	20			40
Remick, Lee	35	50		70
Renaldo, Duncan	50		125	125
Rennie, Michael	125	150		225
Reno, Jean	25	40		50
Renoir, Jean	150	300		400
Reubens, Paul	15			40
Reynolds, Burt	15	25	40	45
Reynolds, Debbie	15	20	40	40
Rhames, Ving	10	20	40	35
Rhett, Alicia	225			
Rhys-Davies, John	20	25	40	40
Ribisi, Giovanni	20			40
Ricci, Christina	20	40		55
Richards, Denise	15	25		40
Richards, Michael	15	20		40
Richardson, Joely	15			30
Richardson, Miranda	20	30		35
Richardson, Natasha	20	30		35
Richardson, Ralph	25			55
Richie, Guy	15	25		35
Richter, Andy	10			30

R

NAME	SIG	DS	ALS	SP
Ringwald, Molly	15	40	50	45
Ritter, John	35	20		70
Ritter, Thelma	55	75		175
Roach, Hal	125	250	300	200
Roach, Jay	15			30
Robards, Jason	20	25		40
Robbins, Tim	20	25		45
Roberts, Doris	15	25	40	35
Roberts, Eric	15	20		30
Roberts, Julia	50	100	200	150
Robertson, Cliff	25	50		50
Robeson, Paul	150	250	300	600
Robinson, Bill "Bojangles"	150	300	450	500
Robinson, Edward G.	75	125		250
Robson, May	50	75		100
Roddenberry, Gene	150	200		250
Rodriguez, Michelle	15			30
Rodriguez, Robert	20			40
Rogers, Buddy	20	25	40	35
Rogers, Ginger	70	175	200	1,500
Rogers, Mimi	15	25		30
Rogers, Roy	70	200		150
Rogers, Will	275	350		1,000
Roland, Gilbert	25			50
Romero, Cesar	50	50		85
Romijn-Stamos, Rebecca	20	40		40
Rooney, Mickey	25	40	50	45
Rossellini, Isabella	20	40		55
Roth, Tim	15	25		45
Roundtree, Richard	15			25
Rourke, Mickey	25	50		60
Rowlands, Gena	20			40
Ruehl, Mercedes	30	50		45
Ruggles, Charles	40	50		75
Russell, Jane	25	50	80	70
Russell, Kerri	10	25		30
Russell, Kurt	15	25		30
Russell, Rosalind	40	55		100

NAME	SIG	DS	ALS	SP
Russo, James	15			30
Russo, Rene	15	25		40
Rutherford, Anne	15	25		40
Rutherford, Margaret	80	150		200
Ryan, Irene	125	200		250
Ryan, Jeri	15	25		50
Ryan, Meg	20	55		80
Ryder, Winona	30	55		75
S				
Sabato, Antonio, Jr.	10		35	30
Sabu	55			175
Saint, Eva Marie	20	40		40
Saint James, Susan	10	15		25
Sampson, Will	100		200	250
San Giacomo, Laura	15	25		30
Sanders, George	100			200
Sarandon, Susan	25	50		50
Scacchi, Greta	10	20		30
Scheider, Roy	25	40		50
Schell, Maximillian	20		35	45
Schepisi, Fred	15			40
Schiff, Richard	15			35
Schlesinger, John	20	40		35
Schneider, Romy	100			150
Schreiber, Liev	20			35
Schroder, Ricky	15	25		35
Schumacher, Joel	20	50		50
Schwarzenegger, Arnold	40	85		85
Schwimmer, David	15	25		35
Sciorra, Annabella	10	15		30
Scofield, Paul	25	40		40
Scorsese, Martin	40	75		75
Scott, George C.	35	55		75
Scott, Randolph	50	125		125
Scott, Ridley	25			60
Scott, Tom Everett	15			30
Scott, Tony	25			40
Scott Thomas, Kristin	20			45

S

S

NAME	SIG	DS	ALS	SP
Seagal, Steven	15	25		40
Seberg, Jean	100			175
Sedgwick, Kyra	15	25		30
Segal, George	10	25		30
Selleck, Tom	15	25		35
Sellers, Peter	125	200	250	250
Selznick, David O.	150	400		350
Sennett, Mack	350	600		800
Serling, Rod	200	250		500
Severance, Joan	10			30
Sevigny, Chloë	20			45
Sewell, Rufus	20			40
Seymour, Jane	15	25		35
Shadyac, Tom	15			40
Shalhoub, Tony	25			45
Shandling, Garry	20			40
Shannon, Molly	20			40
Sharif, Omar	40	55		95
Sharkey, Ray	20			40
Shatner, William	40	75		85
Shaw, Robert	60	75		150
Shawn, Wallace	20			35
Shearer, Harry	20			40
Shearer, Norma	50	200		350
Sheedy, Ally	10	20		30
Sheen, Charlie	15	25		30
Sheen, Martin	20	40	60	50
Shepard, Sam	25			40
Shephard, Cybill	20	45		35
Sheridan, Ann	50			125
Shields, Brooke	25	40		40
Shire, Talia	20	25		40
Shore, Dinah	25		80	50
Shore, Pauly	10	15		20
Short, Martin	15	25		35
Shue, Elizabeth	25	40		40
Signoret, Simone	75	150		200
Silver, Ron	10	20		30

NAME	SIG	DS	ALS	SP
Silverheels, Jay	200	300		350
Silverman, Sarah	20			35
Silvers, Phil	50	75		200
Silverstone, Alicia	20	25		40
Simmons, Jean	10	15		30
Simon, Simone	20			50
Sinatra, Frank	400	600		750
Sinbad	10	20		25
Singer, Lori	15	20		25
Singleton, John	15			35
Sinise, Gary	25	40		55
Sirtis, Marina	20			35
Sizemore, Tom	15			35
Skerrit, Tom	10			30
Skye, Ione	15			30
Slater, Christian	15	25		30
Slater, Helen	20			30
Smart, Amy	15			30
Smith, Jaclyn	10			30
Smith, Kevin	20	40		40
Smith, Maggie	25			55
Smits, Jimmy	10			35
Snipes, Wesley	15	25		35
Soderbergh, Steven	25			60
Somers, Suzanne	15	25	60	35
Sommer, Elke	10	20	40	35
Sorvino, Mira	10	25		40
Sorvino, Paul	10	20		35
Sossamon, Shannyn	20			35
Sothern, Ann	25		40	40
Soto, Talisa	10	25		25
Spacek, Sissy	15	25		50
Spacey, Kevin	15	25	50	65
Spader, James	10	20		30
Spielberg, Steven	40	100	150	100
Spiner, Brent	15	35	60	35
St. Cyr, Lily	10			35
Stack, Robert	10	20		25

S

S

NAME	SIG	DS	ALS	SP
Stallone, Sylvester	25	50	75	75
Stamp, Terence	20	40		40
Stanton, Harry Dean	10	20		20
Stanwyck, Barbara	35	110		100
Steenburgen, Mary	15	25		30
Steiger, Rod	20	40	60	55
Stern, Daniel	10	15		20
Stern, Howard	30	50		45
Stevens, Connie	10			20
Stevens, Stella	10			25
Stiers, David Ogden	50			85
Stiles, Julia	20			40
Stiller, Ben	20			40
Stockwell, Dean	10			30
Stoltz, Eric	10	25		25
Stone, Oliver	20	25		40
Stone, Sharon	25	75	100	70
Stowe, Madeline	15	25		30
Strange, Glenn	200	250		300
Strasberg, Lee	25	45		85
Strasberg, Susan	20		40	25
Strathairn, David	15			35
Stratten, Dorothy	200	250		400
Strauss, Peter	15	25		40
Strauss, Robert	25			50
Streep, Meryl	40	75	150	125
Streisand, Barbra	200	450	450	250
Stroheim, Eric Von	200	325		550
Struthers, Sally	10	20	35	20
Stuart, Gloria	25	40	40	45
Sturges, John	10			20
Sturges, Preston	25	35	70	60
Sullivan, Francis L.	15	25		30
Sutherland, Donald	15	25	40	35
Sutherland, Keifer	15	25		30
Sutton, Frank	100	125		125
Sutton, John	15	20		25
Swain, Dominique	20			45

NAME	SIG	DS	ALS	SP
Swanson, Gloria	60	125	150	175
Swanson, Kristy	15	25		35
Swayze, Patrick	15	25		35
Sweeney, D. B.	15			30
Sweet, Blanche	25		40	40
Swit, Loretta	20	25	60	65
Switzer, Carl "Alfalfa"	600		1,000	1,400
T				
Takei, George	20	35	50	30
Talbot, Lyle	15	20		25
Talmadge, Constance	50	65	75	90
Talmadge, Norma	85	100	200	225
Tamblyn, Russ	15			25
Tambor, Jeffrey	10	20	40	25
Tandy, Jessica	35	55	75	85
Tarantino, Quentin	25	60	60	40
Tate, Sharon	325	500	500	1,000
Taylor, Elizabeth	200	400	600	400
Taylor, Estelle	25	35		50
Taylor, Lili	20	40	60	40
Taylor, Robert	60	125	200	175
Taylor, Rod	15	20		25
Tempest, Marie	35	55		80
Temple, Shirley (as child)	300	600	650	550
Temple-Black, Shirley	25		100	60
Tenant, Victoria	20	25		30
Terhune, Max	125			250
Thalberg, Irving	300	500	750	600
Theron, Charlize	20	50		60
Thewlis, David	20			35
Thiessen, Tiffani Amber	20	25		35
Thomas, Betty	20	40		35
Thomas, Danny	40	60	120	85
Thomas, Dave	15	25		30
Thomas, Heather	10	20	40	30
Thomas, Jonathan Taylor	20	25		35
Thomas, Marlo	20	30	55	30
Thomas, Terry	55	75		155

T

144 Bela Lugosi

145 Jayne Mansfield

146 The Marx Brothers

147 Steve McQueen

148 Jack Nicholson

149 Al Pacino

T

NAME	SIG	DS	ALS	SP
Thompson, Emma	25	40	75	40
Thompson, Lea	15	25		35
Thornton, Billy Bob	30	60	75	55
Three Stooges, The (w/Curly Howard)	2,000	3,500		4,000
Thurman, Uma	25	60	75	55
Tiegs, Cheryl	10	20		30
Tierney, Gene	30	55	75	100
Tilly, Jennifer	20	40	75	40
Tilly, Meg	20	25		30
Tilton, Charlene	10	25		30
Tobias, George	60	75		175
Todd, Ann	20	35		45
Todd, Richard	85			155
Todd, Thelma	225	300	450	550
Toler, Sidney	200	300		400
Tomei, Marisa	30	55	75	45
Tomlin, Lily	15	25	40	30
Tone, Franchot	35	50	75	70
Topol	25			40
Torn, Rip	20	35		35
Torrance, Ernest	100			175
Townsend, Robert	10	25		35
Trachtenberg, Michelle	20			35
Tracy, Spencer	200	300	450	450
Travanti, Daniel J.	10	15		20
Travers, Henry	300			500
Travis, Nancy	20	25		35
Travolta, John	25	40		55
Trejo, Danny	20			40
Trevor, Claire	40	55		60
Tripplehorn, Jeanne	15	25		35
Truffaut, François	75	200		500
Tucker, Chris	25	60	85	55
Tucker, Forrest	40			55
Tucker, Sophie	40			75
Turner, Janine	20	25		35
Turner, Kathleen	20	40		40

T

NAME	SIG	DS	ALS	SP
Turner, Lana	55	85		125
Turpin, Ben	200	300		550
Turturro, John	15	25		35
Tyler, Liv	25	55	75	55
Tyler, Tom	100	200		175
U				
Uggams, Leslie	10	20		20
Ullman, Liv	20	40		35
Ullman, Tracy	25	40	60	40
Umeki, Miyoshi	225			500
Underwood, Blair	15	25		20
Urich, Robert	25	40		45
Ustinov, Peter	35	65	85	70
V				
Vaccaro, Brenda	10	20	40	20
Vadim, Roger	25			55
Valentine, Karen	10	25		30
Valentino, Rudolph	1,100	1,700	1,850	2,200
Vallee, Rudy	15	40	55	45
Van Ark, Joan	10	15	25	20
Van Cleef, Lee	25			55
Van Damme, Jean-Claude	20	40		50
Van Dien, Casper	15	25		40
Van Doren, Mamie	15	25	40	35
Van Dyke, Dick	25	45	65	40
Van Dyke, Jerry	10	20		20
Van Fleet, Jo	25	40	40	40
Van Patten, Dick	10	20	35	20
Van Sant, Gus	20			55
Van Sloan, Edward	125			350
Van Zandt, Philip	55			175
Vance, Courtney B.	15			30
Vance, Vivian	225	250		300
Varney, Jim	15	25		55
Vaughn, Robert	15	25		35
Vaughn, Vince	15	25		35
Veidt, Conrad	100	150		275
Velez, Lupe	100	125		200

W

NAME	SIG	DS	ALS	SP
Verdon, Gwen	10		20	20
Vereen, Ben	20			25
Verhoeven, Paul	20			45
Vidor, King	40			125
Villechaize, Hervé	50	75		75
Vincent, Jan-Michael	10	25		25
Visitor, Nana	15	25		35
Visnjic, Goran	15			40
Voight, Jon	25	40	65	50
Von Sternberg, Joseph	50	75		75
Von Stroheim, Erich	200	350		500
W				
Wagner, Lindsay	15	25		40
Wagner, Robert	25	40	40	35
Wahlberg, Donnie	15	25	40	30
Wahlberg, Mark	20	40		45
Walken, Christopher	25	40	75	55
Walker, Paul	20			45
Walker, Robert, Sr.	55			175
Wallace, Dee	10	25	35	20
Wallach, Eli	15	20		25
Wallis, Hal	25	50		50
Walsh, J. T.	15			55
Walsh, M. Emmet	15			35
Walsh, Raoul	40			80
Walston, Ray	20	25		30
Walters, Julie	10	25		20
Wang, Wayne	20	35		45
Ward, Burt	15	25		25
Ward, Rachel	10			20
Ward, Sela	15	25	40	35
Warden, Jack	10	20		20
Warren, Leslie Ann	15	25	40	30
Warrick, Ruth	15			30
Washington, Denzel	40	75		75
Washington, Isaiah	15			35
Waters, John	20			45
Waterston, Sam	15	25		35

W

NAME	SIG	DS	ALS	SP
Wayans, Damon	20	25		35
Wayans, Keenan Ivory	20			35
Wayans, Marlon	15	25		30
Wayne, Carol	40			175
Wayne, John	450	850	1,250	1,100
Weathers, Carl	15			25
Weaver, Dennis	10	25		25
Weaver, Sigourney	20	55	75	65
Weaving, Hugo	25			55
Webb, Chloe	20			40
Webb, Clifton	40	55		75
Webb, Jack	55	85		125
Weissmuller, Johnny	225	400		550
Weisz, Rachel	20			55
Welch, Raquel	20	45		45
Weld, Tuesday	15		30	30
Weller, Peter	15	25		30
Welles, Orson	250	550	800	450
Wells, Dawn	15	25		30
Wen, Ming-Na	20			40
Werner, Oskar	30	45		55
West, Adam	25	25		35
West, Mae	75	125		350
Wheaton, Wil	25	40		40
Wheeler, Bert	30		75	75
Whitaker, Forest	20			45
White, Alice	25	45		85
White, Betty	15	20	40	30
White, George	75			125
White, Michael Jai	20			40
White, Pearl	200			325
Widmark, Richard	15		25	30
Wiest, Diane	25	55		50
Wilde, Cornel	20	25		40
Wilder, Billy	40	65	75	75
Wilder, Gene	20	25		40
Wilkinson, June	10		25	25
Wilkinson, Tom	20	40		45

W

NAME	SIG	DS	ALS	SP
Willard, Fred	10	20		15
Williams, Billy Dee	15	25		40
Williams, Cindy	10	15		25
Williams, Clarence	25			35
Williams, Esther	15		25	40
Williams, Guy	200	250		375
Williams, Harland	15	25		25
Williams, JoBeth	15			25
Williams, Robin	35	50	75	50
Williams, Treat	15	25		25
Williams, Van	15	25		35
Williams, Vanessa	25	25		40
Williamson, Mykelti	20			35
Willis, Bruce	50	175	150	150
Wilson, Bridgette	15			35
Wilson, Dooley	550	750		1,000
Wilson, Flip	15	25		25
Wilson, Luke	25			50
Wilson, Owen	25			50
Wilson, Peta	20			45
Wilson, Rita	20			45
Winfrey, Oprah	25	70		65
Winger, Debra	15	25		50
Winkler, Henry	10	20		25
Winkler, Irwin	20			55
Winningham, Mare	10			30
Winters, Jonathan	10	25	20	25
Winters, Roland	30	50	75	70
Winters, Shelley	10	20	40	20
Wise, Robert	15	25		30
Withers, Jane	15			25
Witt, Alicia	20			45
Wong, Anna Mae	100	150		225
Wong, B. D.	20			35
Woo, John	25	70		55
Wood, Elijah	40			65
Wood, Lana	15	25		30
Wood, Natalie	225	400		550

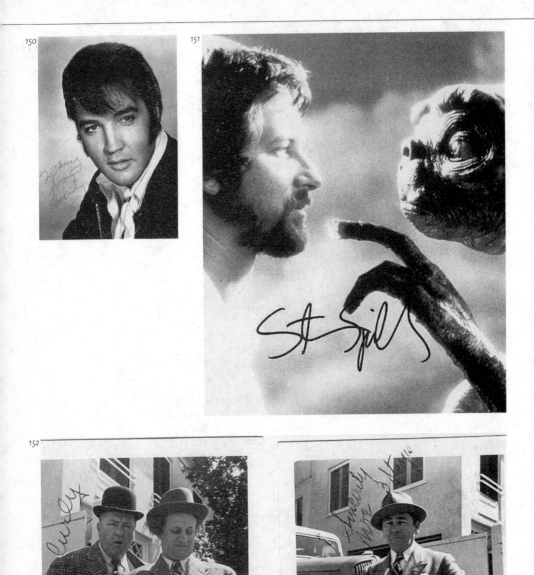

150 Elvis Presley

151 Steven Spielberg

152 The Three Stooges

153

154

153 Elizabeth Taylor

154 Orson Welles

W

NAME	SIG	DS	ALS	SP
Woods, James	15	25	40	35
Woodward, Edward	15	25	40	30
Woodward, Joanne	25	40		45
Wray, Fay	50	75		75
Wright Penn, Robin	20	40		40
Wyatt, Jane	10			20
Wyler, William	40	75		80
Wyle, Noah	20	35		35
Wyman, Jane	20			35
Wynn, Ed	55	125		150
Wynn, Keenan	25	40		45
Y				
Yeoh, Michelle	20	45		45
York, Dick	20	45	25	55
York, Michael	15	20		20
Young, Alan	10	20		20
Young, Burt	15			20
Young, Gig	50	75		95
Young, Loretta	20		25	35
Young, Robert	20			40
Young, Sean	20		40	35
Z				
Zadora, Pia	10	20		25
Zahn, Steve	20			45
Zane, Billy	20	40		40
Zanuck, Darryl F.	60	150	100	100
Zellweger, Renée	20	45		55
Zemeckis, Robert	25	45		60
Zeta-Jones, Catherine	20	40		75
Zimbalist, Efram, Jr.	10			20
Zimbalist, Stephanie	20			25
Zinneman, Fred	40			85
Ziyi, Zhang	20			65
Zukor, Adolph	75	200	250	200
Zwick, Edward	25	50		55

2 Movie Props and Wardrobe

COLLECTING MOVIE PROPS AND WARDROBE

Screen-worn costumes and film-used props have the most direct connection to a famous film or actor in a particular role. The sheer thrill of owning Humphrey Bogart's *Casablanca* tux, John Wayne's six-shooter from *True Grit,* or the "Rosebud" sled from *Citizen Kane* elevates the level of collecting for the film fan far beyond mass-issued posters and action figures. You are, in effect, owning a piece of Hollywood history.

Many of these items have sold in highly publicized auctions in recent years, sometimes fetching astronomical prices. These items are instantly recognizable, and their often one-of-a-kind nature dictates that their value is solely determined by the demand set by the collecting public. The fact that any of these relics have survived the ravages of time to become some of the world's most prized collectibles is astonishing, and is ironically due for the most part to the financial misfortunes of one of the grandest and most lavish movie studios of Golden Hollywood.

In May of 1970, Metro-Goldwyn-Mayer Studios (MGM) was having serious financial troubles, and in an attempt to reclaim some revenue, sold off thousands of original costumes and props from some of their most famous films in a huge auction administered by the David Weisz Company. The sale took place over seventeen days and marked the first time that the general public had an opportunity to own film-used costumes and props. Many of what would turn out to be legendary costumes were in tatters, showing signs of age and neglect. Some bore production tags and star names, and some did not. Many had several tags, evidence that a Civil War battalion jacket may have been worn in multiple films, spanning several decades of Hollywood productions.

It was at this time that what is now considered the world's most cherished and desired piece of Hollywood history was saved from an almost certain and complete extinction. In rummaging through the stacks of items in the costume-packed warehouse on the MGM lot, an MGM employee whom we will name "K.W." found four pairs of the ruby slippers worn by Judy Garland in the 1939 MGM masterpiece *The Wizard of Oz*. It is believed that seven or eight pairs of size 6B slippers were originally made for Garland to wear during filming. *See illustration #155.*

K.W. handed over the pair that were in the worst condition to his supervisor, and, unbeknownst to anyone else at MGM, he removed the remaining three pairs for himself. In the MGM/Weisz auction that followed a few days later, the pair that he turned in were auctioned for $15,000 to an anonymous buyer. In 1979, this pair was donated, once again anonymously, to the Smithsonian Institute in Washington where they reside to this date.

The first of the three "K.W. pairs" was sold to actress Debbie Reynolds. This pair was eventually dubbed the "Arabian Test Pair," as they had a rejected design with curled toes. This pair still remains in Ms. Reynolds's possession. The finest pair was kept by K.W. himself until October 1981, when Christie's auction house auctioned them off for a winning bid of $12,000. The other pair K.W. removed was sold to a friend, Michael Shaw. This information did not become public until February 2, 1971, when the *Houston Chronicle* reported that Shaw owned a pair of the slippers. Sotheby's auctioned the Shaw pair in 1984 for $15,500. This pair is currently on display at Disney-MGM Studios in Los Angeles (ironically their original home).

155

156

155 *The immortal Ruby Slippers
of Oz*
2004 © *Christie's Images*

156 *The Maltese Falcon*
2004 © *Christie's Images*

The most dramatic rise in popularity and in realized prices for movie props and costumes has taken place in the past fifteen years, and is best illustrated by the fifth pair of ruby slippers to surface. In 1940, high school student Roberta Jeffries Bauman won second place in a nationwide contest for submitting her choices for the ten best movies of 1939. Her prize was a pair of ruby red slippers that were marked "double" on the inner label (indicating that they were a duplicate pair for the production). Ms. Bauman kept this pair for almost fifty years, until consigning the pair for auction with Christie's East in June 1988. The winning bid hammered in at $150,000 ($165,000 with buyer's premium), an astonishing price nearly ten times higher than the price realized just four years earlier in the Sotheby's auction. This world record for a Hollywood costume was broken again in May 2000 when the same pair was once again auctioned by Christie's in New York for a final hammer price of $662,846 (including buyer's premium).

The world record price paid for a movie *prop* is held by the sale of the "Maltese Falcon" statue from the 1941 classic of the same name. *See illustration #156.*

An eleven-inch-high falcon made of lead, bearing the original slash marks made by Sydney Greenstreet in the film, hammered home in the Christie's December 1994 auction for $398,600 (including buyer's premium).

The public's fascination with movie costumes and props has grown beyond the auction houses to include the general public. In 1997, the Smithsonian's National Air and Space Museum marked the twentieth anniversary of *Star Wars* by showcasing 250 original movie props, storyboards, models, and costumes. The display included life-size models of Chewbacca and R2-D2, Princess Leia's costumes, Obi-Wan and Darth Vader's light sabers, and original models of the *Millennium Falcon* ship. These props and costumes have remained the property of Lucasfilm and have been rarely exhibited.

Tourist attractions like the Planet Hollywood restaurant chain and the Disney/Universal Studios theme parks have had probably the most direct impact on the increasing popularity in this collectible area. The presentations of classic Hollywood costumes and props in their hundreds of combined global locations have been viewed by millions of tourists yearly.

Even the movie studios themselves have started to use the lure of movie costumes and props in the promotional campaigns of their current releases. Starting with the 1997 Oscar winner, *Titanic,* Paramount launched in 1998 "Titanic on Tour," a 15,000-square-foot touring exhibit of props, sets, and costumes from the film. The props ranged from a forty-four-foot model of the boat used in the filming, all the way down to the "Heart of the Ocean" necklace worn by Kate Winslet's "Rose" in the film. The incredible response to the props led the way for Paramount to sign an exclusive agreement with the J. Peterman catalog company to exclusively sell hundreds of original screen-used props and wardrobe items ranging from life jackets to china place settings. Another example used to stir up even more hype for the release of the *Lord of the Rings: The Fellowship of the Ring* film was an exhibit entitled "A Journey to Middle Earth," set up in Toronto, Canada, in 2001. The exhibit featured over 900 suits of handmade armor, 2,000 pieces of safety (rubber) weaponry, 1,600 pairs of prosthetic feet and ears, and over 20,000 handmade household items used in the film.

This hysteria surrounding movie props and costumes was not always the case, as up until the MGM/Weisz auction, Hollywood costumes and props were just that—sitting in the wardrobe and property departments of the major studios awaiting the next project that required their services.

The Western Costume Company is arguably the largest and most famous Hollywood costume house. The company was started in 1912 as a retailer of American Indian products. Legend has it that cowboy star William S. Hart was in the store when the store owner mentioned to Hart that the costumes worn by the Indians in the Hollywood westerns looked phony. The studio then asked the company to supply them with authentic Indian costumes. That first film turned out to be Cecil B. DeMille's *The Squaw Man* (1913), Hollywood's first full-length feature film, and Hollywood's first box-office smash. The relationship between the Hollywood studios and Western Costume has evolved from then until modern times. The company still exists today, creating and renting out wardrobe for Hollywood's latest and greatest creations. In fact, if you are in Hollywood during the last three weeks of October, Western opens its back doors to the public for rentals of a selection of Hollywood costumes for Halloween parties.

For many years, Universal, Warner Bros., Columbia, and Fox owned the Western Costume Company. As a cost-cutting measure in the early 1980s, they began to sell off their inventory of over five million costumes. These pieces, along with the Weisz/MGM sale pieces, made their way into the hands of true die-hard fans and film historians, as there was absolutely no resale marketplace for these items at the time. The diligent and painstaking task of researching, restoring, and authenticating these pieces of Hollywood history brought life to these articles as viable and collectible objects.

In 1989, the Western Costume Company was sold to Paramount Studios and AHS Trinity Group. The group's specific reason for purchasing the company was to allow the historical value of the remaining inventory to be preserved for future generations of Hollywood fans.

This pretty much stopped the release of material from Western Costume to the collecting marketplace. For the past few decades, the original Western and MGM/Weisz pieces have passed hands through highly publicized auctions held by Sotheby's and Christie's and other auction houses. Most recently, the eBay marketplace has been the home for many auctions of these items.

The main problem facing the average collector looking to purchase quality props and wardrobe is the competition at the auction. The almost-limitless budgets of the Disney/Planet Hollywood mega-complexes created astronomical auction realized prices, indirectly taking the finest collectibles out of the hands of the general collecting community. Another adversary to the average collector is celebrities themselves. A 1994 auction at Sotheby's in London saw U2's Bono pay nearly $56,000 for the Hitler-like suit worn by Charlie Chaplin in the 1940 film *The Great Dictator*. One of the most famous movie prop purchases was made in 1982 at a Sotheby's New York auction. Steven Spielberg purchased the "Rosebud" sled from *Citizen Kane* via telephone for $55,000, and it reportedly still hangs in Spielberg's home. It is interesting to note that this is not the only example of a Rosebud sled to surface—the film's prop masters fabricated several sleds for filming. The sled used for the actual sledding scene in the film was made of pine. The others were made of balsa wood (maybe to help them burn quicker during the film's famous ending); some sources believe that two sleds were destroyed for the cameras. Spielberg owns one of the balsa versions. A pine sled used in the film was sold at auction at Sotheby's in late 1996 for $233,500.

The scarcity of available premier movie props from Hollywood classics is another challenge for the collector. The events of September 11, 2001, prompted George Lucas to donate a few original props to a charity auction to raise money for the September 11 Children's Fund. This marked the first time official *Star Wars* props were offered to the marketplace bearing the Lucasfilm seal of approval (and certificate of authenticity). A collection of fifteen props and models raised over $120,000 in a highly publicized auction on the eBay marketplace. The items in the auction that garnered the most attention were the two authentic movie props offered. These items were a Storm Trooper screen-worn helmet (final bid of $45,111.56) and Darth Maul's light saber (final bid of $35,100.00).

The incredible popularity, historical value, and marketing potential of these props have in effect taken them out of the hands of average collectors. At the same time, some companies have taken to producing reproduction props and wardrobe to satisfy the marketplace. The incredible range of items and values in this collectible area is almost endless. Therefore, when looking to start or add to an existing movie prop and wardrobe collection, it is essential to have a strong understanding of the terminology of these collectibles, as well as the factors that determine value: *authenticity, content,* and *condition*.

Definition of a Movie Prop

There are two distinct terms to describe items used in a film scene: a film *prop* and *set decoration*.

A *prop* (property) is an item that is used in a scene in a film and that is either handled by an actor or specifically made reference to in the scene. For example, an actor talking on a cell phone points to a street sign. The scene cuts to a close-up of the street sign. In this scenario, both the cell phone and the street sign are props.

In a different scenario, the cell phone sat on a table in the background and the street sign was blurred in the background and never made reference to. In these cases, the cell phone and street sign are considered *set decoration*.

Under these distinctions, it is easy to understand why basic set decoration pieces are an inexpensive and fun way to start a movie prop collection. The trouble is being able to clearly attribute a set decoration piece to a specific film. Props, on the other hand, depending on their importance and distinction within a film or a scene, require specific detailing and labeling. The more unusual and original a prop appears within a film, the more distinctive and easy to authenticate and attribute it will be.

Types of Props

Using the following scene as a guideline will allow for an easier illustration of the different types of props.

"A woman at a bar holds up a very rare and expensive bottle of wine. The scene cuts to a close-up of the wine label. A man slams his highly detailed gun on the bar as trade for the wine bottle. The camera cuts to a close-up of the decorative gun. The woman smashes the bottle of wine over the man's head and runs out of the bar. The man grabs the gun and fires two shots at the door."

Backup Prop

A backup prop is a prop that has been replicated several times in the event that it gets dropped or broken. In this scene, the original bottle the woman holds up would be a backup prop (with several exact copies in existence at the time of filming).

Stunt Prop

This refers to a prop that is made out of a durable material (hard rubber for guns) that is able to withstand being dropped or thrown. In this scene, the gun the actor slams down on the bar would be a stunt prop, as well as the bottle of wine that the woman smashes over his head (made out of easily breakable "sugar glass").

Special Effects Model

This would refer to the gun the actor picks up and uses to fire blank shots.

Hero Prop

Hero is movie industry slang for the most identifiable prop variation shown on screen. This is the prop that would require the most detail for a close-up shot. In this scene, the bottle with the highly detailed label and the gun with the ornate detail would be the hero props. There is also the terminology *screen-featured* or *screen-used* to describe these props.

It is important to note that the hero props are the most desired by collectors. Depending upon how often the prop is used throughout the film, and the overall fragility of the item itself, there may be several examples of the same hero prop in existence, therefore not making it one-of-a-kind. These extra props are also referred to as backup props. These are identical to the screen featured prop, but are just not used in the actual filming.

Definition of Movie Wardrobe and Costume

The terms *movie wardrobe* and *costume* refer to an article of clothing worn by an actor or actress in a particular role in a film (or films). These are also referred to as *screen-worn*. There is an area of collecting celebrity wardrobe or personal effects that belonged to a celebrity, but for the purposes of this value guide, we will exclude these items and specifically address the screen-worn items only.

Just as in the case of props, there are usually several exact copies of a set of wardrobe from a film, some in varying degrees of condition depending upon the action that takes place with the character in the film. In the film *Die Hard,* Bruce Willis's character wore a white tank top throughout a large part of the film. As his character got more bruised and bloodied, the tank top became dirtier, sweatier, torn, and bloodstained. To a collector looking for a screen-worn tank top from the film, the desire would be for a more "distressed" example over a clean "untouched" version from the early scenes in the film, as the association with the climactic finale of the film is the key to its appeal. On the other hand, Kate Winslet's stunning gowns made for *Titanic* would be preferred over the water-soaked slip she wore in the climactic rescue at sea.

There are also costumes that have been created for stunt doubles, and some for promotional purposes such as still photographs.

Authenticating Movie Props and Costumes

If you want to purchase a costume or prop, the most important factor to consider is the authenticity of the item in relation to the claim the seller is making regarding it. Questions to ask include:

1. Was the item screen-used?

2. Was it used in a specific film, or several films?

3. Did a specific actor in the film use it?

4. Was it used by the main actor in the film, or a secondary or background player?

5. Is there more than one of these items available?

6. What is the history of ownership?

7. What type of prop is it? Hero, backup, or stunt?

Certificate of Authenticity

A certificate of authenticity (COA) should always accompany the item. The certificate should specifically refer to the piece in question, with added photographs if possible. COAs are only as good as the person signing them—the more reputable the signer, the more reputable the

157 Western Costume tag for an Elvis Presley costume shirt

item. The person signing the certificate should be as closely related to the film and prop/costume as possible. These would include a director of the film studio, director of the film, the actor the item relates to specifically, or the prop master or costume designer from the film.

Behind-the-Scenes Photos

Ask the seller for a few behind-the-scenes photos from the set. If the seller worked on the film, he or she should have these. If the photo details the item, even better.

Studio Tag

A tag attached to a prop that can list any and all of this information—the studio name, production name, actor's name, scene and film title. Some early studio guns have a metal studio tag attached to them. The tags are used by studios for storage purposes, and unfortunately many of them do not survive with the prop.

In regards to costumes, studio tags are usually sewn into a piece of wardrobe. Many pieces from the Western Costume Company may also have a Western tag sewn in as well. *See illustration #157.*

Costumer's Tag

A tag attached to a costume that can list any and all of this information—the studio name, production name, actor's name, scene and film title. Over the years many of these tags have been removed and/or separated from the costumes, and it is usually quite rare to find a vintage costume with an attached costumer's tag.

Actor's Name

The name of the actor (or actress) is almost always handwritten (or sewn in some examples) on the inside collar of any unique costume worn in a film. In fact, this is usually one of the best methods to differentiate between an actor and a stunt costume.

Studio Markings

These are usually etchings found on many prop items. These may list a specific production or actor's name if it is character specific.

When purchasing a costume or prop, purchase only from reputable dealers specializing in movie props and costumes who will offer you a lifetime guarantee to refund your full purchase price if your further research should prove the item not to be authentic as the seller claims.

Refer to the Auction Houses and Retailers directory listed in this book for a selection of established firms, as well as the organizations, collectors' clubs, and publications listings for further aids for the experienced or novice collector.

Condition

Depending on the age and type of item, the factors of condition can be quite severe. Many times, actual film-used props are fabricated of materials that were the most cost effective for the budget of the film. Many props are simply everyday items that were purchased from a local store and then modified for the film. *Star Wars* is a perfect example; made for only $9 million, the original film budget for props was minor. There were twelve models of the famous light sabers used in the film. Prop master Dennis Murren went to an antique camera store and found a box of fifty flash attachments for cameras popular in the 1950s. He bought the lot for $2.50 each. The grips were made from cut-up windshield wiper blades that were glued on. The light saber Darth Vader used to chop off Luke Skywalker's hand in *The Empire Strikes Back* is actually a wooden stick that glows only after the special effects wizards add movie magic to the film. Even the communicator used in *Star Wars Episode 1* was a modified Lady Bic shaver.

It is therefore very important to stress that a screen-used costume or prop that has been distressed (either specifically for the camera or by the use in the film) should not be restored to original condition. Screen-used condition is the most desired by collectors. In fact, prop alterations may be the link to authenticating a prop as being screen used.

Preserving and Displaying Costumes and Props

The most important factor for any item to retain its value is the preservation of its present condition. At the same time, locking up your cherished acquisition can defeat the purpose of enjoying the item while it is in your possession. The combination of proper display and preservation will help maintain its condition and maximize the overall enjoyment you get from your collectibles.

Articles of clothing should be stored at room temperature, as extreme temperature shifts and moisture associated with basements or attics can be harmful to most fabrics. Some collectors prefer to display wardrobe on mannequins. If you choose this method, always position your display out of direct sunlight, as UV rays will cause discoloration or fading. When hanging wardrobe, use padded hangers to protect the fabrics from potential tearing. If you wish to store your items out of view, you can use acid-free tissues and boxes to protect fabrics from the potentially harmful acids found in nonarchival paper.

Other prop items can be displayed in clear Lucite display cases, again kept out of the harmful UV rays of direct sunlight. Some collectors put together elaborate displays featuring photo-

158

158 Face/Off *prop pistol shadow-box display*

graphs of the prop in use in a scene from the film and nameplates with pertinent information. *See illustration #158.*

A shadowbox presentation can be arranged with a local framer. Always insist on acid-free museum-grade materials being used in all displays.

Content

After an item has been determined to be authentic, and the condition has been classified, the next important factor that distinguishes a movie prop or costume from all others in the marketplace is the *content* of the item.

Content refers to the significance of the item in relation to the film and/or celebrity in reference. As an example, Vivien Leigh made over twenty films, with *Gone with the Wind* her most acclaimed. A hat worn by her in that film sold for over $20,000 at auction. Another hat worn by her in a lesser film could probably be purchased for a few hundred dollars. At the same time, a different hat worn in *GWTW*, but worn by a secondary or background player, would sell for much less than the Leigh example, in the $800–$1,000 range. The value of this example would be based purely on the fact that it was worn by this actress in this particular film.

All items with exceptional content are regarded as the Holy Grail pieces of prop and wardrobe collecting. Historically, pieces with the best content appreciate the most in value. When looking to purchase a screen-used item in any format, one should look for the best possible content available in one's price range.

Factors That Determine Long-Term and Future Values

Movie props and costumes are items that have been fabricated to represent a real item when photographed on film. As objects, they do not have a physical value more than their actual cost of materials and manufacturing. Their value is based purely on the factors of supply and demand. The rarer an item is and the greater the number of collectors wanting that item, the more valuable it becomes to the marketplace as a whole.

What makes one prop or costume more valuable than another? Historically, the items associated with Hollywood classics such as *The Wizard of Oz, Gone with the Wind,* as well as the legends—Marilyn Monroe, Charlie Chaplin, and John Wayne (to name just a few)—have fared the best over time. The main reasons for this are a limited supply of very desirable material to a large and continually expanding marketplace of collectors and institutions (museums, theme parks, restaurant chains, etc.) looking to add these pieces to their collections.

Will the Golden Hollywood icons and films mean as much to the cinema fans of twenty or thirty years from now? Will current hit films like *Gladiator, Titanic,* and *Harry Potter* as well as modern stars such as Arnold Schwarzenegger, Russell Crowe, and Tom Cruise become the Hollywood legends of the future?

Modern movie props and costumes are now being offered to the collecting public through charity auctions arranged by the studios, mostly as a publicity vehicle either before or during the initial release of the film. Many collectors are purchasing these items for very high prices (mostly due to "auction fever") that are not based on previous auction results or the time-tested appeal of the film. If a collector is buying an item strictly for their own personal enjoyment and pleasure, then the price they are paying should not be an issue for them in the future.

Collectors should always be comfortable with the price they pay for any item. If and when they make a decision to sell that item in the future, the current generation of market-driving collectors will determine what the value of that item will be.

MOVIE PROP AND WARDROBE PRICE LISTINGS

Because every movie prop and costume is unique, it is impossible to accurately list a set value for these items. Most sellers use an auction format to allow the collecting marketplace to determine the price for an item. The listings in this chapter with an assigned value have been determined from retail prices of several international dealers specializing in movie props and wardrobe.

The majority of the items listed in this chapter were sold at auction through several international auction houses from 1995 to late 2002. In most cases, the examples selected were sold between 1999 and 2002, but some record-setting pieces sold in the mid-1990s had to be included as an invaluable reference.

Each listing contains:

1. The *film* the item was used in

2. The *actor* it belonged to

3. A brief *description* of the item

4. The *date* of the auction

- *Auction Estimate*. Some auction houses provide a presale estimated price range, which is what the auction house has determined to be an expected result. In some cases, the final prices fall below the estimate, and in heated bidding, final prices are in the multiples of the estimates. These figures are very hard to determine, as they are based on previous sales of items that have a comparable interest, which may or may not be reflective of a true market value for a one-of-a-kind item. Where estimates have been available, I have included them in parentheses (est. $2,000–$3,000) before the final realized price.

- *Final Realized Price* ("Buyer's Premium"). Most auction houses charge a bidder a commission on the final invoice. This premium can range from 5 percent up to 20 percent in addition to the final winning bid price. Most auction houses *include the buyer's premium* when they post the final winning prices from their auctions. I personally feel that this figure can be misleading due to the varied ranges of premiums charged by the different houses. As such, I have *excluded* the buyer's premium from the prices listed in this book to reflect the final winning bid. In cases where the premium amount could not be determined and removed, the "incl. buyer's premium" notation has been listed beside the price.

28 Days
White cotton short-sleeve T-shirt (XL) by Jerzees Z w/ Russian woman and lettering; Kayayore Adele; Black Lucky Brand sweatpants (M); black & white sock; and gray suede Italian-made elastic top slip-on sneakers by Gabriel Strehle worn by *Sandra Bullock* as Gwen Cummings. $650.

61*
Full screen-worn New York Yankees uniform; gray Yankees jersey and matching pants, made by Mitchell and Ness, as well as blue knit leggings and period baseball cap, with a white "NY" on the front and the smaller style brim. Jersey and pants have a Western Costume Company stamp inside, with cap stamped inside "W.C.C." In fine condition. May 2002. $824.

8mm
Dark charcoal gray 2-pc Zegna suit; black leather Coach belt; and black Calvin Klein socks worn by *Nicolas Cage* as Tom Welles. $1,000.

A Certain Smile
Black crepe top with light yellow chiffon skirt, handwritten label, as worn by *Joan Fontaine* in the 1957 film. July 2001. (Est. $400–$600) $425.

A Few Good Men
Military hat worn by *Tom Cruise* in the film. October 1997. (Est. $1,000–$1,500) $5,588.

A Few Good Men
White officer's uniform cap, with handwritten label, worn by *Tom Cruise* in the 1992 film. July 2001. (Est. $2,000–$3,000) $1,600.

A Letter to Three Wives
Black crepe gown with handwritten label as worn by *Jeanne Crain* in the 1948 film. April 2002. (Est. $600–$800) $900.

A Perfect Murder

A sculpture/prop used in the 1998 film. May 2000. (Est. $3,000–$5,000) $2,200.

A View to a Kill

Blank prop check 6.75 × 4, from the fictitious Zorin International Bank in Paris, taken out of the original checkbook used by *Christopher Walken* as he portrayed bank president "Max Zorin" in the James Bond film. In very fine condition. August 2001. $349.

A Woman Rebels

Irish lace gown over green taffeta, originally woven in 1885 and designed by Walter Plunkett, as worn by *Katharine Hepburn* in the 1937 film. December 2000. (Est. $6,000–$8,000) $55,000.

Addams Family Values

Black tuxedo jacket with black braid piping and matching pants worn by *Carel Struycken* as "Lurch" in the 1993 film. April 2002. (Est. $1,000–$2,000) $1,000.

Addams Family Values

Dark brown suit jacket with velvet collar, matching pants and cream color shirt worn by *Carel Struycken* as "Lurch" in the 1993 film. April 2002. (Est. $1,000–$1,500) $1,000.

Addams Family Values

Full-length black gown with cobweb motif on sleeves worn by *Anjelica Huston* as "Morticia" in the 1993 film. April 2002. (Est. $3,000–$4,000) $3,000.

Addams Family Values

Gray and black striped suit jacket, pants, and white striped shirt with handwritten label worn by *Raul Julia* as "Gomez" in the 1993 film. April 2002. (Est. $3,000–$4,000) $3,000.

Addams Family Values

Long gray wool button-front trench coat with green velvet collar worn by *Christopher Lloyd* as "Uncle Fester" in the 1993 film. April 2002. (Est. $2,000–$3,000) $2,000.

Addams Family Values

Long sleeve black silk dress with black silk inserts at cuffs worn by *Christina Ricci* as "Wednesday" in the 1993 film. April 2002. (Est. $600–$800) $1,000.

Air Force One

Dark blue Cerrutti 1881 suit: Jacket has two bullet holes in left sleeve; ripped pocket and lining hem torn out at back; and cuffed trousers ripped for harness on both sides at the hip and torn at knee, worn by *Harrison Ford* as "President James 'Jim' Marshall." $2,000.

All The Pretty Horses

Cream color w/ black accents leather riding jacket (size approx. Petite Small) worn by *Penelope Cruz* as "Alejandra de la Rocha." $750.

Amityville Horror

Realty sign used in the original 1979 film about the infamous Long Island murders. Few minor chips, 24 × 18". May 2002. $330.

An Affair to Remember

Black silk organza evening gown with jet bead trim, as worn by *Deborah Kerr* as "Terry McKay" in the 1957 film. December 2000. (Est. $2,000–$3,000) $4,000.

An American in Paris

Blue satin leotard tutu with handwritten label, as worn by *Leslie Caron* as "Lise Bouvier" in the 1951 film. December 2000. (Est. $3,000–$5,000) $2,100.

Anna and the King of Siam

Oriental servant robe of black and gold brocade, with Western Costume typed label, as worn by *Lee J. Cobb* as "Kralahome" in the 1946 film. December 2000. (Est. $1,000–$1,500) $1,600.

Armageddon

Space helmet, gray plastic with silver metal nodules, huge clear plastic face shield arcing over the front, marked "Hero #1" on inside, as worn by *Bruce Willis* in the 1998 film. July 2001. (Est. $2,000–$3,000) $2,500.

Army of Darkness

Costume worn by *Embeth Davidtz* as "Evil Sheila" of a flowing orange dress with leather corset in the 1993 film. April 2002. (Est. $800–$1200) $900.

Army of Darkness

Complete costume worn by *Bruce Campbell* as "Ash" including distressed shirt and trousers with large scarf worn in the 1993 film. April 2002. (Est. $1,500–$2,500) $1,200.

Army of Darkness

Pair of battle helmets made of silver resin and a camouflaged helmet with finial worn by members of the army in the 1993 film. April 2002. (Est. $400–$600) $400.

As Good as It Gets

"Carol's Date Dress & Sweater": Outfit includes black, purple, and dusty rose print nylon blend button-front dress and dusty rose cardigan worn by *Helen Hunt* as "Carol Connelly." $130.

As Good as It Gets

"Simon's Complete Painting Outfit": Complete outfit includes black Hanes T-shirt, LSCA fine striped blue and navy shirt, blue denim jeans (31) by Blue System; and brown canvas and leather work boots. Entire outfit is dirt and paint splattered from filming as worn by *Greg Kinnear* as "Simon Bishop." $1,100.

Austin Powers: The Spy Who Shagged Me

Brown-colored delivery costume worn by the character "Fat Bastard" in the film. The outfit includes the extra, extra large brown Izod polo shirt; the ridiculously enormous brown shorts;

the brown baseball cap with an emblem initialed "FBD" standing for Fat Bastard Delivery; black leather belt; black stirrup leggings; and the black with white striped sneakers (size 12). Accompanied by a letter of authenticity from New Line Cinema. May 2002. $2,310.

Babes in Toyland

Beige wool coat, pants, and cape trimmed with satin, Western Costume labels, as worn by *Tommy Sands* in the 1961 film. July 2001. (Est. $200–$300) $900.

Babes on Broadway

Beige pantsuit with red cummerbund, matching knee-length cape and ornate red brooch with matching leather thigh boots with MGM tag, worn by *Judy Garland* in the 1941 film. July 2001. (Est. $6,000–$8,000) $6,000.

Batman Forever

Black double-breasted suit jacket and matching pants, each having a red painted motif, prototype design for the "Two Face" character portrayed by *Tommy Lee Jones* in the 1995 film. With WB COA. July 2001. (Est. $2,000–$3,000) $1,100.

Batman Forever

Elbow-length silver gloves with attached plastic "fins" on each worn by *Val Kilmer* in the 1995 film. July 2001. (Est. $3,000–$4,000) $1,600.

Batman Forever

Original prop Two Face coin that *Tommy Lee Jones* used to decide whether to be good or bad. Each side with a Liberty head and "E Gothamus Unum," one side intentionally scarred (the "bad" side). In fine condition. February 1999. $395.

Batman Forever

Red and black prop "rocket propelled grenade," painted foam prop, approx. 18" with spent model rocket engine in the tail used in the 1995 film. April 2002. (Est. $200–$300) $200.

Batman Forever

Signature "Question Mark" cane used by "The Riddler," gold plated plastic, approx. 36" long, with WB COA, used by *Jim Carrey* in the 1995 film. July 2001. (Est. $3,000–$4,000) $3,750.

Batman Forever

Silver rubber "sonar" belt with hard plastic buckle with a gold bat insignia worn by *Val Kilmer* as "Batman" in the 1995 film. July 2001. (Est. $2,000–$3,000) $1,200. *See illustration #159.*

Because You're Mine

Two-piece suit with MGM handwritten label, as worn by *Mario Lanza* in the 1952 film. December 2000. (Est. $1,500–$2,000) $1,100.

Silver, rubber sonar belt from Batman

Beckett

Leather-bound pontifical used by *Richard Burton* in the 1964 film. April 2002. (Est. $800–$1,200) $1,500.

Ben-Hur

Brown suede "biblical" belt with lace-up closure and a pair of mid-calf lace-up sandals with brass d-rings with labels, as worn by *Charlton Heston* in the 1959 film. July 2001. (Est. $3,000–$5,000) $6,000.

Ben-Hur

Complete period Roman officer costume; off-white undergarment with red stripe, ornate metal chestplate armor with red tassels, metal helmet with finial, metal sword with scabbard and black leather Roman sandals, as worn in the 1959 film. March 2000. (Est. $2,000–$3,000) $5,500.

Ben-Hur

Four beige sleeveless cotton togas with lace-up front closures worn in the 1959 film. July 2001. (Est. $400–$600) $1,200.

Ben-Hur

Orange wool cape and beige wool tunic with orange stripe at hem, with Western Costume handwritten label, as worn by *Charlton Heston* in the 1959 film. December 2000. (Est. $3,000–$5,000) $4,000.

Ben-Hur

Two screen-used medallions that were part of the Roman soldier costumes in the film. May 1998. (Est. $150–$200) $213.

160

160 *Costume worn by Charlton Heston in* Ben-Hur

Ben-Hur

Leather helmet with matching leather gauntlets and high lace-up leather sandals, worn by *Charlton Heston* in the chariot race in the 1959 film. December 2000. (Est. $10,000–$15,000) $10,000. *See illustration #160.*

Beverly Hills Cop III

Screen-worn Lions football jacket worn by *Eddie Murphy*. Long-sleeve "high school letter-man"–type jacket is black with blue highlights on the collar, cuffs, and waist, with cream colored sleeves. Left lapel has a large football helmet with "Lions" above it, and "67" on both sleeves. In fine condition, with scattered light intentional soiling and distress to sleeves. May 2002. $3,025.

Big Daddy

Cream color suit by Pierre of Paris; yellow tie with gray dogs; taupe socks; and brown belt with gold buckle worn by *Adam Sandler* as "Sonny." $1,200.

Birth of a Nation

Metal bayonet with leather fitting and metal "US" emblem with a canvas and leather Union backpack, very well worn, used in the 1915 film. April 2002. (Est. $800–$1000) $650.

Blade

Screen-featured prop liquid dart, used by *Wesley Snipes* in the film, with blue liquid remnants. February 1999. $349.

Blade Runner

Prop ID plate, 7.75" × 6", painted blue, yellow, and silver with heavy weathering, used in the 1982 film. March 2000. (Est. $600–$800) $500.

Blue Streak

Dirty black cargo pants w/ drawstring ankles and six pockets; belt; black ribbed T-shirt (M) by Kenneth Cole; black wool hat; and black leather gloves worn by *Martin Lawrence* as "Miles Logan." $350.

Bonnie and Clyde

Three-quarter-length button-front linen dress with V-neck as worn by *Faye Dunaway* in the 1967 film. December 2000. (Est. $6,000–$8,000) $6,000.

Braveheart

Scottish warrior's costume of wool plaid kilt, brown overgarment, olive green chestplate armor, period shoes and belt, as worn in the 1995 film. March 2000. (Est. $2,000–$3,000) $4,750.

Bright Leaf

A cognac velvet lounging robe with train, trimmed in soft mink, worn by *Lauren Bacall* as "Sonia" in the 1950 film. December 2000. (Est. $3,000–$5,000) $2,250.

Bull Durham

Wilson A-2000 baseball glove, handwritten "Annie" in black ink on the backside wrist portion, as worn by *Susan Sarandon* as "Annie Savoy" in the 1988 film. December 2000. (Est. $800–$1,200) $600.

Camelot

Two-piece beige wool gown with train, as worn by *Vanessa Redgrave* in the 1967 film. December 2000. (Est. $3,000–$5,000) $2,000.

Casablanca

Wool top with white and gold paisley evening skirt attached, as worn by *Ingrid Bergman* in the 1942 classic. December 2000. (Est. $6,000–$8,000) $7,500.

Charlie's Angels

"Command Room" outfit consisting of a yellow T-shirt with motocross iron-on decal, black pants with silver zippers on knees, black synthetic jacket, and black combat boots, with COA from Sony Pictures, as worn by *Drew Barrymore* in the 2000 film. July 2001. (Est. $1,500–$2,500) $1,500.

Charlie's Angels

Bill Murray's "Bosley" custom flamboyant tuxedo; includes jacket, pants, and tie, as well as a unique jeweled tie clip. Accompanied by a letter directly from the wardrobe department head of Sony Studios on their stationery, attesting to the authenticity of the item. In fine condition. May 2001. $1,100.

Christopher Strong

Metal coat of mail–style long-sleeve gown and matching skullcap (lower half removed), worn by *Katharine Hepburn* in the 1933 film. July 2001. (Est. $3,000–$5,000) $2,500.

Citizen Kane

Pine sled used in the sledding scenes in the film. 1996. $233,500. (incl. buyer's premium).

Clash of the Titans

Gold resin helmet in a leaf motif with two eyeholes, worn by *Harry Hamlin* in the film. July 2001. (Est. $1,200–$1,500) $1,000.

Cleopatra (1934)

Navy blue chiffon period gown with silver lamé floral pattern and heavy bead trim at neck-line with matching cape, as worn by *Claudette Colbert* in the 1934 film. December 2000. (Est. $10,000–$15,000) $7,500.

Cleopatra (1963)

Blue velour Egyptian-style crown with upturned brim and conical point, with handwritten name inside, as worn by *Elizabeth Taylor* in the 1963 film. December 2000. (Est. $1,200–$1,500) $9,500.

Cleopatra (1963)

Elaborate black wool Egyptian wig trimmed with silver and gold on the long braids and crown, with Western Costume label, as worn by *Elizabeth Taylor* in the 1963 film. December 2000. (Est. $1,500–$1,800) $3,750.

Cleopatra (1963)

Metallic blue chiffon jersey over-the-shoulder gown with pleated skirt with ornate belt, Western Costume handwritten label, as worn by *Elizabeth Taylor* in the film. December 2000. (Est. $3,000–$5,000) $6,500.

Cleopatra (1963)

Gold gilt wood Egyptian "Ibis" with wings spread, mounted on a circular pedestal base as used in the 1963 film. December 2000. (Est. $4,000–$6,000) $6,500.

Cleopatra (1963)

Brass-plated double-edged dagger, 9.5" overall, with Ellis Prop COA, as used by *Elizabeth Taylor* as Cleopatra in the 1963 film. July 2001. (Est. $5,000–$6,000) $5,000.

Cleopatra (1963)

Brown and gold painted fiberglass shield with four leather arm straps on the back. April 2002. (Est. $600–$800) $1,400.

Cliffhanger

Long-sleeve Henley thermal shirt, distressed and soiled with studio blood with black stretch pants, as worn by *Sylvester Stallone* as "Gabe Walker" in the 1993 film. December 2000. (Est. $1,000–$1,500) $2,500.

Close Encounters of the Third Kind

Original screen-featured red zipper-front Mayflower jumpsuit. One of only a handful known in private hands. In fine condition, with "Western Costume Company" stamped inside the front. February 1999. $1,600.

Command Decision

Olive green officer's uniform cap with eagle insignia pinned to the crown, brown leather brim and band, as worn by *Clark Gable* as "General K. C. Dennis" in the 1948 film. March 2000. (Est. $3,000–$5,000) $2,500.

Conan the Barbarian

Arnold Schwarzenegger–used sword. May 1998. (Est. $5,500–$6,000) $10,000.

Conan the Barbarian

Special effects sword made of fiberglass and metal, with spring-loaded pump handle to a reservoir in the handle (for fake blood), one of two in existence, used by *Arnold Schwarzenegger* in the 1982 film. July 2001. (Est. $8,000–$10,000) $8,000.

Coney Island

Black tulle and lace period ballgown with sequin, rhinestone, and bugle bead trim and very long train, with handwritten label, with matching fan and hat, as worn by *Betty Grable* in the 1943 film. December 2000. (Est. $2,000–$3,000) $3,000.

Cool Hand Luke

Wooden cane with metal tip carried by "Boss Godfrey" in the 1967 film. April 2002. (Est. $300–$500) $1,600.

Crime School

Two-piece single-breasted three-button suit jacket and matching pants, with WB handwritten label, as worn by *Humphrey Bogart* in the 1938 film. December 2000. (Est. $3,000–$5,000) $3,000.

Cruel Intentions

Ladies' black silk pinstripe pantsuit as worn by *Sarah Michelle Gellar* as "Kathryn Merteuil." $1,500.

Cruel Intentions

Navy blue slip dress as worn by *Reese Witherspoon* as "Annette Hargrove." $950.

Cruel Intentions

Two-piece heather gray Prada cotton blend suit worn by *Ryan Phillippe* as "Sebastian Valmont." $1,200.

Dances with Wolves

Kevin Costner's Union uniform military shirt worn in the Academy Award–winning film. Long-sleeve, size 42" chest, 34" sleeve, and 16" collar. Inside of collar has an original Western Costume Company label bearing his name. In fine condition. June 2001. $3,993.

Dances with Wolves

Screen-featured prop tomahawk with stone head, wooden body, and leather wrappings. In fine condition. February 1999. $358.

Darling Lili

Beige chiffon gown with velvet dots on two tiers, trimmed in floral silk with Western Costume label, as worn by *Julie Andrews* in the 1970 film. July 2001. (Est. $800–$1,200) $650.

Desirée

Burgundy crepe gown with velvet bodice, gold piping with cream satin collar and cuffs, as worn by *Jean Simmons* in the 1954 film. December 2000. (Est. $1,500–$2,000) $1,100.

Desirée

Uniform in the Napoleonic style with coat, trousers, sash, and cape, as worn by *Michael Rennie* in the 1954 film. December 2000. (Est. $2,000–$3,000) $2,750.

Desirée

Gray wool greatcoat worn by *Marlon Brando,* with Western Costume label inside the garment reading "Western Costume Co., M. Brando number 77-2711-2, Chest 40 inch" with sleeve and inseam information also typed in. In fine condition. August 2001. $5,990.

Die Hard III

Screen-worn outfit of *Samuel L. Jackson*; white long-sleeve Saks Fifth Avenue shirt, with one torn sleeve and several blood stains, a pair of black Liz Clairborne pants and a pair of black socks. Both the shirt and pants have Jackson's character name, "Zeus," written on the tags. In fine condition, with expected wear and stress associated with an action film. May 2002. $274.

Doll Face

Nude mesh neckline and midriff costume, with handwritten label, worn by *Carmen Miranda* as "Chita" in the 1945 film. December 2000. (Est. $2,000–$3,000) $2,260.

Dorothy Vernon of Haddon Hall

Coral brocade satin ballgown with gold lace on sleeves, studded with real seed pearls at a cost of $32,000 in 1923 dollars, as worn by *Mary Pickford* in the 1924 film. December 2000. (Est. $20,000–$30,000) $14,000.

Dragonseed

Chinese peasant tunic of black and yellow-striped denim, with MGM cleaning tag and handwritten label, as worn by *Katharine Hepburn* in the 1944 film. July 2001. (Est. $600–$800) $700.

Dubarry Was a Lady

Beige crepe long-sleeve evening gown, adorned with bugle beads, as worn by *Lucille Ball* in the 1946 film. December 2000. (Est. $1,000–$1,500) $1,700.

161 Costume worn by Peter Fonda in Easy Rider

East of Eden

Light beige trousers with blue pinstripes with cuffs and self belt, with WB inside ink stamp and handwritten label as worn by *James Dean* in the 1955 film. December 2000. (Est. $15,000–$18,000) $15,000.

Easy Rider

Long-sleeve, collarless flower and paisley print cotton shirt worn by *Peter Fonda* as "Wyatt/ Captain America" in the 1969 film. July 2001. (Est. $10,000–$15,000) $9,000. *See illustration #161.*

Easy to Love

Brown and beige dress with wool top and brown velour skirt worn by *Esther Williams* in the 1953 film. April 2002. (Est. $400–$600) $1,300.

Easy to Wed

Cream color bellhop-style jacket worn by *Van Johnson* in the 1946 film. July 2001. (Est. $250–$450) $550.

Evita

Period dress and undergarment, labeled "Madonna" and "Eva," worn by *Madonna* in the 1996 film. July 2001. (Est. $3,000–$5,000) $4,250.

Excalibur

Gold toned metal helmet worn by *Robert Addie* in the 1981 film. April 2002. (Est. $3,000–$4,000) $1,800.

Face-Off

Complete prison guard costume of gray coverall and pair of electronic "lock down" boots, as worn in the 1997 film. March 2000. (Est. $1,500–$2,500) $1,000.

Face-Off

Two screen-used prop liquid wood Colt Model 1911 A1 .45 caliber pistols used in the film by *Nicolas Cage*. Pistols were hand painted by the film's weapons coordinator, Rock Galotti, and were used during the first five days of shooting. Accompanied by a letter of authenticity from Galotti. March 2002. $4,875.

Fat Man and Little Boy

Khaki officer's shirt and "pink" military dress pants worn by *Paul Newman* in the 1989 film. Both the shirt and the pants have the original American Costume Company tags sewn inside with the name "Paul Newman" and number 2027 clearly visible on both. The shirt is decorated with the appropriate insignia and tie as seen in the film, and the pants come with a military web belt. In fine condition. Accompanied by a letter of authenticity from the Eastern Costume Company. December 2001. $1,465.

Finding Forrester

Brown/tan patterned alpaca wool H. Herzfeld acetate-lined long coat (XL); white cotton knit long-sleeve turtleneck shirt (XXL) by Amber; charcoal, maroon, and gray vertical striped cotton flannel elastic waist pants (no label /XL); and dark green and tan cashmere fringed scarf worn by *Sean Connery* as "William Forrester." $2,300.

First Knight

Aluminum torso armor with chain mail at shoulders, handwritten "*Richard Gere*—Lancelot" on inside of each half as used in the 1995 film. April 2002. (Est. $1,500–$2,000) $2,250.

First Knight

Custom-made sword with retractable tip, designated the "Hero" sword, 36" long, used by *Richard Gere* in the 1995 film. April 2002. (Est. $3,000–$5,000) $2,000.

First Knight

Fiberglass shield painted gray and silver with royal crest on the front, two leather straps on the back and handwritten "R.G." on the back, as used by *Richard Gere* in the 1995 film. April 2002. (Est. $1,500–$2,000) $2,750.

First Knight

Prop sword constructed of resin and wood, 40" long, used in the 1995 film. July 2001. (Est. $200–$300) $150.

Forever Amber

Black satin cape lined in red satin and trimmed with black seal skin as worn by *Linda Darnell* in the 1947 film. April 2002. (Est. $2,000–$3,000) $1,800.

Forever Amber

Chiffon ballgown with matching headdress, inside handwritten label and S. Goldwyn stamp, as worn by *Linda Darnell* in the 1947 film. December 2000. (Est. $2,000–$3,000) $3,000.

Forrest Gump

Prop box of chocolates printed "Russell Stover Candies The Gift Box" plus a red cotton baseball cap with the front decorated "Bubba Gump Shrimp Co.," both signed by *Tom Hanks*. December 1999. (Est. $700–$1,000) $3,075.

Funny Girl

Barbra Streisand's screen-worn outfit of a hoop-style white and pink, heart-accented costume with ruffled neckline worn prominently in the 1974 film. In fine condition. April 2001. $3,900.

Galaxy Quest

Vox communicator—small silver painted resin prop communicator, 4" in length, with letter of authenticity, used in the 1999 film. July 2001. (Est. $300–$400) $300.

Gaslight

Burgundy wool period dress with lace trim, with MGM cleaning tags and handwritten label, as worn by *Ingrid Bergman* in the 1944 film. December 2000. (Est. $3,000–$5,000) $4,000.

Gentlemen Prefer Blondes

A revealing showgirl leotard encrusted with yellow and black sequins and faux jewels, with fishnet inserts at legs, Fox handwritten label, as worn by *Marilyn Monroe* in the 1953 film. December 2000. (Est. $30,000–$40,000) $31,000.

Get Shorty

Custom-made satin-lined brown wool blend flat-front cuffless trousers (36" × 31") w/ "John Travolta" label inside worn by *John Travolta* as "Chili Palmer." $235.

Get Shorty

Prop book cover *"Weird Tales"* includes book cover and slab of Styrofoam to which covers were attached to make the prop books. Cover can be folded to fit an appropriate sized book for display purposes. $40.

Ghostbusters

Screen-featured remote-controlled prop taxicab, smashed by the Stay Puff marshmallow man. In fine condition. April 1999. $700.

Girl, Interrupted

Custom-made light moss green black cotton-lined suede trousers (30" × 32") with oval stitch front pockets and cream color cotton rib knit long-sleeved scoop neck shirt (S/M). Pants have black dirt marks on leg bottoms and shirt is frayed and stained from use during filming; worn by *Angelina Jolie* as "Lisa Rowe." $1,200.

Girl, Interrupted

Black miniskirt with navysailor-style buttons on front worn by *Winona Ryder* as "Susanna Kaysen." $350.

Gladiator

A Praetorian Guard costume worn by an extra in the film with shield, helmet, wrist and shin guards, leather boots and belt, chest protector with leather laces. The huge shield is adorned with gold-painted laurels. The helmet has two moveable earflaps on either side with eagle motifs with an eagle perched on top. The Praetorian Guards were the Roman emperor's personal elites (bodyguards). May 2002. $800.

Gladiator

Arena helmet made of fiberglass made to resemble silver metal with gold accents from the 2000 film. April 2002. (Est. $1,000–$1,200) $1,200.

Gladiator

Black painted "Praetorian" shield with silver and yellow accents used in the 2000 film. July 2001. (Est. $1,000–$1,500) $600.

Gladiator

Complete costume from the Battle of Carthage scene with long blue shirt, leather boots, spike helmet, leather belt, chain mail vest, and spear. April 2002. (Est. $1,500–$2,000) $1,000.

Gladiator

Full gladiator costume from the training scene, blue tunic with green paint, leather belt, boots and wooden sword used in the 2000 film. April 2002. (Est. $1,000–$1,500) $750.

Gladiator

Metal sword with wooden handle with complete Moroccan costume—sackcloth tunic, boots, and belt as worn in the 2000 film. April 2002. (Est. $1,300–$1,800) $1,000.

Gladiator

Ornate prop ax of gold and silver painted metal with silver knobs on lower handle; semicircular ax head is silver painted rubber with long spike on back side, approx. 34", used by *Russell Crowe* in the 2000 film. July 2001. (Est. $3,000–$5,000) $6,000.

Gladiator

Praetorian costume with full body armor, greaves and gauntlets, helmet, leather boots, purple wool cape, tunic, pants and singulum with shield. April 2002. (Est. $4,000–$6,000) $2,750.

Gladiator

Roman Infantry costume with red shirt and pants, chest and shoulder armor, singulum, greaves, gauntlets, boots, helmet, and cloak with red shield and sword from the 2000 film. April 2002. (Est. $4,000–$6,000) $2,250.

Gladiator

Screen-used prop weapon—a spiked ball on a chain. LOA from "The Prop Store of London." May 2002. $470.

Gladiator

Total package Roman Infantry costume prop complete with helmet (with moveable visor and ear flaps), wrist and shin guards, leather boots and belt, detachable chest and shoulder guards. May 2002. $880.

Goldeneye

Opaque white sign, 54" × 15", with red and black warnings in Cyrillic script, used in the 1995 James Bond film. July 2001. (Est. $300–$500) $400.

Goldeneye

Set of three 32" × 6" placards painted silver with red Russian inscriptions used in the 1995 film. December 2000. (Est. $300–$500) $200.

Goldfinger

A 1937 Phantom III Rolls-Royce used in the 1964 James Bond film. May 2000. (Est. $150,000–$200,000) $402,000 (incl. buyer's premium).

Goldfinger

Gold-painted prop plaster gold bar used in the James Bond film, about 9" × 2.5" × 1.5". In fine condition, with chips of plaster loss and paint loss in areas. October 1998. $375.

Gone with the Wind

Off-white petite hat with upturned brim and thin elastic strap, draped with long black lace, with Selznick Int. Pictures handwritten label, as worn by *Vivien Leigh* as "Scarlett O'Hara" in the 1939 classic. March 2000. (Est. $15,000–$20,000) $12,000.

Grease

Black and white saddle shoes and pale yellow bobby socks worn by *Olivia Newton-John* in the 1978 film. December 2000. (Est. $1,500–$2,500) $8,000.

Halloween H2O

Original prop painted rubber Smith and Wesson AirLite revolver used in the film by both *Adam Arkin* and *Jamie Lee Curtis*. In fine condition. June 1999. $450.

Hamlet (1990)

Rust silk brocade blouse with gold trim, tunic of brown silk, long full trailing cape with matching shoes and belt, worn by *Alan Bates* as "Claudius" in the 1990 film. July 2001. (Est. $2,000–$3,000) $1,600.

Hearts Divided

Dove gray silk jersey gown with floral blue and rose soutache trim, as worn by *Marion Davies* in the 1936 film. December 2000. (Est. $2,000–$3,000) $2,260.

162 *Costume worn by Jim Carrey in*
How the Grinch Stole Christmas

Hello, Dolly!

Period costume of a beige lace and silk blouse, jacket and skirt, each made of period carpet swatches worn over full petticoats with large feathered picture hat, as worn by *Barbra Streisand* in the 1969 film. December 2000. (Est. $3,000–$5,000) $8,000.

Hellraiser

Latex head with sunken eyes and face, hand-detailed and airbrushed, signed by the creator of the prop, from the 1987 film. July 2001. (Est. $1,250–$1,500) $950.

Henry V (1989)

Gray suede court coat, silver jeweled belt, and blue suede pants, with costume labels, as worn by *Kenneth Branagh* in the 1989 film. July 2001. (Est. $400–$600) $550.

How the Grinch Stole Christmas (2000)

Brown wool full-length cloak with caplet and hood, with artificial snow at lower hem, with internal label and COA from Universal, as worn by *Jim Carrey* in the 2000 film. July 2001. (Est. $10,000–$15,000) $9,000. *See illustration #162.*

How the Grinch Stole Christmas (2000)

Christmas toy used by one of the denizens of Whoville in the 2000 version of this film. It actually works, nodding its head and wagging its tail. In amazing near mint condition with an LOA from Premiere Props and Universal Studios. May 2002. $200.

How the Grinch Stole Christmas (2000)

Who "Haddy Golf Caddy" used in the 2000 film. It is full human size (54" from base to the tip of the handle) and sports flashy hubcaps like a mini *Ben-Hur* chariot. It contains four Who designed clubs, a corkscrew club, a pretzel-twisted club, a club with a slight bend, and a club with two flexible rubber joints, all with orange hands for blades. The cart handle is also a hand (a left hand) extended as if to shake the hand of the player. Wonderful EX/MT condition. Accompanied by an LOA from Premiere Props and Universal Pictures. May 2002. $711.

How the West Was Won

Blue vest worn by *John Wayne* as "General William Tecumseh Sherman" in the film. United States Cavalry two-pocket uniform vest, size 46, with nine U.S. Eagle buttons, with a Western Costume Company tag sewn into the back with Wayne's name typed on it as well as a number. In fine condition. July 2001. $5,639.

How the West Was Won

Uniform jacket and vest with Western Costume label, as worn by *John Wayne* in the 1962 film. May 2000. (Est. $7,000–$9,000) $7,000.

How to Marry a Millionaire

Cream cloth evening handbag with handwritten label inside, prominently used in the 1953 film by *Marilyn Monroe*. May 2000. (Est. $6,000–$8,000) $6,000.

How to Marry a Millionaire

Black lamé beret with handwritten label, worn by *Lauren Bacall* in the 1953 film. December 2000. (Est. $1,500–$1,800) $1,300.

Hush

Navy blue silk knit maternity short-sleeve V-necked T-shirt worn by *Gwyneth Paltrow* as "Helen Baring." $250.

I Know What You Did Last Summer

"Festival Crown & Scepter": metal framed crown center is 4" high, ornamented with a seahorse and two large shells, and is composed of green, gold, yellow, and pink rhinestones; the 26" scepter is silver colored metal with teal, olive, pink, green, purple, gold, and yellow rhinestones topped with a large pearl looking ball and seahorse worn by *Sarah Michelle Gellar* as "Helen Shivers." $1,800.

I Know What You Did Last Summer

White cotton rib knit tank top (no label /M) that has special effects blood and dirt on it worn by *Ryan Phillippe* as "Barry Cox." $450.

I Know What You Did Last Summer

Jacket worn by *Ryan Phillippe* in the film. August 1998. $572.

I Love Melvin

Gold lamé accordion-pleated gown with handwritten label, as worn by *Debbie Reynolds* in the 1952 film. July 2001. (Est. $300–$500) $600.

I'd Climb the Highest Mountain

Cotton day dress with flower bouquet motif with handwritten label worn by *Susan Hayward* in the 1951 film. April 2002. (Est. $400–$600) $850.

163

163 *Grail cup from* Indiana Jones and the Last Crusade

Imitation of Life

Rose velvet dress with collar, Universal Int. label, worn by *Lana Turner* in the 1958 film. July 2001. (Est. $800–$1200) $1,600.

Independence Day

Prop rubber stunt machine gun with nylon strap modeled after a Heckler & Koch weapon, used in the 1996 film. April 2002. (Est. $200–$300) $275.

Indiana Jones

Handmade sixteen-plait bullwhip of kangaroo hide, 196" long, used by *Harrison Ford* in all three Indiana Jones films. December 1999. (Est. $4,500–$6,300) $21,150.

Indiana Jones and the Last Crusade

Original red resin stunt Grail cup with gold speckle that was used to pour the last bit of water onto the wounded *Sean Connery* at the end of the film. In fine condition. June 2002. $6,442. *See illustration #163.*

Indiana Jones and the Last Crusade

Original replica German WWII P-08 Luger metal prop pistol; a full weight model carried by one of the Nazis in the film. In fine condition. December 1998. $666.

Indiana Jones and the Temple of Doom

A sword wielded by one of the Thugee guards attempting to kill Indy. Handle is a panther's head with engravings, 35" long. May 2002. $400.

Indiana Jones and the Temple of Doom

Leather-wrapped wooden handle, approx. 22" long, with three braided leather whips fastened to the top, used in the 1986 film. July 2001. (Est. $900–$1,100) $850.

Interview with the Vampire
Light cotton blouse with cavalier sleeves and open chest, handwritten label, as worn by *Tom Cruise* as "Lestat" in the 1994 film. December 2000. (Est. $1,500–$2,000) $1,100.

James Bond
A nonfiring replica of a Luger constructed of steel with real clip, handwritten tag on trigger guard indicates "Pine" for Pinewood studios, used in James Bond films. December 2000. (Est. $500–$700) $1,800.

James Bond
Solid plastic gun painted black with brown faux handles to look like a Walther pistol, used in Bond films. December 2000. (Est. $200–$300) $5,500.

Jeanne Eagels
Kootch costume of a skirt and bra heavily encrusted with pearls and rhinestones and long draping fringe, with matching headpiece, Columbia label, worn by *Kim Novak* in the 1957 film. July 2001. (Est. $900–$1200) $1,700.

Joan of Arc
Cross of St. George battle flag used in the 1948 film, measures 4' × 6'. April 2002. (Est. $200–$300) $500.

Joe Dirt
Joe Dirt's "ACDC Outfit" includes: white w/ blue cotton knit baseball T-shirt (S) w/ orange "ACDC" logo; and blue denim overalls (no label). Outfit is special effects teched w/ dirt to match scenework. Worn by *David Spade* as "Joe Dirt." $300.

Juarez
Burgundy brocade gown worn by *Bette Davis* in the 1939 film. July 2001. (Est. $1,200–$1,500) $1,000.

Jumbo
Pink cotton gown with embroidered eyelet skirt and batiste sleeve and chiffon petticoat, with handwritten label, as worn by *Doris Day* as "Kitty Wonder" in the 1962 film. December 2000. (Est. $2,000 -$3,000) $2,260.

Jurassic Park
Original 3.75" × 8.25" folder promoting the park, used as a prop in the film. A box of these appear with a girl in back of a vehicle as it tries to escape from a dinosaur. The full-color brochure folds out to full color 15.5" × 16.5" visitors' information presentation including map and dinosaur silhouettes. In very fine condition. April 1996. $360.

Kalifornia
Original screen-worn steel-toed boots worn by *Brad Pitt* in virtually every scene in the film. In fine condition (made to look heavily distressed). October 2001. $1,250.

King Kong (1935)

Papier-mâché tribal shield with geometrical design in yellow and rust on the front. Approx. 4' tall, with burlap handle mounted to back and RKO label to left. Used in the 1935 film. April 2002. (Est. $2,000–$3,000) $4,250.

King Kong (1976)

Prop model of King Kong made of brown resin, approx. 19" high, used in the production of the 1976 film. December 2000. (Est. $1,200–$1,400) $1,400.

Kingpin

Complete wardrobe worn by *Woody Harrelson* in the film. February 1999. $578.

Kingpin

Wine red polyester jacket with three front pockets. Comes with matching pants and brown/yellow polyester long-sleeve shirt with wild bird pattern worn by *Woody Harrelson* as "Roy." $750.

L.A. Confidential

Toupee (and wig box) worn by *Kevin Spacey* as "Jack Vincennes." $250.

Ladyhawke

Metal sword approx. 53" with leather-wrapped handle and two metal spikes as used by *Rutger Hauer* in the 1985 film. April 2002. (Est. $1,500–$2,500) $1,600.

Last of the Mohicans

Original film prop 24" tomahawk that was used in the film. In fine condition with overall wear. October 1996. $480.

Latin Lovers

Beige linen sleeveless dress worn by *Lana Turner* in the 1953 film. April 2002. (Est. $400–$600) $2,000.

Law and the Lady

Period dress with checkered taffeta skirt and matching jacket with MGM cleaning tags as worn by *Greer Garson* in the 1951 film. April 2002. (Est. $600–$800) $425.

Legend

Silver-painted fiberglass sword approx. 54" tall, used by *Tim Curry* in the 1985 film. April 2002. (Est. $1,500–$2,500) $1,400.

Let Freedom Ring

Gold brocade silk vest with handwritten MGM label, worn by *Nelson Eddy* in the 1939 film. July 2001. (Est. $200–$300) $450.

Let's Make Love

Black cocktail dress with a bodice of coffee-colored chiffon embroidered with black scrolling foliage and matching cropped jacket, as worn by *Marilyn Monroe* in the 1960 film. October 1999. (Est. $20,000–$30,000) $79,500 (incl. buyer's premium).

Let's Make Love

Black silk jersey cocktail dress as worn by *Marilyn Monroe* in the 1960 film. October 1999. (Est. $15,000–$20,000) $42,000.

Let's Make Love

Gray silk jersey dress with a halter-style neckline with full skirts of layered gray chiffon, as worn by *Marilyn Monroe* in the 1960 film. October 1999. (Est. $15,000–$20,000) $46,000.

Lethal Weapon

Black rubber stunt gun fashioned after a 9mm Beretta automatic, used in the 1987 film. April 2002. (Est. $400–$600) $450.

Letter from an Unknown Woman

Black velvet period gown with very long train, with handwritten label, as worn by *Joan Fontaine* in the 1948 film. July 2001. (Est. $800–$1,200) $1,000.

Lillian Russell

Gray wool full-length period coat with attached caplet trimmed in fox fur with printed label, worn by *Alice Faye* in the 1939 film. July 2001. (Est. $1,500–$1,800) $1,400.

Little Women (1933)

Heavy brown silk skirt with velvet trim and gold blouse with brown bodice, handwritten label, worn by *Katharine Hepburn* as "Jo March" in the 1933 classic. July 2001. (Est. $10,000–$12,000) $10,000.

Little Women (1949)

Black crepe skirt and bodice with inner handwritten label, worn by *June Allyson* as "Jo March" in the 1949 film. December 2000. (Est. $1,000–$1,500) $1,700.

Little Women (1949)

Peach silk organza gown with handwritten label, as worn by *Janet Leigh* as "Meg" in the 1949 film. December 2000. (Est. $2000 -$3000) $1,400.

Lloyds of London

Gold mohair tailcoat with handwritten label, worn by *Tyrone Power* in the 1936 film. July 2001. (Est. $600–$800) $1,000.

Look Who's Talking

Black suede jacket with teal blue leather sleeves, with black jeans, T-shirt, and sneakers as worn by *John Travolta* in the 1989 film. December 2000. (Est. $1,000–$1,500) $700.

Love Me or Leave Me

Kootch costume of halter top and skirt with tassels, sequins, and beads with headband, worn by *Doris Day* in the 1955 film. July 2001. (Est. $800–$1,000) $900.

Mars Attacks

Prop alien mask and glove worn by an actor during stand-in scenes in the film. While all of the on-screen images were done by a computer, this outfit was worn for the dialogue scenes. In fine condition. February 1999. $2,000.

Meet Me in St. Louis

Peach and white lace undergarment overlaid with a sheer nude-colored fabric, handwritten label, as worn by *Judy Garland* as "Esther Smith" in the 1944 film. March 2000. (Est. $2,000–$3,000) $2,000.

Meet the People

Gray wool jumpsuit and off-white cotton blouse, handwritten MGM label, as worn by *Lucille Ball* as "Julie Hampton" in the 1944 film. July 2001. (Est. $800–$1,200) $1,100.

Men in Black

Outfit worn at the beginning of the film includes orange jumpsuit; two white nylon mesh jersey-like shirts; and white Nike sneakers. Outfit also includes jewelry: two silver chains; and silver earring worn by *Will Smith* as "Jay." $4,000.

Men in Black

Outfit worn in the scene where Jay goes to "MIB" for his first day of work. Outfit includes yellow and black motocross racing pants; yellow, gray, and white w/black T-shirt; white socks; and Nike sneakers worn by *Will Smith* as "Jay." $3,500.

Men in Black

Distressed brown coveralls; two distressed brown work shirts; and distressed brown work boots from Edgar, the "alien" that Smith and Jones pursue throughout the film, worn by *Vincent D'Onofrio* as "Edgar the bug." $3,000.

Mission Impossible

Custom-made "gadget" gun (hero prop) that took three months to construct; used by *Jon Voight* in the 1996 film. April 2002. (Est. $4,000–$6,000) $4,000.

Mission Impossible

Full costume of zipper-neck shirt, black synthetic overgarment, pants, helmet, goggles, and padded vest with inner label, worn by *Jon Voight* in the 1996 film. April 2002. (Est. $1,500–$2,500) $1,000.

Mission Impossible

Prop computer watch made of black plastic with clear red inserts, worn by *Tom Cruise* in the 1996 film. July 2001. (Est. $2,500–$3,500) $1,500.

Mission Impossible 2

Hand-painted rubber handgun, prop gun used by *Tom Cruise* in the 2000 film, with COA from the weapons coordinator. July 2001. (Est. $2,000–$3,000) $2,000.

Mission Impossible 2

Hand-painted rubber handgun, used by *Dougray Scott* in all stunt scenes in the 2000 film, with a COA from the weapons coordinator. July 2001. (Est. $1,500–$2,000) $1,500.

Mister Roberts

Light cotton khaki button-front long-sleeve shirt, with handwritten label, as worn by *Henry Fonda* as "Lt. Doug Roberts" in the 1955 film. December 2000. (Est. $2,000–$3,000) $1,700.

Modern Times

Black painted wooden mechanical gear used in the Charlie Chaplin 1936 classic. Approx. 5" in diameter. April 2002. (Est. $1,000-$1,500) $800.

Moulin Rouge (1952)

Black wingtip shoes modified to reduce the height of *José Ferrer* by two feet. April 2002. (Est. $2,000–$3,000) $2,250.

Moulin Rouge (1952)

Wooden cane, 21" long, exhibits cracking in paint from age, end cap missing, used by *José Ferrer*. April 2002. (Est. $300–$500) $1,800.

Moulin Rouge! (2001)

Laminated wooden cane, approx. 30" tall, with colorful painted accents used by *John Leguizamo* in the 2001 film. April 2002. (Est. $800–$1,200) $1,300.

Mutiny on the Bounty (1962)

Black felt period English mariner's uniform hat with satin trim and satin bow over left eye and two brass buttons, with handwritten label, worn by *Marlon Brando* as Fletcher Christian in the film. July 2001. (Est. $3,000–$5,000) $4,000.

My Fair Lady

Hat covered in marabou, with egret feathers on front held with an antique brooch, worn by an extra in the ascot scene in the 1964 film. July 2001. (Est. $400–$600) $325.

My Gal Sal

Burgundy velvet period muff, silk lined, with handwritten label, worn by *Rita Hayworth* in the 1942 film. July 2001. (Est. $300–$500) $600.

Myra Breckenridge

Black sable muff with 12" collar, long sable stole, and a pair of sable cuffs, worn by *Mae West* in the 1970 film. July 2001. (Est. $600–$800) $1,100.

Natural Born Killers

Prop *USA Today* newspaper with front page headline "KILLING COUPLE LEAVES SHAKEN SURVIVOR TO TELL TALE," as used in the 1994 film. March 2000. (Est. $300–$500) $325.

Nixon

Three-piece 1960s-style tuxedo ensemble worn by *Anthony Hopkins* as Richard Nixon in the 1995 motion picture. The Motion Picture Costume labels that have "Anthony Hopkins" typed in are in the coat, vest, and pants; the Anton shirt has a neck label with the initials "A.H." December 2001. $1,465.

Notting Hill

A nineteenth-century blue painted pine door with the number 280 and representing William Thacker's (*Hugh Grant*) front door in the 1999 film. December 1999. (Est. $3,700–$5,400) $4,400.

One Hour with You

Satin spaghetti-strap nightgown with inserts worn by *Jeanette MacDonald* in the 1932 film. April 2002. (Est. $600–$800) $800.

Papillon

Prisoner's uniform made for *Steve McQueen* in the 1973 film, with Western Costume labels and COA from the costume supervisor. July 2001. (Est. $5,000–$6,000) $5,000.

Patton

Green wool military shirt was worn by *George C. Scott* in the 1970 film. The shirt has a Machin label that reads "tailored especially for George Scott" and is decorated with the appropriate insignia and patches and khaki military tie as seen in the film. In fine condition. Accompanied by a letter of authenticity from the Eastern Costume Company. December 2001. $3,575. *See illustration #164.*

Pearl Harbor

Four-piece screen-used and -worn wardrobe by *Ben Affleck:* Army Air Corps officer's shirt, khaki pants, webbed belt, and overseas cap. Accompanied by costumer's tags. In fine condition. August 2001. $1,900.

Picnic

Silk organdy gown with Columbia label, worn by *Kim Novak* for the 1955 film. July 2001. (Est. $800–$1,200) $650.

Pitch Black

Torn gray tank top and custom gray cotton pants worn by *Vin Diesel* as "Riddick." $800.

Portrait of Jennie

White dotted Swiss dress with matching slip, aqua taffeta sash and belt, with Western Costume handwritten label, as worn by *Jennifer Jones* in the 1949 film. December 2000. (Est. $1,500–$2,000) $2,750.

Predator

Combat vest, camouflage shirt, and military web belt worn by *Arnold Schwarzenegger* in the film. June 2000. (Est. $3,000–$5,000) $3,000.

164

164 Costume worn by George C.
Scott as Patton; George C. Scott
as Patton; the shirt label

Predator II

Alien weapon used as a prop in the film, 5" long, cast in metal and finished in gold. In fine condition. July 1997. $354.

Pulp Fiction

Screen-worn suit worn by *Samuel L. Jackson*. Suit consists of a black single-breasted jacket by Perry Ellis and matching pair of black pants. In fine condition, with a bit of light soiling. May 2002. $825.

Queen Bee

Black satin gown with black satin trim, lined in heavy fuchsia cotton with matching cape, as worn by *Joan Crawford* in the 1955 film. July 2001. (Est. $2,000–$3,000) $2,500.

Rambo: First Blood Part 2

Prop shoulder-fired rocket launcher/recoilless rifle, painted olive green, one of only two used by *Sylvester Stallone* as "John Rambo" in the 1985 film. July 2001. (Est. $2,500–$3,500) $1,500.

Rebel without a Cause

Beige wool skirt with handwritten studio label, as worn by *Natalie Wood* as "Judy" to signal the famous drag race in the 1955 film. December 2000. (Est. $4,000–$6,000) $4,250.

Return to Peyton Place

Brown tweed wool dress with long sleeves with Fox handwritten label, worn by *Mary Astor* in the 1961 film. December 2000. (Est. $1,000–$1,500) $700.

Rio Grande

Prop saber used by *John Wayne* in the film. October 1997. (Est. $1,000–$1,500) $3,542.

River of No Return

Three pairs of denim blue jeans with handwritten labels, as worn by *Marilyn Monroe* as "Kay Weston" in the 1954 film. October 1999. (Est. $20,000–$30,000) $37,000.

River of No Return

Emerald green and red saloon-style sleeveless dress with black appliqué and black faux gems, red sewn-in ruffled underskirt, edged in gold ribbon, as worn by *Marilyn Monroe* in the 1954 film. March 2000. (Est. $80,000–$120,000) $42,500. *See illustration #165.*

Robin Hood: Prince of Thieves

Four-piece costume: burlap jacket, white cotton blouse, leather and suede pants, belt, and leather ascot with handwritten label, worn by *Kevin Costner* in the 1991 film. July 2001. (Est. $2,000–$3,000) $4,000.

Robin Hood: Prince of Thieves

Woven leather mesh headpiece adorned with studs, worn by *Sean Connery* in the 1991 film. July 2001. (Est. $800–$1,200) $1,200.

Robocop 2

Stunt costume, complete for the "Robocop" character. May 1998. (Est. $8,000–$11,000) $6,900.

Romeo and Juliet (1936)

Period pants of black wool with gold braid design down one leg, as worn by *Leslie Howard* in the 1936 film. July 2001. (Est. $800–$1,200) $650.

Ronin

Cream dress shirt by Marks & Spencer (size 16); two-piece suit w/ brown/gray two-button jacket by Marks & Spencer; tan raincoat (no label); and black knit cap worn by *Robert DeNiro* as "Sam." $3,000.

Saratoga Trunk

Black silk taffeta period gown with gray and black ribbon trim on bodice and skirt worn by *Ingrid Bergman* in the 1945 film. July 2001. (Est. $1,200–$1,500) $2,500.

Saving Private Ryan

Realistic assemblage of olive drab–colored soldiers' gear includes helmet, dagger, grenade, cloth-covered canteen and cup, etc., used in the 1998 Steven Spielberg–directed WWII drama. May 2002. $400.

Saving Private Ryan

WWII replica field radio and case, as used by *Tom Hanks* in the 1998 film. March 2000. (Est. $4,500–$5,500) $4,000.

Scream

Original costume (ghost faced killer with robe). May 1998. (Est. $4,500–$6,500) $6,000.

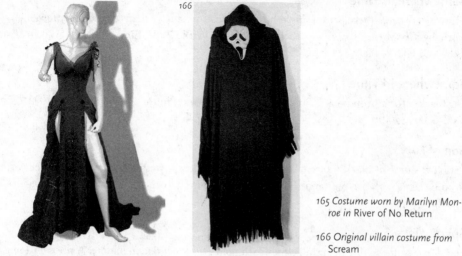

165 Costume worn by Marilyn Monroe in River of No Return

166 Original villain costume from Scream

Scream

Original screen-worn villain costume from the film. Costume consists of a 68-inch-long black hooded robe, a semicircular piece of black cloth and chilling pullover skeleton head mask. In fine condition. Accompanied by a letter of provenance from *Scream*'s costume assistant attesting to the authenticity of the robe. February 2002. $2,000. *See illustration #166.*

Seven Thieves

Off-white spaghetti-strap leotard with fringe and sequin trim, with Fox label, worn by *Joan Collins* in the 1960 film. July 2001. (Est. $400–$600) $500.

Shakespeare in Love

Prop playbill 9.5" × 13" for the *Romeo and Juliet* play in the 1998 film. April 2002. (Est. $400–$600) $300.

Shanghai Express

Black chiffon gown with silver threads in a printed pattern worn by *Marlene Dietrich* in the 1932 film. July 2001. (Est. $4,000–$6,000) $8,000.

Something for the Birds

Blue sharkskin suit jacket with matching skirt with label as worn by *Patricia Neal* in the 1952 film. April 2002. (Est. $400–$600) $350.

Somewhere in Time

Brown wool period bowler hat with grosgrain ribbon trim, as worn by *Christopher Reeve* in the 1980 film. December 2000. (Est. $2,000–$3,000) $4,250.

Somewhere in Time

Brown wool three-piece period single-breasted pinstripe suit, with inside handwritten label, as worn by *Christopher Reeve* as "Richard Collier" in the 1980 film. December 2000. (Est. $3,000–$5,000) $8,000.

Somewhere in Time

Dust jacket for a prop book "*Travels Through Time*" used in the 1980 film. April 2002. (Est. $400–$600) $700.

Son of Fury

Period costume of black moiré taffeta tailcoat and britches, vest, lace dickey, and cape, with costume labels, as worn by *Tyrone Power* in the 1941 film. December 2000. (Est. $3,000–$5,000) $3,250.

Spartacus

Flat metal battle sword with dull edges with gold-painted wooden handle, approx. 24", with metal helmet worn by the Roman legionnaires in the 1960 film. July 2001. (Est. $2,000–$3,000) $2,500.

Spartacus

High brown leather laced sandals with gold leather trim and laces with handwritten label inside, worn by *Laurence Olivier* as "Crassus" in the 1960 film. July 2001. (Est. $600–$800) $1,700.

Spartacus

Prop metal sword with wooden handle, and suede-wrapped scabbard with metal tip, approx. 24" long, used in the 1960 film. April 2002. (Est. $400–$600) $1,300.

Spartacus

Round metal shield with leather strap, approx. 20" in diameter, used in the 1960 film. April 2002. (Est. $400–$600) $800.

Spartacus

Short metal dagger with wooden handle and sheath of metal and wood with suede siding and chain straps, approx. 15" long by 2.5" wide, used in the 1960 film. April 2002. (Est. $300–$500) $750.

Spawn

Screen-used foam clown head prop with hair and arms on a custom base. In fine condition, with the arms showing substantial wear and cracking to the foam. April 1999. $1,700.

Speed

Rubber Colt 1911 prop gun used by *Keanu Reeves* in the 1994 film. In fine condition. Accompanied by a letter of authenticity from the film's weapons coordinator. December 2001. $1,500.

Star Wars

Two-piece suit of black wool with mandarin collar, made for an officer of the Imperial Forces for the 1977 film. December 1999. (Est. $1,800–$2,700) $1,750.

Star Wars

A storm trooper helmet used in *The Empire Strikes Back* and *Return of the Jedi*. December 2001. $45,111.

Star Wars: The Phantom Menace

Stunt Darth Maul light saber used in the film. December 2001. $35,100.

Star!

Black silk dress, encrusted with beads and pearls, worn by *Julie Andrews* as "Gertrude Lawrence" in the 1968 film. July 2001. (Est. $800–$1,200) $1,200.

Stargate

"Ra's ship Top": custom-built of fiberglass, urethane, acrylic, and wood, this is the top of Ra's spaceship. Model is over 4' wide, and approx. the same in height. Has a worn look from the film. $5,000.

Starship Troopers

A 36" long green and black prop hero rifle, constructed of resin and fiberglass, as used in the 1997 film. March 2000. (Est. $800–$1,000) $900.

Stepmom

Jackie's hospital gown worn in the Radiology Lab scene. Beige w/gray wool knit socks included that were worn but not seen, by *Susan Sarandon* as "Jackie Harrison." $200.

Strange Interlude

Black wool double-breasted suit jacket and matching pants, with handwritten label, as worn by *Clark Gable* in the 1932 film. December 2000. (Est. $2,000–$3,000) $900.

Summer Stock

Blue silk dress with pink snowflake print, with handwritten label, as worn by *Judy Garland* as "Jane Falbury" in the 1950 film. December 2000. (Est. $2,000–$3,000) $2,000.

Supergirl

Complete costume worn by *Helen Slater* in the film. May 2000. (Est. $8,000–$10,000) $11,000.

Superman: The Movie

Lucite crystal from the "Fortress of Solitude," used in the first Superman film, approx. 17" long. December 2000. (Est. $300–$500) $275.

Superman: The Movie

Olive khaki canvas backpack with leather and buckle strap closures, used by the adolescent Clark Kent in the 1978 film. July 2001. (Est. $1,500–$2,500) $900.

Superman: The Movie

Three pairs of thigh-high leather boots, black patent, worn by *Jack O'Halloran, Sarah Douglas, Paul Weston* ("Zod" stuntman) as the three villains in the film. March 2000. (Est. $2,500–$3,500) $2,750.

Superman II

Complete costume worn by *Christopher Reeve* as Superman in the film. May 2000. (Est. $30,000–$40,000) $48,000.

Superman II

Dark brown wig of tousled hair, used by *Jack O'Halloran* as "Non" in the film. December 2000. (Est. $1,000–$1,500) $750.

Superman II

Prop *Daily Planet* newspaper with headline "WHITE HOUSE SURRENDERS" used in the 1980 film. March 2000. (Est. $600–$800) $550.

Superman II

Slick brown hair wig with Velcro attachments at the crown and sideburns, as worn by *Terence Stamp* as "General Zod" in the film. December 2000. (Est. $1,000–$1,500) $750.

Superman III

Aqua-color resin Statue of Liberty, approx. 95" tall, used in the 1983 film. March 2000. (Est. $5,000–$7,000) $4,000.

Superman III

Brown wig worn by *Christopher Reeve* in the 1983 film. March 2000. (Est. $2,000–$3,000) $4,000.

Sweet Rosie O'Grady

Black and white checkered taffeta dress, handwritten label, worn by *Betty Grable* in the 1943 film. July 2001. (Est. $800–$1,200) $400.

Take Me Out to the Ballgame

Off-white wool pants with red stripes with MGM cleaning tags and MGM handwritten label, worn by *Gene Kelly* in the 1949 film. July 2001. (Est. $400–$600) $300.

Tarzan

Leather loincloth with leather strap ties, believed to be from one of the first three Tarzan films, as worn by *Johnny Weissmuller*. July 2001. (Est. $8,000–$10,000) $6,500.

Tender Is the Night

Green jersey two-piece dress with cream collar and cuffs, worn by *Jennifer Jones* as "Nicole Diver" in the 1962 film. July 2001. (Est. $600–$800) $500.

Terminator 2: Judgment Day

"T-1000" morphing costume: bright silver foil pants, with matching jacket and officer's helmet, with CRC stamps, as worn by *Robert Patrick* in the 1991 film. March 2000. (Est. $4,000–$6,000) $2,750.

Terminator 2: Judgment Day

Black leather gloves with holes to reveal the endo-skeleton hand, with black rubber prop gun and silver-painted foam bullet hits, gloves, and pistol used by *Arnold Schwarzenegger*, hits worn by *Robert Patrick* in the 1991 film. July 2001. (Est. $3,000–$5,000) $3,000.

Terms of Endearment

Two-piece ensemble, floral print silk blouse with matching knee-length skirt, as worn by *Shirley MacLaine* in the 1983 film. November 2001. (Est. $500–$700) $400.

Texas Chainsaw Massacre Part 2

"Leatherface" mask. May 1998. (Est. $200–$300) $345.

That Wonderful Urge

Satin evening coat with fox trim and belt worn by *Gene Tierney* in the 1948 film. April 2002. (Est. $400–$600) $1,000.

The Addams Family

Black and gold brocade sleeveless and collarless jacket worn by *Christopher Lloyd* as "Uncle Fester" in the 1991 film. April 2002. (Est. $2,000–$3,000) $2,000.

The Addams Family

Black and white striped T-shirt worn by *Jimmy Workman* as "Pugsley" in the 1991 film. April 2002. (Est. $400–$600) $500.

The Addams Family

Black long-sleeve satin shirt with silhouette flower print and white collar with black lace edging worn by *Christina Ricci* as "Wednesday" in the 1991 film. April 2002. (Est. $800–$1,000) $850.

The Addams Family

Purple and lavender paisley print smoking robe with gold braid accents worn by *Raul Julia* as "Gomez" in the 1991 film. April 2002. (Est. $2,000–$3,000) $2,500.

The Adventures of Don Juan

Burgundy wool and satin tunic, burgundy tights, silver metal and red velvet belt, cape of burgundy wool, and gloves worn by *Errol Flynn* in the 1949 film. April 2002. (Est. $8,000–$10,000) $7,000.

The Adventures of Don Juan

Two-piece green velvet costume with gold embroidery worn by *Errol Flynn* in the 1949 film. July 2001. (Est. $8,000–$10,000) $7,000.

The Adventures of Marco Polo

Tunic of green velvet, white cotton shirt, and long gray wool coat, with handwritten costumer's labels, as worn by *Gary Cooper* in the 1938 film. December 2000. (Est. $2,000–$3,000) $1,500.

The Adventures of Robin Hood

Long metal musical horn, approx. 48" long, used in the 1938 film. April 2002. (Est. $300–$500) $275.

The Alamo

Full-size faded Mexican flag used by Santa Anna's troops, measures 4' × 6', used in the 1960 film. April 2002. (Est. $300–$500) $950.

The Alamo

Navy blue long-sleeve western shirt, Western Costume typed label, as worn by *John Wayne* as Davy Crockett in the 1960 film. December 2000. (Est. $3,500–$4,500) $3,500.

The Big Lebowski

Costume worn by *Jeff Bridges* in the film. February 1999. $440.

The Bird Cage

Armand's outfit consists of black (Gap) T-shirt (M) and a two-piece cream silk blend suit worn by *Robin Williams* as "Armand Goldman." $1,100.

The Black Swan

Two-piece beige period suit jacket, with skirt, with handwritten label, worn by *Maureen O'Hara* as "Margaret Denby" in the 1942 film. July 2001. (Est. $1,200–$1,500) $1,300.

The Crow

Black long-sleeve pullover spandex crew shirt, black velvet pants, and long black leather trenchcoat, worn by *Brandon Lee* in the 1994 film. July 2001. (Est. $6,000–$8,000) $6,000.

The Crow

Custom-made black moleskin shirt and vinyl pants worn by *Brandon Lee* during the filming of his final film. In overall fine condition; pants are intentionally distressed, with substantial wear in one area of left leg. Accompanied by a letter of authenticity from the wardrobe supervisor of film. August 2001. $4,500. *See illustration #167.*

The Dirty Dozen

Black rubber "grease gun" submachine gun from the epic 1967 film. April 2002. (Est. $300–$500) $400.

The Flintstones

Prehistoric-looking newspaper slab of the *Bedrock News* used in the 1994 film. May 2000. (Est. $2,000–$3,000) $2,700.

The Forsythe Woman

Black lace and tulle gown with silk roses, inside handwritten label, as worn by *Greer Garson* in the 1949 film. July 2001. (Est. $3,000–$5,000) $2,500.

The Godfather

Black single-breasted three-button jacket with Western Costume label with typed name, as worn by *Al Pacino* as "Michael Corleone" in the famous bathroom killing scene in the 1972 film. December 2000. (Est. $8,000–$10,000) $8,000.

The Godfather

Brown wool single-breasted overcoat with three-button front, with costume label, with gray fedora-style Stetson hat, worn by *Marlon Brando* in the scene where he gets shot in the 1972 film. December 2000. (Est. $6,500–$7,500) $17,000.

The Godfather

Long dress with white squared collar with matching self belt made of orange cotton printed with white hearts with costumer's label, with straw hat, as worn by *Diane Keaton* in the wedding scene at the beginning of the 1972 film. December 2000. (Est. $3,500–$4,500) $3,800.

The Godfather: Part II

Two-piece checkered suit with Western Costume tag, as worn by *Al Pacino* in the 1974 film. May 2000. (Est. $8,000–$10,000) $9,000.

The Godfather: Part II

Two-piece double-breasted three-button suit of very light gray wool, with Western Costume typed label, as worn by *Robert DeNiro* as "Vito Corleone" in the 1974 film. December 2000. (Est. $6,000–$8,000) $6,000.

The Gold Rush

Pair of vintage snowshoes made of wood with leather and sinew lacing, worn by *Tom Murray* in the 1925 Chaplin classic. April 2002. (Est. $1,500–$2,500) $800.

The Great Dictator

Cream colored single-breasted coat with burnt orange collar and cuffs with Western Costume handwritten label, as worn by *Charles Chaplin* as "Adenoid Hynkel" in the 1940 film. December 2000. (Est. $8,000–$10,000) $16,000. *See illustration #168.*

The Green Berets

Green tiger stripe camouflage shirt worn by *John Wayne* as "Colonel Mike Kirby" in the film. Long-sleeve jungle camouflage has two button-up breast pockets and a Western Costume Company tag sewn inside with Wayne's name and a number typed onto it. In fine condition. December 2001. $3,850.

The Harvey Girls

Black and white leather high button ankle boots, with MGM stamp, worn by *Judy Garland* in the 1945 film. July 2001. (Est. $800–$1,200) $1,500.

The Howards of Virginia

Navy and red wool period uniform jacket with tails, worn by *Cary Grant* in the 1940 film. July 2001. (Est. $800–$1,000) $650.

167

168

167 Costume worn by Brandon Lee in The Crow

168 Costume worn by Charlie Chaplin in The Great Dictator

The King and I

Elaborate gold wire headdress worn by *Rita Moreno* as "Tuptim" in the 1955 film. July 2001. (Est. $600–$800) $700.

The Light Touch

Dark blue raw silk suit with inner handwritten label, worn by *Stewart Granger* in the 1951 film. July 2001. (Est. $300–$500) $250.

The Living Daylights

Four burlap medical supply bags linked together at the ends as used in the 1987 James Bond film. July 2001. (Est. $400–$600) $425.

The Maltese Falcon

Cast resin Falcon statuette, weight of 4 lbs, 5.4 ozs, height 11 $\frac{1}{8}$", serial number 90456 WB on the base, used on the set of the film and in promotional photographs for the 1941 film. March 2000. (Est. $100,000–$150,000) $80,000.

The Maltese Falcon

Original prop statue of bird used in the film. December 1994. $398,500 (incl. premium).

The Man in the Iron Mask

Steel double-edged hero sword with ornate clamshell knuckle guard and suede-wrapped handle, with leather scabbard and waist belt, used by *Gerard Depardieu* as "Porthos" in the 1998 film. July 2001. (Est. $2,500–$3,500) $2,500.

The Man in the Iron Mask

A 44" sword with knuckle guard and wire-wrapped handle, with aluminum blade used for fighting scenes, used by *John Malkovich* as "Athos" in the 1998 film. July 2001. (Est. $3,000–$4,000) $3,000.

The Man in the Iron Mask

Concealment costume: black velvet hooded cloak, dark jacket, and heavy overcoat worn by *John Malkovich* in the 1998 film. July 2001. (Est. $2,000–$3,000) $2,000.

The Man in the Iron Mask

Metal prop sword, used by *Leonardo DiCaprio* as King Louis XIV in the 1998 film. December 2000. (Est. $2,500–$3,500) $4,500.

The Man Who Shot Liberty Valance

Signature navy blue wool bib-front shirt, with Western Costume typed label, as worn by *John Wayne* in the 1962 film. March 2000. (Est. $6,000–$8,000) $7,000.

The Manchurian Candidate

Tan military officer's jacket worn by *Frank Sinatra* in the 1962 film. This jacket was worn during the final sequences of the film and during the climactic assassination attempt scene. The jacket has the original Western Costume label sewn into the inside pocket and the name "Frank Sinatra" and "made to order number 2544-2." The piece is decorated with the appropriate officer ribbons and insignia as seen in the film. In fine condition. Accompanied by a letter of authenticity from the Eastern Costume Company. December 2001. $5,640.

The Mark of Zorro

Blue-gray cavalier overjacket, with Western Costume typed label, worn by *Tyrone Power* in the 1940 film (also worn by Nelson Eddy in *The Phantom of the Opera*). December 2000. (Est. $2,000–$3,000) $2,250.

The Mask

Prop mask worn by *Jim Carrey* in the film. October 1997. (Est. $3,000–$5,000) $2,530.

The Mask of Zorro

Cape worn by *Antonio Banderas* in the Hollywood film, 57" long, heavy cotton and polyester fabric with black leather embroidered design around the top of the back. May 2002. $330.

The Mask of Zorro

Pale blue velvet waistcoat w/ black velvet detail on lapels, cuffs, and buttons. Lace trim built into cuffs of coat worn by *Antonio Banderas* as "Alejandro Murrieta/Zorro." $850.

The Mask of Zorro

Wool, lined, gray, waist-length jacket w/ black brocade trim. Gray jacket has black decorative trim around edge of entire jacket. The two (functional) pockets on each side of jacket front are approx. 5" wide × 5" deep and are trimmed in black velvet as worn by *Anthony Hopkins* as "Don Diego de la Vega/Zorro." $950.

The Misfits

A pair of square-toed tan leather cowboy boots as worn by *Marilyn Monroe* in the 1961 film. October 1999. (Est. $4,000–$6,000) $85,000 (incl. buyer's premium).

The Misfits

A sleeveless cocktail dress of black silk jersey and elaborately cut with handwritten label as worn by *Marilyn Monroe* in the 1961 film. October 1999. (Est. $20,000–$30,000) $72,900 (incl. buyer's premium).

The Misfits

A blond wig and hairpiece as worn by *Marilyn Monroe* in the 1961 film. October 1999. (Est. $1,000–$1,500) $26,000.

The Mummy (1999)

Black double-edged dagger with gold Egyptian markings constructed of resin used by *Patricia Velasquez* in the film. April 2002. (Est. $800–$1,000) $800.

The Mummy (1999)

Curved metal hero sword, approx. 36" long, used by *Oded Fehr* in the film. April 2002. (Est. $2,000–$3,000) $1,600.

The Mummy (1999)

Gold-painted foam rubber Egyptian-style sword, approx. 33" long, used in the film. April 2002. (Est. $400–$600) $325.

The Natural

Original New York Knights prop blue and gold baseball pennant from the film. In fine condition with folds. January 1999. $285.

The Natural

Original screen-worn Knights jacket worn by *Robert Redford* in the film. Black wool long-sleeve coat with leather sleeves bears a Knights patch over left breast and "Knights" spelled across the back. Inside of collar bears an Empire Sporting Goods tag, with "Mickey Treanor" in black felt tip across the top. There were only sixteen of these jackets made for the film, with the original custom tailored for Redford, but deemed too small by Redford and the director. This jacket was a bit larger, to give Redford a sickly appearance at the end of the film, the result of his being shot. This jacket was used for that purpose as well as by Treanor. In fine condition. Accompanied by a certificate of authenticity from the film's costume supervisor, James Tyson. March 2002. $4,235.

The Nightmare Before Christmas

A Santa Claus puppet, also known as "Sandy Claus," used in the 1993 film. May 2000. (Est. $1,500–$2,000) $20,000.

The Patriot

Original screen-worn costume worn by *Mel Gibson*. Two-piece outfit consists of a large cream muslin shirt with long "tacked" rolled sleeves and a pair of custom-made black breeches with a tie-up front and buttoned cuffs. Inside of breeches bears a Dominic Gherardi Custom Tailoring tag with "Mel Gibson," and "August 1999," typed on it. Shirt has several areas of special effects blood stains. In fine condition, with expected wear. March 2002. $7,604. *See illustration #169.*

The Patriot

Warthog ivory–handled straight razor used in the film. Ivory handle measures 5" long with silver inlays on either side, steel blade measures 3" and is lightly engraved with a floral pattern. In fine condition, with expected wear. Accompanied by a certificate of authenticity from edged weapon prop designer Tony Swatton, who designed the razor. March 2002. $1,000.

The Patriot

Custom cream muslin long-sleeve shirt bloodied and knife marked from Gabriel's "Wounded and Returning Home Scene." Worn by *Heath Ledger* as "Gabriel Martin." $200.

The Perfect Storm

Set of five main character rain gear uniforms worn by stars *George Clooney, Mark Wahlberg, John C. Reilly, John Hawkes,* and *Allen Payne* in the 2000 film. July 2001. (Est. $1,500–$2,000) $1,000.

The Prince and the Showgirl

Off-white chiffon gown over white satin, encrusted with seed pearls, inside Western Costume handwritten label, as worn by *Marilyn Monroe* in the 1957 film. December 2000. (Est. $20,000–$30,000) $62,500.

The Prince and the Showgirl

Off-white double-breasted formal jacket trimmed with maroon velvet at the collar and cuffs, as worn by *Laurence Olivier* as "Grand Duke Charles" in the 1957 film. March 2000. (Est. $3,000–$5,000) $3,250.

The Private Lives of Elizabeth and Essex

Green silk ball gown with matching bodice, front panel is quilted, with two ruffles at throat, as worn by *Bette Davis* as Queen Elizabeth in the 1938 film. July 2001. (Est. $10,000–$15,000) $10,000.

The Producers

Prop playbill from the musical *Springtime for Hitler* used in the 1968 film. December 2000. (Est. $1,200–$1,500) $1,000.

The Return of Frank James

Blue and white silk period tie, with costume tag, worn by *Henry Fonda* in the 1940 film. July 2001. (Est. $200–$300) $250.

169 *Costume worn by Mel Gibson in* The Patriot

170 *Costume worn by Julie Andrews in* The Sound of Music

The Rock

Black rubber gloves (both right-handed) with studio applied "acid damage" and blood, worn by *Nicolas Cage* in the 1996 film. July 2001. (Est. $700–$1,000) $800.

The Shadow

One of the prop knives used in the film starring *Alec Baldwin*. This particular knife was used in a scene near the end of the movie where the prop was embedded deep in the floor between Baldwin's legs. In very fine condition. Accompanied by a letter of provenance signed by the original owner who obtained it while working on the set. October 1996. $446.

The Sheik

Lead prop shield from the 1949 Paramount film. May 1998. (Est. $275–$375) $259.

The Shining

Prop black and white manipulated photograph, 9" × 11", showing *Jack Nicholson* and other guests attired in 1920s-era clothing as they stand in a ballroom, with COA from the Prop Store, as used in the 1980 film. December 2000. (Est. $1,200–$1,400) $6,000.

The Snows of Kilimanjaro

Red silk 1920s period dress, with Fox handwritten label, with original earrings, necklace, and bracelet, as worn by *Ava Gardner* as "Cynthia Street" in the 1952 film. December 2000. (Est. $2,000–$3,000) $3,500.

The Sound of Music

Earth-tone-beige heavy cotton/linen skirt and cotton/linen blouse with lace cuffs and high collar, with Fox handwritten label, as worn by *Julie Andrews* in the 1965 classic. March 2000. (Est. $10,000–$15,000) $16,000. *See illustration #170.*

The Sun Also Rises

Beige basket-weave short-sleeve silk skirt suit with button front, with handwritten Fox label, as worn by *Ava Gardner* in the 1957 film. July 2001. (Est. $400–$600) $750.

The Taming of the Shrew (1929)

Black cotton period shorts with copper trim and black tights, worn by *Douglas Fairbanks, Sr.*, in the 1929 film. July 2001. (Est. $2,000–$3,000) $1,600.

The Ten Commandments

Brown leather belt with two red stripes and large gold clasp buckle featuring a black jeweled scarab as worn by *Yul Brynner* as "Pharaoh" in the 1956 film. July 2001. (Est. $3,000–$5,000) $4,000.

The Ten Commandments

Forest green rough-hewn cotton, attached to a dark brown leather headband and felt cap, as worn by *Edward G. Robinson* as "Dathan" in the 1956 film. July 2001. (Est. $3,000– $5,000) $7,000.

The Ten Commandments

Heavy cotton short-sleeve tunic, with suede trim at collar, cuffs, and lower hem, worn by *Charlton Heston* as "Moses" in the film. July 2001. (Est. $15,000–$18,000) $17,000. *See illustration #171.*

The Ten Commandments

Light blue sleeveless dress of raw silk, with attached self-belt with matching headpiece, Paramount label, worn by *Debra Paget* as "Lilia" in the 1956 film. July 2001. (Est. $3,000–$5,000) $4,000.

The Ten Commandments

Off-white cloth wrap-style bathing suit top and bottom with Paramount handwritten label, as worn by *Debra Paget* as "Lilia" in the opening scenes of the 1956 film. March 2000. (Est. $1,500–$1,800) $1,100.

The Ten Commandments

Red and green striped sash of woven cotton, approx. 4" wide, worn by *Charlton Heston* as "Moses" in the 1956 film. July 2001. (Est. $4,000–$6,000) $5,000.

The Ten Commandments

Red suede headdress with small gold studs, scallop armor, attached to a gold headband with cobra icon worn by *Henry Brandon* as "Captain of the Charioteers" in the 1956 film. July 2001. (Est. $2,000–$3,000) $3,250.

The Ten Commandments

Rough-hewn fabric, each tied into crowns with long trains and sewn-in headbands with costumer's tag, as worn by *Yvonne DeCarlo* as "Sephora" in the 1956 film. July 2001. (Est. $1,500–$1,800) $3,500.

171 Costume worn by Charlton Heston as Moses in The Ten Commandments

172 Headdress worn by Ian Keith as Ramses I in The Ten Commandments

The Ten Commandments

Set of prop Ten Commandments tablets constructed of fiberglass and other materials, painted a rust color to resemble stone, with early Canaanite-style script, one of the six sets made for the 1956 film. November 2001. (Est. $6,000–$7,000) $10,000.

The Ten Commandments

Red cotton headdress with gold and red piping, attached to a gold headband and cap with eagle and cobra icons on front, worn by *Ian Keith* as Ramses I in the 1956 film. July 2001. (Est. $3,000–$5,000) $5,500. *See illustration #172.*

The Ten Commandments

Two prop swords, one wooden sword painted silver with black cloth tape, and the other one made of wood and covered with cloth, each approx. 21" long. May 1998. (Est. $250–$350) $259.

The Thief of Baghdad

Large brass jailer's key used on screen in the 1924 film. Measures 13" long. April 2002. (Est. $200–$300) $350.

The Two Jakes

Dummy prop double head and shoulders of *Jack Nicholson,* and a pair of arms, used in the explosion scene in the film. In overall fine condition. Accompanied by a letter of authenticity from the makeup artist who worked on the film and created the dummy. December 2001. $900.

The Wild One

Black leather motorcycle cap, with a chrome strap across the crown and front, a steel eagle badge fastened at the front, and chrome edging to the peak, taken by *Marlon Brando* from the

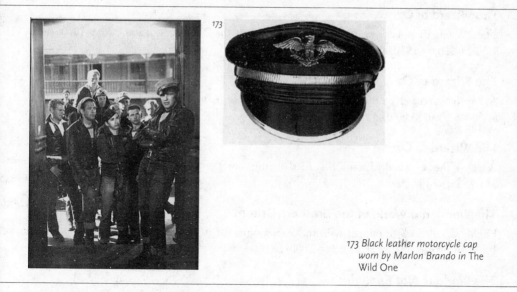

173 *Black leather motorcycle cap worn by Marlon Brando in* The Wild One

wardrobe of the film and kept by him as a souvenir until a recent purchase directly from a member of the family. In fine condition. May 2001. $3,000. *See illustration #173.*

The Wiz

Scarecrow costume of distressed brown tunic of treated crepe with applied banana peels and candy wrappers, attached to matching black pants, orange and white wool stockings, dark brown tights and matching gloves and large animal feet shoes, as worn by *Michael Jackson* in the 1978 film. December 2000. (Est. $1,500–$2,500) $5,500.

The Wizard Of Oz

Pinafore dress of blue and white gingham, with cotton wardrobe label inscribed in black ink "Judy Garland 4228," as worn by *Judy Garland* as "Dorothy Gale" in the 1939 film. December 1999. (Est. $13,000–$18,000) $152,808.

The Wizard of Oz

A few pieces (approximately ten), measuring up to .5" long, of original straw from *Ray Bolger's* "Scarecrow" costume in the film. Includes a letter from Bolger on his personal letterhead attesting to the straw's authenticity from the original costume. In fine condition. June 2001. $1,029.

The Wizard of Oz

One paw-style shoe worn by *Bert Lahr* as the "Cowardly Lion." May 2000. (Est. $20,000–$30,000) $22,000.

The Wizard of Oz

Pair of ruby red slippers worn by *Judy Garland* in the film. May 2000. $666,000 (incl. buyer's premium).

The Wizard of Oz

The "Witch Remover" prop used by *Bert Lahr* as the "Cowardly Lion." May 2000. (Est. $15,000–$20,000) $10,000.

The Wizard of Oz

A hay reaper used in the long shot of the Gale farm in the 1927 film. May 2000. (Est. $1,500–$2,000) $3,000.

The Wizard of Oz

A lock of the "Cowardly Lion's" hair shed during conservation of the costume. May 2000. (Est. $1,000-$1,500) $2,000.

The Wonderful World of the Brothers Grimm

Highly detailed elfish puppet with moveable joints for stop-animation, 13" tall, used in the 1962 film. April 2002. (Est. $1,000–$2,000) $8,000.

The World Is Not Enough

King Industries foreman prop helmet from the film, signed in felt tip by stars *Pierce Brosnan, Sophie Marceau,* and *Robert Carlyle.* The helmet was on the King plant in Kazakhstan. In fine condition, with expected scuff marks of a prop safety helmet. October 2001. $500.

There's No Business Like Show Business

Cream silk jacket, skirt, and pink gloves, with Western Costume label, as worn by *Mitzi Gaynor* as "Katy Donohue" in the 1954 film. December 2000. (Est. $2,000–$3,000) $1,400.

There's No Business Like Show Business

Screen-worn jacket and scarf worn by *Donald O'Connor* in the film. Heavy custom-made decorative waistcoat is highlighted with silver sequins on the front and cuffs and pink and yellow silk sleeves and bears a Western Costume company tag inside of collar with O'Connor's name typed on it along with the number 76-2655-4. In fine condition. April 2002. $1,149.

There's Something About Mary

Complete costume worn by *Ben Stiller* in the opening scene in the film. February 1999. $468.

Three Kings

Four sets of army camouflage fatigues, each consisting of long-sleeve jacket and matching pants, with embroidered name tags and brown T-shirts as worn by *George Clooney, Mark Wahlberg, Spike Jonze,* and *Ice Cube* in the 1999 film. July 2001. (Est. $3,000–$4,000) $3,000.

Titanic

First-class dining room chair used in the film. May 1998. $2,250.

Titanic

Historically accurate prop lifejacket used in the filming. In fine condition. Accompanied by a certificate of authenticity from Twentieth Century Fox. February 1998. $955.

Titanic

Beautiful 10" white china plate used for the first-class dining room scenes in James Cameron's award-winning film. The plate has a blue and gold pattern, gold trim, and a red and gold White Star Line emblem in the center. In fine condition. Accompanied by a certificate of authenticity from Twentieth Century Fox. August 1998. $605.

Titanic

White porcelain dinner plate, 8.75" in diameter, featuring the White Star Line logo in the center and gold/aqua trim around the rim, used in the 1997 blockbuster film's first-class dining room scenes. In very fine condition and accompanied by a certificate of authenticity from Twentieth Century Fox. June 2000. $484.

Tombstone

Black and brown painted resin revolver modeled after a Colt .45 single action pistol, used by *Kurt Russell* in the 1993 film. April 2002. (Est. $1,000–$1,500) $2,250.

Tomorrow Never Dies

Navy blue uniform jacket with gold chevrons on cuffs, matching pants, white shirt, and black tie worn by *Pierce Brosnan* as "James Bond" in the 1997 film. April 2002. (Est. $6,500–$8,500) $7,500.

Torch Song

Blue satin ankle strap pumps, with handwritten note on bottom, as worn by *Joan Crawford* in the 1953 film. July 2001. (Est. $400–$600) $750.

Tower of London

Copper-colored brocade long-sleeve tunic with handwritten inner label, as worn by *Basil Rathbone* in the 1939 film. July 2001. (Est. $800–$1,200) $1,000.

True Grit

Wine-colored long-sleeve shirt with fabric-backed, lined suede vest with collars and elaborate embroidering with Western Costume label worn by *John Wayne*. June 2000. (Est. $7,000-$9,000) $13,000.

Vagabond King

Medieval gown of beige silk with mint green pleated chiffon trim, worn by *Jeanette MacDonald* in the 1930 film. July 2001. (Est. $4,000–$6,000) $3,250.

Vertical Limit

"Promo Rescue" outfit (w/ CT's) includes navy blue polyester Patagonia long underwear/pants (M); black poly blend fleece Patagonia pants (L) with matching black poly blend zip-neck North Face shirt (L); gray nylon Serac snow pants (M) w/ black attached suspenders; gray fleece long-sleeve zip-neck Mountain Equipment Co-op overshirt (L); 100% nylon Serac snow/climbing hooded gold and royal blue jacket (M) w/ flap pockets, zip front, and Teflon closure; one pair of red and black OR gaiters; two-piece glove set, which includes thick black fleece lining gloves (L) and outer nylon gloves (M), by Patagonia; and black knit cap worn by *Chris O'Donnell* as "Peter Garrett." $600.

Very Bad Things

Group lot of props used in the film, including: faux California license plate from the main character's car; pieces of prop broken glass (actually clear rubber) from the hotel scene; two corkscrew blades from the hotel murder scene; and a matchbook from the hotel "Moonlight." In fine condition. April 1999. $605.

Virtuosity

Standard workman's jumpsuit of tan cotton with ID badge "SID 6.7" as worn by *Russell Crowe* in the 1995 film. November 2001. (Est. $800–$1,200) $850.

Wake of the Red Witch

Rugged wooden treasure chest used in the 1948 *John Wayne* film. April 2002. (Est. $800–$1,200) $1,600.

Waterworld

Heavily used prop smoker pistol used in the film. In fine condition, with moderate overall wear. September 1998. $400.

What a Way to Go

Bright green satin gown with matching bra and long arm trains worn by *Shirley MacLaine* in the 1964 film. April 2002. (Est. $600–$800) $1,200.

When a Man Loves

Aqua brocade cape with silver bullion, with a cavalier suit of jackets and pants, with costume label, as worn by *John Barrymore* in the 1927 film. December 2000. (Est. $3,000–$5,000) $1,900.

Where the Sidewalk Ends

Gray wool button-front suit coat and matching skirt with label worn by *Gene Tierney* in the 1950 film. April 2002. (Est. $400–$600) $800.

Wild Things

"Skeet Shooting scene": white dress by Fendissime with brown floral print worn by *Denise Richards* as Kelly Van Ryan. $500.

Willow

A 36" metal sword with leather detail on handle as used in the 1988 film. March 2000. (Est. $600–$800) $600.

Willy Wonka and the Chocolate Factory

Gene Wilder's complete costume as worn in the 1971 film. It is complete with Wilder's rumpled felt top hat, white collared shirt, elaborate brocade vest, original leather belt, and his signature purple velvet frock topcoat. After its use in the film, the costume was used to promote the film on tour around the United States. May 2002. $24,200.

Willy Wonka and the Chocolate Factory

A Wonka Bar featuring yellow letters topped with Willy Wonka's trademark top hat bordered with neon orange and chocolate brown on a pressed cardboard stock, used in the 1971 film. May 2000. (Est. $1,500–$2,000) $3,000.

Willy Wonka and the Chocolate Factory

Miniature boat used in the Chocolate River, hand painted blue and white with red detail, approx. 12", used in the 1970 film. July 2001. (Est. $2,000–$3,000) $2,000.

Willy Wonka and the Chocolate Factory

Costume worn in the film by one of the vertically challenged employees of Mr. Wonka's Chocolate Factory. Complete. May 2002. $4,400.

Wing Commander

Eleven-piece costume of a full body suit, pair of boots, knee-brace armor, chest plate, backpack, and helmet, each airbrushed in red/mauve color, as worn in the 1999 film. December 2000. (Est. $1,500–$2,500) $1,100.

Woman's World

Gray wool button-front jacket and matching over-the-knee skirt, with handwritten label, worn by *Lauren Bacall* in the 1954 film. July 2001. (Est. $600–$800) $650.

Young Bess

Golden velvet period dress with matching waistcoat worn by *Jean Simmons* in the 1953 film. April 2002. (Est. $800–$1,200) $750.

Ziegfeld Follies

Mustard oriental-style dress with handwritten label, as worn by *Lucille Bremer* as "Moy Ling" in the 1946 film. December 2000. (Est. $1,000–$1,500) $900.

3 Movie Art: Posters and Lobby Cards

THE EVOLUTION OF MOVIE ART

There is probably no other type of movie collectible that is more familiar and endearing to cinema buffs and memorabilia collectors than movie art. Since its inception over one hundred years ago, movie art has been the most effective medium used by studios to lure the public into the local movie palace. Vintage movie posters are now regarded as individual works of art created by some of the twentieth century's finest illustrators. Collectors view them as a timeline of the past century of cinema, vividly illustrating how our favorite films and stars were presented to the audiences of their day.

Movie art refers to a vast array of styles and types of advertising paper products used to promote films, including posters and card items such as window and lobby cards. The more common term for these paper items is *movie posters*. There is no other form of movie memorabilia collectible that has so many variations in formats, sizes, reissues, reprints, etc. The collecting of movie art requires an in-depth understanding not only of the terminology associated with this field, but also of the evolution of the materials themselves. *See illustration #174.*

Historians attribute the first movie poster designed for a specific film to the Lumière Brothers' 1896 film *L'Arroseu Arrose;* yet it wasn't until 1905 with the creation of the nickelodeon as a specific venue for viewing movies that the moviemaking industry took off with an explosive growth. In the next two years, nearly five thousand theaters were opened in the United States alone. The highly competitive marketplace required movie-producing studios to create illustrative and effective advertising as a means of promoting their films over those of their competition.

In a move to try to control this burgeoning industry, Thomas Edison joined forces with some of the major studios at the time to form the Motion Picture Patents Company (MPPC).

One of the main initiatives of the company was to unify the printing of all advertising materials from the member studios under a very restrictive set of ethics codes. All MPPC-member studios were also contractually tied to have all of their materials printed with the A. B. See Lithograph Company of Cleveland, Ohio.

The MPPC unification indirectly created the standard size for a movie poster at twenty-seven by forty-one inches (now referred to as a *one-sheet*). These posters generally listed the movie company's name, the film's title, a brief description of the plot, and in some cases a still photograph taken from the film. They were designed to be hung in glass display cases inside and outside the theaters. With the release of each new film, the movie studios purchased the posters from A. B. See and then sold them individually to the nickelodeons that were exhibiting the films. The posters were folded and placed within the film canister containing the actual film, or shipped in large mailing envelopes. The posters were repeatedly used, traveling with the films from venue to venue and city to city.

Up until the late 1940s, the method used to print these posters was called *stone lithography.* Invented in 1798, it was the first new printmaking technique to emerge in about three hundred years. It was also the first printmaking technology that allowed an artist to naturally paint or draw an illustration onto a flat stone. Once the painting was completed, the stone was mois-

174 Metropolis (1926)

tened with water and an oil-based ink was then rolled onto the stone and picked up by the painted sections. Once a piece of paper was pressed onto the stone, the ink was transferred from the stone to the paper. The resulting prints rivaled an original painting in terms of detail, mood, and color variations. Stone litho posters are among the most cherished and sought-after by collectors for these reasons alone.

By the early 1910s, movie viewing had become such a huge phenomenon that the nickelodeons began to be replaced by larger and more luxurious movie theaters. New advertising sizes and formats were soon introduced to complement these venues: *lobby card* sets of eight individual eight-by-ten-inch (and later eleven-by-fourteen) cardstock cards depicting scenes from the movie were issued and hung in the lobby of the theater. *See illustration #204.* Larger poster sizes of forty-one by eighty-one inches (*three-sheet*) and eighty-one by eighty-one inches (*six-sheet*) were also introduced to be displayed in the larger theaters.

The restrictive advertising censorship guidelines imposed on the member studios by Edison's MPPC were lifted with a court-appointed dissolution of the company in 1917. This newfound freedom marked a sharp transformation in the look of movie art advertising, as the limitless possibilities now available to the individual studios were now explored to the fullest. The movie studios began to commission the world's finest commercial artists including Alberto Vargas and Norman Rockwell to create new masterpieces to grab the eye of the moviegoer. *See illustration #176.*

It is at this time that the emergence of the movie star began, and the star's image started to appear more prominently on posters. Film titles and plot descriptions became less emphasized, and luscious portraits of the new gods and goddesses of Hollywood took center stage.

Movie advertising now moved outside the traditional theater lobbies to highway billboards with a poster size of 246 by 108 inches (*twenty-four sheet*). Cardstock posters of fourteen by twenty-

175 Japanese lobby card set from Psycho (1960)

176 The Devil Is a Woman (1935)

177 The Bride of Frankenstein (1935) jumbo window card with theater screening dates printed at top

178 Three design styles for movie art from King Kong (1933)

two inches (*window cards*) were now purchased directly by the theaters themselves and placed anywhere they could find an audience—retail store windows, lamp poles, etc. *See illustration #177.*

To add some variety to their advertising campaigns, the studios produced several distinct styles of movie art for a feature in the one sheet and a smaller twenty-two by twenty-eight half-sheet size. The bigger the film release was, the more styles they would use, but for the most part two styles were generally used. They would differentiate the two styles by a letter-labeling method; Paramount Studios used "Style A" and "Style B"; MGM Studios used "Style C" and "Style D"; and Universal Studios used "Style X" and "Style Y." *See illustration #178.*

By the end of the 1930s, the National Screen Service (NSS) became the sole contracted distributor of all movie paper items for all of the major studios. As a control measure, the NSS instituted a coding system that was tagged to all materials, detailing the year of distribution for the film and the sequential order of the film's release during that year. Although the company ceased operations in the year 2000, this stock-keeping system has become the most valuable resource for modern-day collectors and historians (see NSS Markings under Authenticating Movie Art for more details).

With the onset of World War II, the movie industry was forced to take cost-cutting measures, and advertising budgets were among the first to be cut. With a worldwide shortage of paper, many studios turned to newsprint for their posters. A color offset printing process that was introduced in the mid-1920s now became a more cost-effective alternative to the stone lithography process. Offset printing allowed artwork to be photographed through screens and separated by color, producing images much sharper than the stone litho process but with a loss of color vibrancy. Because this process used duller ink dyes than those used in stone lithography, the colors on the smaller posters looked much better close up, so the overall impact was not lost. This era also saw the birth of the *fanzine*—a movie fan magazine devoted to detailing the studio-fabricated private lives of movie stars with countless reprinted still photographs. This photographic style was soon adopted to movie posters and quickly replaced the painted portrait style of posters from the previous half-century. By the end of the 1940s the stone litho process was virtually extinct in movie art printing.

Movie industry advertising methods and the moviegoing experience as a whole remained pretty much unchanged until the 1980s, with the transition of movie theaters from a one-screen/one-feature setup to a multiplex structure of several smaller screens in one building. Suddenly, the theater lobby had to be divided to house the advertising for all of the films being shown. The studios responded by replacing many of the formats (half-sheets, window cards, etc.) with a more versatile *mini-sheet* format—a smaller poster printed on poster paper in a variety of sizes. Another factor changing the landscape of movie art was the development of the video rental market—effectively replacing the need for reissues of movie prints and posters and creating a whole new industry of movie art (video posters, displays, and boxes).

COLLECTING MOVIE ART

The last fifteen years have seen rare posters adorn the walls of the finest museums and galleries around the world. The buying and selling of movie art has seen exceptional auction results

179 The Mummy *(1932)*

that have effectively taken the finest and rarest examples out of the hands of average collectors. The record for the top five highest prices paid for movie art at auction are:

1) *The Mummy* (1932)   **$453,500**
(March 1997, Sotheby's) *See illustration #179.*

2) *Metropolis* (1926)   **$357,750**
(October 2000, Sotheby's)

3) *King Kong* (1933)   **$244,500**
(April 1999, Sotheby's)

4) *Metropolis* (1926)   **$200,000**
(July 2000, eBay)

5) *Frankenstein* (1931)   **$198,000**
(October 1993, Odyssey)

Vintage movie art has achieved a massive following of collectors for several key reasons:

• The quality of original stone litho prints as a viable art form created by the century's finest illustrators.

• An instant association with iconographic Hollywood films and stars.

• An incredible demand for very limited quantities of artifacts that were never intended to survive beyond their limited promotional purposes.

The incredible range of items and values in this collectible area is almost endless. Therefore, when looking to start or add to an existing movie art collection, it is essential to have a strong understanding of the terminology of these collectibles, as well as the factors that determine value: *authenticity, condition,* and *content.*

Authenticating Movie Art

When looking to purchase a piece of movie art, the most important factor to consider is authenticity. *Authenticity* refers to the claim the seller is making in relation to the actual item. It is also very important to specify what types of movie art are considered noncollectible and which are considered collectible.

Noncollectible Movie Art

This refers to poster artwork that has been licensed to various firms and printed in large quantities for public distribution through worldwide retail outlets. These include:

- *Commercial Posters*: Posters produced in large quantities for sale directly to the public. These are usually issued in the twenty-three by twenty-five- or twenty-four-by-thirty-six-inch sizes.

- *Limited Edition Posters*: Posters released directly to the public in limited quantities, but which are not intended or used by theaters as advertising materials.

- *Reprint Posters*: Reprinted posters measuring twenty-seven by forty inches that have been commercially produced in large quantities for sale to the public. These cause great confusion to novice collectors, as some dishonest sellers have them elaborately framed and try to pass them off as original collectible posters.

- *Video Posters*: These posters have been distributed by movie studios as advertising materials, but are not associated with the initial release of the film to theaters and are therefore not classified under "collectible" movie art.

These items have been specifically created to fill a public demand for film-related collectibles and are not considered collectibles under the definition of collectible movie art covered in this book.

Collectible Movie Art

Collectible movie art refers to items printed in limited numbers by lithographers hired by the movie studios to be used exclusively as advertising materials and subsequently provided to the movie theaters to promote a film. These items were not meant for public distribution and were required to be either returned to the film distributor or destroyed upon completion of the exhibition of the film. There are two main categories of collectible movie art:

1) **Original Issue**: All movie art (various sizes and formats) issued as part of the initial advertising campaign before and up to the actual first release of a film.

2) **Reissue (or Re-release):** Before the advent of the home video rental market, film studios would re-release popular films to the theaters several years after their original releases. With each re-release they would relaunch their advertising campaigns, reissuing movie art of various sizes and formats. The materials were usually duplicates of the original issue materials,

and in some cases they were redesigned completely. In terms of value, the original issue movie art is generally valued higher than reissued art. Additionally, each subsequent reissue is worth less than the reissue before (the earlier the release, the more valuable).

Determining whether a piece of movie art is an original issue or reissue/re-release can be easy or complicated, depending upon the individual piece of art. Here are a few tips:

1) **Check the NSS Number**: Most posters dating from 1940 and onward will have an NSS number marked on them. Look at the bottom right-hand corner of the poster (or side for a 30" x 40"). In most cases, a reissue/re-release poster will have an *R* at the start of the NSS number (indicating "Reissue"). See the NSS Markings section of this chapter for a more in-depth description of using NSS numbers to date an original or reissue/re-release poster.

2) **Check the Copyright Date**: If the copyright date printed on the poster is dated later than the film's original release, you have a reissue/re-release poster.

3) **Look for a Reissue/Re-release Listing**: Sometimes a reissue/re-release poster will have the words "Reissue" or "Re-release" printed directly on it.

4) **Check the Paper Stock**: Glossy paper stocks were not introduced until the mid-1960s; therefore, any glossy finish poster that has an original issue date before the mid-1960s is a reissue/re-release.

5) **Look for Folds**: Before 1985, movie art pieces were *machine folded* before being shipped to movie theaters (with the exception of non–one-sheet sizes). If a poster has never been folded, it is doubtful that it was issued before 1985.

6) **Consider Other Indicators**: Posters that reference awards such as "Academy Award Winner/ Nominee" or "Golden Globe Winner/Nominee" are posters that have been reissued with the re-release of the film to take advantage of the awards. The exception to this is some national and international film festivals such as Sundance or Cannes where many films are screened and awarded prizes before their initial release to the general public.

7) **Consult an Expert If You Are Still Unsure**: Most pre-1940 movie art pieces are very difficult to authenticate and differentiate between original and reissue/re-release mainly due to the lack of NSS coding and the fact that the studios did not generally date the artwork. Always consult an expert for an opinion on any item before making a purchase; the difference in value between an original and reissue/re-release can be substantial.

Factors for Authenticating Collectible Movie Art

Collectible movie art can be authenticated by determining several factors, including:

1) Poster Size

2) Poster Type

3) NSS Markings

The standard movie poster sizes (pre-1985) are as follows:

One-Sheet   (27" x 41")

The one-sheet is the standard size for movie posters in North America and the most popular poster size in terms of both advertising and desirability to collectors. These posters were printed on a paper stock that changed in the 1970s from matte finish that is coarse to the touch to a smooth clay-coated glossy finish. Pre-1985 one-sheets were usually folded and normally had a border. The NSS number is found on the bottom of the poster.

Two-Sheet (also called Subway Poster)   (41" x 54")

The two-sheet is also called the subway sheet or subway poster because it was used as subway advertising. These posters were printed on a cardstock that was thicker than the one-sheets. They were almost always printed in advance of the release of the film and contain advance notice of the film's release. They were released in either a folded or rolled state. They are desired by collectors for several reasons: because they were printed on a thicker paper they are more durable than one-sheets, and they were printed in smaller quantities than the one-sheets and are therefore generally rarer to find.

Three-Sheet   (41" x 81")

These posters were printed on a paper stock that was always folded. They were used for larger theater lobby displays and were typically printed on two pieces of paper that were cut horizontally and when put together made one large display. In these cases, the bottom portion is normally forty-one by fifty-four inches and the top portion is twenty-seven by forty-one (one-sheet size). Because of their size, the printing is generally much coarser than in the smaller formats, and usually lacks clarity when viewed up close. Very few three-sheets were originally printed and very few have survived intact, so they are considered among the rarest of poster sizes to the modern collector. A three-sheet must have both pieces together to be considered collectible and complete.

Six-Sheet   (81" x 81")

These posters were printed on a paper stock consisting of either two or four pieces of paper joined together to make one display. They were used for large advertising areas or as a small billboard. Because of their size, the printing is generally much coarser than in the smaller formats and usually lacks clarity when viewed up close. Very few six-sheets were originally printed, and very few have survived intact. Six-sheets are thus considered the rarest of domestic poster sizes to the modern collector. A six-sheet must have all pieces together to be considered collectible and complete. As an interesting note, the larger size of this art allowed for illustrations of more stars from a film than would generally appear on a smaller-format poster.

Twelve-Sheet   (108" x 144")

These posters were printed on a paper stock comprising numerous pieces and were always folded. They were used for advertising as a small billboard exclusively by Paramount up until the 1940s. Very few twelve-sheets were originally printed, and very few have survived intact (most were destroyed when they were removed from the billboard). They are considered extremely scarce. A twelve-sheet must have all pieces together to be considered collectible and complete.

Twenty-four-Sheet   (246" x 108")

These posters were printed on a paper stock comprising numerous pieces. They were used for advertising as a billboard or placed on the side of a building. Very few twenty-four-sheets were originally printed, and very few have survived intact. Most were destroyed when they were removed from the billboard, and the few surviving examples were usually never used. They are considered extremely scarce. A twenty-four-sheet must have all pieces together to be considered collectible and complete.

Thirty-Sheet   (118" x 285")

These posters were printed on a paper stock comprising numerous pieces. They were used for advertising as a billboard or placed on the side of a building. Very few thirty-sheets were originally printed, and very few have survived intact. Most were destroyed when they were removed from the billboard, and the few surviving examples were usually never used. They are considered extremely scarce. A thirty-sheet must have all pieces together to be considered collectible and complete.

Banners

Banners are printed on paper, cloth, or vinyl and are designed to be displayed in theater lobbies to promote a film. Most are printed horizontally, but some have been printed vertically, and as such sizes do vary. They are produced in minor quantities and are considered quite collectible due to their unique styles.

Half-Sheet   (22" x 28")

These posters were printed horizontally on a cardstock that was thicker than the one-sheets, making them more versatile and durable. They were sent to exhibitors rolled in tubes, but sometimes can be found folded into quarters for mailing as well. Collectors desire them because they were printed on a thicker paper, making them more durable than one-sheets, and they were sometimes released in more than one style, providing an alternative type of artwork to the one-sheet because of that feature. They are also easier to frame than the larger one-sheet.

Inserts   (14" x 36")

These posters were one of the earliest forms of movie advertising, introduced in the 1910s. They were printed on a heavy cardstock that was thicker than the one-sheets, making them more versatile and durable. They were sent to exhibitors rolled in tubes, but sometimes they were folded. They are desired by collectors because they were printed on a thicker paper, making them more durable than one-sheets. In addition, they were usually released with the same artwork as the one-sheet from that feature, and are easier to frame than the larger one-sheet.

Lobby Cards   (11" x 14" Standard, 8" x 10" Mini)

Lobby cards were issued in a series (usually eight) and were displayed in lobbies featuring a pictorial breakdown of the film's narrative. Key cards in the set include the *title card*, featuring main one-sheet artwork or a major star scene (most desired of the set), and *scene cards*, pictorials that make up the majority of the set. Most were numbered with the order in which they were to be displayed in the lobby. Many collectors try to complete a set of all cards issued in the series, and a completed set is always worth more than the combined values of the individual cards. Note: In the mid-1980s most U.S. studios discontinued printing lobby card displays for U.S. theaters; therefore, most modern sets are European.

Standups (or Standees)

These are three-dimensional cardboard displays intended to be displayed in theater lobbies to promote a film. They have been produced in minor quantities and are considered quite collectible due to their unique styles.

Window Cards (14" x 22" Standard, 10" x 18" Mini, 22" x 28" Jumbo)

These posters were printed on a cheaper cardstock that was thicker than the one-sheets, making them more versatile and durable. They were displayed outside the theater in retail store windows, on telephone poles, etc. They were sent to exhibitors in bulk and unfolded. Many have an area at the top that was blank—intended for the theater to write in the show times. Window cards with handwritten show times are not considered of lesser value, but examples that have been trimmed to remove the area are considered of a lesser value. Window cards were printed through several printing houses—some contain the NSS number on them, and these examples are considered more collectible than the non-NSS-issued cards.

Thirty-by-Forty-Inch Posters   (30" x 40")

These posters were printed vertically on a heavy cardstock. They were sent to exhibitors rolled in tubes, and were exhibited both inside and outside the theaters. They are desired by collectors because they were printed on a thicker paper, making them more durable than one-sheets. As well, they were released in the same style as the one-sheet from that feature, but were printed in much smaller quantities than the one-sheet, making them rarer in surviving quantities. An important note for collectors: The NSS number is found on the *side* of the poster as opposed to the bottom for most other formats.

British Quad   (30" x 40")

Not to be confused with the same size thirty-by-forty-inch posters, the British quad posters were printed and distributed in the United Kingdom and were printed horizontally instead of vertically. These posters were printed on a paper stock that changed in the 1970s from matte finish that is coarse to the touch to a smooth clay-coated glossy finish.

Forty-by-Sixty Posters   (40" x 60")

These posters were printed vertically on a heavy cardstock. They were sent to exhibitors rolled in tubes and were exhibited both inside and outside the theaters. They are desired by collectors because they are more durable than one-sheets, and they were released in the same style as the one-sheet from that feature. They were also printed in much smaller quantities than the one-sheet, and are therefore rarer in surviving quantities.

Foreign Market Film Sizes

Film markets other than North America and the United Kingdom have adopted their own universal poster sizes including 23" x 33" (Germany), 47" x 63" (France), 39" x 45" (Italy), and 20" x 29" (Japan).

The standard movie poster sizes post-1985 are as follows:

One-Sheet   (27" x 40")

The one-sheet is the standard movie poster in North America and the most popular poster size in terms of both advertising and desirability by collectors. These posters were trimmed to lose their border after 1985 to a one-inch smaller size of twenty-seven by forty inches. These posters are printed on a clay-coated glossy finish paper stock that is smooth to touch. Post-1985 one-sheets are usually rolled. Most new movie releases since 1985 use this poster size.

Mini-Sheets

These are movie posters that are issued in a variety of sizes, always smaller than the one-sheet but with the same artwork. These posters are printed on poster paper with a clay-coated glossy finish paper stock that is smooth to touch. Mini-sheets are generally given away at movie premieres and during special promotions and are printed in large quantities.

Special Types of Movie Posters

Advance/Teaser Poster

To create momentum for a film's release, movie studios sometimes release what are termed *advance* or *teaser posters*. These are generally in the one-sheet or two-sheet format and may or may not be the same style as the one-sheet that is released with the film. Some indicators that a poster may be an advance/teaser include having the text "Advance," "Teaser," "Adv," "Coming Soon," or a projected release date printed on the poster.

Award Poster

Posters that reference awards such as "Academy Award Winner/Nominee" or "Golden Globe Winner/Nominee" are posters that have been issued with the re-release of the film to take advantage of the awards. The exception to this is some national and international film festivals such as Sundance or Cannes, where many films are screened (and awarded prizes) before their initial release to the general public.

Anniversary Poster

These are posters that mark the anniversary of a film's original release. If the poster was issued to a theater with the re-release of the actual film, it is considered collectible movie art.

Double-Sided Poster

Many theater one-sheets produced after 1985 are printed double-sided, with the artwork on both the front and the back so they can be "backlit" and presented in light boxes in cinema lobbies. Double-sided posters give a more defined appearance than single-sided posters, and many collectors of post-1985 collectible movie art tend to prefer the double-sided versions.

NSS Markings

During the 1930s, the National Screen Service (NSS) became the sole contracted distributor of all movie paper items for all of the major studios. As a control measure, the NSS instituted a coding system in the early 1940s that was applied to all materials, detailing the year of distribution for the film and the sequential order of the film's release during that year. On most post-1940 art, the NSS number can usually be found on the bottom border of the poster. Up until mid-1977, the NSS number consisted of two digits, then a slash (/), and one to four numbers. The first two numbers indicated the year of the release, and the last four digits the sequential order of the movie for that year. For example, *52/140* indicates that the movie was released in 1952 and was the 140th movie title coded by NSS for the year 1952.

In 1977 the NSS changed its numbering system slightly, eliminating the slash from the code. To indicate a poster is a reissue, all NSS numbers contain the letter *R* preceding the number code. Any NSS number containing an *R* in the first position indicates that the poster was reissued or re-released in the year indicated. The National Screen Service ceased operations in September 2000.

Condition

Once a piece of movie art has been authenticated as either an original issue or a reissue/ re-release, and the size and format have been determined, one must then analyze its condition. The condition of an item can severely affect overall value and can play an integral role in determining future value. The condition of an authentic piece of movie art can become the most important factor to the experienced collector when making a decision between purchasing one of several items from the film. In basic terms, the better the condition, the more valuable it is in comparison to other items from the same film and in the same format. The extent to which the condition of an item determines the overall value is directly linked to the popularity of that film and the rarity of that item. The rarer an item is, the more forgiving a collector will be on the condition factors.

The condition of a piece of movie art is determined by the existence of imperfections or blemishes to the piece. These include tears, wrinkles, holes, marks, stains, ink fading, etc. The location of these blemishes on the art is also very important—the more they affect the actual artwork of the poster, the more of a concern they are. If the imperfections are located in the outer border, they are not looked upon as much of a detraction.

Dealers and auction houses use a grading system and basic terminology to clarify the condition of an item. Every dealer has his or her own methods and scales for listing the condition of an item; some use a letter scale from *A* to *F* but most use terms such as "Mint," "Good," all the way down the scale to "Poor." The worse the condition of an item is, the more details you generally will see in an item description.

The following is a brief outline of the various grades (broken down by their term and corresponding letter scale) and their different condition factors:

Mint (or A+)

A poster in *mint* condition looks exactly the way it did when it was first printed (very rare and should be considered suspect in dealing with vintage art). The poster can be machine folded or rolled, depending upon the state in which it was originally shipped by the printing house. A poster that has been hand-folded will not be considered *mint*. The poster will not exhibit any blemishes or tears of any kind.

Near Mint (or A)

A poster in *near mint* condition differs from a mint example in that it may have minor blemishes in the border area only that do not affect the original artwork whatsoever.

Very Good (or B)

A poster in *very good* condition may have blemishes in the border and into approximately one inch of the poster's artwork area. There may also be small tears along the fold lines of the poster only, and the colors may be only slightly faded.

Good (or B– to C)

A poster in *good* condition will have blemishes around the border and into the outer edges of the artwork, but the major areas of the artwork must be free of blemishes. Pieces of the border may be torn or missing.

Fair (or C–)

A poster in *fair* condition will have major blemishes that affect the artwork of the poster. A poster in this condition must be professionally restored.

Poor

A poster in *poor* condition will have major blemishes and will be in such a state that actual handling should be avoided. A poster in this condition must be professionally restored.

Preservation and Conservation

It is very important to understand and adhere to the simple rules of preservation. As you acquire pieces in your collection, you must immediately assess each item's current state of condition. It can be very expensive to restore or improve the present condition of an item; therefore, you should attempt to pinpoint critical condition issues and avoid anything that may promote future deterioration in the condition of the item.

The most destructive forces to movie art are sunlight, heat, and humidity. Always store items in rooms with a humidity factor of 50 to 60 percent and temperatures ranging between 65 and 80 degrees F—generally what we consider comfortable room temperature. Low humidity is a major problem as well—if you run an air conditioner during the summer months, try adding a humidifier in the room to add moisture to the air. Also watch the conditions during the winter months if you heat your home/office. There are a few options for storage of your items:

Flat Storage

One of the most effective ways of storing movie art pieces is flat on top of one another. You may also wish to place a sheet of acid-free paper in between each poster. Always store your posters flat and never folded, as folds will turn into tears over time.

Framing

If you choose to have your posters framed, choose a professional who is familiar with museum-grade framing techniques. Always use nonreflective glass with UV (ultraviolet) protection that will reduce the penetration of light to the item. All items should be adhered to a matte board that is composed of acid-free material (museum board) and that is thick enough to keep the item from touching the glass. Any tape that is used to attach the item to the matte board must be archival tape.

Restoration

If you acquire a vintage piece that has some blemishes—tears, wrinkles, or stains, for example—you may want to consider the option of restoration. This work should never be done by an amateur as this may be more harmful to the poster (and more expensive to fix) than the original blemishes. A professional restorer can do wonders for a poster with condition issues, for example:

- **Bleed-Through Marks**: This is what happens when the ink that has been written on the back of the poster has been absorbed into the paper and has now become visible from the front side. Many times the writing on the back of the poster was done by a theater employee to list screening times, for example. It is possible for a professional restorer to bleach the affected area to remove the ink mark and then reapply a colored ink to the affected area to match the original state.

- **Ink Fading**: This is what happens when a portion of the ink color in the artwork area of the poster has faded due to contact with sunlight. The ink in the faded area is not as vibrant as its original issue state. A professional restorer can restore the ink to its original state by painting the faded areas with a matching paint color.

- **Ink Markings**: This refers to any type of mark found on the artwork of the poster created by a pen, pencil, marker, etc. These were done many times by theater patrons and/or bored children waiting in line for a show. A professional restorer can bleach the affected area, removing the ink mark and then reapplying a colored paint to the affected area to match its original state.

- **Holes and Tears**: Any type of hole or tear that appears on the poster. Most holes have been caused by staples and pins used to hang the posters in theater windows, but this can also refer to worm holes created by storage in a nonprotected area. Tears mostly occur along the fold lines of a poster—repeated folding and unfolding of a poster causes pressure on the weaker fold lines, eventually causing a tear. A professional restorer can patch the affected area using archival tape on the reverse side and then reapply a colored paint to the affected area on the artwork to match its original state.

- **Trimmed Posters**: This refers to the trimming of a poster from its original size to a smaller size. This was usually done for framing purposes or to remove outdated credit information from a previous exhibition and is quite common in the window card format. A professional restorer can restore a trim poster to its original size through a linen backing system described below.

Linen Backing

This is a process used by a professional restorer that is the most effective method not only to restore a poster to a pristine-looking state, but also to help preserve that state for the future. The process involves mounting the poster to a linen or cotton cloth with a sheet of acid-free rice paper in between the poster and the cloth as an acid-neutralizer. This process makes the poster more durable, and at the same time neutralizes the acids in the paper stock.

Content

The term *content* refers to the significance of the item in relation to the collecting marketplace. The more desirable the piece is to the marketplace in terms of its film title, featured stars, and format, the greater the content factor becomes in the overall value of the piece. Historically, pieces with the best content appreciate the most in value. When looking to purchase any piece of movie art, look for the best possible content available in your price range. The following factors should be taken into consideration when determining the content value of any item:

Film

The more popular and cherished the film is, the more desirable the art from that film will be to the marketplace. Art from significant, groundbreaking, and Academy Award–winning films is highly desirable, as is memorabilia from popular collecting genres such as horror, science fiction, and James Bond films.

Featured Actors

Art from a film with major stars is highly desired by collectors. There are many collectors of movie memorabilia who collect items related to specific movie stars, and these collectors will join the demand for movie art featuring these stars beyond what has been created by the collectors of film art only. If the art from a particular film has several styles, the style featuring the major stars in key portraits will be most desired. If a film has several major stars, a style featuring these stars together will also be highly desired.

Format

The varying sizes and formats of movie art from a particular film can be more desirable to different collectors. Most collectors cherish the one-sheet format as the standard poster to collect, but a scarce poster in a scarce format can also be valued by the marketplace due to its rarity.

Future Values

Movie art is cherished by collectors and historians as relics that visually document the evolution of one of our most universally adored art forms. These items were never intended to survive, and were not meant to be collected in the first place. Their value is based purely on the factors of supply and demand. The rarer an item is and the greater the number of collectors wanting that item, the more valuable it becomes to the marketplace as a whole.

Modern releases are very collectible, but most collectors preserve these pieces immediately in pristine states, and these are also collected in numbers that far outweigh the limited supplies of vintage material. Modern films have also not had the luxury of *becoming* classics for future generations. Will the Hollywood legends and films of today mean as much to the cinema fans of twenty or thirty years from now?

Historically, the items associated with Hollywood classics such as *King Kong, The Wizard of Oz,* and *Gone with the Wind,* as well as the horror legends—Boris Karloff and Bela Lugosi (just to name two)—have fared the best over time. The main reasons for this are a limited supply of very presentable material to a large and continually expanding marketplace of collectors and institutions (museums, theme parks, restaurant chains, etc.) looking to add these pieces to their collections. The rarest of these vintage pieces have one or possibly two examples that have survived to this date. It is most probable that these vintage items will remain the future "gems" of the collecting marketplace, and prices will continue to rise as long as there are collectors willing to pay *any* price to obtain a one-of-a-kind piece.

MOVIE ART PRICE LISTINGS

The prices listed in this book reflect current market values for movie art. These values have been determined from retail sales and auction results collected over three years from 1999 to 2002. Each listing contains the following information:

- **Film Title**

- **Year of Release**: (R) denotes year of reissue for listing.

- **Size**: Most listings reference OS (One-Sheet) and LC SET (Lobby Card set) prices for popular titles. When one-sheet listings were not available for a title, the next available format was referenced.

- **Price Range**: The range of prices given for a title reflects price ranges in Mint to Very Good condition. The cases where an individual price and not a range are given denote a record price paid for that item.

MOVIE ART PRICE LISTINGS

A

TITLE	YEAR	SIZE	PRICE RANGE
Abandon Ship	1957	OS	40–60
Abandoned	1949	OS	40–60
Abandoned	1949	LC SET	75–100
Abbott & Costello Go to Mars	1953	OS	600–1,000
Abbott & Costello in Hollywood	1945	OS	600–1,000
Abbott & Costello in Society	1944	OS	200–500
Abbott & Costello in Society	1944	LC SET	300–600
Abbott & Costello in Society	R 1953	INSERT	75–200
Abbott & Costello in the Foreign Legion	1950	OS	100–300
Abbott & Costello in the Foreign Legion	1950	LC SET	200–350
Abbott & Costello Meet Captain Kidd	1953	OS	75–150
Abbott & Costello Meet Captain Kidd	1953	LC SET	150–250
Abbott & Cost. Meet Dr. Jekyll & Mr. Hyde	1953	OS	400–1,000
Abbott & Cost. Meet Dr. Jekyll & Mr. Hyde	1953	LC SET	300–500
Abbott & Cost. Meet Frankenstein	1948	OS	1,500–3,000
Abbott & Cost. Meet Frankenstein	1948	LC SET	2,500–4,000
Abbott & Cost. Meet Frankenstein	R 1956	OS	700–1,000
Abbott & Cost. Meet the Invisible Man	1951	OS	300–1,000
Abbott & Cost. Meet the Keystone Cops	1955	OS	100–300
Abbott & Cost. Meet the Keystone Cops	1955	LC SET	250–500
Abbott & Cost. Meet the Killer	1949	OS	300–800
Abbott & Cost. Meet the Killer	1949	LC SET	500–1,000
Abbott & Cost. Meet the Mummy	1954	OS	500–1,500
Abductors	1957	OS	40–70
Abdullah's Harem	1956	OS	30–70
Abe Lincoln in Illinois	1940	OS	50–100
Abie's Irish Rose	1928	OS	500–900
Abominable Dr. Phibes	1971	OS	50–100
Abominable Dr. Phibes	1971	LC SET	50–100

A

TITLE	YEAR	SIZE	PRICE RANGE
Abominable Snowman	1957	OS	30–75
Abominable Snowman	1957	LC SET	100–300
About Mrs. Leslie	1954	OS	25–75
Above and Beyond	1953	OS	40–75
Above the Law	1988	OS	25–50
Abraham Lincoln	R 1937	OS	100–500
Absence of Malice	1981	OS	30–70
Absent-Minded Professor	1961	OS	40–100
Absent-Minded Professor	R 1967	OS	25–50
Absent-Minded Professor	R 1974	OS	25–45
Absolute Beginners	1986	OS	30–75
Absolute Power	1997	OS	25–50
Accent on Love	1941	OS	25–50
Accent on Youth	1935	OS	300–750
Accident	1967	OS	40–80
Accidental Tourist	1988	OS	25–75
Accidents Will Happen	1938	OS	100–300
According to Mrs. Hoyle	1951	OS	30–60
According to Mrs. Hoyle	1951	LC SET	50–75
Accursed	1958	OS	30–75
Accused	1949	OS	50–100
Accused of Murder	1957	OS	30–75
Ace High	1969	OS	25–75
Ace in the Hole	1951	OS	200–1,000
Ace in the Hole	1951	LC SET	250–450
Ace Ventura Pet Detective	1994	OS	25–50
Across 110th Street	1972	OS	40–150
Across the Pacific	1942	OS	750–2,000
Across the Wide Missouri	1951	OS	50–100
Act of Murder	1948	OS	40–100
Act of Violence	1948	OS	50–200
Action in the North Atlantic	1943	OS	300–500
Action in the North Atlantic	1943	LC SET	300–700
Actress	1953	OS	40–80
Ada	1961	OS	30–80
Adam's Rib	1949	OS	200–500
Addams Family	1991	OS	25–50
Advance to the Rear	1964	OS	25–50

TITLE	YEAR	SIZE	PRICE RANGE
Advance to the Rear	1964	LC SET	25–50
Adventure	1945	OS	200–500
Adventures of Baron Munchausen	1988	OS	25–50
Adventures of Baron Munchausen	1988	LC SET	25–50
Adventures of Buckaroo Bonzai	1984	OS	40–100
Adventures of Buckaroo Bonzai	1984	LC SET	25–50
Adventures of Captain Fabian	1951	OS	75–150
Adventures of Captain Fabian	1951	OS	75–150
Adventures of Don Juan	1949	OS	100–450
Adventures of Frank & Jessie James	1948	OS	75–150
Adventures of Huck Finn	1960	OS	25–50
Adventures of Ichabod & Mr. Toad	1949	OS	100–250
Adventures of Marco Polo	1937	OS	75–200
Adventures of Robin Hood	1938	OS	7,500–20,000
Adventures of Robin Hood	R 1948	OS	400–900
Adventures of Robin Hood	R 1956	OS	250–400
Adventures of Robin Hood	R 1970	OS	100–250
Adventures of Robin Hood	R 1976	OS	75–200
Adventures of Sherlock Holmes	1939	OS	2,000–4,000
Adventure of Sherlock Holmes' Smarter Brother	1975	OS	40–80
Adventures of Tarzan	1921	81 × 81	5,000–11,000
Advise and Consent	1962	OS	150–500
Advise and Consent	1962	LC SET	50–100
Affair in Trinidad	1952	OS	500–2,000
Affair to Remember	1957	OS	300–1,000
Affair to Remember	1957	LC SET	500–900
Africa Screams	1949	OS	100–250
African Queen	1951	OS	1,500–5,500
African Queen	1951	LC SET	300–500
African Queen	R 1968	OS	50–100
After Hours	1985	OS	30–75
After the Fox	1966	OS	30–60
After the Thin Man	1936	OS	1,500–4,000
Against All Flags	1952	OS	75–150
Against All Odds	1984	OS	25–75
Agony and the Ecstasy	1964	OS	50–100

A

A

TITLE	YEAR	SIZE	PRICE RANGE
Aguirre the Wrath of God	1972	OS	25–100
Ain't Misbehavin'	1955	OS	25–50
Air Cadet	1951	OS	30–80
Airplane	1982	OS	25–75
Airport	1970	OS	40–100
Airport	1970	LC SET	25–50
Aka Cassius Clay	1970	OS	150–500
Al Capone	1959	OS	40–100
Aladdin	1992	OS	40–80
Aladdin	1992	LC SET	50–150
Alamo	1960	OS	200–800
Alamo	1960	LC SET	150–250
Alamo	R 1967	OS	50–100
Alexander the Great	1956	OS	25–50
Alexander's Ragtime Band	1938	OS	1,500–2,500
Alexander's Ragtime Band	R 1947	OS	50–100
Alfie	1966	OS	75–400
Algiers	1938	OS	500–1,000
Algiers	R 1953	OS	50–100
Ali Baba and the 40 Thieves	1943	OS	300–700
Alias a Gentleman	1948	OS	50–150
Alias Jesse James	1959	OS	40–75
Alice Doesn't Live Here Anymore	1974	OS	30–80
Alice in Wonderland	1951	OS	500–3,500
Alice in Wonderland	R 1974	OS	25–75
Alice in Wonderland	R 1980	OS	25–60
Alice's Restaurant	1969	OS	30–80
Alien	1979	OS	100–350
Alien	1979	LC SET	50–250
Alien 3	1992	OS	25–70
Alien Resurrection	1998	OS	25–40
Aliens	1986	OS	40–150
All about Eve	1950	OS	800–2,500
All American	1953	OS	50–100
All at Sea	1958	OS	40–75
All in a Night's Work	1961	OS	25–70
All Quiet on the Western Front	1930	OS	15,000–25,000
All That Heaven Allows	1955	OS	50–200

TITLE	YEAR	SIZE	PRICE RANGE
All That Jazz	1979	OS	30–100
All That Jazz	1979	LC SET	25–60
All the Fine Cannibals	1960	OS	40–75
All the King's Men	1949	OS	40–150
All the President's Men	1976	OS	40–100
All the President's Men	1976	LC SET	40–100
All the Right Moves	1983	OS	25–50
All the Right Moves	1983	LC SET	25–40
All through the Night	1942	OS	800–2,500
Allegheny Uprising	1939	OS	25–75
Alligator People	1959	OS	100–250
Alligator People	1959	LC SET	150–300
Along the Great Divide	1951	OS	75–300
Alphaville	1965	47 × 63 FRE	500–1,500
Amadeus	1984	OS	40–125
Amadeus	1984	LC SET	25–40
Amarcord	1974	OS	30–50
Amarilly of Clothesline Valley	1918	OS	600–1,200
Amazing Colossal Man	1957	OS	400–950
Amazing Transparent Man	1959	OS	25–80
Amazing Transparent Man	1959	LC SET	40–80
Amblin	1969	OS	250–500
Ambush at Cimarron Pass	1958	OS	40–100
Ambush Bay	1966	OS	35–50
Ambush Valley	1936	OS	150–300
American Beauty	1999	OS	30–50
American Beauty	1999	LC SET	50–150
American Gigolo	1980	OS	35–60
American Graffiti	1973	OS	125–800
American Graffiti	1973	LC SET	150–250
American Graffiti	R 1978	OS	75–150
American in Paris	1951	OS	500–2,000
American in Paris	R 1963	OS	40–100
American Tail	1986	OS	25–50
American Venus	1926	OS	250–1,000
American Werewolf in London	1981	OS	25–75
American Werewolf in London	1981	LC SET	25–50
Amityville Horror	1979	OS	25–50

A

TITLE	YEAR	SIZE	PRICE RANGE
Among Those Present	1921	OS	500–2,000
Anastasia	1956	OS	50–350
Anatomy of a Murder	1959	OS	350–1,500
Anatomy of a Murder	1959	LC SET	250–400
Anchors Aweigh	1945	OS	250–750
Anchors Aweigh	1945	LC SET	75–200
Anchors Aweigh	R 1955	OS	40–75
And God Created Woman	1957	47 × 63 FRE	150–400
And God Created Woman	1957	LC SET	100–200
And Justice for All	1979	OS	25–50
And Justice for All	1979	LC SET	25–50
And Now for Something Completely Different	1972	OS	25–50
And Now the Screaming Starts	1973	OS	25–75
Andalusian Dog	1929	32 × 47 FRE	1,000–2,200
Anderson Tapes	1971	OS	50–75
Androcles and the Lion	1952	OS	75–350
Andromeda Strain	1971	OS	25–50
Andy Warhol's Bad	1977	OS	100–250
Andy Warhol's Dracula	1974	OS	50–250
Andy Warhol's Dracula	1974	LC SET	50–150
Andy Warhol's Frankenstein	1974	OS	50–200
Andy Warhol's Frankenstein	1974	LC SET	50–200
Angel	1937	OS	1,500–5,000
Angel and the Bad Man	1946	LC SET	500–750
Angel Heart	1987	OS	30–50
Angel Heart	1987	LC SET	30–50
Angel on My Shoulder	1946	OS	250–500
Angel Wore Red	1960	OS	25–50
Angels in the Outfield	1951	OS	25–80
Angels over Broadway	1940	OS	350–950
Angels with Dirty Faces	1938	OS	5,000–7,500
Angels with Dirty Faces	R 1956	OS	100–500
Angry Red Planet	1960	OS	150–600
Angry Red Planet	1960	LC SET	150–250
Animal Crackers	(1930) R 1974	OS	50–200
Animal House	1978	OS	150–450
Anna and the King of Siam	1946	OS	100–300

TITLE	YEAR	SIZE	PRICE RANGE
Anna Karenina	1927	27 × 41 SWE	1,000–2,000
Anna Karenina	1947	OS	150–400
Annie	1982	OS	50–80
Annie Get Your Gun	1950	OS	75–250
Annie Hall	1977	OS	75–250
Annie Hall	1977	LC SET	50–200
Anniversary	1967	OS	30–80
Another Man's Poison	1952	OS	85–150
Any Number Can Play	1949	OS	150–250
Any Which Way You Can	1980	OS	30–75
Anything Goes	1956	OS	40–100
Apache	1954	OS	40–150
Apache Rifles	1964	OS	30–50
Apartment	1960	OS	150–500
Ape	1940	OS	250–500
Ape Man	1943	OS	400–700
Apocalypse Now	1979	OS	100–350
Apocalypse Now	1979	LC SET	100–200
Apollo 13	1995	OS	25–90
Appaloosa	1966	OS	30–75
Appointment with Danger	1951	OS	200–550
Apprenticeship of Duddy Kravitz	1974	OS	30–90
April Love	1957	OS	50–75
Arabesque	1966	OS	50–75
Arch of Triumph	1947	OS	100–450
Aristocats	1971	OS	50–125
Arizona Raiders	1965	OS	25–50
Arizonian	1935	OS	1,500–2,500
Armored Command	1961	OS	30–75
Around the World in a Daze	1963	OS	50–200
Around the World in 80 Days	1956	OS	75–200
Arsenic and Old Lace	1944	OS	750–2,000
Arthur	1981	OS	25–70
Artists and Models	1937	OS	200–400
As Young as You Feel	1951	OS	75–250
Ash Wednesday	1973	OS	25–60
Ashphalt Jungle	1950	OS	100–550
Ashphalt Jungle	R 1954	OS	200–500

A

A

TITLE	YEAR	SIZE	PRICE RANGE
Assault on a Queen	1966	OS	30–60
Astounding She Monster	1958	OS	700–1,150
Asylum	1972	OS	40–80
Atom Man Vs. Superman	1950	OS	2,000–4,000
Attack	1956	OS	40–100
Attack of the Crab Monsters	1957	OS	700–2,000
Attack of the 50 Ft. Woman	1958	OS	4,000–6,500
Attack of the Phantoms	1979	OS	150–400
Attack of the Puppet People	1958	OS	100–200
Auntie Mame	1958	OS	150–550
Babes in Arms	1939	OS	150–500
Babes in Toyland	1934	WC	2,000–5,000
Babes on Broadway	1941	OS	250–700
Babette Goes to War	1960	OS	40–125
Babette's Feast	1988	OS	40–125
Baby Doll	1956	OS	200–550
Baby the Rain Must Fall	1965	OS	75–350
Bachelor and the Bobbysoxer	1947	OS	75–250
Bachelor in Paradise	1961	OS	25–60
Back from the Dead	1957	OS	40–125
Back to Bataan	1945	OS	200–850
Back to the Future	1985	OS	50–250
Back to the Future	1985	LC SET	50–150
Back to the Future 2	1989	OS	50–100
Back to the Future 3	1989	OS	50–100
Backlash	1956	OS	50–75
Bad and the Beautiful	1953	OS	500–1,500
Bad Boys	1982	OS	25–100
Bad Day at Black Rock	1955	OS	200–900
Bad News Bears	1976	OS	25–60
Bad Seed	1956	OS	75–300
Badlands	1974	OS	50–250
Ball of Fire	1941	OS	500–2,000
Ballad of Josie	1968	OS	25–50
Bambi	1942	OS	1,000–2,500
Bambi	R 1948	OS	150–300
Bananas	1971	OS	50–125
Band of Angels	1957	OS	75–300

B

TITLE	YEAR	SIZE	PRICE RANGE
Band Wagon	1953	OS	400–1,500
Bandolero	1968	OS	50–90
Bang the Drum Slowly	1973	OS	40–80
Bank Dick	1940	OS	2,000–5,000
Bar 20	1943	OS	75–350
Barabbas	1962	OS	40–60
Barbarella	1968	OS	150–1,000
Barbarella	1968	LC SET	100–250
Barbarella	R 1977	OS	50–400
Barbarian and the Geisha	1958	OS	50–125
Barbed Wire	1952	OS	50–100
Barefoot Contessa	1954	OS	100–450
Barefoot in the Park	1967	OS	40–90
Barkleys of Broadway	1949	OS	300–1,000
Barretts of Wimpole Street	1934	OS	250–950
Barry Lyndon	1975	OS	50–200
Barry Lyndon	1975	LC SET	50–200
Barton Fink	1991	OS	25–125
Basic Instinct	1992	OS	25–50
Bat	1959	OS	50–150
Bataan	1943	OS	75–150
Batman	1966	OS	200–800
Batman	1989	OS	50–150
Batman and Robin	1997	OS	25–40
Batman Forever	1995	OS	30–50
Batman Returns	1992	OS	20–50
Battle at Apache Brass	1952	OS	25–50
Battle beneath the Earth	1968	OS	30–75
Battle beyond the Sun	1962	OS	40–125
Battle Circus	1953	OS	125–350
Battle for the Planet of the Apes	1973	OS	40–175
Battle for the Planet of the Apes	1973	LC SET	40–75
Battle in Outer Space	1960	OS	50–150
Battle in Outer Space	1960	LC SET	100–250
Battle of Britain	1969	OS	50–250
Battle of the Bulge	1966	OS	40–100
Battlestar Gallactica	1978	OS	25–80
Bayou	1957	OS	25–60

B

TITLE	YEAR	SIZE	PRICE RANGE
Beach Ball	1965	OS	25–80
Beach Blanket Bingo	1965	OS	25–150
Beach Party	1963	OS	75–150
Beast from the Haunted Cave	1959	OS	75–250
Beast from 20,000 Fathoms	1953	OS	700–1,700
Beast with a Million Eyes	1955	OS	400–1,200
Beastmaster	1982	OS	25–50
Beat Generation	1959	OS	50–150
Beat the Devil	1953	OS	75–200
Beatles Come to Town	1964	OS	500–1,400
Beau Brummel	1954	OS	50–90
Beau Geste	1939	OS	5,000–10,000
Beau James	1957	OS	35–150
Beautiful Blonde Bashful Bend	1949	OS	100–250
Beautiful but Dangerous	1957	OS	50–250
Beauty and the Beast	1962	OS	35–75
Beauty and the Beast	1991	OS	50–125
Becket	1964	OS	40–200
Bedazzled	1968	OS	50–275
Bedknobs and Broomsticks	1971	OS	25–50
Bedlam	1946	OS	400–1,000
Bedtime for Bonzo	1951	OS	250–750
Bedtime Story	1941	OS	50–150
Bedtime Story	1964	OS	40–80
Beetlejuice	1988	OS	40–90
Beginning of the End	1957	OS	250–750
Beguiled	1971	OS	50–250
Behave Yourself	1951	OS	50–250
Behind the Green Door	1972	OS	50–200
Being There	1980	OS	50–200
Bell Book and Candle	1958	OS	200–450
Bellboy	1960	OS	25–60
Belle de Jour	1968	OS	400–800
Belle et la Bête	1946	47 × 63 FRE	2,000–7,500
Belle of New York	1952	OS	150–375
Belle Starr	1941	OS	650–1,500
Bells of Coronado	1950	OS	150–300
Bells of Rosarita	1945	OS	300–550

B

TITLE	YEAR	SIZE	PRICE RANGE
Bells of San Angelo	1947	OS	250–400
Bells of St. Mary's	1945	OS	150–400
Beloved Infidel	1959	OS	40–80
Ben-Hur	1959	OS	150–450
Ben-Hur	1959	LC SET	300–500
Ben-Hur	R 1974	OS	40–90
Bend of the River	1952	OS	250–400
Beneath the Planet of the Apes	1970	OS	50–250
Beneath the Planet of the Apes	1970	LC SET	150–250
Beneath the Valley of the Ultra-Vixens	1979	OS	40–250
Benny Goodman Story	1955	OS	70–150
Berserk	1967	OS	25–80
Best Man	1964	OS	25–80
Best of Everything	1959	OS	25–60
Best Years of Our Lives	1946	OS	400–800
Best Years of Our Lives	R 1954	OS	40–100
Betrayed	1954	OS	40–125
Between Heaven and Hell	1956	OS	30–60
Beware My Lovely	1952	OS	75–300
Beyond a Reasonable Doubt	1956	OS	75–375
Beyond Bengal	1933	OS	250–550
Beyond Mombasa	1957	OS	25–60
Beyond the Forest	1949	OS	75–300
Beyond the Limit	1983	OS	25–50
Beyond the Time Barrier	1959	OS	75–300
Beyond the Valley of the Dolls	1970	OS	50–175
Bhowani Junction	1955	OS	50–125
Bible	1967	OS	25–60
Big Bad Mama	1974	OS	40–75
Big Beat	1958	OS	50–120
Big Boodle	1956	OS	50–125
Big Chill	1983	OS	25–100
Big Chill	1983	LC SET	30–75
Big Circus	1959	OS	50–100
Big Clock	1948	OS	200–650
Big Combo	1955	OS	150–550
Big Country	1958	OS	50–350

B

TITLE	YEAR	SIZE	PRICE RANGE
Big Gundown	1968	OS	40–75
Big Hangover	1949	OS	50–175
Big Heat	1953	OS	350–750
Big Jake	1971	OS	50–250
Big Jake	1971	LC SET	150–250
Big Jim McLain	1952	OS	75–175
Big Knife	1955	OS	75–300
Big Parade of Comedy	1964	OS	40–75
Big Red One	1980	OS	25–70
Big Shot	1942	OS	200–750
Big Sleep	1946	OS	1,000–2,200
Big Steal	1949	OS	350–700
Big Store	1941	OS	750–1,250
Big Trouble in Little China	1986	OS	25–60
Big Wednesday	1978	OS	150–550
Big Wednesday	1978	LC SET	150–350
Bigamist	1953	OS	35–75
Bigger than Life	1956	OS	50–125
Biggest Bundle of Them All	1968	OS	50–80
Bikini Beach	1964	OS	50–175
Bill of Divorcement	1932	OS	500–1,250
Billie	1965	OS	50–75
Billion Dollar Brain	1967	OS	25–90
Billy Budd	1962	OS	25–90
Billy Jack	1971	OS	75–125
Bird of Paradise	1932	OS	750–2,000
Birdman of Alcatraz	1962	OS	100–350
Birds	1963	OS	500–1,000
Birds	1963	LC SET	300–650
Birth of a Nation	1915	OS	5,000–8,000
Birth of a Nation	R 1921	OS	4,000–6,300
Birth of a Nation	R 1930	OS	100–150
Bishop's Wife	1948	OS	400–800
Bite the Bullet	1975	OS	25–75
Bitter Victory	1958	OS	50–125
Black Castle	1952	OS	75–175
Black Dragons	1942	OS	200–800
Black Hole	1979	OS	50–150

TITLE	YEAR	SIZE	PRICE RANGE
Black Narcissus	1946	OS	300–450
Black Rain	1989	OS	50–75
Black Rose	1950	OS	150–400
Black Sabbath	1964	OS	75–200
Black Scorpion	1957	OS	75–300
Black Sleep	1956	OS	75–500
Black Stallion	1979	OS	35–70
Black Sunday	1961	OS	150–400
Black Widow	1954	OS	50–125
Black Zoo	1963	OS	50–125
Blackboard Jungle	1955	OS	100–250
Blackout	1940	OS	75–225
Blackwell's Island	1939	OS	75–325
Blacula	1972	OS	40–175
Blade Runner	1982	OS	100–350
Blade Runner	1982	LC SET	250–400
Blaze of Noon	1947	OS	50–150
Blazing Saddles	1974	OS	50–125
Blindfold	1966	OS	40–60
Blob	1958	OS	400–1,000
Blob	1958	LC SET	350–500
Blonde Bait	1956	OS	50–150
Blonde Ice	1948	OS	300–450
Blonde Venus	1932	OS	7,000–10,000
Blood Alley	1955	OS	75–150
Blood and Sand	1922	OS	4,000–7,500
Blood and Sand	1941	OS	400–800
Blood of the Vampire	1958	OS	50–250
Blood on the Sun	1945	OS	200–450
Blood Simple	1985	OS	50–150
Blow Out	1981	OS	50–75
Blow Up	1966	OS	100–275
Blow Up	1966	LC SET	150–350
Blowing Wild	1953	OS	50–175
Blue Dahlia	1946	OS	4,500–6,000
Blue Hawaii	1961	OS	400–700
Blue Hawaii	1961	LC SET	400–600
Blue Lagoon	1949	OS	75–250

B

TITLE	YEAR	SIZE	PRICE RANGE
Blue Lagoon	1980	OS	40–90
Blue Max	1966	OS	50–250
Blue Skies	1946	OS	250–750
Blue Velvet	1986	OS	75–350
Blueprint for Murder	1953	OS	75–200
Blues Brothers	1980	OS	100–350
Blues Brothers	1980	LC SET	50–150
Bobo	1967	OS	25–60
Body and Soul	1947	OS	500–700
Body Double	1984	OS	25–70
Body Heat	1981	OS	25–60
Body Snatcher	1945	OS	2,000–4,000
Bohemian Girl	1936	OS	1,000–2,500
Bolero	1934	OS	7,000–8,500
Bomber's B-52	1957	OS	25–60
Bon Voyage	1962	OS	25–75
Bonjour Tristesse	1958	OS	400–700
Bonnie and Clyde	1967	OS	75–475
Bonnie and Clyde	1967	LC SET	75–200
Boom Town	1940	OS	750–2,500
Boomerang	1947	OS	300–450
Born Losers	1967	OS	50–150
Born Reckless	1959	OS	75–125
Born to Be Bad	1950	OS	75–150
Born to Be Loved	1958	OS	40–75
Born to Kill	1946	OS	500–850
Born Yesterday	1950	OS	100–400
Boston Strangler	1968	OS	50–125
Bounty Hunter	1954	OS	75–125
Bowery at Midnight	1942	OS	500–1,000
Bowery Bombshell	1946	OS	50–90
Boxcar Bertha	1972	OS	25–70
Boy Meets Girl	1938	OS	500–850
Boy on a Dolphin	1957	OS	50–80
Boy Who Cried Werewolf	1973	OS	30–75
Boyfriend	1971	OS	40–70
Boys from Brazil	1978	OS	50–80
Boys in the Band	1970	OS	50–150

B

TITLE	YEAR	SIZE	PRICE RANGE
Brain	1964	OS	40–80
Brain Eaters	1958	OS	300–750
Brain from Planet Arous	1957	OS	250–450
Brain that Wouldn't Die	1962	OS	140–250
Brainstorm	1983	OS	30–70
Brannigan	1974	OS	40–120
Braveheart	1995	OS	50–100
Brazil	1985	OS	75–300
Breakfast at Tiffany's	1961	OS	2,500–8,000
Breakfast Club	1985	OS	40–100
Breaking Away	1979	OS	40–70
Breaking Point	1950	OS	100–175
Breakout	1975	OS	30–70
Breath of Scandal	1960	OS	40–80
Breathless	1959	OS	250–500
Breathless	1959	47 × 63 FRE	1,000–1,850
Bribe	1949	OS	50–250
Bride and the Beast	1958	OS	250–750
Bride of Frankenstein	1935	OS	17,000
Bride of Frankenstein	1935	14 × 36	60,000–85,000
Bride of Frankenstein	1935	LC	7,000–18,000
Bride of the Gorilla	1951	OS	350–750
Bride of the Monster	1955	OS	600–1,500
Bride Wore Black	1967	47 × 63 FRE	300–500
Brides of Dracula	1960	OS	175–450
Brides of Fu Manchu	1966	OS	30–85
Bridge on the River Kwai	1958	OS	300–650
Bridge on the River Kwai	1958	LC SET	250–350
Bridge on the River Kwai	R 1963	OS	75–125
Bridge Too Far	1977	OS	30–80
Bridges at Toko Ri	1954	OS	75–200
Brigadoon	1954	OS	75–300
Bright Road	1953	OS	100–250
Bring Me the Head of Alfredo G	1974	OS	50–150
Bringing Up Baby	1938	OS	3,500–7,500
Bringing Up Baby	R 1955	OS	175–250
Broadcast News	1987	OS	40–70
Broadway Danny Rose	1984	OS	50–90

B

TITLE	YEAR	SIZE	PRICE RANGE
Broken Arrow	1950	OS	150–575
Bronco Billy	1980	OS	30–75
Bronco Billy	1980	LC SET	40–80
Brood	1979	OS	40–80
Brother Orchid	1940	OS	250–600
Brotherhood of Satan	1971	OS	25–60
Brothers Karamazov	1958	OS	50–90
Brothers Rico	1957	OS	25–60
Brubaker	1980	OS	25–80
Brute Force	1947	OS	500–800
Buck Privates	1941	OS	800–1,200
Buck Privates Come Home	1947	OS	300–450
Buck Rogers in the 25th Century	1979	OS	50–80
Bucket of Blood	1959	OS	60–125
Buddy Holly Story	1978	OS	40–80
Buffalo Bill	1944	OS	250–500
Buffalo Bill and the Indians	1976	OS	40–80
Bug	1975	OS	40–60
Bugsy	1991	OS	40–60
Bull Durham	1986	OS	40–80
Bullet for a Badman	1964	OS	50–200
Bullitt	1968	OS	400–700
Bunny Lake Is Missing	1965	OS	150–400
Burglar	1957	OS	70–150
Burn Witch Burn	1962	OS	60–150
Burning Hills	1956	OS	50–125
Burnt Offerings	1976	OS	40–80
Bus Riley's Back in Town	1965	OS	50–80
Bus Stop	1956	OS	500–800
Bus Stop	1956	LC SET	400–700
Bustin' Loose	1981	OS	40–60
But Not for Me	1959	OS	60–150
Butch Cassidy	1969	OS	200–450
Butch Cassidy	1969	LC SET	300–450
Butterfield 8	1960	OS	200–350
Bwana Devil	1952	OS	125–325
By Love Possessed	1961	OS	50–80
Bye Bye Birdie	1963	OS	50–175

TITLE	YEAR	SIZE	PRICE RANGE
Cabaret	1972	OS	75–300
Cabaret	1972	LC SET	75–300
Cabinet of Dr. Caligari	1921	OS	25–80
Cactus Flower	1969	OS	40–75
Caddy	1953	OS	400–650
Caddyshack	1980	OS	50–125
Caesar and Cleopatra	1946	OS	700–1,500
Cafe Metropole	1937	OS	300–500
Cage Aux Folles	1980	OS	25–60
Caged	1950	OS	75–125
Cahill U.S. Marshall	1973	OS	50–125
Caine Mutiny	1954	OS	150–450
Calamity Jane	1953	OS	250–850
Calcutta	1947	OS	500–1,250
California Suite	1978	OS	25–60
Caligula	1980	OS	40–90
Call It Murder	R 1946	OS	200–375
Call Me Bwana	1963	OS	25–60
Call Me Madam	1953	OS	60–150
Call Me Mister	1951	OS	50–90
Call Northside 777	1948	OS	400–700
Call of the Wild	1935	OS	4,000–6,000
Calling Bulldog Drummond	1951	OS	50–90
Calling Dr. Death	1943	OS	150–500
Caltiki	1960	OS	75–275
Camelot	1967	OS	300–550
Camelot	1967	LC SET	200–350
Cameraman	1928	OS	10,500
Cameraman	1928	LC	700–1,500
Camille	1936	OS	700–1,500
Can Can	1960	OS	50–90
Can't Stop the Music	1980	OS	25–70
Canary Murder Case	1929	OS	15,000–22,000
Candidate	1972	OS	60–90
Candleshoe	1977	OS	25–60
Candy	1968	OS	50–150
Cannonball Run	1981	OS	25–60
Cape Fear	1962	OS	150–500

C

C

TITLE	YEAR	SIZE	PRICE RANGE
Cape Fear	1962	LC SET	150–275
Cape Fear	1990	OS	40–125
Capone	1975	OS	25–65
Caprice	1967	OS	25–50
Captain Apache	1971	OS	25–50
Captain Blood	1935	OS	5,000–11,000
Captain Carey USA	1949	OS	125–300
Captain from Castile	1947	OS	125–500
Captain Horatio Hornblower	1951	OS	75–400
Captain January	1936	OS	1,100–2,500
Captain Kronos Vampire Hunter	1973	OS	40–100
Captain Sinbad	1963	OS	35–60
Captains Courageous	1937	OS	750–1,250
Captains of the Clouds	1942	OS	200–500
Captive City	1952	OS	25–50
Captive Wild Woman	1943	OS	850–1,250
Capture	1950	OS	50–150
Car	1977	OS	30–60
Car Wash	1976	OS	50–60
Carbine Williams	1952	OS	50–125
Cardinal	1964	OS	50–175
Career	1959	OS	30–70
Career Girl	1943	OS	50–70
Carefree	1938	OS	1,700–2,750
Caretakers	1963	OS	25–60
Carmen Jones	1954	OS	500–800
Carnal Knowledge	1971	OS	50–90
Carnal Knowledge	1971	LC SET	30–90
Carnival Rock	1957	OS	30–90
Carny	1980	OS	25–60
Carpetbaggers	1964	OS	25–70
Carrie	1952	OS	75–175
Carrie	1976	OS	40–150
Carrie	1976	LC SET	100–175
Casablanca	1942	OS	7,000–17,000
Casablanca	R 1949	OS	1,000–2,200
Casino	1995	OS	40–90
Casino Royale	1967	OS	100–375

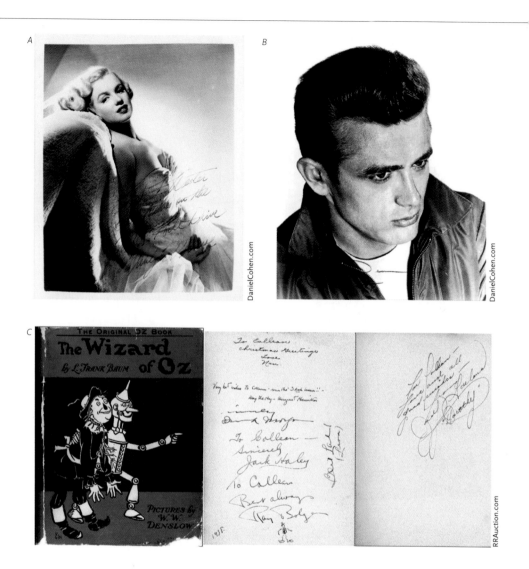

A. *A vintage sepia-toned photograph ca. 1951 signed and inscribed by Marilyn Monroe. July 2001, $9,800.*

B. *A vintage sepia-toned close-up fan club promotional photograph signed by James Dean. June 1999, $7,000.*

C. *A 1903 edition of* **The Wizard of Oz** *by L. Frank Baum which has been boldly inscribed and signed by all six main cast members of the 1939 classic film. Signed for Louis B. Mayer's secretary as a Christmas gift to her niece. July 2000, $49,306.*

D

E

D. *Burgundy silk dress with black chiffon worn by Kate Winslet as Rose DeWitt Bukater in the 1997 film* **Titanic.** *December 2002, $14,040.*

E. *Complete screen-worn Battle of Carthage uniform from the 2000 film* **Gladiator.** *July 2002 $1,884.*

F

G

H

F Tan military officer's jacket worn by Frank Sinatra as Bennett Marco in the 1962 film **The Manchurian Candidate.** *December 2001, $6,484.*

G, H Green tiger stripe camouflage shirt worn by John Wayne as Colonel Mike Kirby in the 1968 film **The Green Berets.** *December 2001, $4,428.*

DanielCohen.com

DanielCohen.com

DanielCohen.com

DanielCohen.com

I   An original movie poster signed by 12 cast members from **Saving Private Ryan**. *December 2002, $1,710.*

J   A photograph of the movie poster signed by 12 cast members from **The Lord of the Rings**. *March 2002, $2,000.*

K   An original shooting script, Fourth Draft, dated 1/1/76 with original blue binder and decal labeled "The Star Wars." *April 2001, $4,000.*

L   An original movie poster signed by five cast members from **A Beautiful Mind**. *October 2002, $860.*

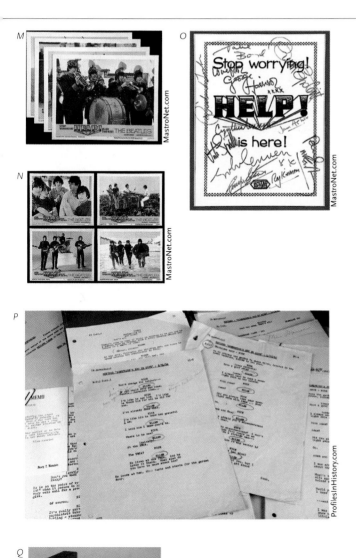

M, N Complete set of eight lobby cards for the 1965 film **Help!** *April 2002, $1,595.*

O A program from the world premiere of the 1965 film **Help!** *signed by all four Beatles plus seven others. April 2002, $9,882.*

P, Q Personal script belonging to Marilyn Monroe from her final, unfinished film, 1962's **Something's Got to Give.** *(Profiles in History.com) Estimate $20,000–$30,000.*

The following posters have set all-time record high prices at established auction houses:

R **The Mummy** *(1932), U.S.A., one-sheet (March 1997, Sotheby's) $453,500.(#1)*

S **Metropolis** *(1926), German, 41 x 81 (October 2000, Sotheby's) $357,750. (#2)*

T **King Kong** *(1933), U.S.A., 41 x 81, Style A (April 1999, Sotheby's) $244,500. (#3)*

U **Frankenstein** *(1931), U.S.A., one-sheet (October 1993, Odyssey) $198,000. (#5)*

V **Men in Black** *(1934), U.S.A., one-sheet (April 1998, Sotheby's) $109,750. (#8)*

W **King Kong** *(1933), U.S.A., one-sheet, Style B (December 1994, Christie's) $98,900. (#9)*

Poster images and statistics courtesy of PosterPrice.com

The following posters have set all-time record high prices at established auction houses:

X Play Ball *(1929), U.S.A., one-sheet (April 1999, Sotheby's) $96,000. (#10)*

Y *Three* Little Pigskins *(1934), U.S.A., one-sheet (April 1999, Sotheby's) $96,000. (#11)*

Z Three Little Pigskins *(1934), U.S.A., one-sheet (April 1999, Sotheby's) $96,000. (#12)*

AA Casablanca *(1942), French, 32 x 47 (March 2000, Christie's) $86,608. (#13)*

Poster images and statistics courtesy of PosterPrice.com

MastroNet.com

BB

CC

DD

EE

BB *An original Courvoisier presenta-*
tion of an original animation cel
from the 1937 film **Snow White**
and the Seven Dwarfs. *April*
2002, $7,139.

CC *An original Courvoisier presenta-*
tion of an original animation cel
from the 1938 film **The Brave**
Little Tailor. *April 2002, $3,025.*

DD *Original Walt Disney blue pencil*
sketch of Mickey Mouse with
inscription and autograph. April
2002, $9,777.

EE *An original Courvoisier presenta-*
tion of an original
animation cel from the 1938 film
The Brave Little Tailor. *April*
2002, $3,328.

8

TITLE	YEAR	SIZE	PRICE RANGE
Casino Royale	1967	LC SET	100–175
Cast a Giant Shadow	1966	OS	40–80
Cat Ballou	1965	OS	75–125
Cat Girl	1957	OS	100–300
Cat O' Nine Tails	1971	OS	25–60
Cat on a Hot Tin Roof	1958	OS	500–1,450
Cat People	1982	OS	40–80
Cat Women of the Moon	1954	OS	200–600
Catch-22	1970	OS	40–175
Catered Affair	1956	OS	40–80
Chad Hanna	1940	OS	150–375
Chain Lightning	1949	OS	200–475
Chalk Garden	1964	OS	40–70
Chamber of Horrors	1966	OS	40–80
Champ	1931	OS	1,500–2,000
Champ	1979	OS	20–60
Champion	1949	OS	125–300
Change of Habit	1969	OS	50–175
Chaplin	1992	OS	50–90
Chapman Report	1962	OS	50–80
Charade	1963	OS	200–575
Charade	1963	LC SET	250–450
Charge of the Light Brigade	1936	OS	400–1,000
Charge of the Light Brigade	1968	OS	40–70
Chariots of Fire	1981	OS	25–70
Charlie Chan at the Wax Museum	1940	OS	300–700
Charlie Chan in London	1934	OS	4,000–7,500
Charlie Chan in Reno	1939	OS	500–850
Charlie McCarthy, Detective	1939	OS	150–500
Charlotte's Web	1972	OS	30–75
Charro	1969	OS	60–150
Charro	1969	LC SET	100–225
Chase	1966	OS	50–90
Cheech and Chong's Next Movie	1980	OS	25–50
Cheech and Chong's Nice Dreams	1981	OS	25–40
Cheers for Miss Bishop	1941	OS	40–80
Cherry Harry and Raquel	1969	OS	40–100
Cheyenne Autumn	1964	OS	50–70

C

C

TITLE	YEAR	SIZE	PRICE RANGE
Cheyenne Social Club	1970	OS	30–70
Child Is Waiting	1963	OS	40–80
Children of the Damned	1964	OS	40–90
Children's Hour	1962	OS	50–175
China Doll	1958	OS	40–80
China Girl	1942	OS	700–1,400
China Syndrome	1979	OS	40–60
Chinatown	1974	OS	200–750
Chinatown	1974	LC SET	250–350
Chinese Connection	1973	OS	100–275
Chinoise	1967	47 × 63 FRE	250–350
Chisum	1970	OS	60–275
Chitty Chitty Bang Bang	1969	OS	40–80
Christine	1983	OS	40–80
Christine	1983	LC SET	40–70
Christmas Carol	1938	OS	400–750
Christmas Carol	1951	OS	60–150
Christmas Eve	1947	OS	75–275
Christmas Holiday	1944	OS	200–475
Christmas Story	1983	OS	50–80
Cimarron	1960	OS	40–80
Cincinnati Kid	1965	OS	50–200
Cinderella	1950	OS	225–500
Cinderella	R 1957	OS	60–125
Cinderella	R 1973	OS	60–90
Cinderfella	1960	OS	50–175
Cinderfella	1960	LC SET	50–100
Cinema Paradiso	1989	OS	50–80
Circus	1928	OS	15,000
Circus of Horrors	1960	OS	50–125
Circus World	1964	OS	50–150
Citizen Kane	1941	OS	7,000–10,000
Citizen Kane	R 1954	OS	1,000–2,000
City Heat	1984	OS	40–60
City Lights	1931	OS	20,000–25,000
City Lights	R 1950	OS	75–200
City Lights	R 1950	LC SET	200–350
City That Never Sleeps	1953	OS	200–600

TITLE	YEAR	SIZE	PRICE RANGE
Clambake	1967	OS	100–250
Clambake	1967	LC SET	100–150
Clash by Night	1952	OS	150–400
Clash of the Titans	1980	OS	40–70
Clash of the Titans	1980	LC SET	30–90
Cleopatra	1917	OS	1,500–4,000
Cleopatra	1934	OS	4,000–6,500
Cleopatra	R 1952	OS	100–300
Cleopatra	1963	OS	250–1,000
Cleopatra	1963	LC SET	250–650
Cleopatra Jones	1973	OS	50–140
Cloak and Dagger	1946	OS	150–525
Clock	1945	OS	550–900
Clockwork Orange	1971	OS	150–450
Clockwork Orange	1971	LC SET	100–500
Clockwork Orange	R 1982	OS	60–200
Close Encounters	1977	OS	50–125
Close Encounters	1977	LC SET	50–90
Clown	1953	OS	80–140
Cocoon	1985	OS	40–60
College Confidential	1960	OS	40–80
Color of Money	1986	OS	50–90
Color Purple	1985	OS	50–125
Colorado Territory	1949	OS	50–250
Colossus of New York	1958	OS	200–550
Colossus of Rhodes	1960	OS	40–70
Coma	1977	OS	40–60
Comancheros	1961	OS	125–300
Combat America	1944	OS	125–300
Come Back Little Sheba	1952	OS	80–150
Come Blow Your Horn	1963	OS	40–70
Come Dance with Me	1960	OS	80–150
Come Fill the Cup	1951	OS	75–150
Come Fly with Me	1963	OS	40–70
Come Live with Me	1941	OS	300–550
Come September	1961	OS	75–120
Comedians	1967	OS	50–120
Comedy of Terrors	1964	OS	75–325

C

C

TITLE	YEAR	SIZE	PRICE RANGE
Coming Home	1978	OS	25–80
Coming to America	1988	OS	40–60
Command Decision	1948	OS	75–200
Commando	1985	OS	40–70
Commandos Strike at Dawn	1942	OS	50–175
Company of Wolves	1984	OS	40–70
Company She Keeps	1950	OS	50–175
Compulsion	1959	OS	75–175
Comrade X	1940	22 × 28	700–1,000
Comrade X	1940	LC SET	750–1,400
Conan the Barbarian	1982	OS	75–125
Conan the Barbarian	1982	LC SET	50–150
Conan the Destroyer	1984	OS	40–70
Conan the Destroyer	1984	LC SET	50–80
Concert for Bangladesh	1972	OS	50–125
Condemned of Altona	1962	OS	25–50
Coney Island	1943	OS	250–500
Confession	1937	OS	400–750
Confidentially Connie	1953	OS	50–90
Conflict	1945	OS	300–550
Conqueror	1956	OS	50–150
Conqueror Worm	1968	OS	40–70
Conquest of Space	1954	OS	300–450
Conquest of the Planet of the Apes	1972	OS	50–200
Conquest of the Planet of the Apes	1972	LC SET	50–125
Conspirator	1949	OS	300–500
Conspirators	1944	OS	225–700
Contact	1997	OS	50–80
Contact	1997	OS	40–80
Contempt	1963	47 × 63 FRE	800–1,700
Conversation	1974	OS	60–175
Coogan's Bluff	1968	OS	50–180
Cool Hand Luke	1967	OS	300–1,200
Corn Is Green	1945	OS	200–375
Cornered	1945	OS	200–500
Corridors of Blood	1962	OS	40–80
Corruption	1968	OS	50–80
Cosmic Monsters	1958	OS	70–200

TITLE	YEAR	SIZE	PRICE RANGE
Cotton Club	1984	OS	40–120
Count	1916	LC	300–600
Count of Monte Cristo	1934	OS	500–900
Count of Monte Cristo	1962	OS	40–70
Countdown	1962	OS	40–70
Countess from Hong Kong	1967	OS	40–70
Country Girl	1954	OS	70–175
County Chairman	1935	OS	200–475
Court Jester	1956	OS	75–200
Court Martial of Billy Mitchell	1956	OS	50–250
Courtship of Eddie's Father	1963	OS	40–80
Cover Girl	1944	OS	400–800
Cowboy and the Lady	1938	OS	800–1,500
Cowboys	1972	OS	50–150
Crack in the Mirror	1960	OS	40–70
Crash Dive	1943	OS	350–750
Crawling Eye	1958	OS	75–200
Creature from the Black Lagoon	1954	OS	6,500–12,500
Creature from the Black Lagoon	1954	LC SET	2,000–3,500
Creature from the Black Lagoon	R 1972	OS	100–350
Creature from the Haunted Sea	1961	OS	50–125
Creature Walks among Us	1956	OS	500–1,150
Creature Walks among Us	1956	LC SET	900–1,100
Creature with Atom Brain	1955	OS	80–150
Creature with Atom Brain	1955	LC SET	100–300
Creeping Flesh	1972	OS	40–80
Creeping Unknown	1956	OS	75–200
Creepshow	1982	OS	40–90
Crime in the Streets	1956	OS	60–175
Crime School	1938	OS	5,000–9,000
Crimes and Misdemeanors	1989	OS	40–70
Crimson Cult	1968	OS	40–90
Crimson Pirate	1952	OS	75–400
Crisis	1950	OS	50–80
Criss Cross	1949	OS	500–1,200
Critic's Choice	1963	OS	50–80
Crocodile Dundee	1986	OS	40–60
Cross of Iron	1977	OS	40–80

C

C

TITLE	YEAR	SIZE	PRICE RANGE
Cross of Iron	1977	LC SET	50–90
Crossed Swords	1953	OS	70–300
Crossfire	1947	OS	500–1,000
Crouching Tiger, Hidden Dragon	2000	OS	40–80
Crow	1994	OS	50–125
Crowded Sky	1960	OS	50–80
Cruising	1980	OS	40–80
Cruising	1980	LC SET	40–80
Crusades	1935	OS	250–400
Cry Baby	1989	OS	40–80
Cry Baby Killer	1958	OS	70–250
Cry Danger	1950	OS	240–400
Cry of the City	1948	OS	500–800
Cry of the Werewolf	1944	OS	500–850
Cry Wolf	1947	OS	150–450
Cuba	1979	OS	40–90
Cujo	1983	OS	25–90
Cul-de-sac	1966	47 × 63 FRE	200–325
Cult of the Cobra	1955	OS	50–325
Curly Top	1935	OS	2,000–3,250
Curse of Frankenstein	1957	OS	150–400
Curse of Frankenstein	1957	LC SET	250–400
Curse of the Cat People	1944	OS	700–1,400
Curse of the Demon	1958	OS	550–1,200
Curse of the Demon	1958	LC SET	400–750
Curse of the Mummy's Tomb	1964	OS	70–150
Curse of the Undead	1959	OS	50–150
Curse of the Undead	1959	LC SET	100–225
Curse of the Werewolf	1961	OS	300–500
Curse of the Werewolf	1961	LC SET	300–450
Curucu, Beast of the Amazon	1956	OS	250–400
Custer's Last Fight	R 1925	OS	400–800
Cycle Savages	1970	OS	40–80
Cyclops	1957	OS	75–225
Cyclops	1957	LC SET	75–325
Cynthia	1947	OS	225–500
Cyrano de Bergerac	1950	OS	70–125
D-Day 6th of June	1956	OS	30–70

TITLE	YEAR	SIZE	PRICE RANGE
D I	1957	OS	50–175
Daddy Long Legs	1955	OS	100–250
Daisy Kenyon	1947	OS	250–400
Dakota Kid	1951	OS	25–75
Damien: Omen 2	1978	OS	30–70
Damn the Defiant	1962	OS	30–70
Damn Yankees	1958	OS	75–175
Damnation Alley	1977	OS	25–60
Damned	1970	OS	30–70
Damsel in Distress	1937	OS	1,500–2,700
Dances with Wolves	1990	OS	30–125
Dancing in the Dark	1949	OS	60–200
Danger Diabolik	1968	OS	50–200
Dangerous	1936	OS	7,000–9,000
Dangerous Liaisons	1988	OS	50–60
Dangerous Profession	1949	OS	50–175
Dangerous When Wet	1953	OS	50–150
Dante's Inferno	1935	OS	1,000–2,200
Dark City	1950	OS	200–450
Dark Crystal	1982	OS	25–60
Dark Passage	1947	OS	1,000–2,250
Dark Past	1948	OS	150–425
Dark Places	1974	OS	25–60
Dark Victory	1939	OS	7,000–10,000
Darkest Africa	1936	OS	1,000–2,200
Darling	1965	OS	50–150
Darling Lili	1970	OS	50–175
Das Boot	1982	OS	25–70
Das Boot	1982	23 × 33 GER	50–275
Date with the Falcon	1941	OS	250–350
Daughter of Dr. Jekyll	1957	OS	70–325
David and Goliath	1961	OS	40–70
David Copperfield	1935	OS	800–1,700
David Copperfield	R 1962	OS	50–80
Davy Crockett	1941	OS	400–700
Davy Crockett King of the Wild	1955	OS	250–600
Davy Crockett King of the Wild	1955	LC SET	400–750
Dawn of the Dead	1979	OS	40–150

D

TITLE	YEAR	SIZE	PRICE RANGE
Dawn Patrol	1938	OS	1,000–2,500
Day at the Races	1937	OS	7,000–10,000
Day at the Races	R 1952	OS	200–750
Day for Night	1973	OS	50–150
Day Mars Invaded Earth	1963	OS	50–225
Day of the Dead	1985	OS	30–70
Day of the Jackal	1973	OS	50–70
Day of the Locust	1974	OS	50–100
Day of the Triffids	1963	OS	150–600
Day of the Triffids	1963	LC SET	150–500
Day the Earth Caught Fire	1962	OS	50–125
Day the Earth Stood Still	1951	OS	4,000–7,000
Day the World Ended	1955	OS	300–550
Days of Heaven	1978	OS	125–300
Days of Thrills and Laughter	1961	OS	25–90
Days of Thunder	1990	OS	50–90
Days of Wine and Roses	1963	OS	50–150
Dead Calm	1989	OS	50–100
Dead End	1937	OS	1,500–3,000
Dead Heat on a Merry-Go-Round	1966	OS	25–60
Dead Men Don't Wear Plaid	1981	OS	25–70
Dead Pool	1988	OS	25–60
Dead Reckoning	1947	OS	1,000–2,200
Dead Ringer	1964	OS	50–125
Dead Ringers	1988	OS	50–80
Dead Zone	1983	OS	40–90
Dead Zone	1983	LC SET	50–100
Deadlier Than the Male	1967	OS	50–80
Deadline at Dawn	1946	OS	200–600
Deadline USA	1952	OS	100–275
Deadly Bees	1967	OS	40–70
Deadly Mantis	1957	OS	200–600
Deadly Mantis	1957	LC SET	300–575
Dear Brigitte	1965	OS	40–70
Dear Ruth	1947	OS	50–125
Death Hunt	1981	OS	25–50
Death in Small Doses	1957	OS	40–70
Death in Venice	1971	OS	50–225

D

TITLE	YEAR	SIZE	PRICE RANGE
Death on the Nile	1978	OS	25–60
Death Race 2000	1975	OS	50–125
Death Wish	1974	OS	30–150
Death Wish	1974	LC SET	50–150
Death Wish 2	1981	OS	25–50
Death Wish 3	1985	OS	25–50
Death Wish 4	1987	OS	25–50
Debbie Does Dallas	1980	OS	50–100
Debtor to the Law	1922	OS	1,000–2,200
Deception	1946	OS	200–500
Decks Ran Red	1958	OS	50–125
Deep	1977	OS	40–90
Deep	1977	LC SET	50–125
Deep in My Heart	1954	OS	50–250
Deep Red	1975	OS	75–175
Deep Red	1975	39 × 55 ITA	150–250
Deep Throat	1974	OS	500–1,000
Deep Valley	1947	OS	50–175
Deep Waters	1948	OS	75–150
Deer Hunter	1978	OS	75–200
Deer Hunter	1978	LC SET	50–150
Defiant Ones	1958	OS	75–200
Delicate Delinquent	1957	OS	40–90
Delicatessen	1991	23 × 33 GER	25–75
Delinquents	1957	OS	60–125
Deliverance	1972	OS	50–150
Deliverance	1972	LC SET	50–125
Dementia 13	1963	OS	50–150
Dementia 13	1963	LC SET	50–200
Demon Seed	1977	OS	25–60
Desert Fox	1951	OS	75–200
Desert Fury	1947	OS	250–400
Desert Fury	R 1958	OS	50–150
Desert Legion	1953	OS	40–90
Desert Rats	1953	OS	50–125
Designing Women	1957	OS	40–125
Desire	1936	OS	5,000–7,000
Desire in the Dust	1960	OS	40–70

D

TITLE	YEAR	SIZE	PRICE RANGE
Desire Me	1947	OS	150–550
Desirée	1954	OS	100–250
Desirée	1954	LC SET	100–175
Desk Set	1957	OS	100–350
Desk Set	1957	LC SET	150–225
Desperate	1947	OS	75–150
Desperate Hours	1955	OS	150–450
Desperate Hours	1955	LC SET	50–175
Desperate Journey	1942	OS	300–450
Desperately Seeking Susan	1984	OS	40–70
Desperately Seeking Susan	1984	LC SET	40–90
Destination Earth	1950	OS	600–900
Destination Tokyo	1943	OS	250–450
Destination Unknown	1933	OS	300–450
Destroy All Monsters	1969	OS	125–300
Destroy All Monsters	1969	LC SET	150–300
Destry Rides Again	1939	OS	1,500–2,000
Detective	1968	OS	50–110
Detective Story	1951	OS	50–175
Detour	1945	OS	1,500–2,750
Devil and Miss Jones	1941	OS	250–400
Devil at 4 O'Clock	1961	OS	40–90
Devil Bat	1941	OS	700–1000
Devil Commands	1941	OS	750–1500
Devil Dogs of the Air	1935	OS	2,000–2,500
Devil Doll	1964	OS	30–80
Devil Girl from Mars	1954	OS	800–1,400
Devil Is a Woman	1935	OS	20,000–40,000
Devil Is a Woman	1935	LC SET	5,000–7,000
Devil Ship Pirates	1964	OS	40–80
Devil Thumbs a Ride	1947	OS	350–625
Devil Within Her	1975	OS	40–70
Devil's Angels	1967	OS	50–80
Devil's Bride	1968	OS	60–175
Devil's Daffodil	1961	OS	60–90
Devil's Disciple	1959	OS	60–90
Devil's Hairpin	1957	OS	50–100
Devil's Hand	1961	OS	40–70

180 Battleship Potemkin *(1925)*

181 The Birth of a Nation *(1915)*

182 The Bride of Frankenstein
(1935)

183 The Cabinet of Dr. Caligari
(1921)

D

TITLE	YEAR	SIZE	PRICE RANGE
Devil's Pass Key	1920	OS	2,000–4,000
Devil's Rain	1975	OS	40–80
Devils	1971	OS	40–70
Devotion	1946	OS	50–90
Diaboliques	1955	47 × 63 FRE	1,200–3,750
Dial 1119	1950	OS	40–70
Dial M for Murder	1954	OS	800–3,000
Dial M for Murder	1954	LC SET	400–750
Diamond Head	1962	OS	40–80
Diamond Horseshoe	1945	OS	300–650
Diamond Queen	1953	OS	350–550
Diamonds Are Forever	1971	OS	200–650
Diamonds Are Forever	1971	LC SET	125–300
Diane	1955	OS	40–90
Diary of a Madman	1963	OS	40–70
Diary of a Madman	1963	LC SET	60–90
Diary of Anne Frank	1959	OS	40–100
Dick Tracy	1937	OS	600–900
Dick Tracy	1945	OS	200–300
Dick Tracy	1990	OS	70–125
Dick Tracy Meets Gruesome	1947	OS	200–550
Dick Tracy Meets Gruesome	1947	LC SET	80–150
Dick Tracy Vs. Crime Inc	1941	OS	300–600
Dick Tracy Vs. Cueball	1946	OS	200–500
Dick Tracy Vs. Phantom Empire	1943	OS	75–200
Dick Tracy Vs. Phantom Empire	R 1952	OS	70–150
Die Hard	1988	OS	40–150
Die Hard 2	1990	OS	40–70
Die Monster Die	1965	OS	60–120
Die Monster Die	1965	LC SET	60–150
Dig That Uranium	1955	OS	30–70
Dillinger	1945	OS	200–550
Dillinger	1973	OS	30–80
Dimples	1936	OS	2,500–4,000
Diner	1982	OS	50–125
Dinner at 8	1933	OS	11,500
Dinner at 8	R 1962	OS	60–90
Dino	1957	OS	60–100

D

TITLE	YEAR	SIZE	PRICE RANGE
Dinosaur	2000	OS	40–80
Dinosaur	2000	LC SET	60–125
Dinosaurus	1960	OS	90–275
Dinosaurus	1960	LC SET	100–225
Diplomatic Courier	1952	OS	40–200
Dirty Dancing	1987	OS	40–80
Dirty Dancing	1987	LC SET	40–80
Dirty Dozen	1967	OS	150–500
Dirty Dozen	1967	LC SET	40–90
Dirty Dozen	R 1973	OS	40–70
Dirty Harry	1971	OS	300–800
Dirty Harry	1971	LC SET	400–700
Dirty Mary Crazy Larry	1974	OS	50–150
Dirty Mingus Magee	1970	OS	40–70
Dirty Rotten Scoundrels	1988	OS	30–60
Discreet Charm of Bourgeosie	1972	OS	60–125
Dishonored Lady	1947	OS	400–800
Disneyland USA	1957	OS	70–225
Disorderly Orderly	1964	OS	40–70
Disputed Passage	1939	OS	225–400
Distant Drums	1951	OS	40–70
Dive Bomber	1941	OS	125–600
Divine Madness	1980	OS	30–60
Divorce American Style	1967	OS	25–50
Dixie	1943	OS	100–250
Django	1966	23 × 33 GER	300–700
Do Not Disturb	1965	OS	40–60
Do the Right Thing	1989	OS	40–70
Do You Love Me	1946	OS	125–300
D.O.A.	1950	OS	600–1,100
D.O.A. (documentary)	1980	OS	70–100
Doc	1971	OS	40–80
Doc Savage	1975	OS	40–80
Doc Savage	1975	LC SET	60–100
Docks of San Francisco	1932	OS	100–300
Doctor and the Girl	1949	OS	40–80
Dr. Blood's Coffin	1961	OS	40–90
Dr. Blood's Coffin	1961	LC SET	40–90

D

TITLE	YEAR	SIZE	PRICE RANGE
Dr. Cyclops	1940	OS	1,000–1,500
Dr. Dolittle	1969	OS	40–80
Dr. Goldfoot and the Girl Bombs	1966	OS	30–70
Dr. Goldfoot and the Girl Bombs	1966	LC SET	60–90
Dr. Goldfoot and the Bikini Machine	1965	OS	30–70
Dr. Jekyll and Mr. Hyde	1920	41 × 81	24,000
Dr. Jekyll and Mr. Hyde	1932	OS	35,000
Dr. Jekyll and Mr. Hyde	1941	OS	600–1,500
Dr. Jekyll and Sister Hyde	1972	OS	60–125
Dr. No	1962	OS	700–2,000
Dr. Phibes Rises Again	1972	OS	40–120
Dr. Strangelove	1964	OS	250–1,000
Dr. Strangelove	1964	LC SET	250–400
Dr. Strangelove	R 1972	OS	150–300
Dr. Terror's House of Horrors	1965	OS	30–70
Dr. Who and the Daleks	1965	OS	30–90
Dr. Who and the Daleks	1965	LC SET	40–80
Doctor X	1932	OS	7,500–10,000
Dr. Zhivago	1965	OS	150–400
Dr. Zhivago	1965	LC SET	150–225
Dodge City	1939	OS	2,000–4,000
Dog Day Afternoon	1975	OS	50–250
Dog's Life	1918	OS	25,000–30,000
Dogs of War	1980	OS	30–60
Dogs of War	1980	LC SET	40–70
Dolce Vita	1960	OS	150–700
Dolemite	1975	OS	100–175
Doll Face	1945	OS	70–125
Dolly Sisters	1945	OS	400–800
Don Q Son of Zorro	1925	OS	2,000–3,000
Don't Bother to Knock	1952	OS	500–2,000
Don't Knock the Rock	1957	OS	200–400
Don't Knock the Twist	1962	OS	40–80
Don't Look Back	1967	OS	500–1,500
Don't Look Now	1973	OS	40–80
Donovan's Brain	1953	OS	100–225
Donovan's Reef	1963	OS	60–175

TITLE	YEAR	SIZE	PRICE RANGE
Doors	1991	OS	40–70
Doors	1991	LC SET	40–80
Double Dynamite	1951	OS	175–300
Double Indemnity	1944	OS	2,000–4,000
Double Life	1947	OS	125–350
Double Trouble	1967	OS	100–350
Doulos	1963	47 × 63 FRE	400–700
Down Three Dark Streets	1954	OS	50–325
Down to Earth	1947	OS	500–1,150
Downhill Racer	1969	OS	150–625
Downhill Racer	1969	LC SET	75–150
Dracula	1931	OS	75,000–80,000
Dracula	1979	OS	50–90
Dracula A.D. 1972	1972	OS	75–150
Dracula—Bram Stoker's	1992	OS	40–70
Dracula—Bram Stoker's	1992	LC SET	40–80
Dracula Has Risen from Grave	1968	OS	60–150
Dracula Prince of Darkness	1966	OS	70–200
Dracula Vs. Frankenstein	1971	OS	50–125
Dracula's Daughter	1936	22 × 28	4,000–6,000
Dracula's Daughter	R 1949	OS	500–750
Dragnet	1954	OS	100–375
Dragon Seed	1944	OS	125–275
Dragonslayer	1981	OS	40–70
Dragonwyck	1946	OS	225–500
Dragstrip Girl	1957	OS	150–400
Dragstrip Riot	1958	OS	250–600
Dragstrip Riot	1958	LC SET	125–225
Draughtman's Contract	1982	OS	50–90
Dream Wife	1953	OS	70–125
Dressed to Kill	1980	OS	30–90
Dressed to Kill	1980	LC SET	40–70
Driving Miss Daisy	1986	OS	40–90
Drowning Pool	1975	OS	40–70
Drugstore Cowboy	1989	OS	40–70
Drum	1976	OS	40–80
Drums of Africa	1963	OS	40–70
Du Barry Was a Lady	1943	OS	200–400

D

D

TITLE	YEAR	SIZE	PRICE RANGE
Duck Soup	1933	OS	9,000–11,000
Duck You Sucker	1972	OS	70–100
Duel	1972	OS	60–200
Duel at Diablo	1966	OS	40–70
Duel in the Sun	1946	OS	150–300
Duel of the Titans	1963	OS	40–80
Duellists	1977	OS	30–60
Dumbo	1941	OS	3,500–7,000
Dune	1984	OS	50–100
Dunkirk	1958	OS	40–90
Each Dawn I Die	1939	OS	900–1,700
Eagle	1925	OS	1,000–3,750
Eagle and the Hawk	1933	OS	1,500–2,250
Eagle with Two Heads	1947	47 × 63 FRE	400–700
Earth Dies Screaming	1964	OS	25–60
Earth Dies Screaming	1964	LC SET	40–80
Earth Vs. Flying Saucers	1956	OS	500–1,400
Earthquake	1974	OS	30–80
East of Eden	1955	OS	400–1,200
East of the River	1940	OS	100–250
East Side, West Side	1949	OS	40–80
Easter Parade	1948	OS	650–1,000
Easy Come, Easy Go	1967	OS	50–170
Easy Living	1949	OS	60–120
Easy Rider	1969	OS	250–600
Easy to Love	1953	OS	40–90
Easy to Wed	1946	OS	200–350
Eating Raoul	1982	OS	40–80
Ebony Parade	1947	OS	750–1,200
Ecco	1965	OS	40–70
Ed Wood	1994	OS	40–80
Ed Wood	1994	LC SET	125–175
Eddie and the Cruisers	1982	OS	40–90
Eddy Duchin Story	1956	OS	50–125
Edge of Darkness	1943	OS	175–400
Edge of the City	1956	OS	75–350
Edward, My Son	1949	OS	40–125
Edward Scissorhands	1990	OS	40–70

E

TITLE	YEAR	SIZE	PRICE RANGE
Egg and I	1947	OS	90–250
Egyptian	1954	OS	200–550
Eiger Sanction	1975	OS	40–90
8 ½	1963	OS	175–250
18 and Anxious	1957	OS	40–80
El Cid	1961	OS	40–70
El Condor	1970	OS	40–70
El Dorado	1966	OS	75–325
El Dorado	1966	LC SET	250–400
Electra Glide in Blue	1973	OS	40–90
Electric Horseman	1979	OS	40–60
Electronic Monster	1960	OS	40–90
Electronic Monster	1960	LC SET	40–125
Elephant Boy	1937	OS	900–1,400
Elephant Man	1980	OS	40–90
Elmer Gantry	1960	OS	80–125
Elmer Gantry	1960	LC SET	90–225
Elvis	1979	OS	100–300
Elvis on Tour	1972	OS	125–350
Elvis: That's the Way It Is	1970	OS	125–300
Embryo	1976	OS	40–80
Emmanuelle	1975	OS	70–190
Emperor of the North	1973	OS	40–70
Empire of the Ants	1977	OS	40–70
Empire of the Sun	1987	OS	40–70
Empire of the Sun	1987	LC SET	30–70
Empire Strikes Back	1980	OS	150–600
Empire Strikes Back	1980	LC SET	100–400
Empire Strikes Back	R 1981	OS	125–300
Empire Strikes Back	R 1982	OS	25–100
Empty Saddles	1936	OS	800–1,200
Enchanted Cottage	1945	OS	60–100
End of the Affair	1955	OS	40–80
Endless Love	1981	OS	40–70
Endless Love	1981	LC SET	40–60
Endless Summer	1966	OS	450–650
Enemy Below	1957	OS	50–80
Enemy from Space	1957	OS	70–125

E

TITLE	YEAR	SIZE	PRICE RANGE
Enforcer	1951	OS	400–700
Enforcer	1976	OS	60–150
Enforcer	1976	LC SET	125–200
English Patient	1996	OS	40–70
Enter the Dragon	1973	OS	125–650
Enter the Dragon	1973	LC SET	125–300
Enter the Dragon	R 1977	OS	100–200
Equus	1977	OS	40–70
Eraserhead	1978	OS	80–150
Errand Boy	1962	OS	40–70
Escape	1940	OS	400–650
Escape from Alcatraz	1979	OS	40–90
Escape from Alcatraz	1979	LC SET	50–150
Escape from Fort Bravo	1953	OS	50–90
Escape from New York	1981	OS	60–150
Escape from New York	1981	LC SET	80–150
Escape from the Planet of the Apes	1971	OS	50–250
Escape from the Planet of the Apes	1971	LC SET	50–150
Escape Me Never	1947	OS	50–250
Escape to Burma	1955	OS	50–80
Esther and the King	1960	OS	40–70
E.T. the Extra-Terrestrial	1982	OS	70–150
E.T. (Bike and Moon Style)	1982	OS	600–1,500
Evel Knievel	1971	OS	40–125
Evel Knievel	1971	LC SET	50–100
Every Girl Should Be Married	1948	OS	150–300
Every Which Way but Loose	1978	OS	40–90
Every Which Way but Loose	1978	LC SET	50–90
Everything I Have Is Yours	1952	SIZE	100–225
Everything You Always Wanted....	1972	OS	40–80
Evil Dead	1983	OS	70–150
Evil Dead 2	1987	OS	40–70
Evil Eye	1964	OS	40–80
Evil of Frankenstein	1964	OS	75–350
Evil That Men Do	1984	OS	40–70
Excalibur	1981	OS	50–125
Excalibur	1981	LC SET	50–150
Executive Action	1973	OS	40–70

F

TITLE	YEAR	SIZE	PRICE RANGE
Executive Suite	1954	OS	80–140
Exodus	1960	OS	100–575
Exorcist	1974	OS	75–250
Exorcist	1974	LC SET	100–225
Exorcist 2: The Heretic	1977	OS	30–60
Experiment in Terror	1962	OS	40–90
Explorers	1985	OS	40–70
Explosive Generation	1961	OS	40–70
Eye for an Eye	1966	OS	40–70
Eye of the Cat	1969	OS	40–60
Eye of the Devil	1967	OS	40–70
Eyes of Laura Mars	1978	OS	30–60
Eyes Wide Shut	1999	OS	50–125
Eyewitness	1981	OS	40–60
F for Sake	1973	OS	40–80
Fabulous World of Jules Verne	1961	OS	40–90
Face behind the Mask	1940	OS	300–500
Face in the Crowd	1957	OS	40–90
Face in the Sky	1933	OS	250–500
Face of Fire	1959	OS	40–60
Face of Fu Manchu	1965	OS	50–125
Face Off	1998	OS	40–70
Face to Face	1975	OS	40–70
Faces	1968	OS	125–250
Facts of Life	1961	OS	40–80
Fahrenheit 451	1967	OS	40–90
Fahrenheit 451	1967	47 × 63 FRE	500–750
Falcon in Danger	1943	OS	400–700
Falcon in Mexico	1944	OS	200–300
Falcon in San Francisco	1945	OS	400–525
Falcon's Adventure	1946	OS	125–350
Fall Guy	1947	OS	75–400
Fall of the Roman Empire	1964	OS	50–125
Fallen Angel	1945	OS	225–525
Fallen Sparrow	1943	OS	125–350
False Colors	1943	OS	250–400
Fame	1980	OS	40–70
Fame	1980	LC SET	40–70

F

TITLE	YEAR	SIZE	PRICE RANGE
Family Jewels	1965	OS	40–65
Family Plot	1976	OS	40–80
Family Plot	1976	LC SET	50–90
Fan	1949	OS	50–150
Fancy Pants	1950	OS	70–125
Fanny	1961	OS	50–125
Fanny Hill	1964	OS	40–70
Fantasia	1940	OS	4,000–7,000
Fantasia	1940	LC SET	3,500–5,000
Fantasia	R 1963	OS	40–90
Fantasia 2000	2000	OS	150–225
Fantastic Planet	1973	OS	40–70
Fantastic Plastic Machine	1969	OS	80–125
Fantastic Voyage	1966	OS	60–225
Fantastic Voyage	1966	LC SET	100–225
Fantomas	1964	OS	40–60
Far Country	1955	OS	250–525
Far from the Madding Crowd	1967	OS	40–70
Farewell, My Lovely	1975	OS	50–125
Farewell to Arms	1957	OS	70–125
Fargo	1996	OS	50–150
Farmer Takes a Wife	1953	OS	75–200
Farmer's Daughter	1947	OS	50–200
Fast and Furious	2001	OS	40–60
Fast and Sexy	1960	OS	40–70
Fast Company	1953	OS	40–70
Fast Times at Ridgemont High	1982	OS	40–125
Faster, Pussycat! Kill! Kill!	1966	OS	800–1,225
Fastest Guitar Alive	1967	OS	50–125
Fat City	1972	OS	40–70
Fat Man	1951	OS	40–80
Fat Spy	1965	OS	40–60
Fatal Attraction	1987	OS	40–60
Fatal Hour	1940	OS	150–350
Fate Is the Hunter	1964	OS	40–60
Father Goose	1964	OS	55–195
Father of the Bride	1950	OS	225–350
Father of the Bride	1950	LC SET	200–400

TITLE	YEAR	SIZE	PRICE RANGE
Father of the Bride	R 1962	OS	60–90
Father's Little Dividend	1951	OS	70–225
Fathom	1967	OS	50–125
FBI Girl	1951	OS	50–225
FBI Story	1959	OS	175–500
Fear and Loathing in Las Vegas	1998	OS	50–80
Fear Strikes Out	1957	OS	40–90
Fearless Vampire Killers	1967	OS	40–125
Feathered Serpent	1948	OS	100–275
Female Animal	1958	OS	40–70
Female on the Beach	1955	OS	50–90
Female Trouble	1975	OS	225–400
Femme Nikita	1990	OS	50–150
Ferris Bueller's Day Off	1986	OS	50–70
Ferris Bueller's Day Off	1986	LC SET	40–60
Ferry Cross the Mersey	1965	OS	50–125
Ferry to Hong Kong	1960	OS	50–70
Ffolkes	1980	OS	40–60
Fiddler on the Roof	1972	OS	40–125
Field of Dreams	1989	OS	40–90
Field of Dreams	1989	LC SET	125–175
Fiend Who Walked the West	1958	OS	50–80
Fiend without a Face	1957	OS	200–500
Fiendish Ghouls	1959	OS	50–80
5th Avenue Girl	1939	OS	250–700
Fifth Element	1997	OS	40–70
Fight Club	1999	OS	40–125
Fight Club	1999	LC SET	40–80
Fighting Kentuckian	1949	OS	250–400
Fighting 69th	1940	OS	300–550
Finders Keepers	1966	OS	40–90
Finian's Rainbow	1968	OS	40–70
Fire and Ice	1983	OS	40–70
Fire down Below	1957	OS	70–150
Fire down Below	1957	LC SET	100–200
Fire Maidens from Outer Space	1956	OS	300–700
Fireball 500	1966	OS	70–90
Firefox	1982	OS	40–80

F

F

TITLE	YEAR	SIZE	PRICE RANGE
Firefox	1982	LC SET	40–70
Firestarter	1984	OS	70–100
First Blood	1982	OS	40–100
First Deadly Sin	1980	OS	40–70
First Man into Space	1959	OS	75–150
First Men in the Moon	1964	OS	75–150
First Spaceship on Venus	1960	OS	150–400
First Spaceship on Venus	1960	LC SET	150–300
Fish Called Wanda	1988	OS	40–70
Fisher King	1991	OS	40–70
Fisher King	1991	LC SET	40–70
Fist	1978	OS	40–60
Fistful of Dollars	1964	OS	600–1,500
Fistful of Dollars	1964	LC SET	125–250
Fistful of Dynamite	1971	OS	75–150
Fists of Fury	1972	OS	75–300
Fists of Fury	1972	LC SET	200–300
Fitzcarraldo	1982	23 × 33 GER	75–250
5 Card Stud	1968	OS	40–80
Five Easy Pieces	1970	OS	40–125
Five Easy Pieces	1970	LC SET	40–70
Five Graves to Cairo	1943	OS	400–1,300
Five Million Years to Earth	1967	OS	50–150
5,000 Fingers of Dr. T	1953	OS	150–400
Fixed Bayonets	1951	OS	75–200
Flame and the Arrow	1950	OS	50–150
Flame over India	1960	OS	40–60
Flaming Frontier	1958	OS	40–60
Flaming Star	1960	OS	150–300
Flash Gordon	1936	OS	30,000–50,000
Flash Gordon	1980	OS	50–90
Flash Gordon's Trip to Mars	1938	OS	3,000–6,000
Flashdance	1983	OS	40–70
Flesh	1969	OS	75–200
Flesh Gordon	1974	OS	40–90
Fletch	1985	OS	40–70
Flight of the Phoenix	1966	OS	40–70
Flight of the Phoenix	1966	LC SET	70–100

TITLE	YEAR	SIZE	PRICE RANGE
Flight to Mars	1951	OS	200–400
Flipper	1963	OS	40–60
Flower Drum Song	1961	OS	50–100
Fly	1958	OS	250–550
Fly	1958	LC SET	250–350
Fly	1986	OS	40–80
Fly	1986	LC SET	40–60
Flying Ace	1923	OS	1,000–2,000
Flying Leathernecks	1951	OS	300–700
Flying Missile	1950	OS	40–90
Fog	1979	OS	40–80
Follow Me, Boys!	1966	OS	40–70
Follow Me, Boys!	1966	LC SET	30–50
Follow That Dream	1962	OS	75–225
Follow the Fleet	1936	OS	4,000–6,500
Follow the Sun	1951	OS	150–325
Food of the Gods	1976	OS	25–60
Footlight Parade	1933	OS	36,000
Footlight Serenade	1942	OS	350–700
Footloose	1984	OS	25–60
Footloose	1984	LC SET	40–80
Footprints on the Moon	1969	OS	50–325
For a Few Dollars More	1966	OS	300–1,000
For a Few Dollars More	1966	LC SET	175–300
For Love of Ivy	1968	OS	40–60
For Men Only	1952	OS	40–70
For Pete's Sake	1974	OS	40–60
For the First Time	1959	OS	40–60
For Those Who Think Young	1964	OS	50–90
For Whom the Bell Tolls	1943	OS	500–1,650
For Your Eyes Only	1981	OS	40–100
For Your Eyes Only	1981	LC SET	60–125
Forbidden Planet	1956	OS	5,000–13,000
Forbidden Planet	1956	LC SET	3,000–4,500
Forbidden Street	1949	OS	100–325
Force of Evil	1948	OS	400–700
Foreign Correspondent	1940	OS	200–650
Foreign Intrigue	1956	OS	60–125

F

F

TITLE	YEAR	SIZE	PRICE RANGE
Forever Darling	1956	OS	125–250
Forever Young	1992	OS	40–70
Formula	1980	OS	40–60
Forrest Gump	1994	OS	50–125
Forrest Gump	1994	LC SET	50–80
Fort Apache	1948	OS	700–1,100
Fort Apache	1948	LC SET	750–1,500
Fort Apache the Bronx	1981	OS	25–50
Fort Ti	1953	OS	50–70
Fort Worth	1951	OS	100–275
Fortune	1975	OS	40–60
Fortune	1975	LC SET	40–60
Fortune Cookie	1966	OS	40–90
48 Hours	1982	OS	40–65
48 Hours	1982	LC SET	40–70
Forty Guns	1957	OS	40–70
Forty Little Mothers	1940	OS	150–250
Forty Pounds of Trouble	1963	OS	40–60
42nd Street	1933	OS	25,000–30,000
Forty Thieves	1944	OS	200–350
Foul Play	1978	OS	40–60
Foul Play	1978	LC SET	30–50
Fountainhead	1949	OS	750–1,450
4-D Man	1959	OS	50–200
4-D Man	1959	LC SET	100–160
Four Days in Naples	1963	OS	40–70
Four Flies on Grey Velvet	1972	OS	60–125
4 for Texas	1964	OS	50–225
Four Horsemen of Apocalypse	1921	OS	3,000–5,000
Four Horsemen of Apocalypse	1961	OS	30–50
Four Muskateers	1975	OS	40–70
Four Muskateers	1975	LC SET	40–80
Four Sons	1940	OS	150–350
Four's a Crowd	1938	OS	175–400
Fox and the Hound	1981	OS	40–70
Foxes	1980	OS	40–60
Foxes	1980	LC SET	50–70
Foxfire	1955	OS	40–70

F

TITLE	YEAR	SIZE	PRICE RANGE
Foxy Brown	1974	OS	100–250
Francis	1949	OS	50–80
Francis Covers the Big Town	1953	OS	50–70
Francis Goes to the Races	1951	OS	70–125
Francis Goes to West Point	1952	OS	40–90
Francis in the Haunted House	1956	OS	40–60
Francis in the Navy	1955	OS	40–60
Frankenstein	1931	OS	198,000
Frankenstein & Monster from Hell	1974	OS	75–150
Frankenstein Conquers World	1966	OS	75–125
Frankenstein Conquers World	1966	LC SET	75–150
Frankenstein Created Woman	1967	OS	75–175
Frankenstein Meets Wolfman	1943	OS	5000–7,500
Frankenstein Must Be Destroyed	1969	OS	40–150
Frankenstein 1970	1958	OS	125–400
Frankenstein's Daughter	1958	OS	250–450
Frankie and Johnny	1966	OS	100–175
Frankie and Johnny	1991	OS	40–60
Freaks	1932	LC	7,000–12,000
Freaks	R 1949	OS	300–700
French Cancan	1955	47 × 63 FRE	750–1,500
French Connection	1971	OS	150–850
French Connection	1971	LC SET	100–200
French Connection 2	1975	OS	50–150
French Lieutenant's Woman	1981	OS	40–60
French Line	1954	OS	100–450
Frenzy	1972	OS	40–80
Frenzy	1972	LC SET	50–90
Friday the 13th	1980	OS	50–125
Friday the 13th	1980	LC SET	50–100
Friendly Persuasion	1956	OS	50–125
Fright Night	1985	OS	25–65
Frisco Kid	R 1942	OS	75–250
Fritz the Cat	1972	OS	75–400
Frogmen	1951	OS	50–80
From beyond the Grave	1973	OS	40–90
From Hell It Came	1957	OS	400–650
From Here to Eternity	1953	OS	600–850

F

TITLE	YEAR	SIZE	PRICE RANGE
From Here to Eternity	1953	LC SET	50–125
From Here to Eternity	R 1958	OS	125–250
From Noon til Three	1976	OS	25–50
From Russia with Love	1964	OS	250–950
From Russia with Love	1964	LC SET	300–600
From the Earth to the Moon	1958	OS	50–150
From the Terrace	1960	OS	40–70
Front	1976	OS	30–80
Front Page	1974	OS	50–150
Frontier Pony Express	1939	OS	600–900
Frozen Ghost	1945	OS	200–500
Fugitive	1993	OS	40–70
Fugitive Kind	1960	OS	50–90
Full Metal Jacket	1987	OS	40–100
Full Metal Jacket	1987	LC SET	80–125
Fun and Fancy Free	1947	OS	200–480
Fun in Acapulco	1963	OS	50–250
Funeral in Berlin	1966	OS	50–225
Funhouse	1981	OS	40–60
Funniest Man in the World	1968	OS	40–80
Funny Face	1957	OS	400–1,400
Funny Face	1957	LC SET	150–300
Funny Girl	1968	OS	250–500
Funny Girl	1968	LC SET	100–200
Funny Lady	1975	OS	40–90
Funny Lady	1975	LC SET	50–80
Funny Thing Happened on the Way to the Forum	1966	OS	50–200
Fury	1979	OS	40–60
Futureworld	1976	OS	40–60
Fuzz	1972	OS	30–50
Fuzzy Pink Nightgown	1957	OS	40–60
FX	1986	OS	40–70
G-Men	1935	14 × 36	15,000
G-Men Vs. the Black Dragon	1943	OS	150–500
Gable and Lombard	1976	OS	40–50
Galaxina	1980	OS	40–90
Gallant Hours	1960	OS	40–70

TITLE	YEAR	SIZE	PRICE RANGE
Gallipoli	1981	OS	40–90
Galloping Ghost	1930	OS	350–450
Gambit	1966	OS	50–125
Gambit	1966	LC SET	50–80
Gambler	1974	OS	40–60
Gambling House	1950	OS	50–90
Game of Death	1979	OS	60–150
Games	1967	OS	40–90
Gamma People	1956	OS	100–250
Gammera the Invincible	1966	OS	60–150
Gandhi	1982	OS	40–60
Gang's All Here	1939	OS	300–700
Garden of Allah	1936	OS	800–2,000
Gaslight	1944	OS	600–1,500
Gaslight	1944	LC SET	500–750
Gathering of Eagles	1963	OS	40–70
Gator	1976	OS	40–60
Gauntlet	1977	OS	50–100
Gauntlet	1977	LC SET	50–80
Gay Divorcee	1934	OS	7,000–9,000
Gazebo	1960	OS	30–60
Geisha Boy	1958	OS	50–80
Gene Krupa Story	1959	OS	40–70
General	1926	22 × 28	15,000–20,000
General Died at Dawn	1936	OS	3,000–5,000
Gengis Khan	1965	OS	40–70
Gentle Giant	1967	OS	40–60
Gentleman Jim	1942	OS	300–700
Gentleman's Agreement	1947	OS	300–600
Gentlemen Prefer Blondes	1953	OS	800–2,250
George Raft Story	1961	OS	40–70
Georgy Girl	1966	OS	50–80
Geronimo	1962	OS	40–90
Get Carter	1971	OS	200–600
Get Shorty	1995	OS	40–60
Get Yourself a College Girl	1964	OS	40–100
Getaway	1972	OS	80–300
Ghidrah	1965	OS	100–350

G

G

TITLE	YEAR	SIZE	PRICE RANGE
Ghost	1990	OS	40–60
Ghost and Mr. Chicken	1966	OS	50–175
Ghost and Mr. Chicken	1966	LC SET	100–200
Ghost and Mrs. Muir	1947	OS	250–500
Ghost Breakers	1940	OS	1,000–2,000
Ghost in the Invisible Bikini	1966	OS	40–90
Ghost of Dragstrip Hollow	1959	OS	125–350
Ghost of Dragstrip Hollow	1959	LC SET	100–325
Ghost of Frankenstein	1942	OS	7,500–10,000
Ghost of Zorro	1959	OS	40–80
Ghost Ship	1943	OS	350–550
Ghostbusters	1984	OS	50–90
Ghostbusters	1984	LC SET	40–100
Ghosts Italian Style	1969	OS	40–80
GI Blues	1960	OS	200–500
GI Blues	1960	LC SET	250–400
Giant	1956	OS	300–700
Giant	1956	LC SET	500–1,000
Giant Behemoth	1959	OS	300–600
Giant Claw	1957	OS	150–400
Giant Claw	1957	LC SET	100–300
Giant Leeches	1959	OS	150–300
Giant Leeches	1959	LC SET	300–450
Giant of Marathon	1960	OS	40–70
Giant of Marathon	1960	LC SET	100–150
Gidget	1959	OS	100–350
Gidget Goes Hawaiian	1961	OS	70–150
Gidget Goes to Rome	1963	OS	40–80
Gift of Love	1958	OS	40–70
Gigantis	1959	OS	75–200
Gigantis	1959	LC SET	150–300
Gigi	1958	OS	500–1,750
Gigot	1962	OS	40–60
Gilda	1946	OS	2,500–5,500
Gilda	1946	LC SET	800–1,200
Gildersleeve's Ghost	1944	OS	75–200
Gimme Shelter	1971	OS	300–600
Ginger and Fred	1985	OS	50–90

TITLE	YEAR	SIZE	PRICE RANGE
Girl Can't Help It	1956	OS	400–600
Girl Crazy	1943	OS	500–900
Girl Happy	1965	OS	70–250
Girl He Left Behind	1956	OS	50–70
Girl in Lover's Lane	1960	OS	40–60
Girl in the Bikini	1952	OS	70–300
Girl in the Kremlin	1957	OS	40–80
Girl in the Red Velvet Swing	1955	OS	40–80
Girl Most Likely	1957	OS	40–80
Girl Named Tamiko	1962	OS	40–60
Girl on the Bridge	1951	OS	75–300
Girl Rush	1955	OS	60–90
Girl Who Had Everything	1953	OS	100–400
Girls! Girls! Girls!	1962	OS	75–300
Girls in Prison	1956	OS	70–100
Girls on the Beach	1965	OS	75–300
Give a Girl a Break	1953	OS	40–90
Gladiator	2000	OS	30–80
Gladiator	2000	LC SET	50–90
Glass Bottom Boat	1966	OS	50–80
Glass Key	1942	OS	2,000–4,500
Glass Slipper	1955	OS	50–125
Glass Web	1953	OS	50–90
Glenn Miller Story	1954	OS	150–400
Global Affair	1964	OS	40–60
Glory	1956	OS	40–70
Glory Alley	1952	OS	40–90
Gnome Mobile	1967	OS	40–80
Go Ape	1974	OS	200–800
Go Go Big Beat	1965	OS	50–150
Go Go Mania	1965	OS	50–125
Go, Johnny, Go!	1958	OS	200–500
Go Naked in the World	1961	OS	40–80
Go West	1925	14 × 36	4,500
Go West	1940	OS	1,500–4,000
God's Little Acre	1958	OS	50–125
Godfather	1972	OS	200–700
Godfather	1972	LC SET	200–350

G

G

TITLE	YEAR	SIZE	PRICE RANGE
Godfather 2	1974	OS	200–400
Godfather 2	1974	LC SET	100–250
Godfather 3	1990	OS	40–100
Gods Must Be Crazy	1984	OS	40–60
Godspell	1973	OS	50–90
Godzilla	1956	OS	2,000–5,000
Godzilla	1956	LC SET	2,000–3,500
Godzilla on Monster Island	1972	OS	50–175
Godzilla Vs. Bionic Monster	1974	OS	100–190
Godzilla Vs. Gigan	1972	OS	80–125
Godzilla Vs. Megalon	1976	OS	150–250
Godzilla Vs. Smog Monster	1972	OS	50–150
Godzilla Vs. the Thing	1964	OS	100–250
Gog	1954	OS	100–300
Going My Way	1944	OS	125–350
Going Steady	1958	OS	40–90
Gold	1974	OS	40–60
Gold for the Caesars	1963	OS	40–60
Gold Rush	1925	OS	71,000
Golden Stallion	1949	OS	100–400
Golden Voyage of Sinbad	1973	OS	40–80
Golden Voyage of Sinbad	1973	LC SET	70–125
Goldeneye	1996	OS	40–60
Goldfinger	1964	OS	500–2,250
Goliath and the Vampires	1964	OS	40–70
Gone in 60 Seconds	1974	OS	40–125
Gone with the Wind	1939	OS	15,000–20,000
Gone with the Wind	1939	LC SET	4,000–5,000
Gone with the Wind	R 1940	OS	2,500–4,000
Gone with the Wind	R 1947	OS	300–450
Good Earth	1937	OS	400–750
Good Neighbor Sam	1964	OS	40–60
Good Sam	1948	OS	100–175
Good, the Bad and the Ugly	1967	OS	400–1,100
Good Times	1967	OS	60–125
Good Times	1967	LC SET	60–125
Good Will Hunting	1997	OS	40–60
Goodbye Charlie	1964	OS	30–50

TITLE	YEAR	SIZE	PRICE RANGE
Goodbye Girl	1977	OS	40–60
Goodbye Mr. Chips	1939	OS	350–600
Goodfellas	1990	OS	150–300
Goonies	1985	OS	75–90
Gore-Gore Girls	1972	OS	50–125
Gorgo	1961	OS	100–400
Gorgo	1961	LC SET	75–150
Gorgon	1964	OS	75–300
Gorilla	1929	OS	800–1,500
Graduate	1967	OS	400–1,250
Grand Hotel	1932	OS	49,000
Grand Hotel	R 1962	OS	50–175
Grand Prix	1967	OS	125–550
Grand Slam	1967	OS	25–60
Grandma's Boy	1922	OS	4,000–6,000
Grapes of Wrath	1940	OS	1,200–4,000
Grass Is Greener	1960	OS	50–125
Grass Is Greener	1960	LC SET	100–200
Grease	1978	OS	100–275
Grease	1978	LC SET	100–225
Grease 2	1982	OS	40–60
Great Bank Robbery	1969	OS	30–60
Great Dictator	1940	OS	1,500–3,500
Great Escape	1963	OS	500–1,100
Great Escape	1963	LC SET	150–225
Great Expectations	1946	OS	200–400
Great Gatsby	1949	OS	300–900
Great Gatsby	1974	OS	40–70
Great Lover	1949	OS	75–150
Great Man	1957	OS	40–90
Great Mouse Detective	1986	OS	40–90
Great Race	1965	OS	40–125
Great Rock and Roll Swindle	1979	30 × 40 UK	150–300
Great Rupert	1950	OS	40–90
Great Scout and Cathouse	1976	OS	50–70
Great Train Robbery	1979	OS	40–70
Great Train Robbery	1979	LC SET	50–90
Great Waldo Pepper	1975	OS	40–70

G

G

TITLE	YEAR	SIZE	PRICE RANGE
Great White Hope	1970	OS	40–70
Greatest	1977	OS	50–125
Greatest Show on Earth	1952	OS	75–250
Greatest Show on Earth	1952	LC SET	100–300
Greatest Story Ever Told	1965	OS	40–80
Green Berets	1967	OS	60–150
Green Dolphin Street	1947	OS	50–350
Green Fire	1955	OS	40–70
Green Hornet	1939	OS	300–900
Green Hornet	1974	OS	150–400
Green Hornet Strikes Again	1940	OS	600–800
Green Mansions	1959	OS	250–450
Green Mile	1999	OS	75–125
Green Mile	1999	LC SET	40–60
Green Slime	1969	OS	75–200
Green Slime	1969	LC SET	75–175
Gremlins	1984	OS	40–70
Gremlins	1984	LC SET	40–60
Greystoke: The Legend of Tarzan	1984	OS	40–60
Grifters	1990	OS	50–150
Groom Wore Spurs	1951	OS	50–125
Grounds for Marriage	1950	OS	40–60
Guess Who's Coming to Dinner	1967	OS	100–350
Guest Wife	1945	OS	50–175
Guilty	1947	OS	150–450
Gulliver's Travels	1939	OS	1,000–2,000
Gun Crazy	1950	OS	2,000–4,000
Gun Glory	1957	OS	40–70
Gun Runners	1958	OS	40–80
Gunfight at the OK Corral	1957	OS	250–550
Gunfight at the OK Corral	1957	LC SET	175–350
Gunfighter	1950	OS	250–650
Gung Ho	1943	OS	100–225
Gunga Din	1939	OS	5,000–7,000
Guns of Navarone	1961	OS	150–350
Guns of Navarone	1961	LC	50–125
Guns of the Magnificent Seven	1969	OS	40–60
Gunslinger	1956	OS	75–250

TITLE	YEAR	SIZE	PRICE RANGE
Guy Named Joe	1943	OS	150–300
Guys and Dolls	1955	OS	250–800
Guys and Dolls	1955	LC SET	150–225
Gypsy	1962	OS	50–90
Gypsy Fury	1950	OS	40–90
H-Man	1959	OS	50–80
Hackers	1995	OS	30–50
Hair	1979	OS	50–90
Hairspray	1988	OS	40–70
Half Angel	1951	OS	50–150
Hallelujah Trail	1965	OS	40–70
Halloween	1978	OS	75–225
Halloween 2	1981	OS	50–125
Hamlet	1948	OS	700–1,250
Hamlet	1990	OS	40–60
Hand of Death	1962	OS	50–90
Hands across the Border	1943	OS	300–400
Hands of the Ripper	1972	OS	40–70
Hands of the Ripper	1972	LC SET	50–80
Hang 'Em High	1968	OS	125–350
Hang 'Em High	1968	LC SET	50–90
Hanging Tree	1958	OS	50–125
Hangman	1959	OS	40–60
Hangover Square	1945	OS	250–575
Hannah and Her Sisters	1986	OS	40–80
Hannibal	1960	OS	40–60
Hannibal	2001	OS	40–60
Hannie Caulder	1972	OS	40–80
Hans Christian Andersen	1952	OS	60–175
Hans Christian Andersen	1952	LC SET	70–125
Happening	1967	OS	40–60
Happiest Millionaire	1967	OS	40–80
Happy Anniversary	1959	OS	40–70
Happy Go Lovely	1950	OS	50–150
Happy Road	1957	OS	50–80
Happy Thieves	1962	OS	40–60
Hard Day's Night	1964	OS	500–1,150
Hard Day's Night	1964	LC SET	800–1,500

H

H

TITLE	YEAR	SIZE	PRICE RANGE
Hard, Fast and Beautiful	1951	OS	100–325
Hard Times	1975	OS	40–70
Hard Way	1943	OS	100–275
Harder They Fall	1956	OS	250–550
Harlow	1965	OS	40–60
Harold and Maude	1972	OS	40–90
Harper	1966	OS	50–150
Harriet Craig	1950	OS	75–275
Harry Potter	2001	OS	40–70
Harry Potter	2001	LC SET	100–150
Harum Scarum	1965	OS	100–250
Harvey	1950	OS	500–1,650
Harvey Girls	1946	OS	300–550
Hasty Heart	1949	OS	50–150
Hatari	1962	OS	75–250
Hatari	1962	LC SET	100–175
Haunted House	1921	OS	18,000–25,000
Haunted Palace	1963	OS	50–200
Haunted Palace	1963	LC SET	200–275
Haunted Strangler	1958	OS	75–225
Haunted Strangler	1958	LC SET	60–90
Haunting	1963	OS	100–400
Have a Wild Weekend	1965	OS	60–125
Have Rocket, Will Travel	1959	OS	60–200
Head	1968	OS	90–250
Headless Ghost	1959	OS	75–300
Headless Ghost	1959	LC SET	80–125
Heart of the Golden West	1942	OS	400–800
Heart of the Rio Grande	1942	OS	200–525
Heartbeat	1946	OS	300–600
Heartbreak Ridge	1986	OS	40–60
Hearts of the West	1975	OS	40–90
Heat	1972	OS	150–350
Heat	1995	OS	50–150
Heat	1995	LC SET	40–80
Heaven Can Wait	1943	OS	300–500
Heaven Can Wait	1978	OS	50–80
Heaven Can Wait	1978	LC SET	50–90

TITLE	YEAR	SIZE	PRICE RANGE
Heaven Knows Mr. Allison	1957	OS	50–175
Heaven's Gate	1980	OS	50–125
Heavenly Body	1943	OS	200–500
Heavy Metal	1981	OS	40–80
Heidi	1937	OS	2,000–3,500
Heiress	1949	OS	300–500
Helen of Troy	1956	OS	50–125
Helicopter Spies	1967	OS	150–400
Hell Divers	1932	OS	1,500–2,500
Hell Is for Heroes	1962	OS	50–175
Hell on Frisco Bay	1956	OS	75–125
Hell's Angels	1930	14 × 36	3,500–4,500
Hell's Angels on Wheels	1967	OS	100–150
Hell's Five Hours	1958	OS	40–75
Hellcats of the Navy	1957	OS	175–250
Hellfighters	1968	OS	50–125
Hellions	1962	OS	40–60
Hello, Dolly!	1969	OS	50–150
Hello, Dolly!	1969	LC SET	50–90
Hello, Frisco! Hello	1943	OS	300–850
Hellraiser	1987	OS	50–200
Help!	1965	OS	300–750
Help!	1965	LC SET	800–1,250
Henry V	1946	OS	100–350
Henry V	1946	LC SET	200–350
Her Cardboard Lover	1942	OS	150–400
Her Twelve Men	1954	OS	50–90
Hercules	1959	OS	150–450
Hercules	1959	LC SET	250–400
Hercules against the Moon Men	1965	OS	50–150
Hercules and Captive Women	1963	OS	50–150
Hercules in New York	1975	OS	50–125
Hercules Unchained	1960	OS	75–150
Here Come the Co-eds	1945	OS	300–700
Here Come the Co-eds	1945	LC SET	250–400
Here Come the Nelsons	1951	OS	50–200
Here Comes the Navy	1934	OS	2,000–3,000
Hero	1923	OS	200–400

H

H

TITLE	YEAR	SIZE	PRICE RANGE
Hey There, It's Yogi Bear	1964	OS	50–150
Hickey and Boggs	1972	OS	40–60
Hidden Hand	1942	OS	40–70
Hideous Sun Demon	1959	OS	100–350
High and the Mighty	1954	OS	150–350
High Anxiety	1978	OS	40–75
High Noon	1952	OS	1,500–3,500
High Noon	1952	LC SET	500–750
High Plains Drifter	1973	OS	250–650
High Plains Drifter	1973	LC SET	200–375
High School Big Shot	1959	OS	40–70
High School Confidential	1958	OS	75–200
High School Hellcats	1958	OS	90–175
High Sierra	1941	OS	1,500–3,500
High Society	1956	OS	500–1,500
High Society	1956	LC SET	350–550
Highlander	1986	OS	50–150
Highlander	1986	LC SET	50–80
Hill	1965	OS	50–80
Hills Have Eyes	1977	OS	40–70
Hindenburg	1975	OS	40–70
His Girl Friday	1939	OS	1,250–3,500
His Kind of Woman	1951	OS	200–550
History of the World	1981	OS	50–125
History of the World	1981	LC SET	40–75
Hit and Run	1957	OS	75–175
Hit the Deck	1955	OS	40–75
Hit the Ice	1943	OS	300–750
Hitchhiker	1953	OS	75–150
Hold On	1966	OS	40–90
Hold That Ghost	1941	OS	2,500–5,000
Hole in the Head	1959	OS	40–95
Holiday	1938	OS	1,500–3,000
Holiday in Havana	1949	OS	50–90
Hollywood Knights	1980	OS	40–70
Hollywood or Bust	1956	OS	50–150
Hombre	1966	OS	40–150
Home from the Hill	1960	OS	50–125

TITLE	YEAR	SIZE	PRICE RANGE
Home Town Story	1951	OS	150–275
Homicidal	1961	OS	50–150
Hondo	1953	OS	800–1,500
Honky Tonk	1941	OS	500–900
Hook	1963	OS	50–80
Hook, Line & Sinker	1969	OS	50–80
Hook, Line & Sinker	1969	LC SET	50–70
Hoosiers	1986	OS	40–80
Hootenanny Hoot	1963	OS	50–125
Horizontal Lieutenant	1962	OS	40–70
Horror	1934	OS	300–750
Horror Castle	1963	OS	75–150
Horror Express	1973	OS	50–175
Horror Hotel	1960	OS	40–90
Horror of Dracula	1958	OS	300–1,000
Horror of Dracula	1958	LC SET	500–950
Horror of Party Beach	1964	OS	100–350
Horrors of Spider Island	1959	OS	50–175
Horse Feathers	1932	OS	7,500–12,000
Horse Soldiers	1959	OS	125–300
Hospital	1971	OS	40–80
Hot Blood	1956	OS	50–125
Hot Car Girl	1958	OS	300–575
Hot Rock	1972	OS	50–175
Hot Rod	1950	OS	300–500
Hot Rods to Hell	1967	OS	50–150
Hot Summer Night	1956	OS	40–70
Hot Water	1924	OS	5,875
Hotel	1967	OS	40–80
Hotel Paradiso	1966	OS	40–125
Houdini	1953	OS	700–1,500
Houdini	1953	LC SET	500–1,000
Hound of the Baskervilles	1939	OS	7,000–10,000
Hound of the Baskervilles	1959	OS	300–750
Hound of the Baskervilles	1959	LC SET	100–300
Hour before the Dawn	1944	OS	300–800
House of Bamboo	1955	OS	75–225
House of Cards	1969	OS	40–80

H

184 Casablanca *(1942)*

185 Casablanca *(1942)*
(Alternate Style)

186 Citizen Kane *(1941)*

187 City Lights *(1931)*

H

TITLE	YEAR	SIZE	PRICE RANGE
House of Dark Shadows	1970	OS	50–100
House of Dark Shadows	1970	LC SET	100–200
House of Dracula	1945	OS	3,000–4,250
House of Fear	1945	OS	500–750
House of Frankenstein	1944	OS	3,000–4,500
House of Frankenstein	R 1950	OS	800–1,800
House of Horrors	1946	OS	750–1,500
House of Strangers	1949	OS	250–400
House of Usher	1960	OS	200–425
House of Usher	1960	LC SET	150–300
House of Wax	1953	OS	50–150
House of Wax	1953	LC SET	150–300
House on Haunted Hill	1958	OS	900–2,250
House on Haunted Hill	1958	LC SET	750–1,150
House That Dripped Blood	1971	OS	50–125
Houseboat	1958	OS	75–150
How Green Was My Valley	1941	OS	1,500–3,000
How I Won the War	1968	OS	75–150
How the West Was Won	1962	OS	150–350
How to Be Very Popular	1955	OS	40–150
How to Make a Monster	1958	OS	250–450
How to Marry a Millionaire	1953	OS	1,500–3,500
How to Murder Your Wife	1965	OS	40–70
How to Save a Marriage	1968	OS	40–70
How to Steal a Million	1966	OS	75–300
How to Stuff a Wild Bikini	1965	OS	50–90
How to Stuff a Wild Bikini	1965	LC SET	60–90
Howling	1981	OS	40–90
Howling	1981	LC SET	80–125
Hud	1963	OS	100–350
Hudson's Bay	1940	OS	200–450
Human Desire	1954	OS	200–650
Humoresque	1946	OS	300–550
Humoresque	1946	LC SET	250–400
Hunchback of Notre Dame	1923	14 × 36	8,000–9,000
Hunchback of Notre Dame	1939	OS	2,500–4,000
Hunchback of Notre Dame	1957	OS	75–200
Hunger	1983	OS	50–90

H

TITLE	YEAR	SIZE	PRICE RANGE
Hunger	1983	LC SET	75–150
Hunt for Red October	1989	OS	40–70
Hunt the Man Down	1950	OS	50–125
Hunted	1947	OS	100–375
Hunter	1980	OS	50–90
Hunter	1980	LC SET	150–225
Hunters	1958	OS	55–125
Hurricane	1938	OS	750–1,250
Hurry Sundown	1967	OS	50–80
Husbands	1970	OS	150–300
Hush . . . Hush, Sweet Charlotte	1965	OS	125–200
Hush . . . Hush, Sweet Charlotte	1965	LC SET	75–250
Hustler	1961	OS	400–750
Hustler	1961	LC SET	500–700
Hustler	R 1964	OS	500–800
I Aim at the Stars	1960	OS	40–80
I Am a Fugitive from a Chain Gang	1932	OS	11,500
I Confess	1953	OS	350–550
I Could Go on Singing	1963	OS	50–125
I Cover the War	1937	OS	500–900
I Don't Care Girl	1953	OS	50–90
I Escaped from Devil's Island	1973	OS	50–125
I Love Trouble	1947	OS	600–900
I Love You Again	1940	OS	150–250
I Love You, Alice B. Toklas!	1968	OS	30–80
I Married a Monster from Outer Space	1958	OS	500–900
I Married a Monster from Outer Space	1958	LC SET	250–500
I Married a Witch	1942	OS	1,250–2,500
I Married a Woman	1958	OS	75–200
I Mobster	1958	OS	50–80
I Remember Mama	1948	OS	50–80
I Saw What You Did	1965	OS	50–90
I Thank a Fool	1962	OS	40–70
I the Jury	1953	OS	75–250
I Walk Alone	1948	OS	250–500
I Walk the Line	1970	OS	40–80

TITLE	YEAR	SIZE	PRICE RANGE
I Walked with a Zombie	1943	OS	1,000–2,000
I Want to Live	1958	OS	50–150
I Wanted Wings	1941	OS	500–900
I Was a Communist for the FBI	1951	OS	80–250
I Was a Male War Bride	1949	OS	50–225
I Was a Teenage Frankenstein	1958	OS	300–900
I Was a Teenage Werewolf	1957	OS	500–850
I Was a Teenage Werewolf	1957	LC SET	450–650
I'll Be Seeing You	1944	OS	100–300
I'll Cry Tomorrow	1955	OS	50–150
I'll Take Sweden	1965	OS	40–70
I'm No Angel	1933	OS	3,000–6,000
I've Lived Before	1956	OS	70–125
Ice Capades	1940	OS	100–250
Ice Station Zebra	1968	OS	40–90
Iceland	1942	OS	125–375
Ideal Husband	1947	OS	50–90
If a Man Answers	1962	OS	50–80
If Winter Comes	1948	OS	40–80
Illegal	1955	OS	50–125
Illustrated Man	1969	OS	50–90
Imagine	1988	OS	50–125
Imitation General	1958	OS	40–90
Imitation of Life	134	OS	800–1,500
Impact	1949	OS	150–350
In a Lonely Place	1950	OS	1,000–2,500
In Cold Blood	1968	OS	50–125
In Enemy Country	1968	OS	40–80
In Harm's Way	1965	OS	75–300
In Harm's Way	1965	LC SET	100–225
In-Laws	1967	OS	50–125
In Like Flint	1967	OS	50–250
In Old Amarillo	1951	OS	150–250
In Old Kentucky	1935	OS	150–300
In Our Time	1944	OS	100–350
In Search of the Castaways	1962	OS	40–95
In the French Style	1963	OS	50–125
In the Good Old Summertime	1949	OS	200–450

TITLE	YEAR	SIZE	PRICE RANGE
In the Good Old Summertime	1949	LC SET	300–500
In the Heat of the Night	1967	OS	50–175
In the Heat of the Night	1967	LC SET	50–150
In the Navy	1941	OS	800–1,200
In This Our Life	1942	OS	300–600
Incendiary Blonde	1945	OS	150–250
Incredible Journey	1963	OS	40–70
Incredible Melting Man	1978	OS	40–80
Incredible Mr. Limpet	1964	OS	75–150
Incredible Mr. Limpet	1964	LC SET	50–90
Incredible Shrinking Man	1957	OS	400–800
Incredible Shrinking Man	1957	LC SET	500–700
Indestructible Man	1956	OS	75–250
Indestructible Man	1956	LC SET	100–200
Indian Fighter	1955	OS	50–125
Indiana Jones Last Crusade	1989	OS	50–100
Indiana Jones Temple of Doom	1984	OS	50–150
Indiana Jones Temple of Doom	1984	LC SET	50–150
Indiscreet	1958	OS	100–350
Inferno	1980	55 × 79 ITA	100–175
Informer	1935	OS	5,000–6,000
Infra Man	1975	OS	50–200
Inherit the Wind	1960	OS	50–175
Inn of the Sixth Happiness	1958	OS	40–90
Innocents	1961	OS	75–150
Innocents	1961	LC SET	100–200
Inside Daisy Clover	1966	OS	40–90
Inside Straight	1951	OS	75–150
Insider	1999	OS	40–70
Inspector General	1949	OS	50–125
Inspector General	1949	LC SET	75–150
Interiors	1979	OS	50–150
Interiors	1979	LC SET	75–125
Interlude	1957	OS	50–70
Intermezzo	1939	OS	500–750
International Lady	1941	OS	50–90
Interview with a Vampire	1994	OS	40–70
Intrigue	1947	OS	40–90

TITLE	YEAR	SIZE	PRICE RANGE
Invaders from Mars	1953	OS	1,500–3,000
Invaders from Mars	1953	LC SET	1,500–2,750
Invasion of the Body Snatchers	1956	OS	500–2,000
Invasion of the Body Snatchers	1956	LC SET	400–850
Invasion of the Body Snatchers	1978	OS	50–80
Invasion of the Body Snatchers	1978	LC SET	50–90
Invasion of the Saucer Men	1957	OS	2,000–3,500
Invasion of the Saucer Men	1957	LC SET	2,500–3,250
Invasion of the Star Creatures	1962	OS	50–125
Invisible Agent	1942	OS	200–550
Invisible Agent	1942	LC SET	400–700
Invisible Boy	1957	OS	200–650
Invisible Invaders	1959	OS	75–300
Invisible Man	1933	OS	60,000–75,000
Invisible Man's Return	1944	OS	500–750
Invisible Ray	1936	OS	44,150
Invisible Stripes	1940	OS	200–550
Invisible Woman	1940	OS	300–750
Invitation to a Gunfighter	1964	OS	40–75
Invitation to the Dance	1956	OS	50–175
Ipcress File	1965	OS	150–550
Irma La Douce	1963	OS	50–125
Iron Mask	1929	OS	1,500–2,500
Iron Mistress	1952	OS	50–90
Iron Petticoat	1956	OS	50–90
Is Paris Burning?	1966	OS	40–70
Island in the Sky	1953	OS	75–250
Island in the Sun	1957	OS	100–225
Island in the Sun	1957	LC SET	50–150
Island of the Doomed Men	1940	OS	200–400
Island of Dr. Moreau	1977	OS	50–90
Island of Dr. Moreau	1977	LC SET	50–80
Isle of the Dead	1945	OS	1,750–2,750
Istanbul	1957	OS	70–125
It Came from beneath the Sea	1955	OS	400–1,150
It Came from beneath the Sea	1955	LC SET	400–750
It Came from Outer Space	1953	OS	700–1,250
It Came from Outer Space	1953	LC SET	1,100–1,500

I

TITLE	YEAR	SIZE	PRICE RANGE
It Conquered the World	1956	OS	700–1,500
It Happened at the World's Fair	1963	OS	150–450
It Happened in Athens	1962	OS	40–80
It Happened One Night	1934	OS	15,000–30,000
It Happened to Jane	1959	OS	40–90
It Should Happen to You	1954	OS	50–125
It Started in Naples	1960	OS	50–125
It Started in Naples	1960	LC SET	50–175
It! Terror from Beyond Space	1958	OS	400–750
It's a Mad Mad Mad Mad World	1963	OS	150–550
It's a Mad Mad Mad Mad World	1963	LC SET	125–225
It's a Wonderful Life	1946	OS	6,000–10,000
It's a Wonderful World	1939	OS	400–650
It's Always Fair Weather	1955	OS	75–225
It's Only Money	1962	OS	50–80
It's the Old Army Game	1926	OS	1,500–2,250
Italian Job	1969	OS	350–1,100
Ivanhoe	1952	OS	50–225
Ivanhoe	1952	LC SET	100–225
Ivy	1947	OS	75–225
Jabberwocky	1977	OS	50–125
Jack and the Beanstalk	1952	OS	50–150
Jack the Ripper	1959	OS	40–70
Jack the Ripper	1959	LC SET	25–50
Jack the Ripper	1976	OS	50–90
Jackie Brown	1997	OS	30–70
Jagged Edge	1985	OS	30–70
Jagged Edge	1985	LC SET	50–100
Jailhouse Rock	1957	OS	1,200–2,750
Jailhouse Rock	1957	LC SET	1,250–2,000
Jamaica Inn	1939	OS	3,000–4,000
James Dean Story	1957	OS	250–600
Jane Eyre	1943	OS	300–600
Janis	1974	OS	50–150
Jason and the Argonauts	1963	OS	75–275
Jason and the Argonauts	1963	LC SET	150–250
Jaws	1975	OS	200–550
Jaws	1975	LC SET	200–325

TITLE	YEAR	SIZE	PRICE RANGE
Jaws 2	1978	OS	50–275
Jazz Singer	1927	OS	25,000–32,000
Jazz Singer	1980	OS	40–60
Jeanne Eagels	1957	OS	50–90
Jeremiah Johnson	1972	OS	75–250
Jerk	1979	OS	50–150
Jerk	1979	LC SET	40–90
Jesse James	1939	OS	3,000–5,000
Jesus Christ Superstar	1973	OS	50–90
Jet over the Atlantic	1958	OS	50–90
Jet Pilot	1957	OS	150–400
Jezebel	1938	OS	10,000–15,000
JFK	1991	OS	50–90
Joan of Arc	1948	OS	250–700
Joe Butterfly	1957	OS	50–70
Joe Kidd	1972	OS	75–150
Joe Kidd	1972	LC SET	75–125
John and Mary	1969	OS	30–70
John Paul Jones	1959	OS	50–150
Johnny Belinda	1948	OS	75–150
Johnny Come Lately	1943	OS	150–400
Johnny Concho	1956	OS	50–90
Johnny Cool	1963	OS	40–70
Johnny Guitar	1954	OS	250–650
Johnny Trouble	1957	OS	50–90
Joker Is Wild	1957	OS	75–350
Jour de Fête	1949	63 × 94 FRE	3,000–4,000
Journey to the Center of Earth	1959	OS	350–500
Journey to the Center of Earth	1959	LC SET	250–450
Journey to the Lost City	1960	OS	50–150
Journey to the 7th Planet	1961	OS	75–225
Journey to the 7th Planet	1961	LC SET	100–200
Joy of Living	1938	OS	250–650
Juarez	1939	OS	750–1,000
Judge Priest	1934	OS	200–400
Judgment at Nuremburg	1961	OS	80–350
Juke Girl	1942	OS	200–350
Jules and Jim	1962	OS	50–250

J

J

TITLE	YEAR	SIZE	PRICE RANGE
Jules and Jim	1962	47 × 63 FRE	800–1,500
Julia	1977	OS	30–60
Julie	1956	OS	50–90
Juliet of the Spirits	1965	39 × 55 ITA	300–700
Julius Caesar	1953	OS	300–600
Jumbo	1962	OS	40–70
June Bride	1948	OS	75–150
Jungle Book	1942	OS	650–800
Jungle Book	1967	OS	150–400
Jungle Book	1967	LC SET	100–200
Jungle Drums of Africa	1952	OS	40–90
Jungle Drums of Africa	1952	LC SET	250–350
Jungle Jim	1948	OS	80–175
Jungle Man Eaters	1954	OS	50–150
Jungle Moon Men	1955	OS	50–175
Jungle Woman	1944	OS	150–400
Junior Bonner	1972	OS	40–90
Jupiter's Darling	1954	OS	50–90
Jurassic Park	1993	OS	40–80
Just a Gigolo	1979	OS	50–150
Just This Once	1952	OS	50–70
Juvenile Jungle	1958	OS	125–275
Kagemusha	1980	20 × 29 JPN	300–750
Karate Kid	1984	OS	40–70
Karate Kid	1984	LC SET	30–70
Kathleen	1941	OS	80–150
Keep 'Em Flying	1941	OS	500–650
Keeper of the Flame	1942	OS	500–750
Kelly's Heroes	1970	OS	150–350
Kentuckian	1955	OS	150–350
Key	1958	OS	40–80
Key Largo	1948	OS	1,500–3,000
Key Largo	1948	LC SET	750–1,250
Key to the City	1950	OS	70–200
Khartoum	1966	OS	50–150
Kid	1921	OS	30,000–45,000
Kid from Brooklyn	1946	OS	125–300
Kid from Left Field	1953	OS	40–80

TITLE	YEAR	SIZE	PRICE RANGE
Kid Galahad	1962	OS	150–400
Kid Rodelo	1965	OS	30–60
Kidnapped	1960	OS	50–90
Kids Are Alright	1979	OS	50–150
Kill Baby Kill	1967	OS	70–150
Kill Baby Kill	1967	LC SET	150–225
Killer Ape	1952	OS	50–70
Killer Elite	1975	OS	40–80
Killer Shrews	1959	OS	150–325
Killer's Kiss	1955	OS	400–550
Killers	1946	OS	350–900
Killers	1964	OS	50–150
Killers from Space	1954	OS	150–250
Killers from Space	1954	LC SET	150–350
Killing	1956	OS	500–850
Killing Fields	1984	OS	40–60
Killing of Sister George	1969	OS	40–60
Kim	1950	OS	75–150
Kind Lady	1951	OS	40–125
King and I	1956	OS	300–750
King and I	1956	LC SET	250–400
King Creole	1956	OS	500–1,250
King Creole	1956	LC SET	500–800
King Kong	1933	OS	80,000–100,000
King Kong	1976	OS	75–250
King Kong	1976	LC SET	50–125
King Kong Escapes	1968	OS	50–125
King Kong Vs. Godzilla	1963	OS	100–450
King of Comedy	1983	OS	50–125
King of Kings	1927	OS	500–800
King of Kings	1961	OS	75–125
King of Marvin Gardens	1972	OS	50–150
King of the Carnival	1955	OS	50–80
King of the Carnival	1955	LC SET	50–70
King of the Congo	1952	OS	50–150
King of the Rocket Men	1949	OS	750–2,000
King of the Underworld	1939	OS	1,200–1,800
King of the Wild	1930	OS	400–1,000

K

K

TITLE	YEAR	SIZE	PRICE RANGE
King Rat	1965	OS	50–100
King Rat	1965	LC SET	40–60
King's Thief	1955	OS	50–90
Kings Go Forth	1958	OS	50–150
Kings of the Sun	1963	OS	40–80
Kismet	1944	OS	200–350
Kismet	1956	OS	75–175
Kiss before Dying	1955	OS	30–70
Kiss in the Dark	1949	OS	50–150
Kiss Me Deadly	1955	OS	150–700
Kiss Me Kate	1953	OS	75–200
Kiss of Death	1947	OS	800–1,500
Kiss of Death	1947	LC SET	350–500
Kiss of the Spider Woman	1985	OS	40–60
Kiss of the Vampire	1962	OS	150–400
Kiss of the Vampire	1962	LC SET	125–250
Kiss the Blood off My Hands	1948	OS	250–750
Kiss the Boys Goodbye	1941	OS	75–275
Kiss Them for Me	1957	OS	75–125
Kiss Them for Me	1957	LC SET	125–225
Kiss Tomorrow Goodbye	1950	OS	50–125
Kissin' Cousins	1964	OS	100–250
Kissing Bandit	1948	OS	50–250
Kitten with a Whip	1964	OS	50–150
Kitty	1945	OS	100–175
Kitty Foyle	1940	OS	200–450
Klute	1971	OS	50–150
Knife in the Water	1961	23 × 33 GER	225–325
Knock on Any Door	1949	OS	250–450
Konga	1961	OS	100–300
Kramer Vs. Kramer	1979	OS	40–70
Kramer Vs. Kramer	1979	LC SET	30–60
Kronos	1957	OS	60–90
Krull	1983	OS	40–60
Kundun	1997	OS	50–150
Kwaheri	1964	OS	40–70
Li'l Abner	1959	OS	40–80
La Bamba	1987	OS	40–70

L

TITLE	YEAR	SIZE	PRICE RANGE
La Bamba	1987	LC SET	30–60
LA Confidential	1997	OS	40–80
LA Confidential	1997	LC SET	70–90
Labyrinth	1986	OS	50–90
Labyrinth	1986	LC SET	40–80
Ladies Man	1961	OS	50–90
Lady and the Monster	1944	OS	400–550
Lady and the Tramp	1955	OS	500–850
Lady Eve	1941	OS	1,500–3,000
Lady Eve	1941	LC SET	1,250–2,500
Lady for a Night	1941	OS	200–350
Lady Frankenstein	1972	OS	40–80
Lady from Nowhere	1936	OS	500–850
Lady from Shanghai	1947	OS	2,500–5,500
Lady Gambles	1949	OS	100–250
Lady Godiva	1955	OS	100–200
Lady Has Plans	1942	OS	300–600
Ladyhawke	1985	OS	50–90
Ladyhawke	1985	LC SET	40–70
Lady in a Cage	1964	OS	50–80
Lady in Cement	1968	OS	65–100
Lady in Question	1940	OS	200–500
Lady in the Dark	1944	OS	350–550
Lady in the Lake	1947	OS	500–850
Lady Is Willing	1942	OS	150–300
Lady L	1966	OS	50–70
Lady on a Train	1945	OS	250–350
Lady Possessed	1951	OS	60–95
Lady Sings the Blues	1972	OS	75–150
Lady Sings the Blues	1972	LC SET	100–200
Lady Takes a Flyer	1958	OS	50–90
Lady Vanishes	1938	OS	9,000–10,000
Lady without a Passport	1950	OS	50–125
Ladykillers	1955	OS	200–350
Lafayette Escadrille	1958	OS	75–150
Land beyond the Law	1926	OS	350–500
Land of the Minotaur	1977	OS	40–80
Land of the Minotaur	1977	LC SET	50–100

L

TITLE	YEAR	SIZE	PRICE RANGE
Land That Time Forgot	1975	OS	50–90
Land Unknown	1957	OS	500–850
Land Unknown	1957	LC SET	250–350
Larceny Inc	1942	OS	350–550
Las Vegas Shakedown	1955	OS	40–90
Las Vegas Story	1952	OS	150–300
Lassie Come Home	1943	OS	750–900
Last American Hero	1973	OS	40–60
Last Angry Man	1959	OS	40–70
Last Challenge	1967	OS	40–70
Last Command	1928	OS	5,000
Last Days of Pompeii	1960	OS	40–70
Last Detail	1973	OS	50–90
Last Detail	1973	LC SET	40–70
Last Emperor	1988	OS	50–100
Last Emperor	1988	LC SET	40–70
Last Exit to Brooklyn	1990	OS	50–90
Last House on the Left	1972	OS	125–300
Last Hurrah	1958	OS	50–90
Last Man on Earth	1964	OS	100–250
Last Man on Earth	1964	LC SET	200–300
Last of the Mohicans	1932	OS	300–500
Last of the Mohicans	1936	OS	300–450
Last of the Mohicans	1992	OS	40–80
Last of the Mohicans	1992	LC SET	50–90
Last of the Secret Agents	1966	OS	40–70
Last of the Vikings	1962	OS	40–70
Last Picture Show	1971	OS	100–275
Last Rebel	1971	OS	40–70
Last Sunset	1961	OS	50–90
Last Tango in Paris	1973	OS	100–200
Last Tango in Paris	1973	LC SET	250–350
Last Temptation of Christ	1988	OS	200–350
Last Time I Saw Archie	1961	OS	50–80
Last Train from Gun Hill	1959	OS	75–150
Last Train from Gun Hill	1959	LC SET	100–200
Last Tycoon	1976	OS	50–80
Last Tycoon	1976	LC SET	50–80

TITLE	YEAR	SIZE	PRICE RANGE
Last Voyage	1960	OS	50–80
Last Waltz	1978	OS	75–150
Last Waltz	1978	LC SET	75–125
Last Woman on Earth	1960	OS	50–75
Late George Apley	1946	OS	100–250
Late Show	1977	OS	75–150
Latin Lovers	1953	OS	125–325
Latitude Zero	1970	OS	50–80
Laughing Policeman	1974	OS	50–70
Laura	1944	OS	5,500–9,000
Lavender Hill Mob	1951	OS	750–1,500
Law and Order	1953	OS	100–325
Law of the Pampras	1939	OS	200–300
Law of the Pampras	1939	LC SET	400–500
Law of the Ranger	1937	OS	450–600
Lawless Eighties	1957	OS	50–90
Lawless Frontier	1934	OS	1,750–2,750
Lawless Range	1935	OS	800–1,400
Lawman	1971	OS	40–80
Lawnmower Man	1992	OS	50–80
Lawrence of Arabia	1962	OS	7,000–11,000
Lawrence of Arabia	1962	LC SET	700–1,400
Le Mans	1971	OS	200–500
Le Mans	1971	LC SET	100–275
League of Gentlemen	1959	27 × 41 UK	100–300
League of Their Own	1992	OS	40–70
Leave Her to Heaven	1945	OS	2,000–4,500
Leech Woman	1960	OS	100–350
Left Hand of God	1955	OS	75–200
Left Handed Gun	1958	OS	50–175
Legend	1985	OS	40–70
Legend of Hell House	1973	OS	40–90
Legend of Lylah Clare	1968	OS	50–90
Legend of the Lone Ranger	1981	OS	40–70
Legend of the Lost	1957	OS	100–190
Legend of 7 Golden Vampires	1974	OS	75–150
Legend of Tom Dooley	1959	OS	40–70
Lemon Drop Kid	1951	OS	150–275

L

L

TITLE	YEAR	SIZE	PRICE RANGE
Lenny	1974	OS	40–70
Lenny	1974	LC SET	60–90
Leopard	1963	OS	50–90
Leopard Man	1943	OS	1,000–1,500
Les Girls	1957	OS	50–150
Les Miserables	1935	OS	200–450
Les Miserables	1952	OS	50–150
Let It Be	1970	OS	250–600
Let's Do It Again	1975	OS	40–60
Let's Face It	1943	OS	125–250
Let's Kill Uncle	1966	OS	40–70
Let's Live a Little	1948	OS	150–250
Let's Make It Legal	1951	OS	75–175
Let's Make Love	1960	OS	300–650
Let's Make Up	1956	OS	50–125
Let's Spend the Night Together	1983	OS	50–125
Let's Spend the Night Together	1983	LC SET	50–90
Lethal Weapon	1987	OS	50–80
Lethal Weapon	1987	LC SET	40–70
Lethal Weapon 2	1989	OS	40–60
Lethal Weapon 3	1992	OS	40–60
Letter	1940	OS	1,500–2,000
Letter from an Unknown Woman	1948	OS	500–750
Letter to Three Wives	1949	OS	250–450
Libel	1959	OS	50–90
Libeled Lady	1936	OS	3,000–4,000
Liberation of L.B. Jones	1970	OS	50–90
License to Kill	1989	OS	50–90
License to Kill	1989	LC SET	40–70
Life and Times of Judge Roy Bean	1972	OS	70–100
Life in the Balance	1955	OS	40–70
Life Is Beautiful	1998	OS	40–60
Life of Brian	1979	OS	70–150
Life of Buffalo Bill	1917	OS	1,000–2,000
Life of Emile Zola	1937	OS	750–1,500
Life of Her Own	1950	OS	40–90
Life with Father	1947	OS	40–90
Lifeboat	1944	OS	1,500–3,000

L

TITLE	YEAR	SIZE	PRICE RANGE
Lifeboat	1944	LC SET	1,000–2,000
Lifeguard	1976	OS	40–70
Light in the Piazza	1961	OS	40–70
Lightning Strikes Twice	1951	OS	50–70
Lightning Strikes West	1940	OS	150–300
Lightning Warrior	1931	OS	400–800
Like Water for Chocolate	1992	OS	75–150
Lili	1952	OS	50–150
Lilies of the Field	1963	OS	50–125
Lilith	1964	OS	40–60
Limelight	1952	OS	300–750
Limelight	1952	LC SET	100–300
Lineup	1958	OS	40–70
Lion in Winter	1968	OS	75–150
Lion in Winter	1968	LC SET	40–90
Lion King	1994	OS	50–150
Lipstick	1976	OS	40–60
Listen Darling	1938	OS	400–650
Lisztomania	1975	OS	50–70
Little Annie Rooney	1925	OS	1,200–2,200
Little Big Man	1970	OS	50–90
Little Colonel	1935	OS	1,000–1,750
Little Egypt	1951	OS	50–90
Little Fauss and Big Halsy	1970	OS	40–70
Little Fauss and Big Halsy	1970	LC SET	50–90
Little Foxes	1941	OS	1,000–2,000
Little Giant	1946	OS	250–400
Little Girl Who Lives Down the Lane	1977	OS	40–60
Little Hut	1957	OS	50–125
Little Mermaid	1989	OS	75–200
Little Mermaid	1989	LC SET	50–90
Little Miss Marker	1934	14 × 36	1,000
Little Old New York	1940	OS	250–400
Little Prince	1974	OS	70–100
Little Princess	1939	OS	450–850
Little Shop of Horrors	1960	OS	150–400
Little Shop of Horrors	1960	LC SET	125–200

L

TITLE	YEAR	SIZE	PRICE RANGE
Little Shop of Horrors	1986	OS	40–60
Little Women	1933	OS	2,000–3,000
Littlest Outlaw	1955	OS	40–70
Littlest Rebel	1935	OS	2,500–3,500
Live a Little, Love a Little	1968	OS	100–250
Live a Little, Love a Little	1968	LC SET	100–150
Live and Let Die	1973	OS	150–400
Live and Let Die	1973	LC SET	50–150
Live Fast, Die Young	1958	OS	250–500
Lively Set	1964	OS	40–80
Lives of a Bengal Lancer	1935	OS	4,000
Living Daylights	1987	OS	50–90
Living It Up	1954	OS	50–175
Lloyds of London	1936	OS	2,000–3,000
Loaded Pistols	1948	OS	200–300
Locket	1946	OS	200–400
Lodger	1944	OS	300–400
Logan's Run	1976	OS	75–90
Logan's Run	1976	LC SET	75–150
Lola	1981	OS	40–60
Lolita	1962	OS	500–1,200
Lolita	1962	LC SET	400–800
Lone Ranger	1938	OS	1,000–2,500
Lone Ranger	1956	OS	600–800
Lone Ranger and the Lost City of Gold	1958	OS	500–750
Lone Ranger Rides Again	1939	OS	1,500–2,250
Lone Star	1951	OS	50–125
Lone Star Lawmen	1941	OS	150–250
Lonely Are the Brave	1962	OS	75–125
Lonely Are the Brave	1962	LC SET	100–150
Lonely Man	1957	OS	40–70
Lonely Hearts	1959	OS	65–90
Lonesome Cowboys	1968	OS	100–250
Lonesome Dove	1991	OS	100–175
Long Good Friday	1982	OS	75–150
Long Goodbye	1973	OS	50–125
Long Gray Line	1955	OS	50–100

TITLE	YEAR	SIZE	PRICE RANGE
Long Haul	1957	OS	50–80
Long Hot Summer	1958	OS	75–250
Long Long Trailer	1954	OS	250–350
Long Night	1947	OS	50–125
Long Riders	1980	OS	50–80
Long Voyage Home	1940	OS	300–650
Longest Day	1962	OS	300–750
Longest Day	1962	LC SET	150–250
Longest Yard	1974	OS	50–80
Looking for Mr. Goodbar	1977	OS	50–90
Looking for Mr. Goodbar	1977	LC SET	50–90
Loophole	1954	OS	75–200
Lord Jim	1964	OS	50–80
Lord of the Flies	1963	OS	100–250
Lord of the Jungle	1955	OS	50–80
Lord of the Rings	1978	OS	50–100
Lord of the Rings	2002	OS	75–125
Lorna	1964	OS	150–250
Los Olivados	1950	27 × 41 MEX	1,200–2,500
Lost Boys	1987	OS	50–70
Lost Boys	1987	LC SET	40–60
Lost City	1935	OS	250–500
Lost City	1935	LC SET	150–225
Lost Continent	1951	OS	125–300
Lost Continent	1968	OS	50–90
Lost Highway	1997	OS	40–70
Lost Horizon	1937	OS	5,000–9,000
Lost Horizon	1972	OS	40–70
Lost in Alaska	1952	OS	150–300
Lost Jungle	1934	OS	300–450
Lost Man	1969	OS	50–80
Lost Missile	1958	OS	60–125
Lost Missile	1958	LC SET	100–275
Lost Moment	1947	OS	100–225
Lost Planet	1953	OS	175–300
Lost Squadron	1932	OS	1,000–2,250
Lost Weekend	1945	OS	3,000–4,000
Lost Weekend	1945	LC SET	400–550

L

L

TITLE	YEAR	SIZE	PRICE RANGE
Lost World	1925	LC	700–1,500
Lost World	1997	OS - W/3-D	350–750
Lost World of Sinbad	1965	OS	50–80
Lottery Bride	1930	41 × 81	800–1,000
Louisiana Purchase	1941	OS	175–350
Love	1919	LC	350–600
Love Affair	1932	LC	900–1,500
Love and Death	1975	OS	75–90
Love and Death	1975	LC SET	50–90
Love and Kisses	1965	OS	75–125
Love before Breakfast	1936	OS	4,000–5,500
Love Bug	1969	OS	50–90
Love Crazy	1941	OS	200–350
Love from a Stranger	1947	OS	75–150
Love God	1969	OS	50–80
Love Happy	1949	OS	500–750
Love Has Many Faces	1965	OS	50–70
Love in a Goldfish Bowl	1961	OS	50–90
Love in the Afternoon	1957	OS	500–850
Love in the Afternoon	1957	LC SET	150–300
Love Is a Ball	1963	OS	50–80
Love Is a Many Splendored Thing	1955	OS	75–200
Love Is Better Than Ever	1952	OS	50–80
Love Is My Profession	1958	OS	75–200
Love Letters	1945	OS	500–850
Love Me or Leave Me	1955	OS	75–250
Love Me Tender	1956	OS	750–1,250
Love Me Tender	1956	LC SET	300–550
Love Nest	1951	OS	150–400
Love on a Pillow	1962	OS	50–125
Love Parade	1929	OS	200–500
Love Slaves of the Amazon	1957	OS	75–175
Love Story	1970	OS	50–75
Love with the Proper Stranger	1963	OS	75–250
Loved One	1965	OS	50–125
Lovely to Look At	1952	OS	50–150
Lovely to Look At	1952	LC SET	100–200
Lover Come Back	1962	OS	50–150

TITLE	YEAR	SIZE	PRICE RANGE
Loves of Carmen	1948	OS	200–550
Loves of Carmen	1948	LC SET	250–350
Loves of Isadora	1968	OS	40–70
Loving You	1957	OS	600–850
Loving You	1957	LC SET	500–750
Luck of the Irish	1948	OS	150–250
Lucky Lady	1975	OS	50–90
Lucky Me	1954	OS	50–125
Lucky Texan	1934	OS	2,500–5,000
Ludwig	1972	OS	50–70
Lulu Belle	1948	OS	75–200
Lumière	1976	OS	50–125
Lure of the Wilderness	1952	OS	50–70
Lured	1947	OS	350–500
Lust for a Vampire	1971	OS	75–300
Lust for Life	1956	OS	75–200
Lusty Men	1952	OS	250–400
Luxury Girls	1953	OS	50–90
Luxury Liner	1948	OS	75–125
M	1931	27 × 41 SWE	7,500
M Butterfly	1993	OS	50–70
Ma and Pa Kettle	1949	OS	100–225
Macabre	1958	OS	150–400
Macabre	1958	LC SET	100–200
Macao	1952	OS	450–600
Macao	1952	LC SET	250–350
Macbeth	1948	OS	600–1,100
Macbeth	1972	23 × 33 GER	70–125
Machine Gun Kelly	1958	OS	150–225
Mack	1973	OS	75–250
Mackenna's Gold	1969	OS	50–80
Mackintosh Man	1973	OS	50–125
Macomber Affair	1947	OS	150–225
Macumba Love	1960	OS	50–90
Mad Dogs and Englishmen	1971	OS	50–125
Mad Executioners	1965	OS	50–70
Mad Ghoul	1943	OS	800–1,300
Mad Magician	1954	OS	150–300

M

M

TITLE	YEAR	SIZE	PRICE RANGE
Mad Max	1979	OS	75–200
Mad Max	1979	LC SET	100–200
Mad Max beyond Thunderdome	1985	OS	50–125
Mad Wednesday	1950	OS	500–800
Madame	1961	OS	50–90
Madame Bovary	1949	OS	75–200
Madame X	1966	OS	50–90
Made for Each Other	1939	OS	500–900
Made in Paris	1966	OS	50–90
Made in Paris	1966	LC SET	40–90
Made in USA	1966	47 × 63 FRE	300–400
Mademoiselle	1966	OS	40–80
Madhouse	1974	OS	50–100
Magic	1978	OS	50–80
Magic Boy	1960	OS	50–150
Magic Christian	1970	OS	50–150
Magic Christian	1970	LC SET	100–175
Magic Face	1951	OS	50–125
Magic Sword	1961	OS	50–90
Magic Town	1947	OS	200–400
Magnetic Monster	1953	OS	200–350
Magnetic Monster	1953	LC SET	75–150
Magnificent Ambersons	1942	OS	3,000–4,000
Magnificent Matador	1955	OS	75–150
Magnificent Obsession	1935	OS	200–450
Magnificent Obsession	1954	OS	50–80
Magnificent Seven	1960	OS	300–700
Magnificent Seven	1960	LC SET	100–275
Magnificent Seven Ride	1972	OS	50–70
Magnolia	1999	OS	50–70
Magnum Force	1973	OS	500–850
Magnum Force	1973	LC SET	75–150
Mahogany	1975	OS	50–100
Main Attraction	1962	OS	50–70
Main Event	1979	OS	50–90
Main Event	1979	LC SET	40–70
Major Dundee	1965	OS	60–90
Make Haste to Live	1954	OS	50–90

M

TITLE	YEAR	SIZE	PRICE RANGE
Make Mine Music	1946	OS	200–400
Malaga	1962	OS	75–200
Malaya	1949	OS	100–175
Male Animal	1942	OS	100–250
Maltese Falcon	1941	OS	5,500–7,000
Mame	1974	OS	70–125
Man Afraid	1957	OS	50–70
Man and a Woman	1966	OS	50–125
Man and a Woman	1966	LC SET	50–100
Man Beast	1955	OS	250–350
Man behind the Gun	1952	OS	100–250
Man Betrayed	1941	OS	400–600
Man Called Flintstone	1966	OS	75–250
Man Called Flintstone	1966	LC SET	75–150
Man Called Horse	1970	OS	40–70
Man Could Get Killed	1966	OS	40–70
Man Crazy	1953	OS	50–150
Man for All Seasons	1966	OS	1,000–1,700
Man for All Seasons	1966	LC SET	75–150
Man from Cairo	1953	OS	50–70
Man from Galveston	1964	OS	40–70
Man from Laramie	1955	OS	250–550
Man from Monterey	1933	OS	5,500–7,000
Man from Planet X	1951	OS	3,500–5,000
Man from the Alamo	1953	OS	75–150
Man from the Diner's Club	1963	OS	50–80
Man from Utah	1934	OS	2,000–3,000
Man Hunt	1941	OS	300–450
Man I Love	1946	OS	350–500
Man in the Attic	1953	OS	40–60
Man in the Dark	1953	OS	125–325
Man in the Grey Flannel Suit	1956	OS	50–90
Man in the Iron Mask	1939	OS	300–550
Man in the Iron Mask	1998	OS	40–50
Man in the Middle	1964	OS	40–70
Man in the Net	1959	OS	50–90
Man in the Shadow	1958	OS	50–90
Man in the White Suit	1951	OS	75–200

M

TITLE	YEAR	SIZE	PRICE RANGE
Man of a Thousand Faces	1957	OS	100–250
Man of a Thousand Faces	1957	LC SET	100–200
Man of La Mancha	1972	OS	60–90
Man of the West	1958	OS	100–225
Man on a Tightrope	1953	OS	50–90
Man on Fire	1957	OS	50–90
Man They Could Not Hang	1939	OS	1,500–2,250
Man Trap	1926	OS	1,000–2,250
Man Trap	1961	OS	40–60
Man Who Came to Dinner	1942	OS	250–500
Man Who Could Cheat Death	1959	OS	50–150
Man Who Could Cheat Death	1959	LC SET	100–200
Man Who Fell to Earth	1975	OS	150–300
Man Who Knew Too Much	1934	OS	300–500
Man Who Knew Too Much	1956	OS	450–700
Man Who Knew Too Much	1956	LC SET	300–400
Man Who Loved Cat Dancing	1973	OS	40–60
Man Who Reclaimed His Head	1934	OS	2,000–3,000
Man Who Shot Liberty Valance	1962	OS	450–850
Man Who Turned to Stone	1957	OS	75–150
Man Who Turned to Stone	1957	LC SET	75–150
Man Who Would Be King	1975	OS	50–125
Man Who Would Be King	1975	LC SET	50–100
Man with a Cloak	1951	OS	200–400
Man with Nine Lives	1940	OS	150–450
Man with the Golden Arm	1956	OS	600–1,250
Man with the Golden Arm	1956	LC SET	300–400
Man with the Golden Gun	1974	OS	300–600
Man with the Golden Gun	1974	LC SET	125–250
Man with the Gun	1955	OS	50–125
Man with the Steel Whip	1954	OS	125–300
Man without a Body	1957	OS	50–90
Man without a Body	1957	LC SET	100–175
Man's Favorite Sport	1964	OS	40–70
Man's Fight	1919	OS	75–150
Manchurian Candidate	1962	OS	300–500
Manchurian Candidate	1962	LC SET	100–150
Mandingo	1975	OS	40–70

TITLE	YEAR	SIZE	PRICE RANGE
Manfish	1956	OS	40–70
Manhattan	1979	OS	200–450
Manhattan	1979	LC SET	100–175
Mania	1961	OS	50–125
Maniac	1963	OS	40–60
Mannequin	1937	OS	750–900
Manpower	1941	OS	150–400
Mara Maru	1952	OS	150–250
Marathon Man	1976	OS	50–90
Marco Polo	1964	OS	40–70
Marie Antoinette	1938	OS	1,500–2,000
Marihuana	1936	OS	450–875
Marilyn	1963	OS	100–200
Marines Let's Go	1961	OS	50–70
Marjorie Morningstar	1958	OS	60–125
Mark of the Devil	1970	OS	50–125
Mark of the Hawk	1958	OS	75–125
Mark of Zorro	1920	22 × 28	750–950
Mark of Zorro	1940	OS	11,500
Marked Woman	1937	OS	3,500–4,000
Marlowe	1969	OS	40–70
Marnie	1964	OS	400–550
Marnie	1964	LC SET	150–300
Marooned	1969	OS	40–70
Marriage Go Round	1960	OS	40–70
Marriage on the Rocks	1965	OS	50–90
Marriage on the Rocks	1965	LC SET	150–225
Marrying Kind	1952	OS	50–80
Mars Attacks	1997	OS	50–90
Mars Attacks	1997	LC SET	50–90
Mars Attacks the World	1938	OS	300–550
Marshal of Cedar Rock	1952	OS	40–90
Marty	1955	OS	100–225
Mary Jane	1968	OS	75–225
Mary Jane	1968	LC SET	70–125
Mary of Scotland	1936	OS	4,500–5,500
Mary Poppins	1964	OS	150–400
Mary Poppins	1964	LC SET	200–350

M

TITLE	YEAR	SIZE	PRICE RANGE
Mary Queen of Scots	1972	OS	50–70
MASH	1970	OS	150–350
MASH	1970	LC SET	40–90
Mask	1961	OS	50–90
Mask	1961	LC SET	100–150
Mask	1985	OS	40–70
Mask of Dimitrios	1944	OS	250–500
Masked Marvel	1943	OS	450–850
Masque of the Red Death	1964	OS	75–175
Masquerade in Mexico	1945	OS	50–125
Masquerader	1933	OS	700–900
Massacre	1934	OS	600–800
Master of Ballantrae	1953	OS	75–300
Master of the World	1961	OS	50–90
Master of the World	1961	LC SET	150–250
Mata Hari	1932	LC	700–900
Matchmaker	1958	OS	50–70
Matrix	1999	OS	50–80
Matrix	1999	LC SET	60–100
Maverick	1952	OS	100–225
Maverick	1994	OS	40–70
Maya	1966	OS	40–70
Maytime	1937	OS	1,000–1,500
McCabe and Mrs. Miller	1971	OS	75–250
McHale's Navy	1964	OS	50–90
McLintock	1963	OS	100–225
McLintock	1963	LC SET	150–250
McQ	1974	OS	50–80
McQ	1974	LC SET	100–150
McVicar	1980	OS	40–70
McVicar	1980	LC SET	40–70
Me Natalie	1969	OS	40–60
Mean Streets	1973	OS	500–800
Mean Streets	1973	LC SET	150–250
Meanest Man in the World	1943	OS	80–150
Meatballs	1979	OS	40–80
Meatballs	1979	LC SET	30–60
Mechanic	1972	OS	40–80

TITLE	YEAR	SIZE	PRICE RANGE
Medea	1970	13 × 28 ITA	100–200
Medium Cool	1969	OS	150–300
Meet Danny Wilson	1952	OS	75–200
Meet John Doe	1941	OS	750–1,750
Meet Me after the Show	1951	OS	75–175
Meet Me at the Fair	1953	OS	50–100
Meet Me in Las Vegas	1956	OS	50–150
Meet Me in St. Louis	1944	OS	1,500–2,000
Meet the People	1944	OS	250–400
Melody Time	1948	OS	250–450
Men	1950	OS	200–350
Men in Black	1997	OS	50–90
Men of Boys Town	1941	OS	250–400
Men of the Fighting Lady	1954	OS	50–150
Men without Souls	1940	OS	150–250
Mermaids of Tiburon	1962	OS	50–150
Merrill's Marauders	1962	OS	50–90
Merrill's Marauders	1962	LC SET	75–125
Merry Andrew	1958	OS	50–90
Merry Christmas Mr. Lawrence	1982	OS	50–90
Merry Christmas Mr. Lawrence	1982	LC SET	50–90
Merry Go Round of 1938	1937	OS	175–400
Merry Widow	1934	14 × 36	1,000–2,000
Mesa of Lost Women	1952	OS	100–200
Meteor	1979	OS	30–60
Metropolis	1926	41 × 81 GER	200,000–350,000
Mexican Hayride	1948	OS	200–300
Mexican Hayride	1948	LC SET	250–400
Mickey Mouse—"New Walt Disney"	1932	OS	41,000
Mickey Mouse—"Technicolor"	1935	OS	18,000
Mickey's Birthday Party	1942	OS	9,000
Mickey's Good Deed	1932	OS	43,000
Mickey's Pal Pluto	1933	OS	31,000
Middle of the Night	1959	OS	50–90
Midnight	1934	OS	1,500–2,000
Midnight Cowboy	1969	OS	300–650

M

TITLE	YEAR	SIZE	PRICE RANGE
Midnight Cowboy	1969	LC SET	75–125
Midnight Express	1978	OS	50–90
Midnight Express	1978	LC SET	50–80
Midnight Lace	1960	OS	40–90
Midnight Manhunt	1945	OS	150–250
Midnight Run	1988	OS	50–90
Midnight Run	1988	LC SET	50–80
Midnight Story	1957	OS	50–90
Midsummer Night's Dream	1935	OS	1,500–2,500
Midsummer Night's Sex Comedy	1982	OS	50–80
Midway	1976	OS	50–80
Midway	1976	LC SET	50–70
Mighty Joe Young	1949	OS	1,500–2,250
Mighty Joe Young	1949	LC SET	800–1,000
Mighty Mouse	1943	OS	500–750
Mighty Ursus	1962	OS	75–200
Mikado	1939	14 × 36	250–600
Mildred Pierce	1945	OS	700–950
Miller's Crossing	1990	OS	75–150
Miller's Crossing	1990	LC SET	50–70
Million Dollar Mermaid	1952	OS	150–400
Million Dollar Mermaid	1952	LC SET	100–200
Millionairess	1960	OS	50–70
Ministry of Fear	1944	OS	400–550
Miniver Story	1950	OS	75–200
Minnie and Moskowitz	1972	OS	75–150
Minotaur	1961	OS	40–60
Minotaur	1961	LC SET	50–90
Minute to Pray, a Second to Die	1968	OS	40–60
Miracle	1959	OS	50–90
Miracle in the Rain	1956	OS	50–90
Miracle of Morgan's Creek	1944	OS	300–650
Miracle of the Bells	1948	OS	350–600
Miracle of the White Stallions	1963	OS	50–80
Miracle on 34th Street	1947	OS	750–1,550
Miracle Rider	1935	OS	750–1,400
Miracle Worker	1962	OS	60–90
Mirage	1965	OS	40–90

188 Cleopatra *(1917)*

189 Dracula *(1931)*

190 Dracula *(1931)*

(Alternate Style)

191 Flash Gordon *(1936)*

M

TITLE	YEAR	SIZE	PRICE RANGE
Misery	1990	OS	40–60
Misfits	1961	OS	650–1,250
Misfits	1961	LC SET	550–700
Miss Grant Takes Richmond	1949	OS	75–200
Miss Sadie Thompson	1953	OS	100–250
Missile Monsters	1958	OS	150–300
Missile to the Moon	1959	OS	200–300
Missing	1982	OS	40–60
Mission	1986	OS	40–80
Mission Impossible	1998	OS	40–70
Mission Mars	1968	OS	40–90
Mississippi	1935	OS	450–600
Mississippi Burning	1988	OS	40–70
Missouri Breaks	1976	OS	50–90
Missouri Traveler	1958	OS	40–70
Mister Roberts	1955	OS	175–375
Mister Rock and Roll	1957	OS	200–350
Misty	1961	OS	40–70
Mixed Nuts	1933	OS	300–400
Mo' Better Blues	1990	OS	40–60
Moby Dick	1956	OS	150–400
Modern Times	1936	OS	13,000–16,000
Modesty Blaise	1966	OS	150–400
Modesty Blaise	1966	LC SET	90–150
Mogambo	1953	OS	450–800
Mole People	1956	OS	750–1,500
Molly Maguires	1970	OS	40–70
Moment to Moment	1966	OS	50–90
Mommie Dearest	1981	OS	50–100
Mommie Dearest	1981	LC SET	50–70
Mona Lisa	1986	OS	40–70
Mondo Cane	1963	OS	50–90
Money from Home	1954	OS	50–150
Money Trap	1965	OS	50–90
Money, Women and Guns	1958	OS	75–125
Monkey Business	1931	OS	7,000
Monkey Business	1931	LC SET	8,625
Monkey Business	1952	OS	300–400

TITLE	YEAR	SIZE	PRICE RANGE
Monkey's Uncle	1965	OS	40–90
Monkeys Go Home	1967	OS	40–70
Monolith Monsters	1957	OS	100–300
Monsieur Beaucaire	1946	OS	150–400
Monsieur Verdoux	1947	OS	400–550
Monsoon	1952	OS	30–50
Monster of Piedras Blancas	1958	OS	200–400
Monster on the Campus	1958	OS	150–350
Monster on the Campus	1958	LC SET	250–400
Monster That Challenged the World	1957	OS	200–500
Monster That Challenged the World	1957	LC SET	150–450
Montana	1950	OS	200–350
Monte Carlo Baby	1953	OS	225–325
Monte Walsh	1970	OS	30–50
Monterey Pop	1968	OS	100–250
Monty Python and Holy Grail	1975	OS	100–200
Monty Python Live at the Hollywood Bowl	1982	OS	40–80
Monty Python Life of Brian	1979	LC SET	50–80
Monty Python's Meaning of Life	1983	OS	40–70
Moon over Miami	1941	OS	4,700–7,000
Moon Spinners	1964	OS	40–80
Moon Zero Two	1970	OS	50–90
Moonfleet	1955	OS	50–90
Moonlighter	1953	OS	150–250
Moonraker	1979	OS	100–200
Moonraker	1979	LC SET	50–90
Moonshine Mountain	1964	OS	50–90
Moonstruck	1987	OS	50–100
Moontide	1942	OS	100–250
More American Graffiti	1979	OS	50–80
More the Merrier	1943	OS	100–225
Morgan the Pirate	1961	OS	40–70
Morocco	1930	OS	21,000
Mosquito Coast	1986	OS	40–70
Mosquito Squadron	1968	OS	40–70
Motel Hell	1980	OS	40–70
Mother and the Law	1919	OS	1,000–2,250

M

M

TITLE	YEAR	SIZE	PRICE RANGE
Mother Goose Goes Hollywood	1938	OS	15,000
Mothra	1962	OS	150–350
Mothra	1962	LC SET	250–450
Motor Psycho	1964	OS	550–800
Motorcycle Gang	1957	OS	150–250
Moulin Rouge	1952	OS	100–225
Moulin Rouge	1952	47 × 63 FRE	600–1,000
Moulin Rouge!	2001	OS	50–80
Mountain	1956	OS	40–70
Mountain Road	1960	OS	60–90
Mourning Becomes Electra	1947	OS	40–150
Mouse on the Moon	1963	OS	40–80
Mouse That Roared	1959	OS	80–150
Move over Darling	1963	OS	40–70
Movie Maniacs	1935	OS	37,000
Mr. and Mrs. North	1941	OS	125–250
Mr. and Mrs. Smith	1941	OS	350–550
Mr. Belvedere Goes to College	1949	OS	60–90
Mr. Belvedere Rings the Bell	1951	OS	30–70
Mr. Blandings Builds His Dream House	1948	OS	150–400
Mr. Bug Goes to Town	1941	OS	400–800
Mr. Deeds Goes to Town	1936	OS	3,000–7,000
Mr. Hobbs Takes a Vacation	1962	OS	40–80
Mr. Imperium	1950	OS	50–100
Mr. Lucky	1943	OS	600–1,150
Mr. Moses	1965	OS	40–70
Mr. Peabody and the Mermaid	1948	OS	200–350
Mr. Ricco	1975	OS	40–60
Mr. Sardonicus	1961	OS	50–90
Mr. Sardonicus	1961	LC SET	75–100
Mr. Skeffington	1944	OS	150–400
Mr. Skitch	1933	OS	250–450
Mr. Smith Goes to Washington	1939	OS	5,000–6,000
Mr. Soft Touch	1949	OS	50–90
Mr. Winkle Goes to War	1944	OS	40–90
Mrs. Brown, You've Got a Lovely Daughter	1968	OS	50–100

TITLE	YEAR	SIZE	PRICE RANGE
Mrs. Miniver	1942	OS	400–600
Mrs. Wiggs of Cabbage Patch	1934	OS	2,500–3,000
Mudhoney	1965	OS	150–300
Mulan	1998	OS	50–90
Mulholland Drive	2001	OS	40–70
Mummy	1932	OS	453,500
Mummy	1959	OS	500–1,250
Mummy Returns	2001	OS	40–70
Mummy's Curse	1944	OS	2,500–3,000
Mummy's Ghost	1944	OS	2,500–3,000
Mummy's Shroud	1967	OS	50–125
Mummy's Tomb	1942	OS	4,000–4,500
Munster Go Home	1966	OS	200–350
Muppet Movie	1979	OS	50–90
Muppets Take Manhattan	1984	OS	40–60
Murder Ahoy	1964	OS	50–125
Murder by Contract	1958	OS	50–150
Murder by Death	1976	OS	50–90
Murder by Decree	1979	OS	40–70
Murder by Decree	1979	LC SET	50–70
Murder by Television	1935	OS	9,600
Murder in Harlem	1934	OS	5,750
Murder Is My Beat	1955	OS	125–350
Murder My Sweet	1944	OS	1,000–2,000
Murder on the Orient Express	1974	OS	50–90
Murder, She Said	1961	OS	70–125
Murderer's Row	1966	OS	50–125
Murderer's Row	1966	LC SET	100–200
Murders in the Zoo	1933	OS	6,800
Murphy's Law	1986	OS	40–60
Muscle Beach Party	1964	OS	50–150
Music Land	1955	OS	75–250
Music Man	1962	OS	250–400
Mutations	1973	OS	40–90
Mutations	1973	LC SET	40–70
Mutiny on the Bounty	1935	OS	3,000–4,000
Mutiny on the Bounty	1962	OS	50–90
Mutiny on the Bounty	1962	LC SET	50–90

M

M

TITLE	YEAR	SIZE	PRICE RANGE
My Best Girl	1927	OS	2,000
My Blood Runs Cold	1965	OS	40–70
My Blue Heaven	1950	OS	50–125
My Cousin Rachel	1952	OS	50–90
My Darling Clementine	1946	OS	1,500–3,000
My Darling Clementine	1946	LC SET	500–850
My Dinner with Andre	1981	OS	40–60
My Fair Lady	1964	OS	350–700
My Fair Lady	1964	LC SET	350–450
My Favorite Brunette	1947	OS	150–450
My Favorite Spy	1942	OS	50–90
My Favorite Wife	1940	OS	1,000–1,500
My Favorite Year	1982	OS	40–90
My Foolish Heart	1949	OS	50–125
My Forbidden Past	1951	OS	200–325
My Friend Irma	1949	OS	250–450
My Friend Irma Goes West	1950	OS	100–350
My Gal Sal	1942	OS	400–650
My Geisha	1962	OS	50–90
My Left Foot	1989	OS	50–80
My Little Chickadee	1940	OS	5,000–6,000
My Man Godfrey	1936	OS	7,150
My Man Godfrey	1957	OS	40–80
My Name Is Nobody	1974	OS	70–125
My Own Private Idaho	1991	OS	50–90
My Pal Trigger	1946	OS	250–450
My Sister Eileen	1942	OS	50–70
My Six Loves	1963	OS	40–60
Myra Beckinridge	1970	OS	50–80
Mysterians	1959	OS	100–250
Mysterians	1959	LC SET	350–500
Mysterious Dr. Satan	1940	OS	350–550
Mysterious Island	1961	OS	75–150
Mysterious Island	1961	LC SET	100–225
Mysterious Island of Capt. Nemo	1973	OS	50–125
Mysterious Lady	1928	OS	6,100
Mysterious Mr. Valentine	1946	OS	75–125
Mysterious Mr. Wong	1935	OS	600–1,250

TITLE	YEAR	SIZE	PRICE RANGE
Mystery Man	1944	OS	100–225
Mystery Mountian	1934	OS	450–750
Mystery of Mr. Wong	1939	OS	700–1,250
Mystery of the Wax Museum	1933	LC SET	7,500
Mystery Street	1950	OS	150–250
Mystery Submarine	1963	OS	40–70
Mystery Train	1989	OS	50–90
Naked Alibi	1954	OS	75–275
Naked and the Dead	1958	OS	50–80
Naked City	1948	OS	550–1,750
Naked Dawn	1955	OS	50–90
Naked Edge	1961	OS	50–90
Naked Gun	1988	OS	40–60
Naked Jungle	1954	OS	40–70
Naked Kiss	1964	OS	300–500
Naked Lunch	1991	OS	75–175
Naked Maja	1959	OS	40–80
Naked Prey	1965	OS	40–70
Naked Runner	1967	OS	50–90
Naked Spur	1953	OS	300–550
Naked under Leather	1968	OS	550–950
Name of the Rose	1986	OS	40–70
Namu the Killer Whale	1966	OS	40–60
Nancy Drew Detective	1938	OS	550–900
Nancy Goes to Rio	1950	OS	50–100
Nanny	1965	OS	50–80
Nanook of the North	1921	OS	9,775
Napoleon	1927	OS	5,750
Narrow Margin	1952	OS	350–500
Nashville	1975	OS	100–250
Nashville	1975	LC SET	40–70
National Lampoon's European Vacation	1985	OS	40–70
National Lampoon's Vacation	1983	OS	100–250
National Lampoon's Vacation	1983	LC SET	50–90
National Velvet	1944	OS	600–1,250
National Velvet	1944	LC SET	1,000–1,500
Natural	1984	OS	50–90

N

TITLE	YEAR	SIZE	PRICE RANGE
Natural	1984	LC SET	40–70
Natural Born Killers	1994	OS	50–90
Naughty Marietta	1935	OS	400–800
Naughty New Orleans	1954	OS	40–70
Naughty Nineties	1945	OS	200–450
Navajo Joe	1966	OS	40–80
Navigator	1924	OS	15,000
Navy Blue and Gold	1937	OS	400–550
Nazarin	1958	47 × 63 FRE	300–550
Neanderthal Man	1953	OS	200–500
Near Dark	1987	OS	40–80
Ned Kelly	1970	OS	75–125
Neptune Factor	1973	OS	40–70
Network	1976	OS	50–125
Network	1976	LC SET	70–90
Nevada Smith	1966	OS	50–175
Never a Dull Moment	1950	OS	50–80
Never a Dull Moment	1968	OS	40–70
NeverEnding Story	1984	OS	40–70
Never Give a Sucker an Even Break	1941	OS	1,000–1,500
Never Let Go	1962	OS	40–70
Never Let Me Go	1953	OS	150–325
Never Let Me Go	1953	LC SET	150–250
Never Love a Stranger	1958	OS	40–80
Never on a Sunday	1960	OS	50–150
Never Say Goodbye	1946	OS	75–250
Never Say Goodbye	1956	OS	75–150
Never Say Never Again	1983	OS	200–400
Never Say Never Again	1983	LC SET	75–125
Never So Few	1959	OS	75–300
Never Steal Anything Small	1958	OS	40–90
Never Wave at a WAC	1953	OS	50–90
New Adv. of Batman and Robin	1949	OS	850–2,000
New Adv. of Tarzan	1935	OS	800–2,500
New Faces	1954	OS	150–250
New Frontier	1935	OS	800–1,500
New Kind of Love	1963	OS	50–90
New Orleans after Dark	1958	OS	50–90

TITLE	YEAR	SIZE	PRICE RANGE
New Orleans Uncensored	1954	OS	50–90
New Spirit	1942	OS	3,500–4,500
New York Confidential	1955	OS	50–90
New York, New York	1977	OS	75–150
New York, New York	1977	LC SET	50–150
New York Town	1941	OS	50–175
News Hounds	1947	OS	50–70
Next Time We Love	1936	OS	1,500–2,500
Next Voice You Hear	1950	OS	50–90
Niagara	1953	OS	1,500–2,500
Nice Little Bank That Should Be	1958	OS	50–70
Nickelodeon	1976	OS	40–70
Night Alarm	1934	OS	300–450
Night and Day	1946	OS	150–400
Night and the City	1950	OS	250–450
Night at the Opera	1935	OS	13,225
Night Creatures	1962	OS	50–125
Night Creatures	1962	LC SET	150–250
Night Fighters	1960	OS	40–70
Night Has a Thousand Eyes	1948	OS	250–500
Night Heaven Fell	1957	OS	75–200
Night in Casablanca	1946	OS	600–800
Night Moves	1975	OS	30–60
Night Must Fall	1937	OS	500–900
Night My Number Came Up	1955	OS	250–550
Night of Dark Shadows	1971	OS	60–100
Night of Dark Shadows	1971	LC SET	75–125
Night of Love	1954	OS	150–300
Night of Terror	1945	OS	50–80
Night of the Blood Beast	1958	OS	300–750
Night of the Blood Monster	1972	OS	50–150
Night of the Following Day	1969	OS	50–80
Night of the Generals	1967	OS	50–90
Night of the Grizzly	1966	OS	50–70
Night of the Hunter	1955	OS	1,100–2,500
Night of the Iguana	1964	OS	50–100
Night of the Lepus	1972	OS	50–90
Night of the Living Dead	1968	OS	400–700

N

311

N

TITLE	YEAR	SIZE	PRICE RANGE
Night of the Living Dead	1968	LC SET	750–1,000
Night of the Quarter Moon	1959	OS	50–150
Night Passage	1957	OS	50–150
Night People	1954	OS	70–125
Night Porter	1974	OS	50–90
Night Porter	1974	LC SET	75–175
Night Runner	1957	OS	50–70
Night Shift	1982	OS	40–60
Night the World Exploded	1957	OS	75–225
Night the World Exploded	1957	LC SET	50–300
Night They Raided Minsky's	1969	OS	50–150
Night Tide	1963	OS	500–900
Night to Remember	1958	OS	150–350
Night Walker	1964	OS	100–250
Night Watch	1973	OS	50–90
Night without Sleep	1952	OS	75–150
Nightcomers	1972	OS	50–80
Nightfall	1956	OS	50–90
Nighthawks	1981	OS	50–70
Nightmare	1956	OS	50–175
Nightmare Alley	1947	OS	500–950
Nightmare before Christmas	1993	OS	75–150
Nightmare before Christmas	1993	LC SET	150–300
Nightmare Castle	1966	OS	75–175
Nightmare in Wax	1969	OS	50–70
Nightmare on Elm Street	1984	OS	50–150
Nightmares	1983	OS	40–60
Nights of Cabiria	1957	OS	150–300
9½ Weeks	1986	OS	50–70
9½ Weeks	1986	LC SET	50–80
Nine Lives of Fritz the Cat	1974	OS	80–125
9 to 5	1980	OS	40–60
1984	1956	OS	175–350
1984	1956	LC SET	150–250
1941	1979	OS	75–125
1941	1979	LC SET	40–70
1900	1976	OS	150–225
99 River Street	1953	OS	40–70

TITLE	YEAR	SIZE	PRICE RANGE
Ninotchka	1939	22 × 28	1,000–2,250
No Down Payment	1957	OS	40–70
No Highway in the Sky	1951	OS	100–250
No Man of Her Own	1950	OS	75–150
No More Ladies	1935	OS	500–750
No, No, Nanette	1940	OS	75–150
No Nukes	1980	OS	40–70
No Room for the Groom	1952	OS	50–100
No Way Out	1950	OS	500–750
No Way Out	1950	LC SET	200–350
No Way Out	1987	OS	50–70
No Way to Treat a Lady	1968	OS	40–70
Noah's Ark	1929	OS	500–800
Nob Hill	1945	OS	150–250
Nobody Lives Forever	1946	OS	300–500
Nocturne	1946	OS	150–300
None but the Brave	1965	OS	50–150
None but the Brave	1965	LC SET	50–90
None but the Lonely Heart	1944	OS	150–250
Noose Hangs High	1948	OS	250–400
Nora Prentiss	1947	OS	150–400
Norma Rae	1979	OS	40–70
Norma Rae	1979	LC SET	75–100
North by Northwest	1959	OS	700–1,200
North by Northwest	1959	LC SET	1,200–1,500
North Dallas Forty	1979	OS	50–90
North Dallas Forty	1979	LC SET	40–70
North of the Great Divide	1950	OS	250–400
North to Alaska	1960	OS	75–250
Northwest Mounted Police	1940	OS	100–250
Northwest Outpost	1947	OS	250–500
Northwest Passage	1940	OS	400–650
Norwood	1970	OS	40–70
Nosferatu the Vampire	1979	OS	75–150
Not as a Stranger	1955	OS	50–125
Not of This Earth	1957	OS	500–1,000
Not of This Earth	1957	LC SET	250–350
Not with My Wife You Don't	1966	OS	40–70

N

313

N

TITLE	YEAR	SIZE	PRICE RANGE
Nothing but the Best	1964	OS	40–70
Nothing but the Night	1972	OS	50–80
Nothing but the Truth	1941	OS	300–500
Nothing but Trouble	1945	OS	500–750
Nothing Sacred	1937	OS	750–1,000
Notorious	1946	OS	3,500–5,500
Notorious	1946	LC SET	2,000–2,500
Notorious Landlady	1961	OS	40–90
Notorious Landlady	1961	LC SET	30–70
Notting Hill	1999	OS	40–60
Now Voyager	1942	OS	1,500–2,000
Number One	1969	OS	40–70
Nun's Story	1959	OS	75–225
Nutty Professor	1963	OS	75–225
Nutty Professor	1963	LC SET	75–150
Nutty Professor	1998	OS	40–70
O Brother, Where Art Thou?	2000	OS	40–60
O Lucky Man	1973	OS	40–60
O'Henry's Full House	1952	OS	125–300
Objective, Burma!	1945	OS	700–950
Oblong Box	1969	OS	50–90
Oblong Box	1969	LC SET	60–100
Obsession	1976	OS	40–60
Ocean's 11	1960	OS	1,250–1,800
Ocean's 11	1960	LC SET	450–700
Ocean's 11	2001	OS	40–60
October Man	1948	OS	100–250
Octopussy	1983	OS	100–175
Octopussy	1983	LC SET	50–70
Odd Couple	1968	OS	75–150
Odd Couple	1968	LC SET	100–150
Odd Man Out	1947	OS	300–500
Odds against Tomorrow	1959	OS	100–225
Ode to Billy Joe	1976	OS	40–60
Odessa File	1974	OS	40–60
Of Human Bondage	1946	OS	100–250
Of Mice and Men	1939	22 × 28	750–1,000
Of Mice and Men	1992	OS	50–90

O

TITLE	YEAR	SIZE	PRICE RANGE
Offence	1973	OS	40–70
Officer and a Gentleman	1982	OS	50–90
Officer and a Gentleman	1982	LC SET	40–70
Oh Dad, Poor Dad	1967	OS	40–60
Oh God	1977	OS	40–70
Oh God	1977	LC SET	50–90
Oh, Men! Oh, Women!	1957	OS	40–80
Oh What a Lovely War	1969	OS	40–70
Oh You Beautiful Doll	1949	OS	50–90
Okinawa	1952	OS	50–175
Oklahoma	1956	OS	75–200
Oklahoma Crude	1973	OS	50–80
Oklahoma Kid	1939	OS	1,500–2,250
Old Acquaintance	1943	OS	300–550
Old Dark House	1963	OS	50–80
Old Dracula	1975	OS	50–90
Old Macdonald Duck	1937	OS	4,300
Old Maid	1939	OS	450–700
Old Maid	1939	LC SET	600–800
Old Man and the Sea	1958	OS	50–175
Old Oklahoma Plains	1952	OS	50–90
Old Spanish Custom	1932	OS	500–850
Old West	1952	OS	75–200
Old Yeller	1957	OS	100–325
Oliver	1968	OS	60–125
Oliver Twist	1948	OS	200–450
Oliver's Story	1978	OS	40–60
Omega Man	1971	OS	100–300
Omega Man	1971	LC SET	50–150
Omen	1976	OS	100–250
On a Clear Day You Can See Forever	1970	OS	100–200
On an Island with You	1948	OS	150–250
On Any Sunday	1971	OS	350–500
On Dangerous Ground	1951	OS	300–500
On Golden Pond	1981	OS	50–90
On Golden Pond	1981	LC SET	50–80
On Her Majesty's Secret Service	1969	OS	350–550

O

TITLE	YEAR	SIZE	PRICE RANGE
On Moonlight Bay	1951	OS	100–225
On Our Merry Way	1948	OS	150–375
On the Avenue	1937	OS	2,875
On the Beach	1959	OS	100–200
On the Double	1961	OS	50–70
On the Old Spanish Trail	1947	OS	350–550
On the Riviera	1951	OS	75–200
On the Threshold of Space	1956	OS	75–125
On the Town	1949	OS	500–850
On the Waterfront	1954	OS	1,500–2,250
On the Waterfront	1954	LC SET	500–900
On Top of Old Smoky	1953	OS	75–200
Once Is Not Enough	1975	OS	40–60
Once More with Feeling	1960	OS	50–70
Once upon a Honeymoon	1942	OS	200–350
Once upon a Time in America	1984	OS	100–350
Once upon a Time in the West	1969	OS	500–750
One A.M.	1916	OS	15,000
One Body Too Many	1944	OS	125–350
One Desire	1955	OS	50–125
One Exciting Week	1946	OS	40–70
One-Eyed Jacks	1961	OS	250–350
One Flew over the Cuckoo's Nest	1975	OS	300–550
One Flew over the Cuckoo's Nest	1975	LC SET	350–600
One Foot in Hell	1960	OS	50–90
One from the Heart	1982	OS	50–90
101 Dalmations	1961	OS	500–850
101 Dalmations	1961	LC SET	400–600
101 Dalmations	1996	OS	40–80
100 Men and a Girl	1937	OS	450–650
100 Rifles	1969	OS	40–90
One Million B.C.	1940	OS	500–1,000
One Million Years B.C.	1966	OS	150–400
One Night in the Tropics	1940	OS	300–500
One Night in the Tropics	1940	LC SET	300–400
One of Our Aircraft Is Missing	1942	OS	300–600
One of Our Spies Is Missing	1966	30 × 40 UK	300–800
One Spy Too Many	1966	OS	200–400

TITLE	YEAR	SIZE	PRICE RANGE
One Spy Too Many	1966	LC SET	75–200
1,001 Arabian Nights	1959	OS	75–200
One Touch of Venus	1948	OS	150–400
One, Two, Three	1961	OS	350–600
Onionhead	1958	OS	40–80
Only Game in Town	1969	OS	40–80
Only Game in Town	1969	LC SET	50–90
Only Two Can Play	1962	OS	40–70
Operation Kid Brother	1967	OS	40–70
Operation Mad Ball	1957	OS	40–70
Operation Pacific	1951	OS	150–350
Operation Petticoat	1959	OS	50–150
Operation Secret	1952	OS	50–70
Operation Snafu	1965	OS	50–80
Operator 13	1934	OS	750–1,000
Opposite Sex	1956	OS	50–90
Optimists	1973	OS	50–90
Orca	1977	OS	50–90
Ordinary People	1980	OS	75–100
Oregon Trail	1936	OS	13,800
Oregon Trail	1959	OS	50–90
Organization	1971	OS	50–80
Orphan's Benefit	1941	OS	5,750
Orphans of the Storm	1922	22 × 28	500–900
Orphée	1950	47 × 63 FRE	700–1,000
O.S.S.	1946	OS	400–700
Othello	1952	OS	350–550
Other	1972	OS	40–70
Our Betters	1933	OS	2,500–3,500
Our Hospitality	1923	LC	750–1,000
Our Man Flint	1966	OS	200–350
Our Man Flint	1966	LC SET	100–250
Our Man in Havana	1960	OS	70–100
Our Miss Brooks	1956	OS	75–125
Our Relations	1936	OS	500–1,500
Out of Africa	1985	OS	75–150
Out of Africa	1985	LC SET	40–90
Out of Sight	1966	OS	50–90

O

O

TITLE	YEAR	SIZE	PRICE RANGE
Out of Sight	1998	OS	40–60
Out of the Fog	1941	OS	150–375
Out of the Past	1947	OS	4,000–6,000
Out of This World	1945	OS	100–300
Out of Towners	1970	OS	50–70
Outland	1981	OS	50–80
Outlaw	1941	OS	15,000
Outlaw Blues	1977	OS	40–60
Outlaw Josey Wales	1976	OS	350–500
Outlaw Josey Wales	1976	LC SET	100–250
Outlawed	1929	OS	3,000
Outlaws Is Coming	1965	OS	50–200
Outrage	1950	OS	40–70
Outrage	1964	OS	50–80
Outside the Law	1921	OS	350–850
Outsider	1962	OS	50–80
Outsiders	1983	OS	50–90
Outsiders	1983	LC SET	75–125
Over-Exposed	1956	OS	150–225
Overland Mail	1942	OS	75–200
Owl and the Pussycat	1970	OS	40–80
Owl and the Pussycat	1970	LC SET	75–125
Ox Bow Incident	1943	OS	350–500
Pack Train	1953	OS	50–150
Pack Up Your Troubles	1932	OS	2,000–4,000
Paddy the Next Best Thing	1933	OS	500–800
Pagan Love Song	1950	OS	75–150
Paint Your Wagon	1969	OS	50–125
Paint Your Wagon	1969	LC SET	75–150
Painted Trail	1938	OS	250–450
Pajama Game	1957	OS	50–125
Pajama Party	1964	OS	50–125
Pal Joey	1957	OS	250–400
Pale Rider	1985	OS	75–200
Paleface	1948	OS	350–600
Paleface	1948	LC SET	350–500
Palm Beach Story	1942	41 × 81	5,750
Pals of the Golden West	1951	OS	200–400

TITLE	YEAR	SIZE	PRICE RANGE
Panama Lady	1939	OS	300–550
Pandora and the Flying Dutchman	1951	OS	200–350
Pandora and the Flying Dutchman	1951	LC SET	200–350
Pandora's Box	1959	OS	75–200
Panic Button	1964	OS	50–125
Panic in Needle Park	1971	OS	50–150
Panic in Needle Park	1971	LC SET	40–100
Panic in the Streets	1950	OS	150–350
Panic in Year Zero	1962	OS	50–200
Panther Girl of the Congo	1955	OS	75–200
Papa's Delicate Condition	1963	OS	50–90
Paper Chase	1973	OS	50–80
Paper Moon	1973	OS	50–90
Paper Moon	1973	LC SET	50–125
Papillon	1974	OS	50–90
Papillon	1974	LC SET	50–100
Paradine Case	1948	OS	300–500
Paradise Alley	1978	OS	40–70
Paradise Canyon	1935	OS	5,280
Paradise Hawaiian Style	1966	OS	75–250
Paradise Hawaiian Style	1966	LC SET	200–350
Parallax View	1974	OS	75–175
Paranoia	1969	OS	50–90
Paranoiac	1963	OS	50–90
Parasite	1982	OS	40–70
Pardners	1956	OS	50–90
Pardon My Sarong	1942	OS	750–1,250
Pardon Us	1931	OS	3,000–5,750
Parent Trap	1961	OS	50–150
Parent Trap	1961	LC SET	50–90
Paris Blues	1961	OS	75–150
Paris Does Strange Things	1956	OS	50–125
Paris Holiday	1958	OS	50–90
Paris Texas	1984	OS	50–175
Paris When It Sizzles	1964	OS	75–275
Parrish	1961	OS	40–70
Party	1968	OS	50–150
Party Crashers	1958	OS	50–90

P

TITLE	YEAR	SIZE	PRICE RANGE
Passage to Marseille	1944	OS	350–1,000
Passenger	1975	OS	40–80
Passenger	1975	LC SET	50–80
Passionate Plumber	1932	OS	850–1,250
Pat and Mike	1952	OS	150–325
Pat Garrett and Billy the Kid	1973	OS	50–150
Patch of Blue	1966	OS	50–90
Paths of Glory	1957	OS	600–900
Patriot	2000	OS	50–125
Patriot	2000	LC SET	40–90
Patsy	1964	OS	50–90
Patterns	1956	OS	40–70
Patton	1970	OS	50–200
Patton	1970	LC SET	50–150
Paula	1952	OS	50–150
Pawnbroker	1965	OS	75–150
Pawnee	1957	OS	40–70
Pay or Die	1960	OS	50–90
Payment on Demand	1951	OS	600–950
Payment on Demand	1951	LC SET	150–250
Pearl Harbor	2001	OS	50–90
Pearl of Death	1944	OS	800–1,000
Pee Wee's Big Adventure	1985	OS	40–90
Peeping Tom	1960	OS	500–850
Peggy Sue Got Married	1986	OS	40–70
Penalty	1920	OS	1,225–2,250
Pendulum	1969	OS	50–90
Penelope	1966	OS	50–90
Pennies from Heaven	1981	OS	40–70
Penny Serenade	1941	OS	350–600
Penthouse	1967	OS	40–70
People against O'Hara	1951	OS	125–300
People That Time Forgot	1977	OS	40–70
People Will Talk	1951	OS	50–125
Percy	1971	OS	30–70
Perfect	1985	OS	40–60
Perfect Furlough	1959	OS	50–80
Perfect Marriage	1946	OS	50–90

TITLE	YEAR	SIZE	PRICE RANGE
Performance	1970	OS	75–150
Perils of Nyoka	1942	OS	400–600
Perils of the Wilderness	1955	OS	50–80
Perri	1957	OS	40–60
Persona	1967	27 × 41 SWE	500–1,250
Personal Property	1937	OS	800–1,500
Pet Semetary	1989	OS	40–60
Pete Kelly's Blues	1955	OS	75–100
Pete's Dragon	1977	OS	40–70
Peter Pan	1953	OS	500–800
Petit Soldat	1963	47 × 63 FRE	250–350
Petty Girl	1950	OS	1,250–2,000
Petulia	1968	OS	40–80
Peyton Place	1957	OS	40–90
Phantasm	1979	OS	100–200
Phantom Creeps	1939	OS	750–1,500
Phantom from Space	1953	OS	75–200
Phantom from 10,000 Leagues	1955	OS	200–450
Phantom from 10,000 Leagues	1955	LC SET	100–200
Phantom Lady	1944	OS	250–350
Phantom of Liberty	1974	OS	40–90
Phantom of the Opera	1925	OS	51,750
Phantom of the Opera	1943	OS	500–1,500
Phantom of the Opera	1962	OS	75–350
Phantom of the Paradise	1974	OS	50–125
Phantom of the Rue Morgue	1954	OS	150–300
Phantom of the West	1930	OS	650–1,100
Phantom Planet	1962	OS	75–150
Phantom Stallion	1954	OS	75–200
Pharaoh's Curse	1956	OS	50–90
Pharaoh's Woman	1961	OS	50–90
Phase IV	1974	OS	40–70
Phenix City Story	1955	OS	150–250
Philadelphia Story	1940	OS	3,000–6,000
Piano	1993	OS	40–60
Pickup	1951	OS	250–550
Pickup Alley	1957	OS	50–150
Pickup on South Street	1953	OS	300–600

P

P

TITLE	YEAR	SIZE	PRICE RANGE
Picnic	1956	OS	200–500
Picnic	1956	LC SET	200–300
Pied Piper	1972	OS	40–70
Pigeon That Took Rome	1962	OS	40–70
Pigskin Parade	1936	OS	300–500
Pillars of the Sky	1956	OS	75–200
Pillow Talk	1959	OS	700–1,000
Pillow to Post	1945	OS	75–225
Pinch Hitter	1917	OS	4,000–5,000
Pink Jungle	1968	OS	40–60
Pink Panther	1964	OS	75–225
Pink Panther	1964	LC SET	125–200
Pink Panther Strikes Again	1976	OS	40–70
Pinky	1949	OS	250–500
Pinocchio	1940	OS	5,000–8,000
Pinocchio	1940	LC SET	6,325
Piranha	1978	OS	50–125
Pirate	1948	OS	600–900
Pirate	1948	LC SET	500–800
Pirates of Blood River	1962	OS	50–90
Pit and the Pendulum	1961	OS	150–400
Pit and the Pendulum	1961	LC SET	300–400
Pitfall	1948	OS	250–400
Pittsburgh	1942	OS	600–850
PJ	1968	OS	40–70
Place in the Sun	1951	OS	1,250–1,550
Place in the Sun	1951	LC SET	750–800
Plan 9 from Outer Space	1958	OS	750–1,500
Planet of the Apes	1968	OS	750–900
Planet of the Apes	1968	LC SET	250–350
Planet of the Apes	2001	OS	40–80
Planet of the Vampires	1965	OS	50–175
Platinum Blonde	1931	LC	700–1,000
Platoon	1986	OS	50–90
Platoon	1986	LC SET	50–80
Play Ball	1929	OS	96,000
Play It Again Sam	1972	OS	50–100
Play It Again Sam	1972	LC SET	50–100

P

TITLE	YEAR	SIZE	PRICE RANGE
Play It Cool	1963	OS	40–70
Play Misty for Me	1971	OS	50–150
Play Misty for Me	1971	LC SET	100–200
Player	1971	OS	175–400
Playgirl after Dark	1962	OS	75–150
Playtime	1967	47 × 63 FRE	200–500
Plaza Suite	1971	OS	40–70
Please Don't Eat the Daisies	1960	OS	50–80
Please Not Now	1961	OS	125–200
Pleasure of His Company	1961	OS	40–80
Pleasure Seekers	1965	OS	40–80
Plenty	1985	OS	40–70
Plymouth Adventure	1952	OS	100–150
Pocahontas	1995	OS	40–90
Pocket Money	1972	OS	40–70
Pocketful of Miracles	1962	OS	50–125
Point Blank	1961	OS	500–850
Pointer	1939	OS	8,050
Police Academy	1984	OS	40–60
Police Call	1933	OS	250–450
Policewomen	1974	OS	25–125
Pollyanna	1920	LC	75–200
Pollyanna	1960	OS	50–90
Poltergeist	1982	OS	40–70
Polyester	1981	OS	200–250
Pony Express	1953	OS	100–200
Pony Soldier	1952	OS	100–150
Poor Cow	1967	OS	50–150
Poor Little Rich Girl	1936	OS	1,500–2,500
Pope of Greenwich Village	1984	OS	50–90
Popeye	1943	OS	250–400
Popeye	1949	OS	750–850
Popeye	1980	OS	50–70
Porgy and Bess	1959	OS	350–500
Pork Chop Hill	1959	OS	75–150
Porky's	1982	OS	40–60
Port of Seven Seas	1938	OS	200–350
Portrait in Black	1960	OS	60–125

P

TITLE	YEAR	SIZE	PRICE RANGE
Portrait of Jennie	1948	OS	250–400
Poseidon Adventure	1972	OS	250–350
Poseidon Adventure	1972	LC SET	50–90
Posse from Hell	1961	OS	50–90
Possessed	1931	LC	500–1,000
Postman Always Rings Twice	1946	OS	3,000–6,000
Postman Always Rings Twice	1981	OS	40–90
Postmark for Danger	1956	OS	40–80
Pot O' Gold	1941	OS	250–400
Power and the Glory	1933	OS	900–1,200
Power and the Glory	1961	OS	40–70
Power and the Prize	1956	OS	40–80
Practically Yours	1944	OS	100–250
Predator	1987	OS	50–90
Prehistoric Women	1966	OS	40–70
Premature Burial	1962	OS	75–200
Presenting Lily Mars	1943	OS	350–700
President's Analyst	1967	OS	50–150
President's Lady	1953	OS	50–90
Pressure Point	1962	OS	40–70
Pretty Baby	1978	OS	50–90
Pretty in Pink	1986	OS	50–90
Pretty Maids All in a Row	1971	OS	50–90
Pretty Poison	1968	OS	50–90
Pretty Woman	1996	OS	50–90
Pride and the Passion	1957	OS	100–225
Pride and Prejudice	1940	OS	1,500–2,250
Pride of St. Louis	1952	OS	250–400
Pride of the Yankees	1942	OS	2,500–4,250
Prime Cut	1972	OS	50–80
Prime of Miss Jean Brodie	1969	OS	40–70
Prince and the Pauper	1937	OS	250–450
Prince and the Showgirl	1957	OS	1,500–2,500
Prince and the Showgirl	1957	LC SET	800–1,700
Prince of Darkness	1987	OS	50–90
Prince of the Foxes	1949	OS	200–325
Prince Valiant	1954	OS	100–225
Prince Who Was a Thief	1951	OS	75–150

TITLE	YEAR	SIZE	PRICE RANGE
Princess Bride	1987	OS	50–90
Princess O'Hara	1935	OS	175–350
Prison Train	1938	OS	50–90
Prisoner of Swing	1938	OS	650–900
Prisoner of War	1954	OS	50–90
Prisoner of Zenda	1937	OS	10,088
Prisoner of Zenda	1952	OS	75–150
Private Benjamin	1980	OS	40–70
Private Benjamin	1980	LC SET	40–70
Private Hell 36	1954	OS	50–175
Private Life of Henry VIII	1933	OS	3,450
Private Life of Sherlock Holmes	1971	OS	40–70
Private Lives of Adam and Eve	1960	OS	50–80
Private Lives of Elizabeth and Essex	1939	OS	1,500–2,250
Private Lives of Elizabeth and Essex	1939	LC SET	700–1,200
Private Parts	1972	OS	40–70
Private Parts	1998	OS	40–70
Private School	1983	OS	50–80
Prize	1963	OS	50–90
Prizzi's Honor	1985	OS	50–90
Prodigal	1955	OS	40–70
Producers	1968	OS	900–1,150
Producers	1968	LC SET	450–600
Professional	1994	OS	40–90
Professionals	1966	OS	75–200
Professor Beware	1938	OS	550–850
Project Moonbase	1953	OS	75–150
Project X	1968	OS	50–80
Prom Night	1980	OS	50–80
Prom Night	1980	LC SET	50–90
Promise Her Anything	1966	OS	40–70
Proud and Profane	1956	OS	50–90
Proud Ones	1956	OS	75–250
Proud Rebel	1958	OS	50–80
Prowler	1951	OS	50–80
Psych Out	1968	OS	150–200
Psyche 59	1964	OS	40–70
Psycho	1960	OS	1,700–2,000

P

P

TITLE	YEAR	SIZE	PRICE RANGE
Psycho	1960	LC SET	750–2,000
Psycho 2	1983	OS	50–80
Psycho 2	1983	LC SET	70–90
Psychopath	1966	OS	40–60
PT 109	1963	OS	50–80
Public Enemy	1931	LC	4,025
Pufnstuf	1970	OS	40–80
Pulp Fiction	1994	OS	150–250
Pumping Iron	1976	OS	250–400
Pumpkin Eater	1964	OS	40–70
Purple Heart	1944	OS	400–700
Purple Rain	1984	OS	40–90
Purple Rain	1984	LC SET	50–90
Purple Rose of Cairo	1985	OS	40–80
Purple Rose of Cairo	1985	LC SET	40–70
Pursued	1947	OS	300–400
Pursuit to Algiers	1945	OS	450–700
Pushover	1954	OS	60–125
Putney Swope	1969	OS	250–500
Pygmalion	1938	OS	1,250–1,750
Pyro	1963	OS	40–70
Quadrophenia	1979	OS	75–150
Quality Street	1937	OS	3,910
Queen Bee	1955	OS	150–300
Queen Christina	1933	OS	4,370
Queen for a Day	1951	OS	50–125
Queen of Babylon	1956	OS	40–90
Queen of Blood	1966	OS	75–225
Queen of Outer Space	1958	OS	750–1,200
Queen of the Jungle	1935	OS	60–90
Queen of the Pirates	1960	OS	50–125
Quentin Durward	1955	OS	50–150
Quest for Fire	1982	OS	40–70
Quick and the Dead	1995	OS	40–70
Quick Gun	1964	OS	40–90
Quiet American	1958	OS	50–90
Quiet Man	1951	OS	750–1,100
Quiller Memorandum	1966	OS	40–70

TITLE	YEAR	SIZE	PRICE RANGE
Quiz Show	1994	OS	70–90
Quo Vadis	1951	OS	200–500
Quo Vadis	1951	LC SET	150–300
Rabbit Run	1970	OS	40–70
Rabbit Trap	1959	OS	40–60
Rabid	1977	OS	50–90
Race for Life	1954	OS	40–80
Race for Your Life Charlie Brown	1977	OS	40–80
Race for Your Life Charlie Brown	1977	LC SET	40–80
Race Street	1948	OS	150–225
Race with the Devil	1975	OS	40–80
Racers	1955	OS	150–300
Rachel and the Stranger	1948	OS	100–250
Rachel, Rachel	1968	OS	40–70
Racing Fever	1964	OS	40–70
Rack	1956	OS	50–90
Racket	1951	OS	250–400
Racket	1951	LC SET	150–300
Racket Busters	1938	OS	800–1,000
Radar Men from the Moon	1952	OS	250–500
Radio Days	1987	OS	40–90
Raffles	1930	LC	300–500
Raffles	1939	OS	600–900
Rage	1966	OS	40–70
Rage at Dawn	1955	OS	50–125
Rage in Heaven	1941	OS	60–125
Rage of Paris	1938	OS	150–300
Raggedy Rose	1926	41 × 81	500–900
Raging Bull	1980	OS	300–500
Raging Bull	1980	LC SET	75–200
Ragtime	1981	OS	40–70
Ragtime	1981	LC SET	40–80
Raiders	1964	OS	40–60
Raiders of the Lost Ark	1981	OS	250–400
Raiders of the Lost Ark	1981	LC SET	150–275
Railroaded	1947	OS	250–400
Rain	1932	22 × 28	1,200–1,800
Rain Man	1988	OS	40–90

R

327

R

TITLE	YEAR	SIZE	PRICE RANGE
Rain People	1969	OS	40–60
Rainbow Island	1944	OS	75–225
Rainbow over Texas	1946	OS	300–500
Rainbow Ranch	1933	OS	1,500–2,000
Rainmaker	1956	OS	50–150
Rains of Ranchipur	1955	OS	50–90
Raintree County	1957	OS	200–450
Raintree County	1957	LC SET	150–300
Raise the Titanic	1979	OS	40–60
Raisin in the Sun	1961	OS	75–150
Raising Arizona	1987	OS	50–150
Rally 'Round the Flag, Boys!	1958	OS	40–70
Rambo	1987	OS	40–60
Rambo 3	1988	OS	40–60
Rambo First Blood 2	1985	OS	50–70
Ramona	1928	OS	800–1,100
Rampage	1963	OS	40–70
Ran	1985	20 × 29 JPN	350–700
Rancho Deluxe	1975	OS	50–80
Rancho Notorious	1952	OS	200–350
Ransom	1955	OS	40–70
Rare Breed	1966	OS	50–125
Rascal	1969	OS	40–60
Rashomon	1951	OS	150–350
Rasputin the Mad Monk	1966	OS	40–70
Rat Race	1960	OS	40–60
Rat Race	1960	LC SET	60–80
Raven	1935	Title Card	12,363
Raven	1963	OS	550–800
Ravishing Idiot	1965	OS	40–90
Raw Deal	1948	OS	1,500–2,500
Raw Meat	1973	OS	40–80
Raw Wind in Eden	1958	OS	40–80
Rawhide	1938	22 × 28	2,950
Rawhide	1951	OS	40–70
Razor's Edge	1946	OS	500–700
Re-Animator	1985	OS	75–175
Real Glory	1939	OS	150–350

TITLE	YEAR	SIZE	PRICE RANGE
Reap the Wild Wind	1942	OS	900–1,250
Rear Window	1954	OS	4,500–6,000
Rebecca	1940	OS	7,000–10,000
Rebel Rousers	1970	OS	50–90
Rebel Set	1959	OS	90–200
Rebel without a Cause	1955	OS	3,500–5,000
Reckless	1935	OS	1,250–2,000
Reckless Moment	1949	OS	200–350
Red Badge of Courage	1951	OS	150–250
Red Barry	1938	OS	500–850
Red Danube	1949	OS	40–90
Red Desert	1964	OS	150–250
Red Dragon	1945	OS	350–500
Red Dust	1932	OS	27,000
Red-Headed Woman	1932	OS	19,500
Red Heat	1988	OS	40–60
Red Light	1949	OS	50–150
Red Line 7000	1965	OS	50–150
Red Line 7000	1965	LC SET	40–70
Red Pony	1949	OS	150–250
Red River	1948	OS	700–1,000
Red Shoes	1948	OS	750–1,400
Red Sonja	1985	OS	40–70
Red Sonja	1985	LC SET	50–80
Red Sun	1972	OS	40–80
Red Sun	1972	LC SET	50–80
Red Tent	1971	OS	40–70
Redhead and the Cowboy	1951	OS	50–80
Reds	1981	OS	40–70
Reds	1981	LC SET	40–60
Reefer Madness	1936	OS	350–600
Reflections in a Golden Eye	1967	OS	50–90
Reform School Girl	1957	OS	50–200
Reivers	1970	OS	50–125
Reivers	1970	LC SET	50–80
Reluctant Astronaut	1967	OS	50–100
Reluctant Debutante	1958	OS	50–90
Reluctant Dragon	1941	OS	350–500

R

192 42nd Street *(1933)*

193 Frankenstein *(1931)*

194 The General (1926)

195 The Gold Rush (1925)

TITLE	YEAR	SIZE	PRICE RANGE
Remains of the Day	1994	OS	40–70
Remains to Be Seen	1953	OS	50–125
Remarkable Mr. Pennypacker	1959	OS	40–70
Remember the Night	1939	OS	800–1,100
Renaldo and Clara	1978	OS	250–400
Renegade Ranger	1938	OS	200–500
Repeat Performance	1947	OS	250–475
Repeat Performance	1947	LC SET	100–200
Repo Man	1984	OS	50–125
Reptile	1966	OS	60–125
Reptile	1966	LC SET	75–125
Reptilicus	1962	OS	75–225
Replusion	1965	23 × 33 GER	75–300
Requiem for a Dream	2000	OS	40–70
Requiem for a Heavyweight	1962	OS	40–90
Rescuers	1977	OS	40–90
Rescuers	1977	LC SET	125–200
Reservoir Dogs	1992	OS	200–350
Restless Years	1958	OS	40–70
Return from Witch Mountain	1978	OS	40–60
Return from Witch Mountain	1978	LC SET	40–70
Return of Chandu	1934	OS	750–1,000
Return of Count Yorga	1971	OS	50–90
Return of Dr. X	1939	OS	750–1,000
Return of Dracula	1958	OS	150–350
Return of Frank James	1940	OS	750–1,500
Return of Mr. Moto	1965	OS	40–70
Return of the Ape Man	1944	OS	1,250–2,000
Return of the Dragon	1974	OS	40–90
Return of the Fly	1959	OS	50–250
Return of the Fly	1959	LC SET	150–400
Return of the Jedi	1983	OS	175–300
Return of the Jedi	1983	LC SET	150–1,250
Return of the Living Dead	1985	OS	40–70
Return of the Pink Panther	1975	OS	50–90
Return of the Seven	1966	OS	40–80
Return of the Vampire	1943	41 × 81	3,250
Return to Paradise	1952	OS	50–125

R

R

TITLE	YEAR	SIZE	PRICE RANGE
Return to Peyton Place	1961	OS	40–60
Return to Treasure Island	1954	OS	40–70
Reunion	1936	OS	50–150
Reunion in France	1942	OS	300–450
Revenge of Frankenstein	1958	OS	200–350
Revenge of the Creature	1955	OS	700–1,150
Revenge of the Creature	1955	LC SET	1,500–2,250
Revenge of the Pink Panther	1978	OS	40–90
Revenge Rider	1935	OS	1,500–3,000
Revengers	1972	OS	40–70
Revolt of Mamie Stover	1956	OS	50–125
Revolt of the Slaves	1961	OS	40–70
Revolt of the Zombies	1936	OS	250–500
Rhapsody	1954	OS	75–150
Rhapsody	1954	LC SET	100–200
Rhapsody in Blue	1945	OS	100–225
Rhinestone	1984	OS	40–60
Rhino	1964	OS	40–60
Rhythm and Weep	1946	OS	3,601
Rhythm on the Range	1936	OS	150–350
Rich Man, Poor Girl	1938	OS	150–250
Rich, Young and Pretty	1951	OS	100–250
Richard III	1955	27 × 41 UK	500–750
Richard Pryor Live Sunset Strip	1982	OS	50–90
Ride a Crooked Trail	1958	OS	50–90
Ride beyond Vengeance	1966	OS	40–70
Ride 'Em Cowboy	1936	OS	1,100–1,750
Ride 'Em Cowboy	1942	OS	500–900
Ride Lonesome	1959	OS	50–90
Ride the High Country	1962	OS	150–250
Ride the Pink Horse	1947	OS	250–500
Ride the Wild Surf	1964	OS	150–300
Ride to Hangman's Tree	1967	OS	40–70
Ride Vanquero	1953	OS	40–70
Rider on the Rain	1970	OS	40–70
Riders to the Stars	1954	OS	50–90
Ridin' for Justice	1931	OS	4,000–6,000
Ridin' Romeo	1921	OS	3,500–4,250

TITLE	YEAR	SIZE	PRICE RANGE
Ridin' the Outlaw Trail	1951	OS	70–125
Riding High	1943	OS	125–250
Riff Raff	1947	OS	100–200
Right Stuff	1982	OS	75–125
Ring	1952	OS	50–90
Ring of Fear	1954	OS	50–90
Ring of Fire	1961	OS	40–70
Rings on Her Fingers	1942	OS	400–600
Rio Bravo	1959	OS	1,000–1,500
Rio Conchos	1964	OS	40–70
Rio Grande	1950	OS	600–1,150
Rio Lobo	1971	OS	250–400
Rio Rita	1942	OS	500–750
Riot in Cell Block 11	1954	OS	50–90
Riot in Juvenile Prison	1959	OS	40–70
Riot on Sunset Strip	1967	OS	40–80
Riptide	1934	OS	800–1,150
Rise and Fall of Legs Diamond	1960	OS	50–100
Risky Business	1983	OS	40–80
Risky Business	1983	LC SET	40–70
River	1985	OS	40–70
River of No Return	1954	OS	500–750
River of No Return	1954	LC SET	350–450
River Runs through It	1992	OS	50–125
Road Agent	1952	OS	40–60
Road Back	1937	OS	300–450
Road House	1948	OS	450–600
Road House	1989	OS	40–60
Road to Bali	1952	OS	300–450
Road to Hong Kong	1962	OS	50–125
Road to Mandalay	1926	OS	2,500
Road to Morocco	1942	OS	500–700
Road to Rio	1948	OS	250–500
Road to the Big House	1947	OS	50–100
Road to Utopia	1945	OS	300–550
Road to Zanzibar	1941	OS	400–650
Road Warrior	1981	OS	50–125
Roadie	1980	OS	40–70

R

R

TITLE	YEAR	SIZE	PRICE RANGE
Roaring Twenties	1939	OS	3,500–5,000
Rob Roy	1953	OS	100–175
Robe	1953	22 × 28	150–300
Roberta	1935	OS	3,000–4,500
Robin and Marian	1976	OS	40–70
Robin and the 7 Hoods	1964	OS	250–400
Robin Hood	1922	OS	13,800
Robin Hood	1973	OS	100–150
Robin Hood: Prince of Thieves	1991	OS	40–60
Robinson Crusoe of Clipper Island	1936	OS	150–400
Robinson Crusoe on Mars	1964	OS	300–450
Robinson Crusoe on Mars	1964	LC SET	100–250
Robocop	1987	OS	40–70
Robocop	1987	LC SET	50–90
Robot Monster	1953	OS	800–1,100
Rock-a-Bye Baby	1958	OS	75–125
Rock-a-Bye Baby	1958	LC SET	75–125
Rock All Night	1957	OS	125–225
Rock and Roll High School	1979	OS	50–80
Rock around the Clock	1956	OS	450–650
Rock around the Clock	1956	LC SET	250–400
Rock Baby: Rock It	1957	OS	250–450
Rock Pretty Baby	1957	OS	50–90
Rock Rock Rock	1956	OS	350–500
Rocketeer	1991	OS	75–125
Rocketship X-M	1950	OS	500–600
Rocky	1976	OS	250–350
Rocky	1976	LC SET	100–250
Rocky 2	1979	OS	200–300
Rocky 2	1979	LC SET	100–150
Rocky 3	1982	OS	50–90
Rocky 3	1982	LC SET	70–125
Rocky 4	1985	OS	40–60
Rocky 5	1990	OS	40–60
Rocky Horror Picture Show	1975	OS	100–200
Rocky Horror Picture Show	1975	LC SET	200–300
Rocky Mountain	1950	OS	100–225
Rodan	1957	OS	200–375

TITLE	YEAR	SIZE	PRICE RANGE
Rodan	1957	LC SET	300–400
Rogue Cop	1954	OS	150–250
Rollerball	1975	OS	350–400
Rollerball	1975	LC SET	50–125
Rolling Thunder	1977	OS	40–70
Roma	1972	39 × 55 ITA	250–550
Roman Holiday	1953	OS	800–1,150
Roman Holiday	1953	LC SET	250–400
Roman Spring of Mrs. Stone	1961	OS	60–125
Romance in Manhattan	1934	OS	2,400
Romance of the Limberlost	1938	OS	125–175
Romance on the High Seas	1948	OS	350–500
Romancing the Stone	1984	OS	40–70
Romanoff and Juliet	1961	OS	40–60
Romantic Melodies	1932	OS	3,000–3,500
Rome Adventure	1962	OS	50–90
Romeo and Juliet	1936	OS	1,700
Romeo and Juliet	1955	OS	75–150
Romeo and Juliet	1968	OS	50–125
Romeo and Juliet	1996	OS	50–90
Romeo Is Bleeding	1993	OS	50–80
Romola	1924	81 × 81	1,652
Romper Stomper	1992	27 × 41 AUZ	200–350
Ronin	1998	OS	40–70
Roogie's Bump	1954	OS	350–500
Rookie	1959	OS	40–70
Rookie	1990	OS	40–70
Rookie Cop	1939	OS	125–225
Room at the Top	1959	OS	50–90
Room for One More	1952	OS	50–125
Room Service	1938	LC	500–750
Room with a View	1986	OS	50–80
Rooster Cogburn	1975	OS	90–275
Rooster Cogburn	1975	LC SET	90–150
Roots of Heaven	1958	OS	50–90
Roots of Heaven	1958	LC SET	75–200
Rope	1948	OS	900–1,250
Rope of Sand	1949	OS	90–150

R

R

TITLE	YEAR	SIZE	PRICE RANGE
Rose	1979	OS	50–90
Rose Marie	1936	OS	250–400
Rose Marie	1954	OS	100–225
Rose Tattoo	1955	OS	50–150
Rose Tattoo	1955	LC SET	50–90
Rosemary's Baby	1968	OS	350–475
Rosemary's Baby	1968	LC SET	40–70
Rosita	1923	LC	150–300
Rough Night in Jericho	1967	OS	50–80
Rough Night in Jericho	1967	LC SET	75–125
Round Midnight	1986	OS	40–70
Round Up	1920	OS	4,600
Rounders	1914	OS	7,050
Rounders	1965	OS	40–70
Rounders	1998	OS	40–70
Roustabout	1964	OS	200–275
Royal Flash	1975	OS	40–60
Royal Scandal	1945	OS	250–400
Royal Wedding	1951	OS	150–300
Royal Wedding	1951	LC SET	200–250
Ruby Gentry	1952	OS	100–250
Ruby Gentry	1952	LC SET	75–200
Rude Boy	1980	OS	150–550
Ruggles of Red Gap	1935	OS	550–950
Ruling Class	1972	OS	75–125
Rumble Fish	1983	OS	50–90
Rumble Fish	1983	LC SET	40–70
Run Angel Run	1969	OS	40–70
Run for Cover	1955	OS	40–70
Run for the Sun	1956	OS	40–60
Run of the Arrow	1957	OS	75–150
Run Silent Run Deep	1958	OS	75–150
Runaway Brain	1995	OS	75–125
Runaway Train	1985	OS	40–70
Running Man	1963	OS	40–70
Running Man	1987	OS	40–70
Running on Empty	1988	OS	40–60
Running Wild	1955	OS	100–175

TITLE	YEAR	SIZE	PRICE RANGE
Russians Are Coming	1966	OS	50–80
Ruthless	1948	OS	75–175
Rx Murder	1958	OS	40–70
Ryan's Daughter	1970	OS	75–150
Sabotage	1936	41 × 81	3,349
Saboteur	1942	OS	750–1,000
Sabrina	1954	OS	750–1,200
Sabrina	1954	LC SET	300–550
Sabrina	1995	OS	40–70
Sad Sack	1957	OS	60–90
Saddle the Wind	1958	OS	75–125
Sadist	1963	OS	40–70
Safari	1940	OS	250–400
Safari Drums	1953	OS	50–80
Safe at Home	1962	OS	750–1,000
Safecracker	1958	OS	40–80
Saga of Hemp Brown	1958	OS	40–80
Sahara	1943	OS	1,500–2,750
Saigon	1948	OS	500–850
Sail a Crooked Ship	1961	OS	50–90
Sailor Beware	1952	OS	75–200
Sailor of the King	1953	OS	50–90
Sailor Who Fell from Grace	1976	OS	50–80
St. Elmo's Fire	1985	OS	40–70
St. Elmo's Fire	1985	LC SET	40–70
Saint in New York	1938	OS	1,000–1,400
Saint John	1957	OS	800–1,100
St. Louis Blues	1958	OS	150–250
St. Louis Kid	1934	OS	3,500–5,500
St. Louis Woman	1934	OS	75–150
Saint Takes Over	1940	OS	450–600
St. Valentine's Day Massacre	1967	OS	50–90
Saint's Girl Friday	1954	OS	50–125
Sainted Devil	1924	OS	8,250
Sally, Irene and Mary	1938	OS	400–800
Sally of the Sawdust	1925	OS	2,750
Salome	1918	OS	10,301
Salome	1953	OS	200–400

S

S

TITLE	YEAR	SIZE	PRICE RANGE
Salome	1953	LC SET	200–325
Salt and Pepper	1968	OS	40–80
Salty O'Rourke	1945	OS	75–150
Saludos Amigos	1943	OS	350–500
Salvador	1985	OS	125–250
Sam Whiskey	1969	OS	40–60
Samar	1962	OS	50–90
Samourai	1967	24 × 32 FRE	700–850
Samson and Delilah	1949	OS	75–175
Samson and the Seven Miracles	1963	OS	50–90
Samson and the Slave Queen	1964	OS	40–60
San Antonio	1945	OS	300–550
San Fernando Valley	1944	OS	600–750
San Francisco	1936	OS	2,000–3,250
San Francisco Story	1952	22 × 28	30–70
San Quentin	1937	OS	5,000
Sanctuary	1961	OS	40–70
Sand Pebbles	1967	OS	75–150
Sandokan the Great	1965	OS	50–90
Sandokan the Great	1965	LC SET	70–100
Sandpiper	1965	OS	75–200
Sandpiper	1965	LC SET	75–150
Sands of Iwo Jima	1950	OS	750–1,250
Sands of Iwo Jima	1950	LC SET	750–900
Sands of the Kalahari	1965	OS	50–90
Sanjuro	1962	20 × 29 JPN	300–500
Santa Claus	1960	OS	40–70
Santa Claus Conquers Martians	1964	OS	50–90
Santa Claus Conquers Martians	1964	LC SET	50–70
Santa Fe Marshal	1940	OS	800–950
Santa Fe Stampede	1938	OS	1,250–2,000
Santa Fe Trail	1940	OS	650–800
Santiago	1956	OS	50–90
Sapphire	1959	OS	50–90
Saps at Sea	1940	OS	550–850
Saraband for Dead Lovers	1948	30 × 40 UK	600–800
Saratoga	1937	OS	850–1,250
Saratoga Trunk	1945	OS	200–450

TITLE	YEAR	SIZE	PRICE RANGE
Satan Bug	1965	OS	40–70
Satan Never Sleeps	1962	OS	40–80
Satan's Sadists	1969	OS	40–60
Satan's Satellites	1958	OS	300–650
Satanic Rites of Dracula	1974	OS	40–90
Satchmo the Great	1957	OS	150–350
Satchmo the Great	1957	LC SET	250–350
Satellite in the Sky	1956	OS	50–90
Saturday Night Fever	1977	OS	100–200
Saturday Night Fever	1977	LC SET	50–150
Saturday Night Kid	1929	LC	350–550
Saturday's Children	1940	OS	150–400
Saturn 3	1980	OS	40–80
Satyricon	1969	OS	75–175
Savage Innocents	1959	OS	40–70
Savage Mutiny	1953	OS	65–125
Save the Children	1973	OS	50–90
Save the Tiger	1973	OS	40–70
Saving Private Ryan	1998	OS	75–150
Saving Private Ryan	1998	LC SET	75–150
Sawdust Trail	1924	OS	1,000–1,500
Say Anything	1989	OS	50–90
Say One for Me	1959	OS	50–90
Say One for Me	1959	LC SET	75–100
Sayonara	1957	OS	250–450
Scalphunters	1968	OS	40–70
Scandal at Scourie	1953	OS	50–90
Scandal Inc.	1956	OS	50–90
Scandal Sheet	1952	OS	250–450
Scanners	1980	OS	50–90
Scanners	1980	LC SET	50–100
Scar	1948	OS	100–225
Scaramouche	1952	OS	150–250
Scaramouche	1952	LC SET	100–200
Scarecrow	1973	OS	40–70
Scared Stiff	1953	OS	200–350
Scared to Death	1946	OS	300–450
Scarface	1932	41 × 81	24,675

S

S

TITLE	YEAR	SIZE	PRICE RANGE
Scarface	1983	OS	250–400
Scarface	1983	LC SET	150–300
Scarlet Claw	1944	OS	1,000–1,750
Scarlet Clue	1945	OS	500–800
Scarlet Coat	1955	OS	50–90
Scarlet Empress	1934	OS	13,800
Scarlet Pimpernel	1935	14 × 36	1,500–3,000
Scarlet Street	1945	OS	850–1,450
Scarlet West	1925	81 × 81	1,650
Scars of Dracula	1971	OS	125–200
Scene of the Crime	1949	OS	50–90
Scent of a Woman	1993	OS	40–70
Schindler's List	1993	OS	150–325
School Daze	1988	OS	40–70
School for Love	1960	OS	50–90
School for Love	1960	LC SET	70–90
School Teacher and the Waif	1912	OS	1,265
Scorpio	1973	OS	75–150
Scotland Yard Inspector	1952	OS	40–70
Scott of the Antarctic	1949	OS	250–400
Scream	1996	OS	40–70
Scream and Scream Again	1970	OS	50–90
Scream and Scream Again	1970	LC SET	50–175
Scream, Blacula, Scream!	1973	OS	75–150
Scream of Fear	1961	OS	75–125
Scream of Fear	1961	LC SET	60–125
Screaming Mimi	1958	OS	75–150
Screaming Skull	1958	OS	350–550
Screaming Skull	1958	LC SET	150–300
Screaming Tiger	1973	OS	40–70
Scrooge	1970	OS	40–70
Scrooged	1988	OS	40–60
Scudda Hoo! Scudda Hay!	1948	OS	300–550
Scudda Hoo! Scudda Hay!	1948	LC SET	150–250
Sea Chase	1955	OS	150–400
Sea Chase	1955	LC SET	200–325
Sea Devils	1937	OS	150–400
Sea Devils	1953	OS	50–90

TITLE	YEAR	SIZE	PRICE RANGE
Sea Hawk	1940	OS	3,000–4,000
Sea Hawk	1940	LC SET	1,500–2,500
Sea of Grass	1947	OS	200–450
Sea of Lost Ships	1953	OS	40–70
Sea of Love	1989	OS	40–60
Sea of Love	1989	LC SET	40–60
Sea Scouts	1939	OS	7,500
Sea Spoilers	1936	OS	1,840
Sea Wife	1957	OS	40–70
Sea Wolf	1941	OS	300–550
Sea Wolves	1980	OS	40–80
Sealed Cargo	1951	OS	75–125
Search	1948	OS	50–90
Search for Bridey Murphy	1956	OS	40–70
Searchers	1956	OS	3,000–5,500
Second Chance	1953	OS	50–150
Second Childhood	1936	OS	2,000–3,500
Second Chorus	1940	OS	300–550
Second Fiddle	1939	OS	350–600
Seconds	1966	OS	75–150
Seconds	1966	LC SET	100–175
Secret Agent	1936	22 × 28	1,250–1,750
Secret Ceremony	1968	OS	50–100
Secret Ceremony	1968	LC SET	40–80
Secret Command	1944	OS	250–550
Secret File Hollywood	1962	OS	50–90
Secret Invasion	1964	OS	40–80
Secret Invasion	1964	LC SET	50–80
Secret Life of an American Wife	1968	OS	40–70
Secret Life of Walter Mitty	1947	OS	75–150
Secret Lives	1937	41 × 81 UK	450–600
Secret of Blood Island	1965	OS	50–90
Secret of Blood Island	1965	LC SET	75–125
Secret of Convict Lake	1951	OS	50–90
Secret of My Success	1965	OS	40–80
Secret of Nimh	1982	OS	50–100
Secret of Santa Vittoria	1969	OS	40–70
Secret Policeman's Ball	1979	OS	40–70

S

TITLE	YEAR	SIZE	PRICE RANGE
Secret Policeman's Other Ball	1982	OS	40–70
Secret Service Darkest Africa	1943	OS	250–400
Secret Seven	1966	OS	40–70
Secret Valley	1936	OS	150–275
Secret Ways	1961	OS	40–70
Secrets	1933	OS	850–1,400
Secrets of Life	1956	OS	40–70
Secrets of Wu Sin	1932	OS	300–500
Seems like Old Times	1980	OS	40–80
Semi Tough	1977	OS	40–70
Semi Tough	1977	LC SET	40–70
Seminole	1953	OS	40–70
Seminole Uprising	1955	OS	40–70
Send Me No Flowers	1964	OS	50–90
Send Me No Flowers	1964	LC SET	60–90
Senior Prom	1958	OS	40–70
Sensations of 1945	1944	OS	200–350
Sentinel	1977	OS	40–70
Separate Tables	1958	OS	75–200
September Affair	1951	OS	40–70
September Storm	1960	OS	40–70
Serenade	1956	OS	40–80
Sergeant Madden	1939	OS	150–300
Sergeant Rutledge	1960	OS	40–70
Sergeant Ryker	1968	OS	40–70
Sergeant York	1941	OS	800–1,100
Sergeants 3	1962	OS	250–400
Serpent of the Nile	1953	OS	40–70
Serpent of the Nile	1953	LC SET	40–60
Serpico	1974	OS	200–325
Serpico	1974	LC SET	100–200
Servant	1963	OS	400–575
Set It Up	1949	OS	200–350
Seven	1996	OS	40–70
Seven Angry Men	1955	OS	40–70
Seven Brides for Seven Brothers	1954	OS	50–125
Seven Brides for Seven Brothers	1954	LC SET	40–80
Seven Brothers Meet Dracula	1974	OS	40–70

TITLE	YEAR	SIZE	PRICE RANGE
Seven Chances	1925	14 × 36	5,500
Seven Cities of Gold	1955	OS	50–90
Seven Days in May	1964	OS	50–90
Seven Days in May	1964	LC SET	50–90
Seven Faces of Dr. Lao	1964	OS	75–175
Seven Hills of Rome	1958	OS	50–90
711 Ocean Drive	1950	OS	40–70
Seven Little Foys	1955	OS	100–250
Seven Men from Now	1956	OS	50–90
Seven Miles from Alcatraz	1942	OS	100–200
Seven Minutes	1971	OS	75–200
Seven Percent Solution	1976	OS	40–70
Seven Percent Solution	1976	LC SET	50–90
Seven Samurai	1954	OS	350–550
Seven Sinners	1940	OS	450–700
Seven Slaves against the World	1965	OS	40–70
Seven Thieves	1959	OS	40–70
Seven Ups	1973	OS	40–70
Seven Ways from Sundown	1960	OS	50–90
Seven Women from Hell	1961	OS	40–70
Seven Year Itch	1955	OS	1,750–3,000
Seven Year Itch	1955	LC SET	750–1,450
7th Cavalry	1956	OS	75–125
7th Commandment	1960	OS	40–70
Seventh Cross	1944	OS	400–650
7th Dawn	1964	OS	40–70
Seventh Heaven	1927	OS	650–950
Seventh Seal	1957	OS	50–125
Seventh Sin	1957	OS	40–80
7th Voyage of Sinbad	1958	OS	250–400
7th Voyage of Sinbad	1958	LC SET	750–1,250
Sex and the Single Girl	1965	OS	50–80
Sex Kittens Go to College	1960	OS	50–90
Sex Kittens Go to College	1960	LC SET	75–200
Sex, Lies, and Videotape	1989	OS	75–125
Sexy Beast	2000	OS	50–80
Sgt. Pepper's Lonely Hearts Club Band	1978	OS	50–125

S

S

TITLE	YEAR	SIZE	PRICE RANGE
Shack out on 101	1955	OS	50–70
Shadow	1937	14 × 36	150–450
Shadow of a Doubt	1943	OS	2,000–3,500
Shadow of a Doubt	1943	LC SET	1,500–2,250
Shadow of the Cat	1961	OS	50–125
Shadow of the Eagle	1955	OS	40–70
Shadow of the Law	1930	22 × 28	700
Shadow of the Thin Man	1941	OS	750–1,500
Shadow on the Wall	1949	OS	50–90
Shadowed	1946	OS	250–400
Shadows	1922	LC	350–700
Shadows	1959	OS	400–600
Shadows and Fog	1992	OS	40–70
Shadows on the Stairs	1941	OS	50–125
Shadows over Chinatown	1946	OS	500–800
Shaft	1971	OS	400–575
Shaft	1971	LC SET	75–200
Shaft in Africa	1973	OS	100–250
Shaft in Africa	1973	LC SET	75–150
Shaft's Big Score	1972	OS	150–200
Shaft's Big Score	1972	LC SET	75–150
Shaggy	1948	OS	50–80
Shaggy DA	1976	OS	40–70
Shaggy Dog	1959	OS	75–125
Shaggy Dog	1959	LC SET	100–200
Shake Hands with the Devil	1959	OS	50–70
Shakedown	1950	OS	175–275
Shakespeare in Love	1999	OS	50–100
Shakiest Gun in the West	1968	OS	40–70
Shalako	1968	OS	40–70
Shall We Dance	1937	OS	3,500–4,250
Shall We Dance	1937	LC SET	2,000–3,000
Shampoo	1975	OS	50–100
Shampoo	1975	LC SET	75–150
Shamus	1972	OS	40–70
Shane	1953	OS	1,200–1,650
Shane	1953	LC SET	200–400
Shanghai Cobra	1945	OS	1,000–1,650

TITLE	YEAR	SIZE	PRICE RANGE
Shanghai Express	1932	22 × 28	3,000–3,750
Shanghai Gesture	1941	OS	500–850
Shanghaied	1915	OS	2,600
Shark	1970	OS	40–70
Shark's Treasure	1975	OS	40–70
Sharkfighters	1956	OS	50–90
Sharky's Machine	1981	OS	40–70
Shatter	1974	OS	40–70
Shawshank Redemption	1994	OS	75–150
She	1935	41 × 81	1,650
She	1965	OS	150–250
She Couldn't Say No	1954	OS	75–125
She Couldn't Take It	1935	LC	75–150
She Creature	1956	OS	750–2,000
She Creature	1956	LC SET	550–700
She Demons	1958	OS	100–225
She Demons	1958	LC SET	300–400
She Devil	1957	OS	150–400
She Devil	1957	LC SET	200–400
She Devils on Wheels	1968	OS	100–250
She Done Him Wrong	1933	OS	7,187
She Freak	1967	OS	75–150
She Gets Her Man	1945	OS	50–90
She Gods of Shark Reef	1958	OS	90–200
She Gods of Shark Reef	1958	LC SET	50–125
She Loves Me Not	1934	OS	500–750
She Married Her Boss	1935	OS	3,300
She Played with Fire	1957	OS	40–80
She Wolf of London	1946	OS	350–600
She Wore a Yellow Ribbon	1949	OS	1,500–3,000
She's Gotta Have It	1985	OS	75–150
She's Working Her Way through College	1952	OS	100–250
She's Working Her Way through College	1952	LC SET	50–125
Sheepman	1958	OS	50–90
Sheik	1921	OS	13,800
Sheltering Sky	1990	OS	50–150

S

S

TITLE	YEAR	SIZE	PRICE RANGE
Shenandoah	1965	OS	100–175
Shepherd of the Hills	1941	OS	350–600
Sheriff of Fractured Jaw	1959	OS	60–125
Sherlock Holmes	1922	OS	11,550
Sherlock Holmes	1932	OS	1,500–2,500
Sherlock Holmes Faces Death	1943	OS	1,500–2,250
Sherlock Holmes in Washington	1942	OS	500–800
Sherlock Holmes and the Secret Weapon	1942	OS	750–1,200
Sherlock Holmes and the Spider Woman	1944	OS	1,000–2,000
Sherlock Jr.	1924	LC	1,000–1,750
Shine	1996	OS	50–90
Shine on Harvest Moon	1938	OS	350–700
Shine on Harvest Moon	1944	OS	300–500
Shining	1980	OS	200–350
Shining	1980	LC SET	100–200
Ship Ahoy	1942	OS	275–450
Ship of Fools	1965	OS	75–250
Ship of Fools	1965	LC SET	75–125
Ship of Wanted Men	1933	OS	150–300
Shock Corridor	1963	OS	500–650
Shock Treatment	1964	OS	50–90
Shocking Miss Pilgrim	1946	OS	75–200
Shockproof	1949	OS	250–400
Shoes of the Fisherman	1968	OS	40–70
Shoot the Moon	1982	OS	40–70
Shoot the Piano Player	1960	OS	150–300
Shootist	1976	OS	200–350
Shootist	1976	LC SET	200–300
Shootout	1971	OS	50–70
Shootout at Medicine Bend	1957	OS	40–70
Shop around the Corner	1940	OS	650–1,400
Shopworn Angel	1929	OS	350–550
Shopworn Angel	1938	OS	600–800
Short Cut to Hell	1957	OS	70–100
Short Cuts	1993	OS	75–200
Shot in the Dark	1964	OS	100–175

TITLE	YEAR	SIZE	PRICE RANGE
Shot in the Dark	1964	LC SET	50–70
Shoulder Arms	1918	LC	450–700
Show Boat	1929	OS	2,000–3,000
Show Business	1944	OS	150–375
Show Business	1944	LC SET	100–225
Show Folks	1928	OS	700–1,150
Show Them No Mercy	1934	OS	1,200
Showboat	1936	OS	4,025
Showboat	1951	OS	150–300
Showdown	1940	OS	750–1,000
Showdown	1963	OS	40–70
Showdown	1973	OS	40–70
Showdown at Abilene	1956	OS	50–80
Showdown at Boot Hill	1958	OS	40–70
Showdown at Boot Hill	1958	LC SET	50–90
Shrek	2001	OS	50–90
Shriek in the Night	1933	OS	1,000–2,250
Shrike	1955	OS	40–70
Shuttered Room	1967	OS	40–80
Sicilian Clan	1969	OS	40–70
Sid and Nancy	1986	OS	75–150
Side Street	1950	OS	175–400
Side Hackers	1959	OS	40–70
Sidewalks of London	1939	OS	500–750
Siege of the Saxons	1963	OS	40–70
Sierra Sue	1941	OS	250–400
Sign of Four	1932	OS	1,200–2,000
Sign of the Cross	1932	OS	300–450
Sign of the Gladiator	1959	OS	100–175
Sign of the Pagan	1954	OS	40–70
Sign of the Times	1987	OS	40–80
Sign of the Wolf	1931	OS	40–70
Sign of the Wolf	1941	OS	100–175
Sign of Zorro	1960	OS	200–300
Signpost to Murder	1965	OS	40–70
Silence of the Lambs	1991	OS	200–300
Silence of the Lambs	1991	LC SET	150–225
Silencers	1966	OS	75–175

S

S

TITLE	YEAR	SIZE	PRICE RANGE
Silencers	1966	LC SET	150–225
Silent Barriers	1937	OS	150–400
Silent Call	1961	OS	40–70
Silent Death	1962	OS	150–300
Silent Enemy	1959	OS	40–90
Silent Men	1933	OS	1,000–1,500
Silent Movie	1976	OS	40–80
Silent Movie	1976	LC SET	50–90
Silent Night, Evil Night	1975	OS	40–70
Silent Raiders	1954	OS	40–80
Silent Running	1972	OS	75–150
Silent Running	1972	LC SET	75–150
Silent World	1956	OS	75–150
Silk Stockings	1957	OS	500–800
Silken Affair	1956	OS	40–80
Silkwood	1983	OS	40–70
Silly Symphony	1933	OS	5,000–6,000
Silver Bullet	1985	OS	40–70
Silver Canyon	1951	OS	150–350
Silver Chalice	1955	OS	60–90
Silver Chalice	1955	LC SET	50–90
Silver on the Sage	1939	OS	600–900
Silver River	1948	OS	150–300
Silver River	1948	LC SET	250–350
Silver Spurs	1936	OS	800–1,250
Silver Spurs	1943	OS	450–700
Silver Streak	1976	OS	40–70
Silver Streak	1976	LC SET	40–70
Silver Valley	1927	OS	1,000–2,500
Silverado	1985	OS	75–150
Sin of Nora Moran	1933	22 × 28	1,500–3,000
Sinbad and the Eye of the Tiger	1977	OS	40–80
Sinbad and the Eye of the Tiger	1977	LC SET	75–125
Sinbad the Sailor	1946	OS	750–1,400
Since You Went Away	1944	OS	300–650
Sincerely Yours	1955	OS	50–200
Sing and Swing	1964	OS	40–75
Sing Boy Sing	1958	OS	40–90

TITLE	YEAR	SIZE	PRICE RANGE
Sing Sister Sing	1935	OS	1,500–2,250
Singapore	1947	OS	1,500–2,750
Singer, Not the Song	1961	OS	50–90
Singin' in the Rain	1952	OS	2,000–2,750
Singin' in the Rain	1952	LC SET	800–1,000
Singing Fool	1928	41 × 81	5,865
Singing Hill	1941	OS	400–700
Singing Nun	1966	OS	50–80
Singing Outlaw	1937	OS	200–450
Single Room Furnished	1968	OS	75–150
Singles	1992	OS	40–70
Sink the Bismark	1960	OS	40–70
Sink the Bismark	1960	LC SET	50–80
Sinners in the Sun	1932	OS	1,000–2,000
Sins of Jezebel	1953	OS	50–90
Sins of Rachel Cade	1961	OS	50–90
Sins of the Children	1936	OS	100–225
Sioux Blood	1929	OS	1,500–3,000
Sioux City Sue	1946	OS	450–750
Sirens of Atlantis	1947	OS	450–700
Sirens	1994	OS	40–80
Sirocco	1951	OS	450–600
Sister Kenny	1946	OS	100–175
Sisters	1938	OS	2,000–3,000
Sisters	1973	OS	50–90
Sitting Pretty	1948	OS	150–225
Six Black Horses	1962	OS	50–90
Six Bridges to Cross	1955	OS	50–90
Six Lessons from Madame Lason	1940	OS	75–200
Six of a Kind	1934	OS	1,725
633 Squadron	1964	OS	50–175
Sixteen Candles	1984	OS	40–80
Sixteen Candles	1984	LC SET	50–90
Sixth Sense	1999	OS	40–70
Sixth Sense	1999	LC SET	40–70
Skammen	1969	OS	75–150
Ski Party	1965	OS	50–90
Ski Troop Attack	1960	OS	40–70

S

S

TITLE	YEAR	SIZE	PRICE RANGE
Skirts Ahoy	1952	OS	75–225
Skirts Ahoy	1952	LC SET	100–175
Skull	1965	OS	40–80
Skull	1965	LC SET	75–150
Sky Commando	1953	OS	40–80
Sky Dragon	1949	OS	400–650
Sky Full of Moon	1952	OS	75–150
Sky Murder	1940	OS	200–450
Sky Trooper	1942	OS	4,300
Skyjacked	1972	OS	40–70
Skyscraper Souls	1932	OS	750–2,000
Slacker	1991	OS	40–80
Slapshot	1977	OS	150–250
Slattery's Hurricane	1949	OS	75–200
Slaughter	1972	OS	75–150
Slaughter on 10th Ave.	1957	OS	50–90
Slaughter's Big Rip Off	1973	OS	50–90
Slave	1917	11 × 20	3,162
Slave Girls	1966	OS	50–90
Slave Son of Spartacus	1963	OS	50–90
Slaves in Bondage	1937	OS	350–500
Sleep My Love	1947	OS	300–500
Sleeper	1974	OS	100–200
Sleeper	1974	LC SET	50–90
Sleeping Beauty	1959	OS	900–1,200
Sleeping Car Murder	1965	OS	50–125
Sleepless in Seattle	1992	OS	50–125
Sleepy Hollow	1999	OS	50–90
Sleepy Hollow	1999	LC SET	40–80
Slender Thread	1965	OS	50–90
Sleuth	1972	OS	50–90
Sleuth	1972	LC SET	50–80
Slight Case of Larceny	1953	OS	50–90
Slightly Dangerous	1943	OS	400–750
Slightly French	1948	OS	40–70
Slightly Scarlet	1956	OS	100–225
Slim	1937	OS	200–375
Slime People	1963	OS	50–90

TITLE	YEAR	SIZE	PRICE RANGE
Sling Blade	1996	OS	50–150
Small Town Girl	1953	OS	100–175
Smart Girl	1935	OS	300–450
Smart Politics	1948	OS	40–70
Smart Woman	1948	OS	50–125
Smash Up	1946	OS	750–1,150
Smashing Time	1968	OS	40–80
Smile Please	1924	OS	150–450
Smiles of a Summer Night	1957	OS	50–90
Smiley	1956	OS	50–90
Smilin' Through	1922	OS	150–300
Smoke	1995	OS	40–70
Smoke Lightning	1933	OS	750–1,000
Smoke Signal	1955	OS	50–90
Smokey and the Bandit	1977	OS	50–90
Smokey and the Bandit	1977	LC SET	40–70
Smokey and the Bandit 2	1980	OS	40–60
Smoky	1966	OS	40–70
Snafu	1945	OS	50–125
Snake Pit	1948	OS	400–650
Snake Woman	1960	OS	75–150
Snake Woman	1960	LC SET	40–70
Snatch	2000	OS	40–60
Sniper	1952	OS	50–150
Snoopy Come Home	1972	OS	50–80
Snorkel	1958	OS	40–70
Snow Job	1972	OS	150–300
Snow White	1937	OS	15,000–30,000
Snow White	1937	LC SET	9,200
Snow White and the Three Stooges	1961	OS	150–300
Snows of Kilimanjaro	1952	OS	100–225
So Big	1953	OS	50–125
So Dark the Night	1946	OS	150–300
So Dear to My Heart	1949	OS	450–700
So Ends Our Night	1941	OS	150–275
So Goes My Love	1946	OS	150–350
So Proudly We Hail	1943	OS	200–550
So This Is Love	1953	OS	50–90

S

TITLE	YEAR	SIZE	PRICE RANGE
So This Is New York	1948	OS	50–90
So's Your Old Man	1926	22 × 28	1,500
Sob Sister	1931	OS	500–750
Social Celebrity	1926	LC	750–1,000
Society Dog Show	1939	OS	11,500
Sock a Bye Baby	1934	OS	3,105
Sodom and Gomorrah	1963	OS	50–90
Sol Madrid	1968	OS	50–80
Sold Out Appetite	1928	OS	11,750
Soldier Blue	1970	OS	40–70
Soldier in the Rain	1963	OS	50–125
Soldier in the Rain	1963	LC SET	50–125
Soldier of Fortune	1955	OS	75–200
Soldier of Fortune	1955	LC SET	150–300
Soldier's Three	1951	OS	50–90
Solid Gold Cadillac	1956	OS	75–225
Solid Gold Cadillac	1956	LC SET	100–175
Solomon and Sheba	1959	OS	100–175
Some Blondes Are Dangerous	1937	OS	300–650
Some Came Running	1958	OS	450–600
Some Kind of Wonderful	1987	OS	40–70
Some Like It Hot	1959	OS	2,500–4,000
Some Like It Hot	1959	LC SET	1,000–1,750
Somebody up There Likes Me	1956	OS	100–175
Somebody up There Likes Me	1956	LC SET	100–200
Something for the Birds	1952	OS	40–70
Something for the Boys	1944	OS	150–300
Something in the Wind	1947	OS	40–70
Something of Value	1957	OS	75–150
Something to Live For	1952	OS	50–90
Something Wicked This Way Comes	1983	OS	40–70
Something Wild	1962	OS	40–70
Something Wild	1986	OS	50–75
Sometimes a Great Notion	1971	OS	40–70
Somewhere I'll Find You	1942	OS	275–550
Somewhere in the Night	1946	OS	500–850
Somewhere in Time	1980	OS	100–175

TITLE	YEAR	SIZE	PRICE RANGE
Son of Dr. Jekyll	1951	OS	75–200
Son of Dracula	1943	OS	2,500–4,000
Son of Dracula	1943	LC SET	1,000–2,250
Son of Flubber	1963	OS	75–125
Son of Frankenstein	1939	OS	28,750
Son of Fury	1942	OS	300–550
Son of Paleface	1952	OS	300–550
Son of Samson	1961	OS	75–200
Son of Sinbad	1955	OS	50–125
Son of the Sheik	1926	OS	16,100
Son of Zorro	1947	OS	200–400
Song Is Born	1947	OS	75–125
Song of Arizona	1946	OS	500–850
Song of Bernadette	1943	OS	750–900
Song of Freedom	1936	OS	2,000–3,000
Song of Russia	1944	OS	150–300
Song of Songs	1933	OS	29,900
Song of the Islands	1942	OS	500–700
Song of the Open Road	1944	OS	250–450
Song of the South	1946	OS	600–800
Song of the South	1946	LC SET	600–950
Song of the Thin Man	1947	OS	900–1,100
Song Remains the Same	1976	OS	75–150
Song without End	1960	OS	40–70
Sons of Katie Elder	1965	OS	200–350
Sons of Katie Elder	1965	LC SET	150–300
Sons of the Desert	1933	22 × 28	12,075
Sons of the Pioneers	1942	OS	450–600
Sons of the Saddle	1930	OS	450–600
Sophie's Choice	1982	OS	40–70
Sorcerer	1977	OS	40–80
Sorcerers	1967	OS	75–200
Sorority Girl	1957	OS	125–250
Sorority Girl	1957	LC SET	100–200
Sorrell and Son	1927	OS	500–750
Sorry Wrong Number	1948	OS	750–1,250
Sorry Wrong Number	1948	LC SET	350–500
SOS Coast Guard	1942	OS	1,000–1,750

S

S

TITLE	YEAR	SIZE	PRICE RANGE
SOS Pacific	1960	OS	40–80
Soul of a Monster	1944	OS	250–450
Souls at Sea	1937	OS	500–750
Sound and the Fury	1959	OS	40–70
Sound of Music	1965	OS	1,000–1,450
Sound of Music	1965	LC SET	750–1,000
Sound of Speed	1960	OS	150–350
Sounder	1972	OS	40–70
Soup and Fish	1934	OS	1,500–2,750
South of Caliente	1951	OS	350–550
South of Santa Fe	1942	OS	750–900
South of the Rio Grande	1932	OS	4,850
South Pacific	1959	OS	100–250
South Pacific	1959	LC SET	75–150
South Pacific Trail	1952	OS	50–90
South Park	1999	OS	50–70
South Sea Woman	1953	OS	75–125
Southern Star	1968	OS	40–70
Southwest Passage	1954	OS	50–90
Soylent Green	1973	OS	75–200
Soylent Green	1973	LC SET	50–90
Space Children	1958	OS	75–175
Space Children	1958	LC SET	75–125
Space Jam	1996	OS	50–90
Spaceballs	1987	OS	40–70
Spacemaster X-7	1958	OS	50–150
Spacemaster X-7	1958	LC SET	100–200
Spaceways	1952	OS	75–200
Spanish Affair	1957	OS	40–70
Spartacus	1960	OS	750–900
Spartacus	1960	LC SET	400–600
Spawn of the North	1938	OS	1,000–1,750
Speak Easily	1932	LC	500–850
Special Agent	1935	22 × 28	1,500
Special Agent	1949	OS	50–90
Species	1995	OS	50–90
Speed	1994	OS	50–90
Speed Crazy	1958	OS	150–350

TITLE	YEAR	SIZE	PRICE RANGE
Speedway	1929	OS	300–450
Speedway	1968	OS	200–375
Speedy	1928	OS	3,000–5,500
Spellbound	1945	OS	2,500–3,000
Spellbound	1945	LC SET	850–1,000
Spencer's Mountain	1963	OS	50–90
Spider	1958	OS	350–600
Spider Woman	1944	OS	750–900
Spider Woman Strikes Back	1946	OS	750–1,000
Spiderman	1977	OS	75–150
Spiderman	1977	LC SET	50–90
Spiderman	2002	OS	75–150
Spiderman Strikes Back	1978	OS	50–90
Spiderman Strikes Back	1978	LC SET	50–80
Spies	1928	LC SET	3,680
Spike's Gang	1974	OS	40–70
Spin a Dark Web	1955	OS	75–200
Spinout	1966	OS	100–250
Spiral Road	1962	OS	40–70
Spiral Staircase	1945	OS	150–300
Spirit Is Willing	1967	OS	40–70
Spirit of St. Louis	1957	OS	150–350
Spirits of the Dead	1968	OS	50–90
Spiritualist	1948	OS	75–200
Spitfire	1934	OS	2,500–3,250
Spitfire	1942	OS	600–800
Splash	1984	OS	50–90
Splash	1984	LC SET	50–80
Splendor in the Grass	1961	OS	150–400
Split	1968	OS	40–70
Spoilers	1942	OS	750–1,100
Spoilers of the Plains	1951	OS	250–500
Spook Chasers	1957	OS	70–100
Spooks	1942	OS	400–650
Spooks Run Wild	1941	OS	1,000–1,250
Spree	1967	OS	50–175
Springfield Rifle	1952	OS	100–200
Springtime in the Rockies	1942	OS	600–750

S

TITLE	YEAR	SIZE	PRICE RANGE
Springtime in the Sierras	1947	OS	300–500
Spy Chasers	1955	OS	75–125
Spy Hunt	1950	OS	75–150
Spy in the Green Hat	1967	30 × 40 UK	350–600
Spy in the Sky	1966	OS	40–70
Spy Who Came in from the Cold	1966	OS	75–150
Spy Who Loved Me	1977	OS	75–200
Spy Who Loved Me	1977	LC SET	75–150
Spy Who Shagged Me	1999	OS	40–70
Spy with My Face	1966	30 × 40 UK	350–700
Square Jungle	1955	OS	40–70
Square Ring	1955	OS	50–90
Sssssss	1973	OS	40–80
Stage Door	1937	OS	1,500–2,250
Stage Door Canteen	1943	OS	150–400
Stage Fright	1950	OS	550–900
Stage Struck	1925	22 × 28	500–750
Stage Struck	1958	OS	40–80
Stage to Blue River	1951	OS	50–90
Stage to Thunder Rock	1964	OS	50–90
Stagecoach	1939	OS	1,250–2,250
Stagecoach to Fury	1956	OS	40–70
Stagecoach War	1940	OS	350–700
Staircase	1969	OS	40–70
Stakeout	1987	OS	40–70
Stalag 17	1953	OS	100–250
Stalking Moon	1968	OS	40–70
Stallion Road	1947	OS	400–750
Stand by Me	1986	OS	40–80
Stand by Me	1986	LC SET	50–90
Stand Up and Cheer	1934	OS	700–1,000
Standing Room Only	1944	OS	100–175
Star	1953	OS	250–400
Star	1968	OS	40–80
Star	1968	LC SET	50–80
Star Dust	1940	OS	400–650
Star 80	1983	OS	40–70
Star 80	1983	LC SET	50–90

196 Gone with the Wind *(1939)*

197 Gone with the Wind *(1939)*
(Alternate Style)

198 Grand Hotel *(1932)* Grunts

199 Grips, Grunts and Groans
(Three Stooges) *(1937)*

S

TITLE	YEAR	SIZE	PRICE RANGE
Star in the Dust	1956	OS	50–90
Star Is Born	1937	OS	1,150
Star Is Born	1954	OS	500–900
Star Is Born	1954	LC SET	450–700
Star Is Born	1976	OS	75–175
Star Is Born	1976	LC SET	50–90
Star of Midnight	1935	OS	7,700
Star Packer	1934	OS	1,500–2,500
Star Spangled Rhythm	1942	OS	250–450
Star Trek	1979	OS	75–150
Star Trek	1979	LC SET	75–90
Star Trek 2: Wrath of Khan	1982	OS	50–150
Star Trek 2: Wrath of Khan	1982	LC SET	75–90
Star Trek 3: Search for Spock	1984	OS	40–70
Star Trek 3: Search for Spock	1984	LC SET	50–80
Star Trek 4: Voyage Home	1986	OS	40–70
Star Trek 4: Voyage Home	1986	LC SET	50–90
Star Trek 5: Final Frontier	1989	OS	40–70
Star Trek 6: Undiscovered Country	1991	OS	40–70
Star Trek 7: Generations	1994	OS	40–70
Star Trek 8: First Contact	1996	OS	40–60
Star Trek Insurrection	1998	OS	40–60
Star Wars	1977	OS	600–1,000
Star Wars	1977	LC SET	150–400
Star Wars Phantom Menace	1999	OS	50–80
Stardust	1975	OS	50–80
Stardust Memories	1980	OS	50–90
Stardust Memories	1980	LC SET	40–70
Stardust on the Sage	1942	OS	250–400
Stark Fear	1962	OS	40–70
Starman	1984	OS	40–70
Starman	1984	LC SET	40–70
Stars and Stripes Forever	1952	OS	100–175
Stars Looking Down	1939	OS	250–400
Starship Troopers	1997	OS	40–70
Start Cheering	1937	OS	700–950
Starting Over	1979	OS	40–70
State Fair	1962	OS	40–70

TITLE	YEAR	SIZE	PRICE RANGE
State of Grace	1990	OS	40–70
State of the Union	1948	OS	450–600
Station Six Sahara	1964	OS	40–70
Statue	1970	OS	40–70
Stay Away Joe	1968	OS	100–175
Stay Away Joe	1968	LC SET	50–125
Stay Hungry	1976	OS	40–70
Stay Hungry	1976	LC SET	50–90
Staying Alive	1983	OS	40–70
Staying Alive	1983	LC SET	40–70
Steamboat Bill Jr.	1928	14 × 36	4,025
Steel Fist	1952	OS	40–70
Steel Helmet	1951	OS	250–550
Steel Magnolias	1989	OS	40–70
Steel Town	1952	OS	70–125
Stella	1950	OS	40–90
Stella Dallas	1925	22 × 28	500–800
Stella Dallas	1937	OS	1,500–2,250
Step Lively	1944	OS	200–450
Stepford Wives	1975	OS	40–80
Sterile Cuckoo	1969	OS	40–70
Stiletto	1969	OS	40–70
Still Smokin'	1983	OS	40–70
Sting	1973	OS	500–700
Sting	1973	LC SET	150–300
Sting 2	1983	OS	40–70
Stingaree	1934	OS	250–450
Stir Crazy	1980	OS	50–90
Stolen Face	1952	OS	350–600
Stolen Hours	1963	OS	40–70
Stolen Hours	1963	LC SET	50–90
Stolen Life	1946	OS	100–350
Stooge	1952	OS	100–200
Stooge	1952	LC SET	75–150
Stop! Look! and Laugh!	1960	OS	100–250
Stop Making Sense	1984	OS	100–200
Stopover Tokyo	1957	OS	40–80
Stork Club	1945	OS	250–400

S

S

TITLE	YEAR	SIZE	PRICE RANGE
Storm Center	1955	OS	50–150
Storm Fear	1956	OS	40–70
Storm over the Nile	1956	OS	40–70
Storm Warning	1950	OS	100–225
Stormy Weather	1943	OS	4,125
Story of Dr. Wassell	1944	OS	200–400
Story of Dr. Wassell	1944	LC SET	150–300
Story of Esther Costello	1957	OS	50–90
Story of GI Joe	1945	OS	100–1,500
Story of Mankind	1957	OS	100–225
Story of Molly X	1949	OS	50–90
Story of O	1975	OS	50–90
Story of Robin Hood	1952	OS	100–250
Story of Seabiscuit	1949	OS	150–400
Story of Vernon & Irene Castle	1939	OS	1,000–1,400
Story of Will Rogers	1952	OS	75–150
Story on Page One	1960	OS	40–70
Stowaway	1936	OS	1,250–1,750
Stowaway Girl	1957	OS	40–90
Strada	1954	OS	75–225
Straight No Chaser	1989	OS	100–250
Straight Story	1999	OS	40–70
Straight Time	1978	OS	40–70
Straight Jacket	1964	OS	100–150
Strange Adventure	1956	OS	40–70
Strange Affair of Uncle Harry	1945	OS	250–400
Strange Bedfellows	1964	OS	60–90
Strange Brew	1983	OS	50–80
Strange Cargo	1940	OS	1,500–2,250
Strange Case of Dr. Rx	1942	OS	125–250
Strange Door	1951	OS	150–250
Strange Intruder	1956	OS	40–90
Strange Lady in Town	1955	OS	50–90
Strange Love of Martha Ivers	1946	OS	350–550
Strange Woman	1946	OS	80–150
Stranger	1946	OS	900–1,400
Stranger	1946	LC SET	450–600
Stranger in My Arms	1959	OS	40–70

TITLE	YEAR	SIZE	PRICE RANGE
Stranger in Town	1968	OS	40–70
Stranger Wore a Gun	1953	OS	75–150
Strangers All	1934	OS	250–400
Strangers on a Train	1951	OS	900–1,750
Strangers on a Train	1951	LC SET	400–650
Strangers When We Meet	1960	OS	40–80
Strangler	1964	OS	50–90
Stranglers of Bombay	1960	OS	70–100
Strategic Air Command	1955	OS	50–90
Stratton Story	1949	OS	125–250
Straw Dogs	1972	OS	200–350
Straw Dogs	1972	LC SET	75–125
Strawberry Blonde	1941	OS	700–900
Strawberry Statement	1970	OS	40–70
Street Angel	1928	OS	1,430
Street of Chance	1942	OS	175–300
Street with No Name	1948	OS	350–500
Streetcar Named Desire	1951	OS	750–1,500
Streetfighter	1975	OS	75–125
Streets of Fire	1984	OS	50–150
Streets of Laredo	1949	OS	250–450
Streets of Sorrow	1925	LC	550–800
Strictly Dishonorable	1951	OS	50–90
Strings of Steel	1925	OS	200–400
Stripes	1981	OS	50–100
Stripes	1981	LC SET	50–90
Striporama	1953	OS	75–100
Stripper	1963	OS	40–90
Stroker Ace	1983	OS	40–60
Stromboli	1950	OS	150–300
Student Prince	1954	OS	40–70
Studs Lonigan	1960	OS	40–70
Study in Terror	1966	OS	80–125
Stuff	1985	OS	40–70
Stunt Man	1978	OS	50–90
Submarine Command	1951	OS	50–90
Submarine Patrol	1938	OS	200–450
Submarine Seahawk	1959	OS	50–90

S

TITLE	YEAR	SIZE	PRICE RANGE
Subterraneans	1960	OS	40–70
Succubus	1969	OS	40–70
Such Good Friends	1971	OS	70–100
Sudan	1945	OS	250–500
Sudden Danger	1956	OS	40–80
Sudden Fear	1952	OS	150–275
Sudden Impact	1983	OS	70–100
Sudden Impact	1983	LC SET	50–125
Suddenly	1954	OS	125–300
Suddenly It's Spring	1946	OS	200–375
Suddenly Last Summer	1959	OS	250–450
Suddenly Last Summer	1959	LC SET	200–325
Suds	1920	OS	2,300
Sugarland Express	1974	OS	75–150
Suicide Battalion	1958	OS	40–70
Sullivan's Travels	1941	OS	4,500–7,500
Summer and Smoke	1961	OS	50–90
Summer Holiday	1963	OS	75–150
Summer Love	1958	OS	40–90
Summer Lovers	1982	OS	40–60
Summer Magic	1963	OS	40–90
Summer of '42	1971	OS	50–90
Summer Place	1959	OS	100–275
Summer Place	1959	LC SET	125–225
Summer Stock	1950	OS	200–350
Summer Stock	1950	LC SET	400–500
Summertime	1935	OS	500–750
Summertime	1955	OS	100–250
Sun Also Rises	1957	OS	125–325
Sun Also Rises	1957	OS	100–225
Sun Comes Up	1948	OS	75–150
Sun Valley Serenade	1941	OS	400–600
Sunday Dinner for a Soldier	1944	OS	75–150
Sunday in New York	1963	OS	40–70
Sundown	1941	OS	550–700
Sundowners	1960	OS	50–90
Sundowners	1960	LC SET	50–90
Sunnyside	1919	OS	11,500

TITLE	YEAR	SIZE	PRICE RANGE
Sunrise at Campobello	1960	OS	50–90
Sunset Boulevard	1950	OS	3,500–6,500
Sunset Boulevard	1950	LC SET	1,500–2,000
Sunset in El Dorado	1946	OS	300–450
Sunset in the West	1950	OS	250–400
Sunset in Wyoming	1941	OS	250–400
Sunset of Power	1935	OS	850–1,150
Sunset Serenade	1942	OS	350–550
Sunshine Boys	1975	OS	40–70
Superfly	1972	OS	150–350
Supergirl	1984	OS	50–90
Superman	1948	OS	1,500–2,250
Superman and the Mole Men	1951	OS	3,500–4,250
Superman Flies Again	1954	OS	1,200–2,000
Superman in Scotland Yard	1954	OS	1,200–2,000
Superman the Movie	1978	OS	150–300
Superman the Movie	1978	LC SET	100–175
Superman the Movie 2	1981	OS	75–125
Superman the Movie 2	1981	LC SET	50–90
Superman the Movie 3	1983	OS	40–70
Superman the Movie 3	1983	LC SET	40–60
Superman the Movie 4	1987	OS	40–70
Supernatural	1933	OS	40,890
Supervixens	1975	OS	75–150
Support Your Local Gunfighter	1971	OS	40–70
Support Your Local Sheriff	1969	OS	50–125
Sure Thing	1985	OS	50–125
Surf Party	1964	OS	200–450
Surprise Package	1960	OS	30–70
Surrender Hell	1959	OS	40–70
Susan and God	1940	OS	500–900
Susan Slept Here	1954	OS	40–70
Susanna Pass	1949	OS	500–850
Suspect	1944	OS	400–750
Suspect	1944	LC SET	300–500
Suspicion	1941	OS	6,000
Suspiria	1977	OS	125–175
Suzanna	1922	22 × 28	450–600

S

TITLE	YEAR	SIZE	PRICE RANGE
Suzy	1936	OS	1,750
Svengali	1931	LC	300–650
Svengali	1955	OS	50–90
Swamp Thing	1982	OS	40–70
Swamp Thing	1982	LC SET	50–70
Swamp Water	1941	OS	150–300
Swamp Women	1956	OS	150–325
Swan	1956	OS	125–225
Swan	1956	LC SET	75–150
Swanee River	1939	OS	500–800
Sweet Bird of Youth	1962	OS	50–90
Sweet Charity	1969	OS	40–70
Sweet Charity	1969	LC SET	50–90
Sweet Hereafter	1997	OS	40–70
Sweet Kill	1970	OS	50–90
Sweet November	1968	OS	40–70
Sweet Ride	1968	OS	40–80
Sweet Rosie O'Grady	1943	OS	300–550
Sweet Smell of Success	1957	OS	850–1,250
Sweet Smell of Success	1957	LC SET	400–700
Sweet Sweetback	1971	OS	250–400
Sweetheart of the Campus	1941	OS	200–400
Sweethearts	1938	OS	650–900
Swept Away	1975	OS	100–325
Swimmer	1968	OS	50–90
Swing Fever	1944	OS	450–650
Swing High, Swing Low	1937	22 × 28	250–450
Swing Parade of 1946	1946	OS	50–150
Swing Shift	1984	OS	40–60
Swing Shift Cinderella	1945	OS	3,700
Swing Shift Maisie	1943	OS	250–450
Swing Time	1936	OS	5,500–7,000
Swinger	1966	OS	50–90
Swingers	1996	OS	40–60
Swiss Family Robinson	1960	OS	50–125
Swiss Family Robinson	1960	LC SET	50–90
Swiss Miss	1938	OS	1,000–1,450
Sword and the Dragon	1960	OS	50–90

TITLE	YEAR	SIZE	PRICE RANGE
Sword and the Sorcerer	1982	OS	40–70
Sword in the Stone	1963	OS	100–250
Sword of Ali Baba	1965	OS	40–70
Sword of Monte Cristo	1951	OS	75–125
Sword of Sherwood Forest	1961	OS	40–70
Swordsman of Siena	1962	OS	40–70
Sylvia	1965	OS	50–70
Symphony Hour	1942	OS	6,325
Synanon	1965	OS	40–70
Syncopation	1942	OS	75–200
System	1953	OS	50–90
T Bird Gang	1959	OS	100–150
T Bone for Two	1942	OS	2,875
T-Men	1947	OS	600–900
Tabu	1931	LC	617
Taggart	1965	OS	40–70
Tailspin	1938	OS	250–400
Take a Giant Step	1960	OS	50–90
Take a Girl Like You	1970	OS	40–70
Take a Hard Ride	1975	OS	40–70
Take Care of My Little Girl	1951	OS	50–95
Take Her, She's Mine	1963	OS	50–90
Take Me Out to the Ball Game	1949	OS	250–450
Take Me to Town	1953	OS	400–650
Take My Life	1941	OS	650–1,000
Take One False Step	1949	OS	275–450
Take the Money and Run	1969	OS	75–150
Taking of Pelham 123	1974	OS	75–150
Taking of Pelham 123	1974	LC SET	40–80
Tale of Two Cities	1935	OS	800–1,150
Tale of Two Cities	1935	LC SET	600–750
Tale of Two Cities	1958	OS	75–175
Talented Mr. Ripley	1999	OS	75–125
Tales from the Crypt	1972	OS	50–175
Tales from the Crypt	1972	LC SET	75–200
Tales of Hoffman	1951	OS	350–550
Tales of Manhattan	1942	OS	550–850
Tales of Terror	1962	OS	50–150

T

T

TITLE	YEAR	SIZE	PRICE RANGE
Tales That Witness Madness	1973	OS	50–125
Talk about a Lady	1946	OS	125–200
Talk of the Town	1942	OS	1,000–1,400
Talk Radio	1988	OS	50–75
Talkartoon	1932	OS	6,600
Tall in the Saddle	1944	OS	450–750
Tall Men	1955	OS	75–200
Tall Story	1960	OS	50–150
Tall T	1957	OS	75–200
Tamahine	1962	OS	40–70
Tamango	1959	OS	50–90
Tami Show	1964	OS	150–300
Taming of the Shrew	1967	OS	55–175
Tammy and the Bachelor	1957	OS	50–125
Tammy and the Doctor	1963	OS	50–90
Tammy and the Millionaire	1967	OS	40–70
Tammy Tell Me True	1961	OS	50–80
Tampico	1944	OS	75–200
Tangier	1946	OS	400–850
Tank	1984	OS	40–70
Tank Commandos	1959	OS	40–60
Tank Girl	1995	OS	40–60
Tanned Legs	1929	OS	5,500
Tap Roots	1948	OS	100–275
Taps	1981	OS	50–80
Tarantula	1955	OS	1,400–2,000
Tarantula	1955	LC SET	800–1,450
Taras Bulba	1962	OS	50–70
Tarawa Beachhead	1958	OS	40–70
Target	1952	OS	100–175
Target Earth	1954	OS	500–650
Target Unknown	1951	OS	50–90
Targets	1968	OS	75–150
Tarnished Angels	1957	OS	150–300
Tarzan	1999	OS	60–100
Tarzan	1999	LC SET	40–80
Tarzan and His Mate	1936	OS	9,200
Tarzan and the Amazons	1945	OS	800–1,750

TITLE	YEAR	SIZE	PRICE RANGE
Tarzan and the Great River	1967	OS	50–90
Tarzan and the Huntress	1947	OS	500–750
Tarzan and the Jungle Boy	1968	OS	75–100
Tarzan and the Leopard Woman	1946	OS	500–900
Tarzan and the Lost Safari	1957	OS	150–250
Tarzan and the Mermaids	1948	OS	450–750
Tarzan and the Slave Girl	1950	OS	150–300
Tarzan and the Valley of Gold	1966	OS	75–125
Tarzan Escapes	1936	OS	75–200
Tarzan Finds a Son	1939	OS	1,500–3,000
Tarzan Goes to India	1962	OS	40–70
Tarzan of the Apes	1918	OS	12,650
Tarzan the Ape Man	1932	OS	20,700
Tarzan the Fearless	1933	OS	3,000–4,500
Tarzan the Magnificent	1960	OS	75–200
Tarzan Triumphs	1943	OS	750–1,000
Tarzan's Magic Fountain	1949	OS	250–400
Tarzan's New York Adventure	1942	OS	350–550
Tarzan's Secret Treasure	1941	OS	500–850
Tarzan's Three Challenges	1963	OS	50–90
Task Force	1949	OS	50–175
Taste of Honey	1961	OS	100–225
Taste the Blood of Dracula	1970	OS	75–225
Tattoo	1981	OS	40–90
Taxi	1932	LC	1,500–2,000
Taxi Dancer	1953	22 × 28	500–800
Taxi Driver	1976	OS	750–1,150
Taxi Driver	1976	LC SET	175–400
Tea and Sympathy	1956	OS	75–150
Tea for Two	1950	OS	50–125
Teacher's Pet	1958	OS	75–200
Teahouse of the August Moon	1956	OS	90–275
Tear Gas Squad	1940	OS	100–225
Teenage Caveman	1958	OS	450–650
Teenage Caveman	1958	LC SET	350–450
Teenage Doll	1957	OS	75–150
Teenage Millionaire	1961	OS	75–125
Teenage Monster	1957	OS	75–150

T

T

TITLE	YEAR	SIZE	PRICE RANGE
Teenage Rebel	1956	OS	75–150
Teenage Thunder	1957	OS	150–300
Teenagers from Outer Space	1959	OS	200–475
Telefon	1977	OS	40–70
Telefon	1977	LC SET	40–70
Telegraph Trail	1933	OS	1,447
Tell Them Willie Boy Is Here	1969	OS	50–90
Tell It to the Marines	1926	LC	1,500
Tell-Tale Heart	1960	OS	40–70
Tembo	1952	OS	100–225
Tempest	1928	OS	1,265
Tempest	1959	OS	75–175
Temptation	1946	OS	75–175
Temptress	1926	LC	650–800
10	1979	OS	50–125
10	1979	LC SET	40–70
Ten Commandments	1923	OS	1,500
Ten Commandments	1956	OS	950–2,000
Ten Commandments	1956	LC SET	175–325
Ten Little Indians	1966	OS	75–225
Ten Men Wanted	1954	OS	50–90
Ten Nights in a Barroom	1931	OS	150–250
10 North Frederick	1958	OS	50–90
Ten Seconds to Hell	1959	OS	40–90
Ten Tall Men	1951	OS	75–150
10,000 Bedrooms	1957	OS	60–125
Ten Who Dared	1960	OS	40–90
Tenant	1976	OS	50–90
Tender Comrade	1944	OS	100–325
Tender Is the Night	1961	OS	75–175
Tender Mercies	1983	OS	40–90
Tender Trap	1955	OS	90–175
Tender Years	1947	OS	75–150
Tennessee Champ	1954	OS	40–80
Tennessee's Partner	1955	OS	50–175
Tension	1949	OS	150–225
Tension at Table Rock	1956	OS	250–425
10th Avenue Angel	1947	OS	175–275

TITLE	YEAR	SIZE	PRICE RANGE
Teorema	1968	OS	50–175
Tequila Sunrise	1988	OS	40–70
Term of Trial	1962	OS	75–125
Terminator	1984	OS	75–175
Terminator	1984	LC SET	50–90
Terminator 2: Judgement Day	1994	OS	75–125
Terminator 2: Judgement Day	1994	LC SET	40–70
Termites of 1938	1939	OS	27,600
Terms of Endearment	1983	OS	50–90
Terms of Endearment	1983	LC SET	50–80
Terror	1920	OS	2,475
Terror	1963	OS	150–300
Terror	1963	LC SET	200–325
Terror at Midnight	1956	OS	50–90
Terror by Night	1946	OS	750–1,000
Terror by Night	1946	LC SET	750–1,000
Terror from the Year 5000	1958	OS	450–700
Terror from the Year 5000	1958	LC SET	225–325
Terror Island	1920	LC	3,910
Terror of the Tongs	1961	OS	75–125
Terror Train	1980	OS	40–70
Terrorists	1975	OS	40–70
Terrornauts	1967	OS	40–70
Tess	1981	OS	75–150
Test Pilot	1938	OS	700–1,000
Testament of Orpheus	1959	47 × 63 FRE	1,500–2,250
Tex	1982	OS	40–70
Texans	1938	OS	750–1,100
Texans Never Cry	1951	OS	75–150
Texas	1941	41 × 81	450–650
Texas across the River	1966	OS	40–70
Texas Badman	1932	OS	2,656
Texas Carnival	1951	OS	75–125
Texas Chainsaw Massacre	1974	OS	350–500
Texas Chainsaw Massacre 2	1986	OS	50–90
Texas Masquerade	1944	OS	150–300
Texas Rangers	1951	OS	50–90
Texas Trail	1937	OS	250–400

T

T

TITLE	YEAR	SIZE	PRICE RANGE
Texican	1966	OS	40–90
Thank God It's Friday	1978	OS	40–70
Thank Your Lucky Stars	1943	OS	250–450
That Certain Feeling	1956	OS	40–70
That Certain Woman	1937	OS	150–400
That Cold Day in the Park	1969	OS	40–60
That Darn Cat	1965	OS	40–70
That Darn Cat	1965	LC SET	50–80
That Forsyte Woman	1949	OS	300–650
That Funny Feeling	1965	OS	40–70
That Hagen Girl	1947	OS	200–350
That Hamilton Woman	1941	OS	900–1,250
That Kind of Woman	1957	OS	40–90
That Man from Rio	1964	OS	50–90
That Man in Istanbul	1964	OS	40–90
That Midnight Kiss	1949	OS	150–300
That Naughty Girl	1956	OS	75–250
That Night in Rio	1941	OS	900–1,250
That Obscure Object of Desire	1977	OS	50–125
That Tennessee Beat	1966	OS	40–80
That Touch of Mink	1962	OS	300–450
That Uncertain Feeling	1941	OS	150–275
That Wonderful Urge	1948	OS	100–225
That's Dancing	1985	OS	50–80
That's Entertainment	1974	OS	50–125
That's Entertainment 2	1975	OS	50–90
That's My Boy	1932	OS	350–650
That's My Boy	1951	OS	75–175
That's My Man	1946	OS	40–80
That's the Way It Is	1971	OS	125–200
Theatre of Blood	1973	OS	85–150
Theatre of Blood	1973	LC SET	100–225
Thelma and Louise	1991	OS	50–90
Thelma Jordan	1949	OS	100–225
Them	1954	OS	1,500–2,250
Them	1954	LC SET	800–950
Theodora Goes Wild	1935	OS	500–750
There Was a Crooked Man	1970	OS	40–70

TITLE	YEAR	SIZE	PRICE RANGE
There's a Girl in My Soup	1970	OS	40–70
There's Always a Woman	1938	OS	250–450
There's Always Tomorrow	1934	41 × 81	550–700
There's Always Tomorrow	1956	OS	40–80
There's No Business Like Show Business	1954	OS	550–750
There's Something about Mary	1998	OS	50–90
These Are the Damned	1962	OS	40–90
These Are the Damned	1962	LC SET	50–90
These Three	1936	OS	1,000–1,400
These Wilder Years	1956	OS	50–90
They All Kissed the Bride	1942	OS	200–400
They Call It Sin	1932	OS	1,704
They Call Me Mr. Tibbs	1970	OS	50–90
They Call Me Trinity	1971	OS	50–70
They Came from Within	1975	OS	75–125
They Came from Within	1975	LC SET	50–90
They Came to Cordura	1959	OS	50–90
They Dare Not Love	1941	OS	100–225
They Died with Their Boots On	1941	OS	2,000–3,250
They Drive by Night	1940	OS	850–1,250
They Gave Him a Gun	1937	OS	150–375
They Got Me Covered	1942	OS	400–575
They Live by Night	1948	OS	1,000–1,750
They Made Me a Criminal	1939	OS	1,500–2,250
They Only Kill Their Masters	1972	OS	40–60
They Shoot Horses, Don't They?	1969	OS	60–90
They Were Expendable	1945	OS	450–700
They Won't Believe Me	1947	OS	300–550
Thief	1952	OS	100–325
Thief	1981	OS	40–70
Thief of Bagdad	1924	22 × 28	6,900
Thief of Bagdad	1940	OS	850–1,000
Thief of Bagdad	1961	OS	50–125
Thief of Damascus	1952	OS	50–90
Thief of Venice	1952	OS	75–225
Thieves' Highway	1949	OS	75–150
Thieves like Us	1973	OS	50–125

T

T

TITLE	YEAR	SIZE	PRICE RANGE
Thin Ice	1937	OS	300–550
Thin Man	1934	22 × 28	25,850
Thin Man Goes Home	1944	OS	650–800
Thin Red Line	1964	OS	40–70
Thin Red Line	1998	OS	75–100
Thing	1982	OS	75–125
Thing	1982	LC SET	75–100
Thing from Another World	1951	OS	850–1,150
Thing that Couldn't Die	1958	OS	150–500
Thing that Couldn't Die	1958	LC SET	150–300
Thing with Two Heads	1972	OS	50–125
Things Are Tough All Over	1982	OS	40–60
Things to Come	1936	OS	8,510
Think Fast Mr. Moto	1937	OS	1,500–2,250
Third Day	1965	OS	40–80
Third Finger Left Hand	1940	OS	50–90
3rd Man	1949	OS	1,000–1,750
3rd Man	1949	LC SET	650–1,250
13 Frightened Girls	1963	OS	50–90
13 Ghosts	1960	OS	100–225
13 Ghosts	1960	LC SET	150–275
13 Rue Madeleine	1946	OS	1,000–1,400
13 West Street	1962	OS	40–70
Thirteenth Hour	1947	OS	75–125
Thirty Day Princess	1934	OS	750–900
30 Foot Bride of Candy Rock	1959	OS	50–125
39 Steps	1935	41 × 81 UK	9,400
30 Seconds over Tokyo	1944	OS	75–200
36 Hours	1965	OS	50–125
30 Years of Fun	1963	OS	75–175
This Above All	1942	OS	1,150–1,750
This Boy's Life	1993	OS	40–70
This Could Be the Night	1957	OS	40–70
This Earth Mine	1959	OS	60–90
This Gun for Hire	1942	OS	22,325
This Is Elvis	1981	OS	60–100
This Is My Love	1954	OS	50–90
This Is Russia	1958	OS	40–70

TITLE	YEAR	SIZE	PRICE RANGE
This Is Spinal Tap	1984	OS	100–150
This Is the Army	1943	OS	150–225
This Is the Life	1943	OS	75–150
This Is Your Army	1954	OS	75–150
This Island Earth	1955	OS	1,500–2,250
This Island Earth	1955	LC SET	1,400–2,250
This Land Is Mine	1943	OS	100–325
This Man's Navy	1945	OS	300–550
This Prosperity Is Condemned	1966	OS	75–125
This Prosperity Is Condemned	1966	LC SET	50–125
This Sporting Age	1932	OS	1,000–1,500
This Sporting Life	1963	OS	250–400
This Time for Keeps	1942	OS	50–150
This Time I'll Make You Rich	1974	OS	40–60
This Woman Is Dangerous	1952	OS	90–150
This Woman Is Mine	1941	OS	75–200
Thomas Crown Affair	1968	OS	600–800
Thoroughbreds Don't Cry	1937	OS	300–450
Thoroughly Modern Millie	1967	OS	50–100
Those Calloways	1965	OS	40–70
Those Love Pangs	1914	41 × 81	2,025
Those Magnificent Men in Their Flying Machines	1965	OS	50–80
Thousand Clowns	1966	OS	50–150
Thousands Cheer	1943	OS	200–325
Threat	1949	OS	100–225
Three Amigos	1986	OS	40–70
Three Bad Sisters	1955	OS	80–125
Three Bites of the Apple	1967	OS	40–70
Three Blind Mice	1938	OS	250–450
Three Caballeros	1944	OS	450–650
Three Came Home	1949	OS	50–90
Three Cases of Murder	1955	OS	200–450
Three Coins in the Fountain	1954	OS	50–125
Three Daring Daughters	1948	OS	100–175
Three Days of the Condor	1975	OS	75–175
Three Faces of Eve	1957	OS	75–150
Three Faces of Eve	1957	LC SET	40–90

T

T

TITLE	YEAR	SIZE	PRICE RANGE
3 for Bedroom C	1952	OS	75–150
Three for the Show	1954	OS	75–225
Three for the Show	1954	LC SET	100–225
3 Godfathers	1936	OS	75–200
3 Godfathers	1948	OS	500–800
Three Hours to Kill	1954	OS	40–70
300 Spartans	1962	OS	150–325
Three in the Attic	1968	OS	40–70
Three in the Cellar	1970	OS	40–70
Three Little Girls in Blue	1946	OS	100–325
Three Little Pigskins	1934	OS	96,000
Three Little Words	1950	OS	150–325
Three Little Words	1950	LC SET	75–150
Three Loves Has Nancy	1938	OS	75–250
Three Men and a Baby	1987	OS	40–60
Three Met by Moonlight	1957	OS	200–400
Three Musketeers	1933	OS	850–1,250
Three Musketeers	1948	OS	250–400
Three Musketeers	1948	LC SET	300–400
Three Musketeers	1974	OS	60–90
Three Musketeers	1974	LC SET	40–90
Three of a Kind	1944	OS	200–300
Three on a Couch	1966	OS	40–70
Three on a Match	1932	OS	3,750
Three Secrets	1950	OS	75–150
Three Stooges Fun O Rama	1959	OS	60–125
Three Stooges in Orbit	1962	OS	250–500
Three Stooges in Orbit	1962	LC SET	125–175
Three Stooges Meet Hercules	1961	OS	150–225
Three Strangers	1946	OS	200–450
Three Texas Steers	1939	OS	1,500–2,250
Three Violent People	1957	OS	40–80
Three Weekends	1928	LC	400–600
3 Women	1977	OS	75–125
3 Worlds of Gulliver	1960	OS	75–125
3 Worlds of Gulliver	1960	LC SET	50–90
Thrill of It All	1963	OS	40–80
Through the Back Door	1921	LC	150–275

TITLE	YEAR	SIZE	PRICE RANGE
Throwback	1935	OS	1,750–2,750
Thunder Afloat	1939	OS	200–375
Thunder Alley	1967	OS	40–80
Thunder Alley	1967	LC SET	40–70
Thunder Bay	1953	OS	100–275
Thunder Birds	1942	OS	500–750
Thunder in Carolina	1960	OS	40–80
Thunder in the City	1937	OS	300–475
Thunder in the East	1953	OS	50–90
Thunder in the Sun	1959	OS	50–90
Thunder Mountain	1935	OS	400–550
Thunder of Drums	1961	OS	40–70
Thunder on the Hill	1951	OS	150–325
Thunder over Hawaii	1957	OS	75–150
Thunder Road	1958	OS	350–550
Thunderball	1965	OS	1,500–2,000
Thunderball	1965	LC SET	1,000–1,400
Thunderbirds Are Go	1967	OS	75–225
Thunderbolt and Lightfoot	1974	OS	75–175
Thunderbolt and Lightfoot	1974	LC SET	50–125
Thunderstorm	1956	OS	50–90
THX 1138	1970	OS	225–400
Ticket to Tomahawk	1950	OS	75–175
Tickle Me	1965	OS	200–300
Ticklish Affair	1963	OS	40–80
Tie Me Up, Tie Me Down	1989	OS	50–90
Tiger Walks	1964	OS	40–70
Tiger Woman	1944	OS	400–800
Tight Shoes	1941	OS	100–175
Tight Spot	1955	OS	90–200
Tightrope	1984	OS	50–90
Tightrope	1984	LC SET	40–70
Till the Clouds Roll By	1946	OS	400–650
Till We Meet Again	1944	OS	100–275
Tillie	1922	22 × 28	300
Tillie's Punctured Romance	1914	OS	250–400
Tim Tyler's Luck	1937	OS	2,125
Timber	1941	OS	5,175

T

T

TITLE	YEAR	SIZE	PRICE RANGE
Timberjack	1955	OS	40–70
Timbuktu	1959	OS	40–70
Time after Time	1979	OS	40–70
Time after Time	1979	LC SET	50–90
Time Bandits	1980	OS	40–80
Time Bandits	1980	LC SET	75–100
Time Machine	1960	OS	800–1,250
Time Machine	1960	LC SET	830
Time of Their Lives	1946	OS	175–450
Time of Your Life	1948	OS	50–90
Time to Sing	1968	OS	75–125
Time Travellers	1964	OS	75–150
Time Travellers	1964	LC SET	50–90
Timetable	1956	OS	40–70
Tin Drum	1979	OS	50–90
Tin Pan Alley	1940	OS	250–400
Tin Star	1957	OS	150–300
Tingler	1959	OS	350–600
Tingler	1959	LC SET	150–225
Tip Off	1931	OS	450–600
Tip Off Girls	1938	OS	250–400
Tish	1942	OS	40–80
Titanic	1943	OS	450–650
Titanic	1953	OS	200–325
Titanic	1953	LC SET	200–300
Titanic	1997	OS	50–90
Titfield Thunderbolt	1953	OS	200–450
To Be or Not to Be	1942	OS	750–900
To Be or Not to Be	1983	OS	40–70
To Catch a Thief	1955	OS	2,000–2,750
To Catch a Thief	1955	LC SET	500–650
To Die For	1995	OS	40–70
To Each His Own	1946	OS	550–800
To Have and Have Not	1944	OS	2,000–2,750
To Have and Have Not	1944	LC SET	2,050
To Hell and Back	1955	OS	350–550
To Kill a Mockingbird	1963	OS	1,500–2,000
To Kill a Mockingbird	1963	LC SET	500–650

TITLE	YEAR	SIZE	PRICE RANGE
To Mary with Love	1936	OS	350–575
To Please a Lady	1950	OS	250–400
To Sir with Love	1967	OS	75–150
To the Devil a Daughter	1976	OS	75–150
To the Devil a Daughter	1976	LC SET	100–175
To the Ends of the Earth	1948	OS	150–325
To Trap a Spy	1966	OS	150–300
Toast of New Orleans	1950	OS	200–325
Toast of New Orleans	1950	LC SET	75–175
Tobacco Road	1941	OS	1,250–1,500
Tobor the Great	1954	OS	1,250–1,750
Tobor the Great	1954	LC SET	450–600
Tobruk	1967	OS	40–80
Tokyo Joe	1949	OS	75–150
Tokyo Rose	1946	OS	150–300
Tom and Jerry	1952	OS	250–500
Tom Brown's School Days	1940	OS	300–425
Tom Dick and Harry	1941	OS	200–325
Tom Horn	1980	OS	40–80
Tom Jones	1963	OS	250–325
Tom Thumb	1958	OS	175–325
Tomb of Ligeia	1965	OS	75–150
Tomb of Ligeia	1965	OS	75–175
Tomb Raider	2001	OS	50–90
Tombstone	1993	OS	60–110
Tombstone	1993	LC SET	40–70
Tommy	1975	OS	75–125
Tommy Boy	1995	OS	40–70
Tommy Boy	1995	LC SET	40–60
Tomorrow Is Forever	1945	OS	300–450
Tomorrow Never Dies	1997	OS	40–70
Tomorrow the World	1944	OS	50–75
Tomorrow We Live	1942	OS	50–90
Tonight and Every Night	1944	OS	300–550
Tonight We Sing	1953	OS	50–125
Tony Rome	1967	OS	75–125
Too Hot to Handle	1938	OS	450–700
Too Late Blues	1962	OS	75–125

T

T

TITLE	YEAR	SIZE	PRICE RANGE
Too Late Blues	1962	LC SET	50–90
Too Late for Tears	1949	OS	200–400
Too Late the Hero	1969	OS	40–90
Too Many Blondes	1941	OS	150–400
Too Many Girls	1940	OS	150–250
Too Much Too Soon	1958	OS	75–150
Too Soon to Love	1960	OS	40–80
Tootsie	1982	OS	50–90
Top Gun	1955	OS	40–70
Top Gun	1986	OS	75–150
Top Gun	1986	LC SET	75–150
Top Hat	1935	OS	11,050
Top O' the Morning	1949	OS	40–80
Top of the Town	1937	OS	600–750
Top Secret	1984	OS	40–70
Top Secret Affair	1957	OS	40–80
Topaz	1969	OS	75–150
Topaze	1933	OS	1,325
Topeka	1953	OS	75–150
Topkapi	1964	OS	150–250
Topper	1937	OS	1,250–1,500
Tora! Tora! Tora!	1970	OS	75–150
Tora! Tora! Tora!	1970	LC SET	75–125
Torch Song	1953	OS	150–250
Tormented	1960	OS	75–150
Torn Curtain	1966	OS	175–325
Torn Curtain	1966	LC SET	50–150
Torpedo Bay	1964	OS	40–80
Torpedo Run	1958	OS	50–90
Torrent	1926	LC	750–900
Torrid Zone	1940	OS	400–750
Tortilla Flat	1942	OS	400–650
Torture Garden	1967	OS	75–125
Total Recall	1990	OS	40–80
Total Recall	1990	LC SET	50–75
Touch	1971	OS	40–80
Touch of Class	1973	OS	40–80
Touch of Evil	1958	OS	1,750–2,500

TITLE	YEAR	SIZE	PRICE RANGE
Touch of Evil	1958	LC SET	400–675
Touch of Larceny	1960	OS	40–70
Touchdown Mickey	1932	OS	79,800
Toughest Gun in Tombstone	1958	OS	50–75
Toughest Man in Arizona	1952	OS	50–80
Tovarich	1937	OS	750–975
Toward the Unknown	1956	OS	50–90
Tower of Lies	1925	OS	950–1,100
Tower of London	1939	OS	650–850
Tower of London	1962	OS	50–90
Towering Inferno	1974	OS	150–250
Towering Inferno	1974	LC SET	200–325
Town Tamer	1965	OS	40–70
Town without Pity	1961	OS	50–80
Toxic Avenger	1985	OS	40–70
Toy Story	1995	OS	75–125
Toy Story 2	1999	OS	50–75
Toy Wife	1938	OS	250–400
Toys in the Attic	1963	OS	40–70
Toys in the Attic	1963	LC SET	65–90
Track of the Cat	1954	OS	350–500
Track the Man Down	1955	OS	40–70
Trade Winds	1938	OS	200–425
Trader Horn	1931	OS	3,450
Trader Mickey	1932	OS	31,625
Trading Places	1983	OS	40–70
Trading Places	1983	LC SET	50–75
Traffic	1971	OS	150–300
Traffic	2000	OS	50–90
Traffic in Souls	1913	OS	2,415
Trail Beyond	1934	81 × 81	5,000
Trail Drive	1933	OS	750–1,000
Trail Dust	1936	OS	450–700
Trail of the Lonesome Pine	1936	OS	450–600
Trail of the Pink Panther	1982	OS	40–70
Trail of the Yukon	1949	OS	50–90
Trail to San Antone	1947	OS	300–550
Trailing North	1933	OS	350–500

T

TITLE	YEAR	SIZE	PRICE RANGE
Train	1965	OS	100–225
Train	1965	LC SET	75–150
Train Robbers	1973	OS	75–200
Train Robbers	1973	LC SET	100–150
Trainspotting	1996	OS	50–90
Tramp	1915	41 × 81	10,925
Transatlantic	1931	OS	1,400–2,000
Transatlantic Tunnel	1935	OS	2,500–2,750
Transformers	1986	OS	50–150
Trap	1947	OS	500–800
Trap	1959	OS	40–80
Trapeze	1956	OS	250–500
Trapp Family	1960	OS	40–70
Trapped	1949	OS	300–375
Trapped by Boston Blackie	1948	OS	200–375
Trapped in Tangiers	1960	OS	40–70
Trash	1970	OS	75–150
Trauma	1962	OS	40–70
Travels with My Aunt	1972	OS	100–175
Treason	1933	OS	1,100–1,400
Treasure Island	1919	LC	300–400
Treasure Island	1934	OS	1,500–2,250
Treasure Island	1972	OS	50–80
Treasure of Ruby Hills	1955	OS	40–70
Treasure of Golden Condor	1953	OS	40–70
Treasure of the Sierra Madre	1948	OS	4,750–5,500
Tree Grows in Brooklyn	1945	OS	300–400
Tremors	1989	OS	40–70
Trent's Last Case	1953	OS	150–300
Trespasser	1929	OS	3,335
Trespasser	1947	OS	75–150
Trial of Mary Dugan	1941	OS	75–200
Tribes	1971	OS	50–80
Tribute	1980	OS	50–80
Tribute to a Bad Man	1956	OS	75–125
Tribute to a Bad Man	1956	LC SET	75–150
Trigger Fingers	1939	OS	50–125
Trip	1967	OS	175–250

TITLE	YEAR	SIZE	PRICE RANGE
Trip	1967	LC SET	75–125
Trip to Chinatown	1926	81 × 81	1,069
Triple Trouble	1918	LC	450–650
Tristana	1970	OS	150–300
Trog	1970	OS	50–90
Trojan Women	1971	OS	75–150
Tron	1982	OS	75–125
Tron	1982	LC SET	75–150
Tropic Holiday	1938	OS	250–400
Tropic of Cancer	1970	OS	40–80
Tropic Zone	1953	OS	150–325
Tropical Heatwave	1952	OS	50–90
Trouble along the Way	1953	OS	75–125
Trouble Chasers	1945	OS	75–175
Trouble for Two	1936	OS	350–500
Trouble in the Glen	1953	OS	125–250
Trouble in the Sky	1961	OS	40–70
Trouble Makers	1949	OS	50–90
Trouble Man	1972	OS	200–300
Trouble with Angels	1966	OS	125–200
Trouble with Girls	1969	OS	250–325
Trouble with Girls	1969	LC SET	100–175
Trouble with Harry	1955	OS	500–750
Truant Officer Donald	1941	OS	4,312
True Confession	1937	OS	800–1,000
Treu Confessions	1981	OS	40–70
True Glory	1945	OS	300–375
True Grit	1969	OS	225–325
True Grit	1969	LC SET	200–300
True Romance	1993	OS	75–100
True Story of Jesse James	1957	OS	50–90
True to Life	1943	OS	150–300
Truman Show	1998	OS	50–80
Truth	1960	OS	150–275
Truth about Spring	1965	OS	40–70
Truth or Dare	1991	OS	40–70
Tucker	1988	OS	50–90
Tumbleweed	1953	OS	50–90

T

T

TITLE	YEAR	SIZE	PRICE RANGE
Tumbleweeds	1925	LC	300–400
Tunnel of Love	1958	OS	40–70
Tunnel Vision	1976	OS	40–70
Turnabout	1940	OS	150–350
Turning Point	1952	OS	200–300
Turning Point	1977	OS	50–90
12 Angry Men	1957	OS	125–200
12 Angry Men	1957	LC SET	150–250
Twelve Chairs	1970	OS	40–70
Twelve Monkeys	1995	OS	50–90
Twelve O'Clock High	1949	OS	800–1,000
Twelve O'Clock High	1949	LC SET	300–400
Twelve to the Moon	1960	OS	40–70
20th Century	1934	OS	23,100
20 Million Miles to Earth	1957	OS	250–400
20 Million Miles to Earth	1957	LC SET	250–400
Twenty Million Sweethearts	1934	OS	800–1,000
27th Day	1957	OS	75–150
20,000 Leagues under the Sea	1954	OS	400–550
20,000 Men a Year	1939	OS	300–550
20,000 Years in Sing Sing	1932	14 × 36	4,000
Twice Told Tales	1963	OS	50–100
Twilight for the Gods	1958	OS	50–90
Twilight for the Gods	1958	LC SET	75–100
Twilight in the Sierras	1950	OS	350–500
Twilight in the Sierras	1950	LC SET	250–350
Twilight of Honor	1963	OS	40–70
Twilight on the Rio Grande	1947	OS	175–275
Twilight Zone	1983	OS	40–70
Twilight Zone	1983	LC SET	40–75
Twin Peaks	1990	OS	40–70
Twin Peaks: Fire Walk with Me	1992	OS	50–70
Twinkle and Shine	1961	OS	40–70
Twins of Evil	1971	OS	150–225
Twins of Evil	1971	LC SET	100–175
Twist All Night	1962	OS	40–70
Twist around the Clock	1961	OS	50–90
Twist of Fate	1954	OS	50–90

TITLE	YEAR	SIZE	PRICE RANGE
Twist of Sand	1968	OS	60–90
Twisted Nerve	1969	OS	40–70
Two Faced Woman	1941	OS	450–700
Two for the Road	1967	OS	300–475
Two for the Seesaw	1962	OS	50–70
Two Girls and a Sailor	1944	OS	75–150
Two Gun Justice	1938	OS	350–525
Two Gun Lady	1956	OS	75–100
200 Motels	1971	OS	75–150
200 Motels	1971	LC SET	50–100
Two Jakes	1990	OS	50–90
Two Lane Blacktop	1971	OS	250–350
Two Little Bears	1961	OS	50–125
Two Lovers	1928	14 × 36	800–1,000
Two Mrs. Carrolls	1947	OS	550–800
Two Mrs. Carrolls	1947	LC SET	350–550
Two Mules for Sister Sara	1970	OS	125–200
Two of a Kind	1951	OS	125–225
Two on a Guillotine	1965	OS	50–90
Two Rode Together	1961	OS	50–125
2001 (Style A)	1968	OS	900–1,250
2001 (Style B)	1968	OS	850–1,250
2001 (Style C)	1968	OS	2,500–3,250
2001 (Eye Style)	1968	OS	16,920
2001	1968	LC SET	875–1,400
2,000 Maniacs	1964	OS	175–250
2010	1984	OS	50–90
2010	1984	LC SET	40–70
Two Tickets to Paris	1962	OS	40–70
Two Tickets to Paris	1962	LC SET	40–60
Two Weeks in Another Town	1962	OS	50–90
Two Weeks in September	1967	OS	85–175
Two Weeks with Love	1950	OS	75–150
Two Women	1960	OS	50–90
Two Women	1960	LC SET	50–90
Twonky	1953	OS	75–150
Tycoon	1947	OS	350–550
Typhoon	1940	OS	850–1,150

U

200 The Invisible Man *(1933)*

201 The Invisible Ray *(1936)*

202 It Happened One Night *(1934)*

203 The Jazz Singer *(1927)*

TITLE	YEAR	SIZE	PRICE RANGE
U Boat 29	1939	OS	400–550
U Boat Prisoner	1944	OS	100–325
U Turn	1997	OS	40–60
U2: Rattle and Hum	1988	OS	50–90
UFO	1956	OS	50–90
Ugly American	1963	OS	50–90
Ugly Daschund	1965	OS	50–90
Ugly Duckling	1939	OS	6,900
Ugly Ones	1968	OS	40–70
UHF	1989	OS	40–70
Ultimate Warrior	1975	OS	40–70
Ulysses	1955	OS	75–200
Ulysses	1955	LC SET	50–125
Ulzana's Raid	1972	OS	50–90
Umbrellas of Cherbourg	1964	OS	150–325
Unbearable Lightness of Being	1988	OS	40–60
Unbreakable	2000	OS	50–90
Uncertain Glory	1944	OS	450–600
Uncle Tom's Cabin	1927	OS	1,265
Uncommon Valor	1983	OS	40–60
Unconquered	1947	OS	700–1,000
Undead	1957	OS	175–300
Undefeated	1969	OS	75–200
Undefeated	1969	LC SET	75–125
Under Capricorn	1949	OS	250–450
Under Fiesta Stars	1941	OS	300–500
Under Fire	1988	OS	40–70
Under My Skin	1950	OS	200–325
Under Nevada Skies	1946	OS	300–475
Under Secret Orders	1943	OS	50–90
Under Siege	1992	OS	40–70
Under Ten Flags	1960	OS	50–90
Under the Gun	1951	OS	50–90
Under the Red Sea	1952	OS	75–100
Under the Tonto Rim	1933	OS	500–700
Under the Volcano	1984	OS	60–90
Under the Yum Yum Tree	1963	OS	80–125
Under Two Flags	1936	OS	700–1,000

U

TITLE	YEAR	SIZE	PRICE RANGE
Under Western Skies	1945	OS	40–80
Under Western Stars	1938	OS	3,680
Undercover Maisie	1947	OS	50–90
Undercover Man	1936	OS	300–450
Undercover Hero	1975	OS	40–70
Undercurrent	1946	OS	500–700
Undersea Girl	1957	OS	50–90
Undersea Kingdom	1936	OS	4,850
Undertow	1949	OS	100–225
Underwater	1955	OS	350–550
Underwater City	1961	OS	40–70
Underwater Warrior	1958	OS	50–90
Underworld Story	1950	OS	50–70
Underworld USA	1961	OS	50–90
Unearthly	1957	OS	200–350
Unearthly	1957	LC SET	100–250
Unearthly Stranger	1964	OS	50–90
Unemployed Ghost	1931	OS	350–550
Unfaithful	1931	OS	150–300
Unfaithfully Yours	1948	OS	700–950
Unfaithfully Yours	1948	LC SET	350–500
Unfaithfuls	1960	OS	40–70
Unfinished Dance	1947	OS	40–80
Unforgiven	1960	OS	250–325
Unforgiven	1992	OS	150–225
Unguarded Moment	1956	OS	50–125
Unholy Partners	1941	OS	100–175
Unholy Three	1930	OS	4,000–5,000
Unholy Wife	1957	OS	50–90
Uninvited	1944	OS	450–700
Union Pacific	1939	OS	700–900
Union Station	1950	OS	75–125
Unknown	1946	OS	150–300
Unknown Terror	1957	OS	75–150
Unknown Terror	1957	LC SET	50–125
Unseen	1944	OS	200–325
Unsinkable Molly Brown	1964	OS	50–90
Unsuspected	1947	OS	75–175

TITLE	YEAR	SIZE	PRICE RANGE
Untamed	1929	LC	200–350
Untamed	1940	OS	75–200
Untamed Youth	1957	OS	150–275
Until the End of the World	1991	OS	40–70
Until They Sail	1957	OS	50–90
Untouchables	1987	OS	50–90
Unveiling Hand	1919	OS	200–475
Unwed Mother	1958	OS	50–90
Up	1972	OS	75–125
Up from the Beach	1965	OS	40–70
Up in Arms	1944	OS	75–225
Up in Central Park	1948	OS	75–200
Up in Smoke	1978	OS	50–125
Up in the Cellar	1970	OS	50–70
Up Periscope	1959	OS	50–90
Up the River	1930	LC	1,500
Up the Sandbox	1972	OS	75–125
Up to His Ears	1965	OS	40–70
Upper Hand	1966	OS	75–125
Upstairs Downstairs	1961	OS	40–70
Uptown New York	1932	OS	300–550
Uptown Saturday Night	1974	OS	50–70
Urban Cowboy	1980	OS	50–70
Urban Cowboy	1980	LC SET	40–60
Usual Suspects	1995	OS	75–200
Utah	1945	OS	500–900
Utah Baline	1957	OS	40–70
Utah Wagon Train	1951	OS	75–125
Utopia	1954	OS	300–400
Utopia	1954	LC SET	150–200
Vagabond	1916	OS	1,550
Vagabond King	1956	OS	50–90
Valachi Papers	1972	OS	50–90
Valachi Papers	1972	LC SET	50–75
Valdez Is Coming	1971	OS	50–90
Valentino	1951	OS	75–125
Valentino	1977	OS	50–90
Valerie	1957	OS	50–125

V

V

TITLE	YEAR	SIZE	PRICE RANGE
Valiant	1962	OS	40–70
Valley Girl	1983	OS	40–70
Valley Obscured by Clouds	1972	OS	125–300
Valley of Eagles	1951	OS	50–90
Valley of Fire	1951	OS	75–125
Valley of Gwangi	1969	OS	150–225
Valley of Head Hunters	1953	OS	50–90
Valley of Head Hunters	1953	LC SET	100–200
Valley of Hell	1927	OS	350–650
Valley of Mystery	1967	OS	40–70
Valley of the Dolls	1967	OS	300–450
Valley of the Dragons	1961	OS	50–90
Valley of the Kings	1954	OS	40–70
Valley of the Redwoods	1960	OS	50–70
Valley of the Zombies	1946	OS	550–700
Valley of Vengeance	1944	OS	150–250
Valmont	1989	OS	50–90
Vampire	1957	OS	75–175
Vampire	1957	LC SET	85–150
Vampire and the Ballerina	1962	OS	75–150
Vampire Bat	1933	OS	125–300
Vampire Circus	1972	OS	75–150
Vampire Circus	1972	LC SET	70–90
Vampire Lovers	1970	OS	150–200
Vampire Lovers	1970	LC SET	150–200
Vampire's Ghost	1945	OS	200–350
Vanishing American	1955	OS	50–90
Vanishing Body	R 1953	OS	300–450
Vanishing Men	1937	OS	300–500
Vanishing Pioneer	1928	OS	350–550
Vanishing Point	1971	OS	250–450
Vanishing Point	1971	LC SET	75–125
Vanquished	1953	OS	50–90
Varan the Unbelievable	1962	OS	75–150
Variety Girl	1947	OS	200–400
Vault of Horror	1973	OS	75–125
Vault of Horror	1973	LC SET	80–125
Velvet Vampire	1971	OS	75–125

TITLE	YEAR	SIZE	PRICE RANGE
Vendetta	1950	OS	150–350
Vendetta for the Saint	1969	OS	40–70
Venetian Affair	1966	OS	75–125
Vengeance	1918	OS	450–650
Vengeance of Fu Manchu	1968	OS	50–90
Vengeance of Fu Manchu	1968	LC SET	75–125
Vengeance of She	1968	OS	75–125
Vengeance Valley	1950	OS	150–250
Venom	1982	OS	40–70
Vera Cruz	1955	OS	250–400
Verboten!	1959	OS	40–70
Verdict	1946	OS	100–225
Verdict	1946	LC SET	500–650
Verdict	1982	OS	40–70
Verdict	1982	LC SET	40–70
Veronica Voss	1982	OS	40–70
Vertigo	1958	OS	4,000–5,250
Very Private Affair	1962	OS	75–150
Very Private Affair	1962	LC SET	150–225
Very Special Favor	1965	OS	40–70
Via Pony Express	1934	OS	400–550
Vice Raid	1960	OS	75–125
Vice Squad	1953	OS	75–125
Vicki	1953	OS	40–70
Victim	1961	OS	40–70
Victor Victoria	1982	OS	75–125
Victors	1963	OS	40–70
Victory	1940	OS	75–150
Victory	1981	OS	40–70
Victory through Air Power	1943	OS	650–900
Videodrome	1983	OS	75–125
Videodrome	1983	LC SET	75–90
View from the Bridge	1962	OS	40–70
View to a Kill	1985	OS	75–175
View to a Kill	1985	LC SET	50–90
Vigil in the Night	1940	OS	450–650
Vigilante Terror	1953	OS	50–90
Vigilantes Are Coming	1936	OS	500–800

V

V

TITLE	YEAR	SIZE	PRICE RANGE
Viking Queen	1967	OS	50–90
Viking Queen	1967	LC SET	50–90
Viking Women and Sea Serpent	1957	OS	250–425
Viking Women and Sea Serpent	1957	LC SET	150–250
Vikings	1958	OS	450–575
Villa Rides	1968	OS	50–90
Village of the Damned	1960	OS	100–175
Village of the Damned	1960	LC SET	150–275
Village of the Giants	1965	OS	75–125
Village Smithy	1941	OS	3,737
Village Vampire	1916	OS	1,350
Villain	1971	OS	50–80
Vintage	1957	OS	40–80
Violators	1957	OS	50–90
Violent Road	1958	OS	40–70
Violent Saturday	1955	OS	40–70
V.I.P.s	1963	OS	100–175
Virgin Queen	1955	OS	75–175
Virgin Queen	1955	LC SET	100–175
Virginia City	1940	OS	1,955
Virginian	1929	OS	13,200
Viridiana	1961	OS	100–300
Virtue	1932	OS	3,000
Visit	1964	OS	50–90
Visit to a Small Planet	1960	OS	50–90
Visit to a Small Planet	1960	LC SET	50–80
Viva James Bond	1970	OS	125–225
Viva Knievel	1977	OS	40–70
Viva Knievel	1977	LC SET	50–90
Viva Las Vegas	1964	OS	750–1,000
Viva Las Vegas	1964	LC SET	150–400
Viva Maria	1965	OS	50–90
Viva Maria	1965	LC SET	75–150
Viva Villa	1934	LC	200–350
Viva Zapata	1952	OS	3,300
Vixen	1968	OS	150–225
Voice in the Mirror	1958	OS	50–90
Voice of the Turtle	1947	OS	125–200

TITLE	YEAR	SIZE	PRICE RANGE
Voice of the Turtle	1947	LC SET	200–250
Volga Boatman	1926	LC SET	200–275
Volpone	1940	47 × 63 FRE	2,500
Von Ryan's Express	1965	OS	150–300
Voodoo Island	1957	OS	175–375
Voodoo Man	1944	OS	500–750
Voodoo Tiger	1952	OS	100–250
Voodoo Woman	1957	22 × 28	175–300
Voodoo Woman	1957	LC SET	100–200
Voyage of the Damned	1976	OS	40–70
Voyage of the Damned	1976	LC SET	75–100
Voyage to the Bottom of the Sea	1961	OS	100–175
Voyage to the Bottom of the Sea	1961	LC SET	75–150
Voyage to the End of the Universe	1964	OS	100–200
Voyage to the End of the Universe	1964	LC SET	75–150
Vulture	1966	OS	40–70
Wabash Avenue	1950	OS	250–500
Wackiest Ship in the Army	1960	OS	50–75
Waco	1966	OS	40–70
Wag the Dog	1997	OS	50–80
Wages of Fear	1953	OS	200–350
Wagon Master	1950	OS	400–575
Wagon Master	1950	LC SET	250–350
Wagon Team	1952	OS	150–225
Wagons Roll at Night	1941	OS	500–750
Wait until Dark	1967	OS	100–200
Waiting for Guffman	1996	OS	40–70
Wake Island	1942	OS	250–450
Wake Me When It's Over	1960	OS	40–70
Wake of the Red Witch	1948	OS	350–475
Wake Up and Dream	1946	OS	75–150
Wake Up and Live	1937	OS	350–500
Walk a Crooked Mile	1948	OS	250–400
Walk a Tightrope	1964	OS	40–70
Walk Don't Run	1966	OS	40–80
Walk in the Spring Rain	1970	OS	50–80
Walk into Hell	1957	OS	50–90
Walk like a Dragon	1960	OS	50–90

W

W

TITLE	YEAR	SIZE	PRICE RANGE
Walk on the Wild Side	1962	OS	150–300
Walk Softly Stranger	1950	OS	100–225
Walk the Proud Land	1956	OS	50–90
Walkabout	1971	OS	100–175
Walkabout	1971	LC SET	50–90
Walking Dead	1936	OS	1,500
Walking My Baby Back Home	1953	OS	75–125
Walking My Baby Back Home	1953	LC SET	125–200
Walking Stick	1970	OS	40–60
Walking Tall	1973	OS	40–60
Wall	1982	OS	150–200
Wall	1982	LC SET	75–125
Wall of Noise	1963	OS	40–60
Wall Street	1987	OS	75–150
Wall Street	1987	LC SET	75–125
Wall Street Cowboy	1939	OS	1,536
Walls Came Tumbling Down	1946	OS	75–125
Walls of Jericho	1948	OS	75–175
Waltz of the Toreadors	1962	OS	40–80
Wanda Nevada	1979	OS	40–70
Wanderer of the Wasteland	1945	OS	75–125
Wanderers	1979	OS	75–125
Wanted Dead or Alive	1951	OS	50–90
War against Mrs. Hadley	1943	OS	50–125
War and Peace	1956	OS	100–195
War and Peace	1956	LC SET	150–300
War between the Planets	1971	OS	50–90
War between the Planets	1971	LC SET	50–90
War Drums	1957	OS	40–80
War Games	1983	OS	40–70
War Games	1983	LC SET	40–60
War Gods of the Deep	1965	OS	75–150
War Gods of the Deep	1965	LC SET	50–125
War Hunt	1962	OS	50–90
War Is Hell	1964	OS	50–90
War Italian Style	1966	OS	40–80
War Lord	1965	OS	40–70
War Lover	1962	OS	50–90

TITLE	YEAR	SIZE	PRICE RANGE
War Lover	1962	LC SET	75–125
War of the Colossal Beast	1958	OS	400–650
War of the Roses	1989	OS	40–70
War of the Satellites	1958	OS	150–250
War of the Satellites	1958	LC SET	150–225
War of the Wildcats	1943	OS	400–550
War of the Worlds	1953	OS	6,000
War of the Worlds	1953	LC SET	1,495
War of the Zombies	1965	OS	75–150
War of the Zombies	1965	LC SET	75–125
War Wagon	1967	OS	200–325
War Wagon	1967	LC SET	400–475
Warlock	1959	OS	50–90
Warlords of Atlantis	1978	OS	50–90
Warm December	1973	OS	50–90
Warm Reception	1916	OS	500–850
Warning Shot	1967	OS	40–70
Warrens of Virginia	1915	OS	600–850
Warrior and the Slave Girl	1959	OS	50–70
Warrior Empress	1960	OS	40–90
Warrior Empress	1960	LC SET	50–90
Warriors	1955	OS	75–150
Warriors	1955	LC SET	75–125
Warriors	1979	OS	75–150
Warriors	1979	LC SET	75–125
Warriors Five	1962	OS	40–70
Washington Story	1952	OS	75–125
Wasp Woman	1959	OS	4,000
Wasp Woman	1959	LC SET	750–1,100
Watch the Birdie	1950	OS	75–150
Watcher in the Woods	1980	OS	50–90
Watcher in the Woods	1980	LC SET	75–100
Waterhole #3	1967	OS	40–70
Waterloo	1971	OS	75–125
Waterloo	1971	LC SET	50–90
Waterloo Bridge	1940	OS	1,750–2,400
Watermelon Man	1970	OS	50–90
Watership Down	1978	OS	50–90

W

W

TITLE	YEAR	SIZE	PRICE RANGE
Watership Down	1978	LC SET	75–150
Waterworld	1995	OS	40–70
Wattstax	1973	OS	75–150
Watusi	1959	OS	40–80
Way Down East	1920	OS	5,175
Way of a Gaucho	1952	OS	50–90
Way of a Man	1923	OS	900–1,250
Way of a Woman	1919	OS	150–450
Way of the Dragon	1973	LC SET	150–250
Way out West	1937	22 × 28	3,450
Way out West	1937	LC SET	2,875
Way to the Gold	1957	OS	40–70
Way Way Out	1966	OS	50–80
Way We Were	1973	OS	50–125
Way We Were	1973	LC SET	75–150
Way West	1967	OS	40–80
Wayne's World	1992	OS	40–70
Wayward Bus	1957	OS	150–250
Wayward Canary	1932	OS	31,625
Wayward Girl	1957	OS	50–90
W.C. Fields and Me	1976	OS	50–70
We Are Not Alone	1939	OS	300–550
We Live Again	1934	OS	2,200
We Were Dancing	1942	OS	250–500
We Were Strangers	1949	OS	75–150
We Who Are Young	1940	OS	75–150
We'll Bury You	1962	OS	40–80
We're No Angels	1955	OS	75–200
We're No Angels	1989	OS	40–70
We're Not Married	1952	OS	75–200
Weapon	1956	OS	50–80
Web of Evidence	1959	OS	50–90
Wedding	1978	OS	50–90
Wedding March	1928	OS	6,600
Wedding March	1928	LC SET	3,450
Wedding Night	1935	14 × 36	800
Wee Willie Winkie	1937	OS	6,800
Weekend at Dunkirk	1965	OS	40–70

W

TITLE	YEAR	SIZE	PRICE RANGE
Weird Science	1985	OS	40–70
Weird Woman	1944	OS	250–450
Welcome Danger	1929	OS	1,150
Welcome to Hard Times	1967	OS	40–70
Welcome to L.A.	1977	OS	40–70
Welcome to My Nightmare	1975	OS	75–200
Welcome to the Dollhouse	1996	OS	50–90
Well Groomed Bride	1946	OS	75–150
Werewolf	1956	OS	150–250
Werewolf	1956	LC SET	200–350
Werewolf in a Girl's Dorm	1963	OS	50–90
Werewolf in a Girl's Dorm	1963	LC SET	100–200
Werewolf of London	1935	14 × 36	15,000
Werewolves on Wheels	1971	OS	50–90
West Point Story	1950	OS	75–225
West Side Story	1961	OS	950–1,250
West Side Story	1961	LC SET	350–600
Westbound	1959	OS	50–90
Western Union	1941	OS	450–600
Westerner	1940	OS	1,250–2,000
Westward Ho	1935	OS	1,250–1,750
Westworld	1973	OS	100–225
What a Way to Go	1964	OS	75–125
What a Widow	1930	OS	300–550
What Did You Do in War, Daddy?	1966	OS	40–90
What Ever Happened to Baby Jane?	1962	OS	250–400
What Happened to Rosa	1920	OS	400–650
What Price Glory	1952	OS	75–150
What's Buzzin', Cousin?	1943	OS	175–250
What's Eating Gilbert Grape	1994	OS	40–70
What's New, Pussycat	1965	OS	100–225
What's New, Pussycat	1965	LC SET	50–90
What's Up, Doc?	1972	OS	75–150
What's Up, Doc?	1972	LC SET	75–175
What's Up, Tiger Lily?	1966	OS	75–200
Whatever Happened to Aunt Alice?	1969	OS	50–90
Wheeler Dealers	1963	OS	50–90
When Dinosaurs Ruled Earth	1970	OS	50–90

W

TITLE	YEAR	SIZE	PRICE RANGE
When G-Men Step In	1938	OS	250–350
When Harry Met Sally	1989	OS	100–150
When Hell Broke Loose	1958	OS	50–90
When in Rome	1951	OS	50–90
When Ladies Meet	1941	OS	300–500
When My Baby Smiles at Me	1948	OS	250–400
When My Baby Smiles at Me	1948	LC SET	150–200
When Strangers Marry	1933	OS	400–550
When the Boys Meet the Girls	1965	OS	75–175
When the Boys Meet the Girls	1965	LC SET	50–90
When Willie Comes Marching Home	1950	OS	75–150
When Women Had Tails	1970	OS	50–90
When Worlds Collide	1951	OS	1,116
When You're in Love	1937	OS	400–650
Where Angels Go, Trouble Follows	1968	OS	50–90
Where Danger Lives	1950	41 × 81	2,000–3,250
Where Do We Go from Here?	1945	OS	150–250
Where Eagles Dare	1968	OS	250–400
Where Love Has Gone	1964	OS	75–150
Where the Boys Are	1960	OS	75–125
Where the Hot Wind Blows	1960	OS	50–90
Where the North Begins	1923	OS	750–900
Where the Sidewalk Ends	1950	OS	250–500
Where There's Life	1947	OS	75–150
Where's Charley	1952	OS	50–90
Where's Poppa?	1971	OS	50–90
While New York Sleeps	1937	OS	250–400
While the City Sleeps	1956	OS	50–120
Whipsaw	1935	OS	2,000
Whirlpool	1949	OS	350–500
Whirlwind	1933	OS	450–675
Whispering Shadow	1933	OS	950–1,150
Whispering Smith	1949	OS	300–375
Whistle down the Wind	1961	OS	100–325
Whistling in Brooklyn	1943	OS	300–450
Whistling in Dixie	1942	OS	150–250
White	1994	OS	50–90

TITLE	YEAR	SIZE	PRICE RANGE
White Cargo	1942	OS	250–500
White Christmas	1954	OS	650–800
White Christmas	1954	LC SET	250–325
White Cliffs of Dover	1944	OS	250–400
White Heat	1934	OS	150–325
White Heat	1949	OS	700–850
White Lightning	1973	OS	40–70
White Line Fever	1975	OS	40–70
White Sister	1923	41 × 81	8,250
White Slave Ship	1962	OS	40–70
White Warrior	1961	OS	50–90
White Witch Doctor	1953	OS	50–90
White Zombie	1932	OS	2,500
Who Done It?	1942	OS	900–1,400
Who Framed Roger Rabbit	1988	OS	100–175
Who Framed Roger Rabbit	1988	LC SET	125–175
Who Killed Gail Preston?	1938	OS	500–800
Who Was That Lady?	1960	OS	50–70
Who'll Stop the Rain	1978	OS	40–70
Who's Afraid of Virginia Woolf?	1966	OS	150–250
Who's Afraid of Virginia Woolf?	1966	LC SET	125–200
Who's Been Sleeping in My Bed?	1963	OS	40–80
Who's Got the Action?	1962	OS	50–90
Who's Minding the Mint?	1967	OS	50–70
Who's Minding the Store?	1963	OS	40–70
Who's Minding the Store?	1963	LC SET	50–80
Who's That Girl?	1987	OS	40–70
Who's That Knocking at My Door?	1968	OS	300–500
Whoopee	1930	OS	2,875
Whoopee Party	1932	OS	28,750
Why Bother to Knock	1965	OS	40–70
Why Must I Die?	1960	OS	40–70
Why Worry?	1923	LC	200–450
Wichita	1955	OS	50–90
Wicked As They Come	1956	OS	50–90
Wicked City	1950	OS	75–125
Wicked Dreams of Paul Schultz	1968	OS	40–70
Wicked Go to Hell	1960	OS	50–80

W

W

TITLE	YEAR	SIZE	PRICE RANGE
Wicked Lady	1946	OS	250–400
Wicked Woman	1953	OS	100–225
Wicked Woman	1953	LC SET	50–125
Wicker Man	1974	OS	50–125
Wicker Man	1974	LC SET	100–175
Wide Open Faces	1938	OS	150–225
Wide Open Spaces	1947	OS	2,900
Wife, Doctor and Nurse	1937	OS	250–450
Wife, Doctor and Nurse	1937	LC SET	250–350
Wife of Monte Cristo	1946	OS	50–90
Wilby Conspiracy	1975	OS	40–70
Wild and the Innocent	1959	OS	50–90
Wild and Wonderful	1964	OS	40–70
Wild and Woolly	1917	OS	1,035
Wild Angels	1966	OS	150–250
Wild Angels	1966	LC SET	125–225
Wild at Heart	1990	OS	40–70
Wild Bunch	1968	OS	500–750
Wild Bunch	1968	LC SET	250–400
Wild Child	1970	OS	40–70
Wild Country	1947	OS	50–90
Wild Dakotas	1956	OS	50–80
Wild for Kicks	1961	OS	125–175
Wild Geese	1978	OS	50–90
Wild Geese	1978	LC SET	40–70
Wild Guitar	1962	OS	50–90
Wild Harvest	1947	OS	500–750
Wild Heart	1952	OS	75–125
Wild Horse Ambush	1952	OS	40–70
Wild in the Country	1961	OS	200–325
Wild in the Streets	1968	OS	40–70
Wild Is the Wind	1957	OS	40–70
Wild North	1952	OS	40–70
Wild One	1954	OS	750–900
Wild One	1954	LC SET	150–250
Wild Orchid	1990	OS	40–70
Wild Orchids	1929	LC	700–950
Wild Party	1929	OS	3,162

TITLE	YEAR	SIZE	PRICE RANGE
Wild Racers	1968	OS	40–70
Wild Ride	1960	OS	90–150
Wild River	1960	OS	50–90
Wild Rovers	1971	OS	40–70
Wild Seed	1965	OS	50–70
Wild Stallion	1952	OS	50–90
Wild Strawberries	1956	OS	150–350
Wild Things	1998	OS	50–90
Wild West Days	1937	OS	350–500
Wild Wild Planet	1967	OS	50–90
Wild Wild Winter	1966	OS	40–70
Wild Wild World of J. Mansfield	1968	OS	75–150
Wild Women of Wongo	1958	OS	100–175
Wildcat Saunders	1936	OS	250–350
Will Penny	1968	OS	50–90
Will Success Spoil Rock Hunter?	1957	OS	75–200
Willard	1971	OS	75–175
Willow	1988	OS	50–90
Willow Tree	1920	OS	800
Willy Wonka	1971	OS	250–325
Willy Wonka	1971	LC SET	150–200
Wilson	1944	OS	250–450
Winchester 73	1950	OS	1,200–1,750
Wind across the Everglades	1958	OS	40–80
Wind and the Lion	1975	OS	50–90
Wind Cannot Read	1958	OS	40–80
Windjammer	1937	OS	100–175
Window	1949	OS	300–550
Winged Victory	1944	OS	75–225
Wings	1927	OS	4,950
Wings in the Dark	1934	LC SET	1,150
Wings of Desire	1988	OS	75–200
Wings of Eagles	1957	OS	75–200
Wings of Eagles	1957	LC SET	150–225
Wings of the Morning	1937	OS	350–550
Wings of the Navy	1939	OS	750–1,100
Winners of the West	1940	OS	150–325
Winnie the Pooh and Tigger Too	1974	OS	150–250

W

TITLE	YEAR	SIZE	PRICE RANGE
Winning	1969	OS	75–125
Winning	1969	LC SET	50–90
Winning of the West	1953	OS	125–275
Winning Team	1952	OS	200–325
Winter Meeting	1948	OS	150–250
Winter Meeting	1948	LC SET	100–150
Wintertime	1943	OS	250–400
Witch's Curse	1963	OS	40–70
Witchcraft	1964	OS	75–200
Witches	1966	OS	100–175
Witches of Eastwick	1987	OS	40–90
With a Song in My Heart	1952	OS	100–250
With a Song in My Heart	1952	LC SET	100–150
With Six You Get Egg Roll	1968	OS	40–70
Withnail and I	1988	OS	400–750
Without Love	1945	OS	200–450
Without Reservations	1946	OS	200–350
Witness	1985	OS	50–90
Witness	1985	LC SET	50–70
Witness for the Prosecution	1958	OS	100–225
Witness for the Prosecution	1958	LC SET	75–150
Wives and Lovers	1963	OS	40–70
Wiz	1978	OS	40–90
Wiz	1978	LC SET	50–75
Wizard of Baghdad	1960	OS	40–70
Wizard of Oz	1939	22 × 28	25,300
Wizard of Oz	1939	LC SET	25,000
Wizards	1977	OS	75–150
Wolf Call	1939	OS	125–200
Wolf Dog	1958	OS	40–70
Wolf Man	1924	81 × 81	2,136
Wolf Man	1941	OS	17,600
Wolfen	1981	OS	40–70
Woman	1918	OS	350–600
Woman Eater	1959	OS	80–150
Woman Haters	1934	OS	41,400
Woman in Green	1945	OS	750–1,250
Woman in Green	1945	LC SET	1,050

TITLE	YEAR	SIZE	PRICE RANGE
Woman in Hiding	1949	OS	50–95
Woman in Red	1938	OS	2,588
Woman in Red	1984	OS	40–70
Woman in the Window	1944	OS	600–850
Woman Is a Woman	1961	47 × 63 FRE	350–500
Woman like Satan	1959	OS	50–90
Woman Obsessed	1959	OS	50–90
Woman Obsessed	1959	LC SET	50–90
Woman of Affairs	1928	OS	3,220
Woman of Paris	1923	LC	250–400
Woman of Straw	1964	OS	50–90
Woman of Straw	1964	LC SET	50–90
Woman of the Year	1942	OS	2,000–2,500
Woman of the Year	1942	LC SET	800–950
Woman on the Beach	1946	OS	250–400
Woman They Almost Lynched	1953	OS	50–90
Woman Time Seven	1967	OS	40–70
Woman to Woman	1929	OS	500–800
Woman under the Influence	1974	OS	650–850
Woman Who Wouldn't Die	1965	OS	50–90
Woman's Devotion	1956	OS	50–90
Woman's Face	1941	OS	150–300
Woman's Secret	1949	OS	300–450
Women	1939	OS	2,750–3,250
Women in Love	1970	OS	75–125
Women of Pitcairn Island	1956	OS	40–70
Women of Prehistoric Planet	1966	OS	50–90
Women's Prison	1954	OS	75–150
Wonder Man	1945	OS	150–325
Wonderful Country	1959	OS	50–90
Wonderful Country	1959	LC SET	75–150
Wonderful to Be Young	1962	OS	40–70
Wonderful World Brothers Grimm	1963	OS	40–70
Wonders of Aladdin	1961	OS	40–70
Woodstock	1970	OS	300–550
Words and Music	1948	OS	250–400
Working Girl	1988	OS	40–70
World and the Flesh	1932	OS	150–350

W

W

TITLE	YEAR	SIZE	PRICE RANGE
World for Ransom	1954	OS	50–90
World in His Arms	1952	OS	150–300
World in My Corner	1956	OS	50–90
World Is Not Enough	1999	OS	40–90
World of Abbott and Costello	1965	OS	75–200
World of Henry Orient	1964	OS	50–90
World of Suzie Wong	1960	OS	75–125
World of Suzie Wong	1960	LC SET	100–175
World Premiere	1941	OS	150–250
World, the Flesh and the Devil	1959	OS	50–90
World without End	1956	OS	700–950
World without End	1956	LC SET	350–450
World without Sun	1964	OS	50–90
World's Greatest Athlete	1972	OS	40–70
Wrath of God	1972	OS	40–70
Wreck of the Mary Dear	1959	OS	75–125
Wreck of the Mary Dear	1959	LC SET	75–150
Wrecking Crew	1969	OS	250–325
Written on the Wind	1956	OS	400–550
Wrong Box	1966	OS	40–70
Wrong Man	1957	OS	1,150–1,450
Wrong Man	1957	LC SET	750–1,000
WUSA	1970	OS	40–70
Wuthering Heights	1939	OS	850–1,250
Wuthering Heights	1970	OS	40–70
W.W. and the Dixie Dancekings	1975	OS	40–70
Wyatt Earp	1994	OS	50–125
Wyatt Earp	1994	LC SET	75–100
Wyoming	1940	OS	400–650
Wyoming Outlaw	1939	OS	250–450
Wyoming Roundup	1952	OS	50–90
X Files	1998	OS	75–125
X Files	1998	LC SET	50–90
X Men	2000	OS	50–90
X Men	2000	LC SET	40–70
X the Man with the X Ray Eyes	1963	OS	750–1,150
X the Man with the X Ray Eyes	1963	LC SET	75–200
X the Unknown	1956	OS	75–175

TITLE	YEAR	SIZE	PRICE RANGE
X, Y and Zee	1972	OS	40–70
X-15	1961	OS	50–90
Xanadu	1980	OS	75–125
Xanadu	1980	LC SET	50–90
Xtro	1983	OS	125–200
Yakuza	1975	OS	350–400
Yank at Oxford	1938	OS	400–750
Yank at Oxford	1938	LC SET	50–175
Yank in the R.A.F.	1941	OS	300–500
Yank in the R.A.F.	1941	LC SET	100–225
Yank in Vietnam	1964	OS	40–70
Yankee Doodle Dandy	1942	OS	950–1,750
Yanks	1979	OS	40–70
Year of Living Dangerously	1983	OS	40–80
Year of the Dragon	1985	OS	40–70
Yearling	1946	OS	75–200
Yellow Cab Man	1950	OS	40–90
Yellow Canary	1963	OS	40–70
Yellow Jack	1938	OS	150–300
Yellow Mountain	1954	OS	40–70
Yellow Rolls-Royce	1965	OS	50–90
Yellow Rose of Texas	1944	OS	300–500
Yellow Sky	1948	OS	250–400
Yellow Submarine	1968	OS	3,160
Yellow Submarine	1968	LC SET	650–800
Yellow Tomahawk	1954	OS	40–70
Yellowstone Cubs	1963	OS	40–70
Yellowstone Kelly	1959	OS	40–70
Yentl	1983	OS	40–70
Yentl	1983	LC SET	40–80
Yesterday, Today and Tomorrow	1964	OS	40–70
Yesterday's Enemy	1959	OS	50–90
Yog: Monster from Space	1970	OS	50–90
Yojimbo	1961	22 × 28	100–250
You Are What You Eat	1968	OS	50–90
You Belong to Me	1941	OS	200–350
You Came Along	1945	OS	75–150
You Can't Beat Love	1937	OS	300–500

Y

Y

TITLE	YEAR	SIZE	PRICE RANGE
You Can't Cheat an Honest Man	1939	OS	6,900
You Can't Get away with Murder	1939	OS	2,750–3,250
You Can't Take It with You	1938	OS	1,500–2,000
You Gotta Stay Happy	1948	OS	90–175
You Know Me	1915	OS	2,350
You Only Live Once	1937	OS	1,250–1,750
You Only Live Twice	1967	OS	750–1,150
You Were Meant for Me	1948	OS	75–125
You Were Never Lovelier	1942	OS	750–1,250
You Were Never Lovelier	1942	LC SET	1,200
You'll Never Get Rich	1942	OS	1,000–1,400
You're in the Army Now	1937	OS	500–750
You're in the Navy Now	1951	OS	100–175
You're My Everything	1949	OS	50–90
You're Never Too Young	1955	OS	50–90
You're Never Too Young	1955	LC SET	100–150
You're Telling Me	1934	OS	1,525
Young and Wild	1958	OS	75–200
Young at Heart	1955	OS	150–275
Young Bess	1953	OS	75–200
Young Cassidy	1965	OS	50–70
Young Dillinger	1965	OS	40–70
Young Doctors	1961	OS	40–70
Young Donovan's Kid	1931	OS	750–950
Young Dr. Kildare	1938	OS	250–400
Young Frankenstein	1974	OS	175–250
Young Frankenstein	1974	LC SET	150–300
Young Guns	1956	OS	40–70
Young Guns	1988	OS	40–70
Young Land	1958	OS	50–90
Young Lions	1958	OS	100–250
Young Lovers	1964	OS	40–70
Young Man with a Horn	1950	OS	300–550
Young Mr. Lincoln	1939	OS	650–850
Young People	1940	OS	175–250
Young Philadelphians	1959	OS	50–90
Young Racers	1963	OS	50–90
Young Racers	1963	LC SET	100–150
Young Runaways	1968	OS	40–70

204 The Kid *(1921)*

205 The Klondike Kid *(1932)*

206 The Phantom of the Opera
(1925)

207 Son of Frankenstein *(1939)*

Y

TITLE	YEAR	SIZE	PRICE RANGE
Young Savages	1961	OS	40–70
Young Widow	1946	OS	95–175
Youngblood Hawke	1964	OS	40–70
Your Cheatin' Heart	1964	OS	75–125
Yours, Mine and Ours	1968	OS	50–90
Yukon Flight	1940	OS	400–700
Z	1969	OS	40–70
Zabriskie Point	1970	OS	150–250
Zachariah	1971	OS	50–90
Zarak	1956	OS	40–70
Zardoz	1974	OS	50–90
Zaza	1938	OS	300–450
Zazie	1960	OS	40–70
Zebra in the Kitchen	1965	OS	40–70
Zelig	1983	OS	40–70
Zelig	1983	LC SET	50–75
Zenobia	1939	OS	200–350
Zeppelin	1971	OS	40–70
Zero Hour	1957	OS	40–70
Ziegfeld Follies	1945	OS	2,250–2,750
Ziegfeld Girl	1941	OS	650–950
Ziggy Stardust	1982	OS	50–125
Zombie	1979	OS	75–125
Zombies of Mora Tau	1957	OS	50–90
Zombies of Mora Tau	1957	LC SET	50–150
Zombies of the Stratosphere	1952	OS	200–275
Zombies of the Stratosphere	1952	LC SET	100–175
Zombies on Broadway	1945	OS	300–450
Zorba the Greek	1964	OS	50–90
Zorba the Greek	1964	LC SET	50–90
Zorro	1976	OS	50–70
Zorro Rides Again	1937	OS	500–750
Zorro the Gay Blade	1981	OS	40–70
Zorro's Black Whip	1944	OS	450–650
Zotz	1962	OS	50–90
ZPG	1972	OS	40–70
Zulu	1964	OS	650–950
Zulu	1964	LC SET	150–250
Zulu Dawn	1979	OS	40–70

4 Animation Art

COLLECTING ANIMATION ART

One of the most popular types of movie memorabilia collecting is the collecting of animation art from Hollywood's finest illustrated masterpieces. Animation is created in films using several mediums, from Claymation to computer-generated images. One of the earliest and most cherished formats is the hand-painting of still drawings on clear celluloid sheets (*cels*). An outline drawing is either traced (hand-inked) or photocopied (photomechanically reproduced) from an original onto the front of the sheet and then hand-painted in color on the reverse side. The sheets are then placed over a background illustration and photographed. When a sequence of these photographed images is projected back at a speed of twenty-nine frames per second, the result is an animated moving picture that gives life to an otherwise two-dimensional flat surface. *See illustration #208.*

The birth of this medium as a collectible can be traced back to 1937 and a small fine art dealer in San Francisco named Guthrie Courvoisier. Walt Disney Studios had just released its first full-length animated feature, *Snow White and the Seven Dwarfs,* to an instantaneous success, and Courvoisier had a vision. He believed that the hand-painted cels used to make the Disney films represented a work of important artistic expression and that the individual cels had an enormous sales potential if they were promoted on a fine art level.

Animators operated on very small production budgets and routinely stripped the ink and paint from a photographed celluloid sheet so it could be repainted and photographed again in the same film or in a future production. Even Walt and Roy Disney (who had already started what would become the universal model for cartoon character merchandising by this time) had to be convinced of the potential sales that existed in these otherwise discarded items.

On July 19, 1938, Courvoisier came to an agreement with Disney, granting the Courvoisier Gallery the exclusive rights to market the original Disney animation art from *Snow White* to art galleries and museums in major cities all over the world. As part of the agreement, Disney set up a specific crew of artists from the animation department to select and assemble the pieces. This was a very detailed process, as an average ninety-minute animated film requires a minimum of 75,000 individually hand-painted cels.

The Courvoisier Gallery pieces ranged in price from a few dollars up to $75 for the most elaborate pieces that included original backgrounds and multiple cels (*cel setup*) within one presentation. The nitrate sheets were often trimmed to the outline of the character image, glued to the background, covered with a protective top cel sheet, and matted in a simple off-white matte board with the character name penciled in. Rather than having a drawing framed against a white card background, Courvoisier created what would become its signature background: a genuine sheet of wood veneer hand-rubbed to accentuate the grain. Courvoisier also provided lushly airbrushed multicolored backgrounds to give the display a three-dimensional quality. *See illustration #209.*

Courvoisier Gallery cels can also be identified by an "Original WDP" seal that was rubber-stamped at the lower right corner of the mat opening, as well as a similar seal, without the word *Original* on the background. Two small labels on the reverse side, a construction paper backing, and a large label can also identify these with the name of the film either printed or

208

209

208 Production drawing and matching painted cel from Lady and the
Tramp

209 Original Courvoisier Snow
White cel

210 Courvoisier Gallery cel label

211 Pencil production drawing of
Mickey Mouse

Images © Walt Disney Co.

handwritten on it. The gallery would also frame pieces at the customer's request. *See illustration #209.*

Throughout 1938, the Disney/Courvoisier program was limited to the sale of cels from *Snow White.* The incredible success of the program was instantaneous, and it was soon expanded to include hand-painted original backgrounds, story sketches, and original source drawings from *Snow White* as well as other Disney films. By March 1939 (just eight months after the program was launched) over 8,000 cels, 150 backgrounds, and 500 animation drawings from *Snow White* and over 5,000 cels from previous Disney productions were sold by Courvoisier.

The gallery closed in 1947, with the cels from *Song of the South* being the last Disney pieces sold. Courvoisier and Disney's act of transforming used animation cels and drawings into permanent works of art not only was a good business decision, but also marked the first time a production-used item from a film became a marketed collectible. Most important of all, the Courvoisier vision saved these treasures from an inevitable destruction, undertaking the most important single act of preservation in Hollywood history.

The Boom

For the next forty years, the collecting of animation art was conducted almost exclusively among a select group of animation enthusiasts and Disney collectors with a passion for the films and their original art. Pieces were sold privately through collecting clubs set up by dealers and collectors. In 1981, the Whitney Museum of American Art in New York exhibited a collection of Disney animation art to an incredible public reaction. Animation art was once again projected into the mainstream as a respected art form, picking up from where the original Courvoisier vision had left off.

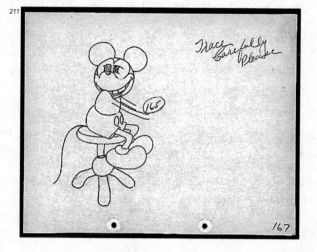

210

This is an original pointing on celluloid from the Walt Disney Studios, actually used in the filming of "Snow White and the Seven Dwarfs."

Only a very limited number have been selected to be placed on the market.

WALT DISNEY.

211

A feeding frenzy took place among a new breed of collecting public, with speculators around the world clamoring to purchase animation art. Celebrities like Steven Spielberg and Michael Jackson became the poster children of the new collecting group, and their influence, as well as their limitless budgets, pushed prices up into multiples of their previously established highs.

By 1984, Christie's auction house began producing two sales a year devoted entirely to animation art, and world record prices for animation art began to be broken as quickly as they could be set. Christie's currently holds two world auction records for animation art: $286,000 for an animation cel from Disney's 1934 *Orphan's Benefit* set in 1989, and $101,500 for an animation drawing from Disney's 1929 *The Plow Boy* set in 1995.

The original Courvoisier/Disney pieces quickly became the Holy Grail of animation art collectibles to the marketplace. This was mostly due to the fact that the early nitrate sheets used up until the 1950s did not age very well, with most responding to the elements by yellowing, rippling, and cracking. Most cels simply did not survive the forty-plus-year trek to their rebirth in the 1980s. As the demand for vintage material far outweighed the supply, collectors began looking at other vintage animation items to fill the void. Penciled production drawings, original hand-painted backgrounds, and original character model sheet drawings all began to take their place in the higher echelon of collections and auction results. *See illustration #211.*

Collectors became interested in studios other than Disney, such as Warner Bros. (Looney Tunes), Walter Lantz Studio (Woody Woodpecker), Metro-Goldwyn-Mayer (Tom and Jerry), Depatie-Freleng (The Pink Panther), Hanna-Barbera (Yogi Bear), and United Artists Studios (mostly for the Beatles' *Yellow Submarine*).

Animation galleries began to pop up in the late 1980s and early 1990s around the world. These outlets carried few vintage pieces, as the steep prices they were now commanding took them out of the hands of the average collector. The main focus of their inventory centered on newly created "limited edition" fine art reproductions of original cels that were now being produced by the Disney and Warner Bros. companies. Limited edition cels are hand-painted cels that have been created specifically for collectors and are produced in limited quantities ranging from 300 to 750 per edition. Each piece has been hand-numbered and usually hand-signed by the animator. Some of these have been designed to resemble original production cels of famous key scenes, while others feature several key characters in an original pose.

As the popularity of animation art collecting continued to swell, the studios quickly escalated the number of designs and increased edition sizes to match the demand set by the ever-increasing number of new collectors and retailers to the market. Prices for the limited editions also increased to a level that excluded the budget-minded and novice collectors. As an antidote, studios began issuing *serigraph cels* (sericels) consisting of a silk-screened cel that was similar in appearance to a limited edition cel, but without any work actually being done by hand. Most sericels are produced in editions of 2,500 up to 5,000. Because of the larger edition size, sericels have quickly become the most affordable type of animation art for the novice collector.

And Now the Bad News

By the mid-1990s, the collectors' market was flooded with both sericels and the animation galleries themselves. In fact, the two main studios producing animation art for the retail market had set up their own retail outlets, the Disney Store and the Warner Brothers Studio Store. Most of the independent retailers depended upon the new editions from Disney and Warner Bros., and both of these companies began to concentrate the distribution of their releases (sometimes exclusively) to their own retail outlets as well as on their own Web sites. By the end of the decade, animation art had lost its mass appeal and sales decreased commensurately. In 2001, both Disney and Warner Bros. closed their art programs entirely for the year, ending the supply of new editions to any of the retailers. Many independent animation art retailers soon began closing their doors, and even Warner Bros. closed its retail stores in 2001.

The hysteria surrounding the collecting of vintage animation art began to cool around 1995, with stagnated prices in the auction market (you will note that the two world records were set in 1989 and 1995 and have not been touched since). Collectors who strictly follow trends, and the celebrities and speculators that lead them, turned their attention to new fads (Beanie Babies for one). This has taken the auction fever element out of the auction market and has allowed prices for vintage material to come down to more respectable and affordable levels. Most major auction houses rarely devote entire sales to animation art anymore, choosing to combine them with other entertainment memorabilia such as props, wardrobe, and autographs.

The Future

It is once again affordable for true collectors to acquire the vintage material that eluded them during the hot market of the past two decades. Many of the rare vintage Courvoisier pieces are selling for 25 to 50 percent of their peak prices from a decade ago. The Internet has proven to be an unparalleled sales channel and an amazing comparative shopping and research vehicle for both experienced and novice collectors. The downturn in the retail area has also led independent retail galleries to focus their inventories on the vintage production items.

As a renewed passion for collecting the once-again obtainable vintage pieces continues to grow within the marketplace, the prices will eventually rise to match the demand. The very limited number of new releases from Disney and Warner Bros., and the flooding of second-hand sericels and even some of the later limited editions to eBay, should keep prices for these items flat for some time to come. Only until the day arrives that the vintage material is no longer affordable to the masses will these items appreciate.

With this in mind, it is important to stress that, as in all collecting areas, you should always collect what you love and purchase only the best available items in your price range. When looking to start or add to an animation art collection, it is essential to have a strong understanding of the terminology of these collectibles, as well as the factors that determine value.

ANIMATION ART TERMINOLOGY

Production Art

Cel
A sheet of clear cellulose acetate or nitrate that has been hand-painted with an image of a character.

Production Cel
An individual cel used in the actual production of an animated film.

Nitrate
Material used in cels up until the early 1950s.

Acetate
Material used in cels up to the present day (more stable than nitrate).

Hand-Inked Cel
Outline drawing traced in ink, on front side, from original pencil drawing and painted in color on verso.

Xeroxed Cel
Outline drawing photomechanically transferred to front side of cel.

12-Field
Refers to the size of the cel or drawing; 10.5" × 12.5" is standard size.

16-Field
Refers to the size of the cel or drawing, 12" × 16".

Pan (Cinemascope)
Refers to the size of the cel or drawing, 12" × 30".

Registration Holes (Peg Holes)
Holes punched in cels and drawings to keep them in line with the camera. Can be used to date artwork (2 holes = 1928–35, 5 holes= 1935–50, 3 holes = 1950–present)

Cel Setup (Multi-Cel Setup)
The combination of multiple layers of individual cels with a single character or part of a character painted on each.

Color Model
Cel created by the ink and paint department of a studio and used for accurate color referencing during production.

Color Test
Cels with color tests on characters that are different from the final character colors.

Courvoisier
A Disney cel setup sold by the Courvoisier Gallery between 1938 and 1947. Most vintage Disney cels are Courvoisier.

Lamination
The sealing of a cel between two thin sheets of plastic for preservation.

Vintage Disney
Refers to animation art from the 1960s and prior from Disney.

Disneyland Art Corner
Cels sold at Disneyland from the mid-1950s to the early 1970s. Cels are trimmed with a gold seal attached to the back of the matte.

Pencil Animation Drawing
An original pencil drawing by an animator on paper that is eventually transferred to a cel.

Rough Animation Drawing
Drawing by an animator indicating position and pose.

Clean-up Drawing
Drawing done over a rough drawing that will become the trace for the painted cel.

Key Master Setup
A cel or cels paired with the original matching background as they appeared in the actual film—most desired by collectors.

Master Setup
A cel or cels paired with a background from the same film, but not from the same scene in the film.

Production Background

A background created for use in the production of an animated film.

Presentation Background (hand-prepared)

A newer background created by an artist to complement an existing cel.

Reproduction Background

A Xerox, lithograph, or photographic copy of an original production background used to complement an existing cel.

Photographic Background

A photograph used as a background.

Studio Seal

An authenticity seal applied to a cel by a studio when it is released for sale to the public.

Reproduction Art

Scene Cel (Publicity Cel)

A cel hand-painted by the studio to publicize the characters to the media, usually used for posters, postcards, etc.

Limited Edition Cel

A nonproduction hand-painted cel created specifically for sale as an art form.

Serigraph Cel (Sericel)

Silk-screen printed cel (not hand-painted) created specifically for sale as a mass-produced art form.

TIPS ON BUYING ANIMATION ART

There are several venues available for purchasing animation art:

Studio Stores

Studio stores are retail stores run by the animation studios themselves (Disney and Warner Bros.). Their selections are limited to mostly new limited editions and sericels. They rarely carry vintage pieces or sold-out editions of earlier limited edition and sericel releases. Guarantees of authenticity are issued, but the store's staff may not be too knowledgeable about vintage production animation art.

Independent Galleries

These are privately owned and operated establishments that source their inventory from other dealers, auction houses, and private collections. Their assortment of pieces will be based on their own interests and those of their clientele. The staff will generally be educated about the art form and will be the best source for information for the novice collector. Once you become a customer, they will be more than happy to keep a "want list" for you to source anything you may be looking to add to your collection. They will also be very helpful in framing your art, offering appraisals, and maybe even purchasing pieces from your collection if you decide to sell something in the future. Always insist on a certificate of authenticity from the gallery, and most should offer some form of guarantee in regards to authenticity as well as the date and film the cel is from. The only negative with purchasing from these vendors is that the prices they charge may or may not be competitive with other galleries. Shop around and look for local animation galleries in your phone directory and on the Internet.

On-line Independent Galleries

Many of the larger independent gallery stores have Web sites on the Internet. In fact, some retailers have closed their retail stores to concentrate solely on on-line sales. Most of these sites offer a current and complete inventory available for viewing and purchasing. The benefits to shopping with these operators are the same as with retail outlets, but you have the convenience of shopping twenty-four hours a day, every day, with sellers located around the world. You also have the luxury of comparative shopping on a grand scale. The negatives are that you are not able to see the actual piece in person, and you must rely on the scans and descriptions offered on the site. Shipping costs (and duty if you are purchasing from overseas) may be expensive in relation to the amount of your purchase. Always insist on finding out the complete costs of shipping *before* you place an order. Ask the seller to provide a certificate of authenticity and a guarantee in regards to authenticity, and have your shipments insured for full value.

Auction Houses

The major auction houses such as Christie's and Sotheby's have been scaling back the frequency and number of offerings in their sales. Most offer very limited selections, mostly of premier vintage material. The benefits of purchasing through major auction houses are that you have the opportunity to purchase some of the finest vintage items available to collectors. You also have the opportunity of previewing the material in person before the sale. You are also benefiting from the knowledge of the appraisers and staff. The negatives are there as well—catalog descriptions can sometimes be vague, especially in the area of condition. You must also pay a buyer's premium on your final bid—sometimes as high as 20 percent—as well as shipping, insurance, and applicable taxes.

On-Line Auctions

In these venues you do business in a person-to-person transaction. You will be offered pieces from some experienced collectors and dealers, some novices, and some flat-out thieves. The benefit of purchasing through on-line auctions is that you may be able to get pieces for better prices than if you were to shop with a retailer or auction house. The winning bidder will determine the final price. Presently there are no buyer's premiums charged through these sites. However, these have become the most fraudulent venues in all collectible categories—let the buyer beware! It is imperative to be aware of whom you are actually purchasing from—the more reputable the seller, the safer your transaction will be. You may or may not be offered a certificate of authenticity (only as good as the person signing it), and a refund may or may not be available.

Content

Content refers to the significance of the item in relation to the character and film depicted in the cel. Historically, pieces with the best content appreciate the most in value. When looking to purchase a piece of animation art, look for the best possible content available in your price range. The following factors should be taken into consideration when determining the content value of any piece of animation art:

Film

The more popular and cherished a film is, the more desirable the art from that film will be to the marketplace. Art from significant or groundbreaking films can be highly desirable, as can art from a film that marks the first appearance of a famous character.

Character

The most popular characters (generally the main characters) are most desired by collectors. There are some exceptions, notably famous secondary characters like the Queen from *Snow White and the Seven Dwarfs*.

Pose

The pose that the character is displaying in the cel is very important to collectors. The better the pose is (full length as opposed to half-length, full portrait as opposed to profile), the more valuable that cel is to the marketplace.

Background

The type of background presented with the cel is a very important factor. A *master background* (one that appeared in the same film as the cel) will increase the overall price of the cel by up to ten times that of a cel without the background or with a reproduction background. A master background is most desired, followed by a production background from another film featuring the same character. Hand-painted and color laser reproduction backgrounds do not add much monetary value to a piece but can make them much more presentable and enjoyable than just the plain cel.

Signatures

The signature of Walt Disney on a matte board surrounding the cel is very desirable for Disney collectors and can add up to $2,000 to the price of the piece. The more common studio signatures ("Walt Disney" signatures signed by Disney artists on Walt's behalf) add about $250 to the piece (*make sure the autograph is authentic before buying the piece*—see the Walt Disney autograph reference guide in this book). Signatures of famous animators like Marc Davis can add up to $75 per signature to a piece. *See illustration #212.*

Condition

The condition of an item can severely affect overall value and can play an integral role in determining future value. Dealers and auction houses use a grading system and/or basic terminology to clarify the condition of an item. The extent to which the condition of an item determines the overall value is directly linked to the rarity and desirability of that item. The rarer an item is, the more forgiving a collector will be on the condition factors.

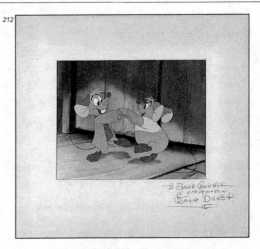

212 Walt Disney signed Cinderella *cel*

Cels

Vintage animation cels were painted on nitrate with water-based paints, whereas modern cels are acetate with acrylic paint. Extreme temperature changes to the vintage cels can cause the paint to crack and peel or become completely separated from the cel. A professional can restore vintage cel paint, but cracking to the cel itself is not repairable. If the area of damage can be creatively hidden by the mount, it is still acceptable, but if the cracking is located on any area of the character, it is considered major damage and the overall value of the piece will be severely affected.

Drawings

The effects of direct sunlight and acids from nonarchival storage can affect the overall presentation and value of a drawing. Tears to the paper can be restored (again by a professional) on the reverse side of the drawing using acid-free museum tape.

Preservation and Conservation

The condition of a piece of animation art is one of the most important factors in determining present and future value, so it is very important to understand and adhere to the simple rules of preservation. As you acquire pieces in your collection, you must immediately assess each new item's current state of condition. It is very difficult and can be very expensive to restore or improve the present condition of an item. You should attempt to pinpoint any current problem areas and try to avoid anything that may promote future deterioration in the condition of the item. What you should be trying to accomplish is to freeze the current state of condition of the item for the future. If the preservation of the present condition of a vintage item requires more involvement, you may wish to consult a conservation specialist in your area (try contacting your local museum), although the relatively high cost of this should be reserved for museum-quality pieces only.

Cels

One of the greatest rewards of collecting animation art is displaying your treasured items on the walls of your home or office. The biggest problem with displaying animation is that contact with changes in temperature can be a disaster. Framed cels should be hung in rooms with a humidity factor of 50 to 60 percent and temperatures ranging between 65 and 80 degrees Fahrenheit—generally a comfortable room temperature. Humidity is a major problem for framed cels as it can cause moisture condensation inside the frame. Monitor the room's condition during the winter months if you run heating in your home/office.

Always hang all pieces out of direct sunlight. Remember that indirect and reflected daylight will cause fading. Watch for any reflected light coming from hallway mirrors or glass tables.

If you are going to have an animation cel framed, try to locate a professional who is familiar with animation art and museum-grade framing techniques. Always use nonreflective glass with UV (ultraviolet) protection that will reduce the penetration of light to the item. You can also use UV-filtered Plexiglas instead of glass—it will not break if the frame is dropped and will be necessary if you will be shipping your piece in the future. Plexiglas is easy to scratch, however, and should be cleaned with just water and a clean cloth. All items should be adhered to a matte board that is composed of acid-free material (also termed *museum board*) and is thick enough to keep the item from touching the glass. Any tape that is used to attach the item to the matte board must be archival tape.

Vintage cels that are in their original vintage frames were not matted and framed using acid-free material. However, a Courvoisier setup is highly desired by collectors, and these mattes and frames should not be removed and replaced with acid-free materials.

If you choose to bypass framing, you should be very careful when handling the individual cels—in fact, you really should not handle the cels at all if possible. When required, wear clean cloth gloves and handle the cels by the edges. Cels can also be stored directly in acid-free Mylar sheets that can be purchased from a local animation gallery. Place a sheet of acid-free tissue against the back of the cel (painted side) in between the cel and the Mylar to prevent the cel from sticking to the Mylar sleeve. Another alternative to framing is matting cels within an acid-free matte-board mount. Use archival tape to attach the cels to the matte boards. Matted cels can also be stored in larger acid-free Mylar sleeves. This is a good idea if you plan to store your cels stacked, as the matte board mounts (and not the actual cels) will absorb the weight of the stacked cels. Store all unframed cels upright in acid-free boxes in consistent room temperature conditions.

Whether your cels are framed on your wall, or stored in acid-free boxes, you should always monitor the condition of your cels on a regular basis, especially during changes in temperature. Watch for any signs of paint separation from the back of the cel, rips in the paint, and any portion of paint that is chipping from the cel. If you notice any changes in the appearance of your cel, contact your local animation gallery for an immediate opinion; restoration may be an option.

A word about restoration: Opinions on restoration are highly divided. Visually, a restored cel (a cel that has had its paint re-wet and filled into an area of paint loss, or partially repainted with matching paint) looks much better than a cel with paint deterioration. There have been many cases of restored cels selling for figures at the same level as nonrestored cels of the same type and content. There are also many collectors who will refuse to purchase a restored cel on the basis that they feel it is no longer original. If you choose to have a cel restored, check references and choose a qualified expert—never try to restore a cel yourself.

Drawings

Paper items such as drawings have their most destructive force built within them: the *acid* content in the paper. The acid that exists in the wood content of the paper (pulp) can cause the paper to yellow and become more brittle, eventually crumbling into pieces. The acid content of other paper products coming into contact with your drawing (a file folder, other pages on top of or below the page) will also react with the paper. Acid can actually be physically extracted from a page, but this should only be trusted to a professional conservator, and can be a very expensive process.

The easiest way to lessen the effects of the acid in paper is to store the item in an acid-free environment. Your local comic book and sports card collectible stores offer acetate comic bags and acid-free cardboard backers that will store your items safely. You can also purchase acetate sheets that have been three-hole punched for storage in a binder (also referred to as *sheet protectors* or *print protectors*). These are offered by a variety of manufacturers in different quality grades. Before using any of these products, contact the manufacturer's customer service departments and ask them to specify which of their products are guaranteed as acid-free or archival.

A more presentable method of protecting drawings is by matting them within a mount. Use only acid-free mounts, as the acid in a nonarchival matte board will cause a burning to the paper surrounding the drawing. Use archival tape to attach the drawing to the matte boards. Matted drawings can also be stored in larger acid-free Mylar sleeves.

Never store any paper item folded, as a fold will in time deteriorate into a tear. If a page has been torn, you may be able to repair the tear by using the archival tape on the reverse side of the item. This should be attempted only by an experienced conservator. Many experts would suggest leaving the tear as it is, storing the item in a way that will not cause the tear to extend further along the page. Remove all staples and paper clips from any pages, as these will rust in time, causing discoloration and stain to the pages. Store each page individually in acetate sheets.

The rules of framing and displaying your drawings are the same as they are for cels: always use acid-free mounts, UV-protected glass, or Plexiglas; watch the room humidity and temperature levels; and avoid direct sunlight.

ANIMATION ART PRICE LISTINGS

The items featured in the listings of this book reflect *screen-used production animation art only.*

Vintage animation art prices have taken a dramatic shift from the auction madness of the 1980s and early 1990s to the more educated and realistic retail prices of the last eight to ten years. As such, many of the prices listed in this chapter reflect current retail prices sourced from several major animation art retailers. Auction houses still feature animation art in their sales, and auction-realized prices are an excellent comparative study. Several of the listings have been extracted from auction results dating from 1999 through 2002 from several international auction houses.

Each listing contains:

- The *film* the item was used in

- The *date* of the film

- A brief *description* of the item

- The *retail value* of the item

In the case of auction results:

- The *date* of the auction.

- *Auction estimate*: A presale estimated price range. Where estimates have been available, I have included them in parentheses (est. $2,000–$3,000) before the final realized price.

- The *final realized price* ("buyer's premium"): Auction houses charge a bidder a commission on the final invoice that can range from 5 percent up to 20 percent in addition to the final winning bid price. I have *excluded* the buyer's premium from the prices listed in this book to reflect the final winning bid. In cases where the premium amount could not be determined and removed, the "incl. buyer's premium" notation has been listed beside the price.

Walt Disney Studios: Original Production Cels

Beach Party (1931)
Master background. Unframed. 11" × 13" (image size 5" h × 11"w). $4,200.

Mickey's Circus (1936)
Production cel of Donald Duck. Image sealed with nail polish. Unframed. 11" × 13". $3,500.

Snow White and the Seven Dwarfs (1937)
Courvoisier cel of Dopey and Doc. Some paint separation. Unframed. 11" × 13" (image size 7" h × 6" w). $16,500.

Snow White and the Seven Dwarfs (1937)
Master setup of Doc with production background used in the1937 film. Unframed. $19,000.

Snow White and the Seven Dwarfs (1937)
Master setup of the Wicked Witch paired with a production background used in the 1937 film. Framed. $29,000.

Snow White and the Seven Dwarfs (1937)
Master setup of Happy including diamonds ready to be collected from the mine on a separate cel. Unframed. $18,000.

213

213 *Production cel of Prince and
Snow White from* Snow White
and the Seven Dwarfs
© Walt Disney Co.

Snow White and the Seven Dwarfs (1937)

Production cel of the Prince and Snow White with original Courvoisier background, labels, and mat and original Disney labels on reverse. May 2002. $7,139. *See illustration #213.*

Snow White and the Seven Dwarfs (1937)

Courvoisier cel of Grumpy and Happy. Grumpy having flowers put on his head by Happy, Sleepy, and Sneezy. Unframed. 11" × 13" (image size 7" h × 8.5" w). $8,500.

Snow White and the Seven Dwarfs (1937)

Courvoisier cel of Dopey and Doc. Multicharacter setup of the dwarfs from the bed-building scene. Framed. Image size 5" h × 8" w. $9,500.

Snow White and the Seven Dwarfs (1937)

Production multicel setup of the Witch offering Snow White the poisoned apple applied to a Courvoisier airbrushed background. Unframed. 7.5" × 9.5". December 2001. (Est. $7,300–$10,000) $6,750.

Snow White and the Seven Dwarfs (1937)

Courvoisier cel of Snow White. Unframed. $6,500.

Snow White and the Seven Dwarfs (1937)

Courvoisier cel of Snow White and Bashful. In original Courvoisier mat. Unframed. Image size 7.75" h × 7" w. $9,500.

Snow White and the Seven Dwarfs (1937)

Courvoisier cel of Dopey. Framed. $5,500.

Snow White and the Seven Dwarfs (1937)

Production multicel setup of Dopey applied to a Courvoisier airbrushed background. Unframed. 6.75" × 8.75". December 2001. (Est. $2,700–$3,600) $1,250.

Snow White and the Seven Dwarfs (1937)

Production cel of Grumpy applied to a Courvoisier wood veneer background. Unframed. 7.25" × 5.5". December 2001. (Est. $2,700–$3,600) $1,350.

Snow White and the Seven Dwarfs (1937)

Production cel of Dopey on Courvoisier background with pencil notation and original labels. Unframed. 9" × 9". May 2002. $2,002.

Snow White and the Seven Dwarfs (1937)

Production cel of Dopey applied to a Courvoisier wood veneer background. Unframed. 7.25" × 7.25". December 2001. (Est. $3,700–$5,100) $2,000.

Snow White and the Seven Dwarfs (1937)

Courvoisier cel of Happy and Sneezy. Cute setup of the dwarfs and their musical instruments signed by Walt Disney. Framed. $7,500.

Snow White and the Seven Dwarfs (1937)

Color model cel of Snow White. Large color model cel of Snow White in a reflective pose. Unframed. 11" × 13". $4,500.

Snow White and the Seven Dwarfs (1937)

Color model cel of Snow White. Pretty color model cel of Snow White walking down the steps of the dwarfs' cottage. Unframed. 11" × 13". $4,500.

Snow White and the Seven Dwarfs (1937)

Production cel of Snow White. Framed. 11" × 13" (image size 7.5" h × 5.5" w). $7,500.

Snow White and the Seven Dwarfs (1937)

Courvoisier cel of Dopey and Sneezy. Framed. Aperture size is 10" × 6.75". (image size 9" h × 4" w). $5,900.

Snow White and the Seven Dwarfs (1937)

Courvoisier cel. Original animation cel of a doe and her fawn. Unframed. $2,400.

Snow White and the Seven Dwarfs (1937)

Color model cel of Snow White. Wonderful color model cel of a skipping Snow White. Unframed. 11" × 13". $4,000.

Snow White and the Seven Dwarfs (1937)

Production cel of Doc. Image of a deer nudging a slow-moving Doc onward. Signed by Frank Thomas and Ollie Johnston. Framed. $4,500.

Snow White and the Seven Dwarfs (1937)

Production cel of Dopey. Framed (image size 4" h × 3" w). $3,500.

Snow White and the Seven Dwarfs (1937)

Production cel of Sneezy with original Courvoisier background, labels, and mat and original Disney labels on reverse. May 2002. $3,661.

Snow White and the Seven Dwarfs (1937)

Production cel of a few animals with original Courvoisier background, labels, and mat and original Disney labels on reverse. May 2002. $1,000.

Snow White and the Seven Dwarfs (1937)

Courvoisier setup of the Hag and the Raven (cels trimmed) with original Courvoisier mat with the label on the back. Unframed. 11" × 12". $9,000.

Snow White and the Seven Dwarfs (1937)

Courvoisier setup featuring Prince Charming (cel trimmed) and applied to the airbrushed wood veneer background with original Courvoisier mat and label on the back. Unframed. 11" × 10.5". $5,500.

Snow White and the Seven Dwarfs (1937)

Courvoisier setup featuring Dopey and the Fly (cels trimmed) and attached to the original Courvoisier paper background. There is some water staining to the background, but the cels are unaffected. Image size 4" × 4". $3,500.

Donald's Better Self (1938)

Production cel of Donald Duck. Unframed. 11" × 13". $1,800.

The Brave Little Tailor (1938)

Original production cel of Mickey Mouse in full figure with original Courvoisier background and mat and original Disney labels on reverse. May 2002. $3,328. *See illustration #214.*

The Brave Little Tailor (1938)

Original production cel of Minnie Mouse in full figure with original Courvoisier background and mat and original Disney labels on reverse. May 2002. $3,025.

The Practical Pig (1939)

Original production cel of two images of Practical Pig and one other pig in full figure with original Courvoisier mat. 11.5" × 9.5" May 2002. $1,612.

The Pointer (1939)

Courvoisier cel of Mickey Mouse and Pluto in the middle of a hunt. Framed. $7,500.

The Pointer (1939)

Original production cel of Pluto. Framed to 10.5" × 9". May 2002. $1,198.

214

214 Production Cel of Mickey Mouse
from The Brave Little Tailor
© Walt Disney Co.

The Pointer (1939)

Original production cel of Mickey Mouse hunting in the forest with Pluto with a Disney prepared background with original Courvoisier background, labels, and mat and original Disney labels on reverse. Matted and framed to 14" × 16.5". July 2000. $10,000.

Fantasia (1940)

Courvoisier cel of Mickey Mouse. Signed by Walt Disney. Framed. Image size 6.5" h × 3" w. $18,000.

Fantasia (1940)

Courvoisier cel of Hyacinth Hippo and Ali Gator. From the sequence "Dance of the Hours." Unframed. 11" × 13". (image size 9" h × 6" w). $5,500.

Fantasia (1940)

Courvoisier cel of Jacchus and Bacchus. "Studio" Disney signature. Unframed. 7" × 7.5" (image size 5.5" h × 6" w). $4,800.

Fantasia (1940)

Production cel of Pegasus on a Courvoisier background. Unframed. 11" × 13". $4,900.

Fantasia (1940)

Two-cel setup featuring the Centaurettes from the Pastoral Sequence (slightly trimmed). Unframed. 13.5" × 12". $1,800.

Fantasia (1940)

Production cel of the Sound Wave produced by the Trumpet. Unframed. 16" × 12.5". (image size 9.5" × 5.5"). $1,300.

Fantasia (1940)

Production cel of milkweed pods floating in a scene from "Toccata and Fugue in D Minor" sequence with Courvoisier background. Framed. 14" × 9.5". May 2002. $1,854.

Fantasia (1940)

Two-cel setup featuring the Dancing Milkweeds and effects. Unframed. 12.5" × 15.5" (small pieces of tape around the tips of each Milkweed to protect the paint). $1,000.

Fantasia (1940)

Four-character group as they flee the Thunderbolts of Zeus in the "Pastoral Symphony" segment (trimmed). Unframed. 10.25" × 11.75" (laminated and some lifting and chipping in the paint). $1,000.

Pinocchio (1940)

Master setup of Jiminy Cricket and Lampwick. Framed. 11" × 13". $12,000.

Pinocchio (1940)

Courvoisier cel of Pinocchio and Jiminy Cricket. Close-up of Pinocchio and Jiminy, as Pinocchio listens to Jiminy telling him to "Always let your conscience be your guide." Unframed. Image size 6.5" h × 5.75" w. $8,500.

Pinocchio (1940)

Rare production cel featuring three of the main villains from the film, placed on a custom watercolor background (plus cel of the Moneybag re-created for effect). Unframed. 10" × 14" Image size 3.5" × 7.5". $5,500.

Pinocchio (1940)

Production cel of a full-figured Pinocchio smiling. Unframed. 10" × 12". December 2001 (Est. $2,200–$2,900) $900.

Pinocchio (1940)

Production cel of Figaro hiding between Gepetto's legs. Courvoisier setup in the original frame and mat with the Courvoisier label on the back. Image size 3.5" × 3". $1,500.

Pinocchio (1940)

Courvoisier setup featuring Jiminy Cricket in the original frame and mat with the Courvoisier label on the back. Image size 4" × 3.5". $2,500.

Pinocchio (1940)

Production cel of Pinocchio as a marionette. Framed. 11" × 13". $ 4,900.

Pinocchio (1940)

Courvoisier cel of Jiminy Cricket. Framed. 11" × 13" (image size 4" h × 5" w). $4,500.

A Gentleman's Gentleman (1941)

Production cel of Pluto. Some paint cracking. Framed. 11" × 13". $850.

Dumbo (1941)

Courvoisier cel of Mother Kangaroo and Baby with a Courvoisier background. Unframed. 11" × 13" (image size 4.25" h × 3.25" w). $1,500.

Dumbo (1941)

Production cel of Dumbo and his mother as she protects him from the teasing boys (trimmed to image). Unframed. Applied to a 10.5" × 12.5" cel (image size 6.5" × 7"). $2,800.

Dumbo (1941)

Production cel of Dumbo sitting on his mother's trunk applied to a Courvoisier airbrushed background. Unframed. 9.5" × 7.5". December 2001. (Est. $1,800-$2,200) $2,500.

Dumbo (1941)

Production cel of Timothy Mouse as he sheds a tear. Unframed. Trimmed to 8.5" × 10.5" and slightly wrinkled (image size 4" × 2.25"). $1,200.

The Art of Skiing (1941)

Production cel of Goofy showing his form on the slopes with Courvoisier background and labels. Framed. 8.5" × 9". May 2002. $2,796.

The Reluctant Dragon (1941)

Production cel of Goofy being stripped of his underwear by a horse, with Courvoisier background and labels. Framed. 12.5" × 9.5". May 2002. $1,318.

Bambi (1942)

Key master setup of Bambi and Flower on a preliminary oil production background. Cels have been trimmed and applied to a cel and Bambi has been restored. The background is full and untrimmed with studio marks and camera notations. Unframed. $15,000.

Bambi (1942)

Courvoisier cel of Bambi and Thumper in the original Courvoisier mat. Framed. Image size 5" h × 4" w. $6,900.

Bambi (1942)

Courvoisier cel of Bambi pondering a butterfly. Framed. $5,500.

Bambi (1942)

Courvoisier cel of Thumper and Miss Bunny. Framed. Image size 4" h × 6" w. $4,900.

Bambi (1942)

Courvoisier cel of Faline on a Courvoisier background and original Courvoisier frame. $2,500.

Bambi (1942)

Production cel of Bambi. Signed by Frank Thomas and Ollie Johnston. Framed. Image size 6" h × 5.5" w. $3,300.

Bambi (1942)

Courvoisier cel of Bambi and Bambi's mother. Framed; aperture opening is 5" × 5.25" (image size 4.5" h × 4.5" w). $1,500.

Bambi (1942)

Production cel of Thumper. Trimmed to 3.5" × 5.25". Unframed. Image size 1.5" × 2". $900.

Bambi (1942)

Production cel of Bambi trimmed to image and placed on a color copy background. Unframed. Image size 2" × 1.75". $2,500.

Saludos Amigos (1943)

Production cel of Donald Duck and Jose Carioca, Jose chatting away as Donald scratches his head and looks confused. Unframed. 11" × 13" (image size 3" h × 3" w). $1,800.

Springtime for Pluto (1944)

Production cel of Pluto with his ear raised. Framed. 11" × 13". $1,800.

The Three Caballeros (1945)

Production cel of Aracuan Bird. Unframed. Image size 6" × 6". $600.

The Three Caballeros (1945)

Production cel of Panchito. Unframed. Image size 8" × 8". $600.

The Three Caballeros (1945)

Production cel of Gauchito on a Courvoisier background. Unframed. Image size 3.5" × 2". $600.

Bath Day (1946)

Production cel of Minnie Mouse and Figaro. Framed. 11" × 13". $2,500.

Melody Time (1948)

Production multicel setup featuring color models of the Bee and Piano Keys from "Bumble Bee Boogie" sequence. Unframed. 12.5" × 15.5". $850.

Melody Time (1948)

Production cel and hand-painted production background from the "Once upon a Wintertime" sequence. Trimmed and applied to the background at the studio, original studio mat with an "Original WDP" stamp on the mat. Unframed. 13.5" × 14.5". $4,000.

So Dear to My Heart (1949)

Cel and key master background setup featuring Jeremiah and the Owl. Trimmed and applied to the background at the studio, still in its original studio presentation mat with the "original WDP" stamp on the front and a studio sticker on the back. Unframed. 15" × 16.5" (image size 8.5" × 10.5"). $6,000.

Cinderella (1950)

Master setup of Cinderella and Bruno. Framed. $14,000.

Cinderella (1950)

Master setup of Lucifer getting ready to get into some mischief. Framed. 11" × 13". $8,500.

Cinderella (1950)

Production cel of Cinderella. Unframed. 11" × 13". $10,500.

Cinderella (1950)

Production cel of Jacques the mouse on a color copy background. Unframed. 10.5" × 12" (image size 4.5" × 2.75"). $1,200.

Cinderella (1950)

Production cel of mice Gus and Jacques with color photo background. Framed. 10" × 9". May 2002. $847.

Cinderella (1950)

Production cel of the King and the Duke. Paint professionally restored. Unframed. 11" × 13". $1,250.

Melody Time (1950)

Production cel of Johnny Appleseed. Unframed. 11" × 13". $1,100.

Alice in Wonderland (1951)

Production cel of Alice. Paint professionally restored. Unframed. 11" × 13". $3,200.

Alice in Wonderland (1951)

Production cel of Alice. Framed. 11" × 13" (image size 7.5" h × 8.5" w). $4,500.

Alice in Wonderland (1951)

Production cel of Alice looking up at the Queen, matted and framed. Signed on the matte by animator Bill Justice. Framed. Image size 8.5" × 5.5". May 2002. $1,183.

Alice in Wonderland (1951)

Two-cel setup featuring the Carpenter and the Shack as it is being built. The cel of the carpenter has been trimmed to image and placed on the cel of the shack with a color copy background. Unframed. 12.5" × 16.5". $650.

Alice in Wonderland (1951)

Production cel of the Rare Red Rose placed on a color photographic background. Unframed. 10.5" × 12.5". $2,000.

Alice in Wonderland (1951)

Production cel of one of the singing Pansies slightly trimmed to 6.5" × 4.5" and placed on a custom background. Unframed. $350.

Alice in Wonderland (1951)
Production cel of one of the Violets trimmed to 8" × 10". Unframed. Image size 4.5" × 3.5". $400.

Alice in Wonderland (1951)
Production cel of members of the Jury. Trimmed to image and applied to a color copy background. Unframed. $600.

Alice in Wonderland (1951)
Production cel of the Yellow Tulip trimmed to 9" × 11.5" and placed on a custom background. Unframed. $450.

Alice in Wonderland (1951)
Two-cel setup featuring Alice and a very rare cel of the Caterpillar as a Butterfly. The cel of Alice is full-figure, trimmed to image and applied to the cel of the Butterfly. Unframed. 12.5" × 15". $1,000.

Man's Best Friend (1952)
Production cel of Goofy walking his dog. With original production background. Framed. 11" × 13". $2,500.

Peter Pan (1953)
Production cel of Peter Pan flying over the pirate ship with a knife in hand. Framed. 11" × 13" (image size 4" h × 5" w). $2,900.

Peter Pan (1953)
Production cel of Captain Hook and Peter Pan. Unframed. $4,900.

Peter Pan (1953)
Production cel of a full-figure Captain Hook. Unframed. 11" × 13". $3,800.

Peter Pan (1953)
Production cel of Tinkerbell. Four-cel setup of the playful pixie. Unframed. $3,000.

Peter Pan (1953)
Production cel of a full-figure Peter Pan. Unframed. 12.5" × 16". December 2001. (Est. $1,400–$1,700) $900.

Peter Pan (1953)
Production cel of Tinkerbell applied to a reproduction painted background. Unframed. 12.5" × 16". December 2001. (Est. $730–$1,000) $900.

Peter Pan (1953)
Production multicel setup of Captain Hook. Framed. Image size 13.25" × 9.25". May 2002. $949. *See illustration #215.*

Peter Pan (1953)

Production cel of the Lost Boys. Foxy and three of the Indians the Lost Boys encounter. Framed. 11" x 13". $950.

Peter Pan (1953)

Walt Disney Studio production setup. Original production cel of Peter on an original gouache/watercolor production background. Framed. $15,000.

Peter Pan (1953)

Production cel of Hook as he threatens Tiger Lily. Trimmed to 11" × 14.5". Unframed. Image size 10.5" × 9". $2,500.

Peter Pan (1953)

Production cel of Tinkerbell. Framed. 11" × 13" (image size 7" h × 5.5" w). $950.

Peter Pan (1953)

Production cel of Mr. Smee. Unframed. 10.5" × 12.5". $800.

Peter Pan (1953)

Two-cel setup featuring Peter Pan marching with Tiger Lily close behind. Tiger Lily is a trimmed cel, and both have been placed on a color copy background. Unframed. $2,000.

Peter Pan (1953)

Production cel of John placed on a hand-painted production background from the film. The entire background measures 10.5" × 12". The background image size is 7.5" × 9.5". John's image size is 6.5" × 3". Unframed. $2,400.

Peter Pan (1953)

Production cel of one of the Lost Boys. Slightly trimmed and triple matted. Unframed. $400.

Simple Things (1953)

Production cel of Mickey Mouse casting off a fishing line. Framed. 11" × 13". $1,900.

Lady and the Tramp (1955)

Two production cels of Lady and the Tramp in the street applied to a studio background. Unframed. 9" × 29". December 2001. (Est. $7,300–$10,000) $4,300.

Lady and the Tramp (1955)

Production cel of Tramp. Trimmed and unframed. 12.5" × 16". $1,200.

Lady and the Tramp (1955)

Production cel of Lady with matching animation drawing. Unframed. 12" × 10". May 2002. $949.

Lady and the Tramp (1955)

Production two-cel setup of Lady and Tramp with laser background of Tony's. Unframed. 15" × 12". May 2002. $1,554.

215 Production multicel setup of Captain Hook

216 Production cel of Lady and Tramp

© *Walt Disney Co.*

Lady and the Tramp (1955)

Production cel of Lady and Tramp. Cels have been professionally restored and applied to a new cel. Cels have been trimmed to figure and applied to a new piece of acetate. The paint has been professionally restored. Unframed. 11" x 13". $2,900. *See illustration #216.*

Lady and the Tramp (1955)

Production cel large image of Tramp placed on a color copy background. Tramp's image size is 6.75" × 7". Unframed. $2,200.

Lady and the Tramp (1955)

Production cel of a very sad Lady. Art Corner setup is still attached to its original backing board with the Gold Disneyland Label. Unframed. Trimmed to 9" × 12". Lady's image size is 3" × 5". $1,300.

Lady and the Tramp (1955)

Production cel setup featuring Tramp, the Cop, and the Gentleman at the Zoo placed on a color copy background. The total image size of the characters is 7.5" × 10". Unframed. $1,700.

Lady and the Tramp (1955)

Production cel of Tramp, trimmed to figure and reapplied to a new piece of acetate. Unframed. 11" × 13" (image area 5.5" h × 3" w). $750.

Lady and the Tramp (1955)

Production cel of Tramp, trimmed to 7" high × 8" wide (image area 5.5" h × 4" w). Unframed. $795.

Lady and the Tramp (1955)

Production cel of Peg. The cel has been professionally restored and trimmed and applied to a new cel. The paint has been professionally restored. Unframed. 11" × 13". $1,200.

Lady and the Tramp (1955)

Production cel of Lady. The paint has been professionally restored. Unframed. Image size 5.5" h × 5" w. $1,500.

Lady and the Tramp (1955)

Disneyland cel setup of Peg. In original Disneyland mat with gold Art Corner label. Unframed. $795.

Lady and the Tramp (1955)

Production cel of some puppies and Jim Dear. Unframed. $1,200.

Lady and the Tramp (1955)

Disneyland cel setup of Lady and Tramp. Happy cel of Lady chasing Tramp. Unframed. Image size 5.75" h × 3" w. $2,200.

Lady and the Tramp (1955)

Production cel of Tramp lying on the floor chewing on an invisible bone. Very small paint chip toward hind legs. Unframed. 11" × 13" (image size 2.5" h × 6" w). $1,600.

Lady and the Tramp (1955)

Production cel of Lady in shock at the mess of the fish bowl being knocked over. Framed. 11" × 13". $1,250.

Lady and the Tramp (1955)

Production cel of Peg. A crease on the right side from top to bottom. Cel has been trimmed. The paint has been professionally restored. Unframed. Image size 5" h × 6.5" w. $950.

Lady and the Tramp (1955)

Production cel of Jock and Toughy. Framed. 11" × 13". $850.

Lady and the Tramp (1955)

Production cel of Peg in the dog pound. Framed. 11" × 13". $450.

The Truth about Mother Goose (1957)

Disneyland cel setup of Mary Queen of Scots being toasted from the Mary Mary Quite Contrary segment of this featurette. Original Disneyland mat with gold Art Corner label; some paint separation. Unframed. $400.

The Truth about Mother Goose (1957)

Production cel of Mary Queen of Scots. Unframed. 11" × 13". $325.

Sleeping Beauty (1959)

Key master setup of Briar Rose in wonderful interior shot of the cottage, just before they make the cake and dress. Framed. $18,000.

Sleeping Beauty (1959)

Master setup of Maleficent and Fairies; background is a production background but did not appear under the camera. Unframed. $16,000.

Sleeping Beauty (1959)

Disneyland cel setup of Maleficent. Matted. $3,200.

Sleeping Beauty (1959)

Production cel of the Queen. Color laser background. The paint has been professionally restored. Unframed. 11" × 13". $1,250.

Sleeping Beauty (1959)

Original production cel of Sleeping Beauty and a few of her forest helpers. Matted and framed to 11" × 11". May 2002. $1,129.

Sleeping Beauty (1959)

Color model cel of Maleficent and Fairies (Diablo, King Stefan, the Queen, King Hubert, the young Prince, the three fairies, and the castle). Framed. $6,500.

Sleeping Beauty (1959)

Original production cels of Flora and Fauna with reproduction background and original Disney labels on reverse. Unframed. 12" × 14". May 2002. $886.

Sleeping Beauty (1959)

Color model cel of Briar Rose. Her bodice is brown, as this piece is a color model cel. Signed by Frank Thomas, Ollie Johnston, and Marc Davis. Unframed. Image size 6" h × 2" w. $1,600.

Sleeping Beauty (1959)

Production cel of Briar Rose. Unframed. Image area 5" h × 3" w. $1,400.

Sleeping Beauty (1959)

Production cel of the Jester. Body has begun to separate as has the feather in his hat. Unframed. 11" × 13". $650.

Sleeping Beauty (1959)

Production cel of Merryweather. A few delicate sparkles around her wand. On a color laser background. Unframed. 11" × 13". $950.

Sleeping Beauty (1959)

Production cel of the Jester showing the Kings the blueprint for the Prince's new castle. Unframed. 11" × 13" (trimmed to 12.5" h × 12.25" w). $650.

Sleeping Beauty (1959)

Production cel of Flora with very beautiful transparent wings. Unframed. 11" × 13" (trimmed, as it was a pan cel still 12.5" h × 16.5" w). $695.

Sleeping Beauty (1959)

Production cel of Owl as Mock Prince. Color laser background. Unframed. 11" × 13". $2,500.

Sleeping Beauty (1959)

Production cel of King Stefan. Unframed. $595.

Sleeping Beauty (1959)

Disneyland cel setup of Flora in peasant clothing. Nice wand action! Signed by Frank Thomas and Ollie Johnston. Unframed. Image size 7" h × 4" w. $795.

Sleeping Beauty (1959)

Production cel of Merryweather with wand in hand. Unframed. 11" x 13" (image size 7" h × 5" w). $750.

Sleeping Beauty (1959)

Disneyland cel setup of Merryweather. Unframed. Image size 5" h × 5" w. $750.

Sleeping Beauty (1959)

Production cel of Prince Philip as he searches for Briar Rose. Unframed. 13" × 16" (image size 6" h × 3.5" w). $595.

Sleeping Beauty (1959)

Production cel of Merryweather looking up inside the castle. Unframed. 11" × 13" (image size 6.5" h × 6" w). $495.

Sleeping Beauty (1959)

Production cel of one of Briar Rose's forest friends. Unframed. Image size 6" h × 2" w. $250.

Sleeping Beauty (1959)

Production cel featuring Briar Rose and the Owl. Trimmed pan cel measures 15" × 11.25" and is placed on a color copy background. Briar Rose's image size is 6.5" × 4.25". Unframed. $1,700.

Sleeping Beauty (1959)

Production cel of Maleficent hand-signed by Marc Davis. Unframed. $2,500.

Sleeping Beauty (1959)

Production cel of the King's Guards. A reflection you see in the scan is from the frame. The image of the Guards measures 16" × 7.5". Framed. $750.

Goliath II (1960)

Disneyland cel setup of Goliath the Elephant in original Art Corner mat. The cel and paint have been professionally restored. Unframed. Image size 7 $^3/_4$" h × 5 $^{11}/_{16}$" w. $500.

Goliath II (1960)

Disneyland cel setup of Goliath the Elephant in an original Art Corner mat. Unframed. Image size 3.5" h × 4.5" w. $450.

101 Dalmatians (1961)

Production cel of Cruella De Vil. Unframed. Image size 6" h × 6.5" w. $3,800.

101 Dalmatians (1961)

Disneyland cel setup of Cruella De Vil. Paint separation on the bottom of coat and a small amount on her face above her mouth. Unframed. Image size 7" h × 5.5" w. $2,400.

101 Dalmatians (1961)

Production cel of a large image of Pongo. Art Corner setup on its original litho background and backing board with the gold label on the back. Unframed. Image size 6.5" × 6.5". $1,400.

101 Dalmatians (1961)

Production cel of a full-figure image of one of the Puppies. Art Corner setup on its original backing board with the gold label on the back. Unframed. 7.5" × 10" (image size 4.5" × 4"). $750.

101 Dalmatians (1961)

Three production cels of Sergeant Tibbs and two others. Unframed. 12.5" × 16" (image size 5.5" × 4.25"). December 2001. (Est. $220–$290) $150.

101 Dalmatians (1961)

Production cel of a full-figure image of Patch. Art Corner setup and in its original mat with the gold label on the back. Unframed. 8" × 9.5" (image size 3.5" × 3"). $950.

101 Dalmatians (1961)

Production cel of Nanny. Sixteen-field cel has been hand-signed by Marc Davis, Frank Thomas, and Ollie Johnston. Image size 5.5" × 4". $475.

101 Dalmatians (1961)

Production cel of Jasper and Horace. Art Corner setup (sold at Disneyland) placed on a litho background, and still in its original mat with the gold label on the back. Unframed. Image size 6.5" × 9". $500.

101 Dalmatians (1961)

Production cel of the Colonel (some paint lifting). Unframed. Image size 11" × 7". $400.

101 Dalmatians (1961)

Production cel setup from the finale of Pongo and Roger. Art Corner setup in its original mat with the Disneyland gold label on the back. Unframed. 12" × 14" (image size 6" × 9.5"). $1,350.

101 Dalmatians (1961)

Production cel of Cruella's car and the truck carrying the Dalmatians, from the climactic scene of the film. Unframed. Truck image size 4" × 4". Cruella's car image size 2" × 4". $450.

101 Dalmatians (1961)

Disneyland cel setup of Pongo; small paint separation. Unframed. (Image size 6" h × 6.5" w. $795.

The Sword in the Stone (1963)

Production cel of Merlin winding up an airplane, as his beard gets caught in the propeller. Unframed. 11" × 13" (image size 7" h × 11" w). $950.

The Sword in the Stone (1963)

Disneyland cel setup of Merlin and Archimedes. Unframed. Image size 8" h × 9" w. $750.

The Sword in the Stone (1963)

Production cel of Madam Mim. Paint has been restored. Unframed. 11" × 13". $295.

The Sword in the Stone (1963)

Production cel of Wart scrubbing the floor before being rescued by Merlin. Unframed. 11" × 13". $450.

The Sword in the Stone (1963)

Production cel of Merlin and Wart. Art Corner setup (sold at Disneyland) with a color print background. Framed. 15" × 17" (image size 8.5" × 9.5"). $750.

The Sword in the Stone (1963)

Production cel of Merlin. Unframed. $400.

The Sword in the Stone (1963)

Production cel of Wart. Unframed. $250.

The Jungle Book (1967)

Production cel of Baloo and some monkeys. Unframed. 11" × 13". $1,800.

The Jungle Book (1967)

Production cel of Bagheera applied to a key studio background. Unframed. 8.5" × 11". December 2001. (Est. $4,400–$7,300) $2,340.

The Jungle Book (1967)

Production cel of Mowgli and Baloo playing in the jungle applied to a key pan background. Unframed. 11" × 19". December 2001. (Est. $11,000–$14,000) $6,300.

The Jungle Book (1967)

Production cel of Mowgli and Flunkey Monkey. Unframed. 11" × 13". $1,100.

The Jungle Book (1967)

Production cel of King Louie swinging from a branch in a cel trimmed to about 4"x 10". Unframed. Image size 5.5" h × 3" w. $950.

The Jungle Book (1967)

Production cel of Baloo in full-figured pose. Signed by Frank Thomas and Ollie Johnston. Unframed. Image size 7" h × 5.5" w. $1,200.

The Jungle Book (1967)

Production cel of Mowgli and Baloo. Framed. 11" × 13" (image size 7" h × 9" w). $1,800.

The Jungle Book (1967)

Key master setup of Baloo and Mowgli. Framed. 11" × 13". $12,500.

The Jungle Book (1967)

Production cel of Mowgli and Kaa. Framed. 11" × 13" (image size 6" h × 5" w). $1,800.

The Jungle Book (1967)

Production cel of Kaa trimmed to 10" × 7.5" (image size 6.5" × 3.5"). Unframed. $450.

The Jungle Book (1967)

Production two cel setup featuring Mowgli and one of the Elephants. From part of a Disneyland Art Corner setup trimmed to 10" × 11.75". Unframed. The elephant measures 7.5" × 4.5". Mowgli measures 4.5" × 2.5". $800.

The Jungle Book (1967)

Production cel of one of the Vultures. Unframed. 12.5" × 16" (image size 7" × 7.5"). $450.

The Jungle Book (1967)

Production cel of a large image of Baloo with a Disney seal. Unframed. 12.5" × 16" (image size 6.5" × 9"). $900.

The Jungle Book (1967)

Production cel of King Louie's right-hand man. Art Corner setup trimmed to 8" × 10". Unframed. The Monkey's image size is 6.5" × 5". $400.

The Jungle Book (1967)

Production cel of one of King Louie's monkey sidekicks with a Disney seal. Unframed. Image size 4.5" × 4". $400.

Blustery Day (1968)

Disneyland cel setup of Christopher Robin and Owl. Slight cracking. Unframed. $450.

The Aristocats (1970)

Production cel of Napoleon and Edgar. Unframed. 12.5" x16" (image size 7" × 6"). $200.

The Aristocats (1970)

Production cel of Abigail Gabble and Amelia Gabble. Unframed. 11" × 13" (image size 7" h × 8" w). $550.

The Aristocats (1970)

Disneyland cel setup of Duchess and Amelia Gabble with original Disneyland backmatting and gold seal. Unframed. $595.

The Aristocats (1970)

Production cel of Berlioz and Frou Frou. Unframed. Image size 5" × 8". $300.

The Aristocats (1970)

Production cel of Toulouse and Marie. Unframed. 11" × 13" (image size 4.25" h × 6.5" w). $450.

The Aristocats (1970)

Production cel of Berlioz. Unframed. 11" × 13" (image size 2.5" h × 4.5" w). $350.

The Aristocats (1970)

Production cel of O'Malley. Paint has been professionally restored. Unframed. Image size 7" h × 4.7" w. $250.

The Aristocats (1970)

Production cel of Amelia Gabble. Unframed. 13" × 16" (image size 7.5" h × 4.5" w). $295.

The Aristocats (1970)

Production cel of Edgar. Unframed. 11" × 13" (image size 8" h × 5" w). $150.

Bedknobs and Broomsticks (1971)

Production cel of the Fisherman Bear. Unframed. 12.5" × 16" (image size 8" × 7"). $300.

Bedknobs and Broomsticks (1971)

Production cel of one of the King's soccer players. Unframed. 12.5" × 16" (image size 6.5" × 5"). $200.

Bedknobs and Broomsticks (1971)

Production cel of the King. Unframed. 12.5" × 15.5" with Disney seal (image size 9" × 5.5"). $450.

Bedknobs and Broomsticks (1971)

Production cel of the Kanagaroo and the Hyena from the Soccer Match. Unframed. 12" × 15" with a Disney seal (image size 7.5" × 8.5"). $375.

Bedknobs and Broomsticks (1971)

Production cel of the Kangaroo Soccer Player. Unframed. Image size 4" × 5". $200.

Robin Hood (1973)

Production two-cel setup featuring Robin and Prince John. Unframed. 12.5" × 16" with Disney seal (image size 7" × 5"). $800.

Robin Hood (1973)

Production cel of Prince John with a Disney seal and laminated by the studio and hand-signed by Frank Thomas and Ollie Johnston. Unframed. 12.5" × 16" (image size 9" × 11"). $300.

Robin Hood (1973)

Production multicel setup of Friar Tuck with the Church Mice with Disney seal and laminated by the studio. Unframed. 12.5" × 16" (image size 9.5" × 13"). $275.

Robin Hood (1973)

Production two-cel setup featuring the Sheriff and Sir Hiss matted with Disney seal. Image size 7.5" × 9". $550.

Robin Hood (1973)

Production cel of the Sheriff of Nottingham matted with Disney seal. Unframed. Image size 9" × 9". $400.

Robin Hood (1973)

Production two-cel setup of Friar Tuck. Unframed. Image size 11" × 8". $400.

Robin Hood (1973)

Production cel of Robin Hood and Maid Marian. Cels have been laminated and stapled together in the upper left corner. Unframed. 13" × 16". $975.

Robin Hood (1973)

Production cel of Maid Marian and Lady Kluck with original Disneyland Disneyana certificate of authenticity. Unframed. 11" × 13". $750.

Robin Hood (1973)

Production cel of Maid Marian with original Disneyland Disneyana certificate of authenticity. Unframed. 13" × 16". $650.

Robin Hood (1973)

Production cel of Maid Marian with original Disneyland Disneyana certificate of authenticity. Unframed. 11" × 13". $550.

The Rescuers (1977)

Production cel of Orville, the proprietor, pilot, and "plane" of Albatross Air Charter Service with original Disney certificate of authenticity and seal. Unframed. 11" × 13". $395.

The Rescuers (1977)

Production cel of Bernard and Bianca with original Disneyland Disneyana certificate of authenticity. Unframed. 13" × 16". $695.

The Rescuers (1977)

Production cel of Bernard and Bianca with original Disneyland Disneyana certificate of authenticity. Unframed. 11" × 13". $650.

The Rescuers (1977)

Production cel of Bianca with original Disneyland Disneyana certificate of authenticity. Unframed. 11" × 13". $495.

The Rescuers (1977)

Production cel of Medusa with Disney seal. Unframed. 12.5" × 16" (image size 8" × 7"). $450.

The Rescuers (1977)

Production cel of Bernard and Bianca with Disney seal. Unframed. 12.5" × 16" (image size 10" × 12.5"). $400.

The Rescuers (1977)

Production cel of Medusa hand-signed by animators Frank Thomas and Ollie Johnston. Unframed. Image size 7" × 8.5". $450.

The Rescuers (1977)

Production cel of Medusa and the preacher Owl with Disney seal. Unframed. Image size 6.5" × 9.5". $400.

The Fox and the Hound (1981)

Production cel of Vixey and Tod with original Disneyland Disneyana certificate of authenticity. Unframed. 11" × 13". $450.

The Fox and the Hound (1981)

Production model cel with two images of the Badger. Unframed. Image size 4" x 8". $150.

The Black Cauldron (1985)

Production cel of Gurgi with a Xerox line background and a Disney seal. Unframed. 12" × 16" (image size 7" × 6.5"). $450.

The Black Cauldron (1985)

Production cel of the three witches with a Disney seal. Unframed. Image size 8" × 13.5". $450.

The Black Cauldron (1985)

Production model cel of Burny. Unframed. Image size 4.5" × 5". $200.

The Black Cauldron (1985)

Production cel of Creeper with a Disney production stamp. Unframed. Image size 4" × 5.5". $200.

The Black Cauldron (1985)

Production cel of Dallben with a Disney production stamp. Unframed. Image size 6" × 7". $200.

The Great Mouse Detective (1986)

Production cel of Ratigan with a Disney seal. Unframed. 12.5" × 16" (image size 8" × 9.5"). $450.

The Great Mouse Detective (1986)

Production multicel setup featuring Ratigan and Bartholomew with a Disney seal. Unframed. 10.5" × 12.5" (image size 9" × 10"). $350.

The Great Mouse Detective (1986)

Production multicel setup featuring Basil and Dawson with a Disney seal. Unframed. 15.5" × 12.5" (image size 7" × 11.5"). $425.

The Great Mouse Detective (1986)

Production cel of Dawson and a Lady Mouse from the bar scene with a Disney seal. Framed. Image size 7.5" × 5.5". $400.

The Great Mouse Detective (1986)

Production cel of Basil at work in the lab with a Disney seal. Unframed. Image size 8.5" × 8". $400.

Oliver and Company (1988)

Production multicel setup of Fagin with Syke's Dobermans, Roscoe, and DeSoto with a Disney seal. Unframed. 12.5" × 17" (image size 8" × 13"). $400.

Oliver and Company (1988)

Production cel of Tito on a color copy background with a Disney seal. Unframed. Image size 5.5" × 4.5". $400.

Who Framed Roger Rabbit (1988)

Production cel of Jessica Rabbit with a Disney seal and placed on a black-and-white photographic background. Unframed. 16.5" × 12.5" (image size 6" × 5"). $3,000.

Who Framed Roger Rabbit (1988)

Production cel of Jessica Rabbit. Unframed. 13" × 16". $1,400.

Who Framed Roger Rabbit (1988)

Production cel of Jessica Rabbit applied to a reproduction studio background. Unframed. 8" × 11". December 2001. (Est. $880–$1,200) $495.

Who Framed Roger Rabbit (1988)

Production cel of Eddie's bullets with a Disney seal and frame and placed on a black-and-white photographic background. Framed. Image size 3" × 8". $750.

The Little Mermaid (1989)

Production cel of Triton on a color laser background. Unframed. Image size 8.5" × 12". $950.

The Little Mermaid (1989)

Production cel of Ariel. Framed. 11" × 13". $2,100.

The Little Mermaid (1989)
Production cel of Ariel. Unframed. 13" × 16". $1,400.

The Little Mermaid (1989)
Production cel of Ursula. Framed. 11" × 13". $1,800.

The Little Mermaid (1989)
Production cel of Ariel on land with Eric and Max. Unframed. 11" × 13". $1,900.

The Little Mermaid (1989)
Production cel of Ursula. Unframed. 13" × 16". $1,250.

The Little Mermaid (1989)
Production cel of Scuttle. Unframed. 11" × 13". $750.

The Little Mermaid (1989)
Production background of night sky showing the shoreline with twinkling star clusters. Unframed. 11" × 13". $1,800.

The Little Mermaid (1989)
Master setup; key master setup of either Flotsam or Jetsam. Unframed. 11" × 13". $2,500.

Tarzan (1999)
Master setup of Terk. Original animation master background used in the film with a re-created cel of Terk. Framed. $2,500.

Walt Disney Studios: Original Production Drawings
Steamboat Willie (1928)
Production drawing of Mickey Mouse and Peg Leg Pete in a two-drawing set. Unframed. 10" × 12" (image size 7" × 5"). $8,500.

The Barn Dance (1929)
Production drawing of Mickey Mouse. Framed. 9.5" × 8.25". May 2002. $484.

Mother Goose Melodies (1931)
Production drawing of the Mother Goose and the Goose. Unframed. Image size 4.5" × 4". $190.

Mother Goose Melodies (1931)
Production drawings of Little Miss Muffet and the Spider. Unframed. $200.

The Beach Party (1931)
Production drawing of an Octopus. Unframed. 10" × 12" (image size 3" × 6"). $50.

The Cactus Kid (1931)

Two production drawings of Mickey Mouse playing the piano. Framed. 12" × 9.5". May 2002. $484.

The Clock Shop (1931)

Production drawing. Unframed. 10" × 12" (image size 3" × 2"). $60.

Babes in the Woods (1932)

Production drawing. Unframed. 10" × 12" (image size 2.5" × 3.5"). $75.

Babes in the Woods (1932)

Production model drawing of the peasant children. Unframed. 11" × 13" (image size 9" × 11"). $1,800.

Bugs in Love (1932)

Production drawing of the main characters. Unframed. 11" × 13". $395.

Bugs in Love (1932)

Production drawing. Unframed. 9" × 11" (image size 2" × 1.5"). $40.

Mickey's Good Deed (1932)

Production drawing; original pencil model sheet of a kitten. Unframed. 11" × 13". $1,400.

Mickey's Good Deed (1932)

Production drawing of Adelbert. Unframed. 11" × 13" (image size 8" × 11"). $1,700.

Mickey's Mellerdrammer (1932)

Production drawing of Mickey Mouse and Minnie Mouse. Unframed. 11" × 13" (image size 4" × 4"). $900.

Mickey's Mellerdrammer (1932)

Production drawing of Mickey Mouse and Minnie Mouse dancing. Unframed. 12" × 9.5". May 2002. $291.

Mickey's Nightmare (1932)

Production drawing of a very young Mickey Mouse. Unframed. 11" × 13". $3,500.

The Klondike Kid (1932)

Production drawing of Minnie Mouse and Peg Leg Pete. Unframed. 11" × 13". $1,250.

The Whoopee Party (1932)

Production drawing of Mickey Mouse. Framed. 11" × 13". $795.

Trader Mickey (1932)

Production drawing of Mickey Mouse jumping on a board. Unframed. 11" × 13" (image size 4" × 4"). $750.

Trader Mickey (1932)

Production drawing of the King of the Cannibals. Unframed. 11" × 13". $250.

Mickey's Gala Premiere (1933)

Production drawing of Joe E. Brown. Unframed. 10" × 12" (image size 5.5" × 7.5"). $75.

Mickey's Mechanical Man (1933)

Production drawing of the Robot. Unframed. 10" × 12" (image size 4.5" × 7"). $75.

Mickey's Pal Pluto (1933)

Production drawing of Mickey Mouse. Unframed. 11" × 13". $850.

On Ice (1933)

Very detailed production drawing of Mickey Mouse. Unframed. 11" × 13" (image size 4" × 6"). $4,900.

On Ice (1933)

Production drawing of Mickey Mouse and Minnie Mouse. Unframed. 11" × 13" (image size 4" × 5"). $2,900.

Puppy Love (1933)

Production drawing of Mickey Mouse and Minnie Mouse. Unframed. 11" × 13" (image size 4" × 5"). $1,250.

The Mad Doctor (1933)

Production drawing of Mickey Mouse and Pluto. Unframed. 11" × 13". $1,200.

The Steeplechase (1933)

Production drawing of Mickey Mouse. Layout drawing. Unframed. 11" × 13" (image size 6" × 7.75"). $1,250.

Gulliver Mickey (1934)

Production drawing of Mickey Mouse. Unframed. Image size 3.5" × 5.5". $400.

Gulliver Mickey (1934)

Production drawing; model sheet of the General and the People. Unframed. 11" × 13". $1,650.

Mickey Plays Poppa (1934)

Production drawing of Mickey Mouse. Unframed. 11" × 13". $750.

Mickey's Steamroller (1934)

Production drawing of Mickey Mouse having some technical difficulties. Unframed. 11" × 13". $2,400.

Mickey's Steamroller (1934)

Production drawing of Mickey Mouse. Unframed. 11" × 13". $695.

Orphans Benefit (1934)

Production drawing of Clara Cluck. Unframed. Image size 6.5" × 8". $350.

The Big Bad Wolf (1934)

Production drawing of Red Riding Hood and the Big Bad Wolf. Unframed. 10" × 12" (image size 5" × 9"). $450.

The Flying Mouse (1934)

Production drawing of the Fairy. Unframed. 10" × 12" (image size 9" × 7"). $125.

Broken Toys (1935)

Production drawing of of one of the discarded toys from the city dump in graphite and colored pencil. Unframed. 11" × 13". $295.

Cock o' the Walk (1935)

Production drawing. Unframed. Image size 6" × 4". $250.

Cookie Carnival (1935)

Production drawing. Layout drawing with lovely color highlights. Unframed. 11" × 13". $1,200.

The Robber Kitten (1935)

Production drawing. Unframed. 10" × 12" (image size 5" × 3"). $80.

The Tortoise and the Hare (1935)

Production drawing of the Tortoise. Unframed. Trimmed to 8" × 11" (image size 2.25" × 2.5"). $200.

The Tortoise and the Hare (1935)

Production drawing of the Hare. Unframed. Trimmed to 8" × 11" (image size 5.5" × 4"). $225.

Alpine Climber (1936)

Production drawing of Mickey Mouse. Unframed. 11" × 13" (image size 4" × 4"). $950.

Elmer the Elephant (1936)

Production drawing of Elmer. Unframed. Image size 5" × 4". $175.

Elmer the Elephant (1936)

Production drawing of Joey Hippo. Unframed. Image size 4" × 4". $125.

Elmer the Elephant (1936)

Production drawing of Elmer's animal friends. Unframed. Image size 3.5" × 11". $100.

Mickey's Circus (1936)

Production drawing of Donald Duck all wet. Unframed. 11" × 13". $495.

Mickey's Elephant (1936)

Production drawing of Pluto. Unframed. 11" × 13". $350.

Mickey's Rival (1936)

Production drawing of Mickey Mouse. Unframed. 11" × 13". $750.

Mickey's Rival (1936)

Production drawing of Minnie Mouse. Unframed. 11" × 13" (image size 4" × 3"). $650.

Mickey's Rival (1936)

Production drawing of Mortimer. Unframed. 11" × 13". $295.

The Hockey Champ (1936)

Production drawing of Donald Duck in red and graphite pencil. Unframed. 11" × 13" (image size 5" × 4.75"). $450.

Clock Cleaners (1937)

Production drawing of Mickey Mouse. Unframed. 10" × 12" (image size 3.5" × 4.5"). $400.

Clock Cleaners (1937)

Production drawing of Goofy. Unframed. 10" × 12" (image size 6.5" × 4"). $400.

Donald's Ostrich (1937)

Production background layout. Unframed. 10" × 12" (image size 8" × 10"). $75.

Donald's Ostrich (1937)

Production drawing—storyboard. Unframed. 11" × 13" (image size 5" × 6"). $850.

Little Hiawatha (1937)

Production drawing of Little Hiawatha. Unframed. 11" × 13". $550.

Little Hiawatha (1937)

Production drawing of Little Hiawatha. Unframed. Image size 3" × 3.5". $350.

Magician Mickey (1937)

Production drawing of Mickey Mouse in a tuxedo. Unframed. 11" × 13" (image size 4" × 5"). $650.

Magician Mickey (1937)

Production drawing of Mickey Mouse putting Donald into a gun. Unframed. Image size 8.5" × 9.5". $1,500.

Modern Inventions (1937)

Production drawing of Donald Duck. Unframed. 11" × 13" (image size 7.5" × 7"). $600.

Snow White and the Seven Dwarfs (1937)

Original production drawing of the Witch polishing an apple. 15.5" × 12.5". May 2002. $949.

Snow White and the Seven Dwarfs (1937)

Production drawing of the Wicked Witch holding the poison apple. Unframed. 11" × 13". $2,400.

Snow White and the Seven Dwarfs (1937)

Production drawing of some Dwarfs (color reference drawing). Unframed. 11" × 13". $1,600.

Snow White and the Seven Dwarfs (1937)

Production drawing of the Queen just before she turns into the Witch with swirl effects drawing. Unframed. 13" × 16". $3,900.

Snow White and the Seven Dwarfs (1937)

Production drawing of five Dwarfs. Unframed. 10" × 12" (image size 8.5" × 6.75"). December 2001. (Est. $1,100–$1,300) $810.

Snow White and the Seven Dwarfs (1937)

Production drawing of Dopey. Unframed. 10" × 12" (image size 8.5" × 8"). May 2002. $587.

Snow White and the Seven Dwarfs (1937)

Production drawing of Snow White. Unframed. 11" × 13". $1,250.

Snow White and the Seven Dwarfs (1937)

Production drawing of the Wicked Witch with the famous poisoned apple with references to the different colors that the ink and paint departments were to use when painting the cels. Unframed. 13" × 16". $2,500.

Snow White and the Seven Dwarfs (1937)

Production drawing of all Seven Dwarfs. Framed. 11" × 13" (image size 5"h × 6" w). $2,200.

Snow White and the Seven Dwarfs (1937)

Two production drawings of Snow White and Prince with signatures of Frank Thomas, Ollie Johnston, and Marc Davis. Framed. 11" × 13". $2,000.

Snow White and the Seven Dwarfs (1937)

Production drawing of Sneezy with his beard tied up so he doesn't wake the sleeping Snow White. Unframed. 11" × 13". $800.

Snow White and the Seven Dwarfs (1937)

Production drawing of Snow White as she sings. Unframed. 11" × 13". $1,100.

Snow White and the Seven Dwarfs (1937)

Production drawing of Snow White with excessive wear. Unframed. 11" × 13". $850.

Snow White and the Seven Dwarfs (1937)

Production drawing of Sneezy and soap. Unframed. $295.

Snow White and the Seven Dwarfs (1937)

Production drawing of Doc from the scene by the bed where he argues with Grumpy. Freddie Moore rough drawing. Unframed. 11" × 13". $600.

Snow White and the Seven Dwarfs (1937)

Production drawing of Bashful. Unframed. 11" × 13". $600.

Snow White and the Seven Dwarfs (1937)

Production drawing of a squirrel. Unframed. 11" × 13". $350.

Boat Builders (1938)

Production drawing of Mickey Mouse. Unframed. 11" × 13" (image size 8" × 7"). $950.

Ferdinand the Bull (1938)

Production drawing of the Matador. Unframed. 11" × 13" (image size 6" × 3.5"). $295.

Ferdinand the Bull (1938)

Production drawing of Ferdinand. Unframed. 10" × 12" (image size 5" × 8"). $275.

Mickey's Parrot (1938)

Production drawing of Mickey Mouse from the scene where Mickey goes to shoot the bird he thinks is bad; the gun is bigger than he is. Unframed. $2,100.

Mickey's Surprise Party (1939)

Production drawing of Minnie Mouse. Unframed. Image size 4" × 3". $300.

Mickey's Surprise Party (1939)

Production drawing of Fifi. Unframed. 11" × 13". $195.

Mickey's Surprise Party (1939)

Production drawing of Minnie Mouse. Unframed. 11" × 13". $450.

Society Dog Show (1939)

Production drawing of full-figured Mickey Mouse and Pluto. Unframed. 11" × 13" (image size 5" × 10"). $2,200.

Society Dog Show (1939)

Production drawing of Mickey Mouse, Pluto, and a Judge. Unframed. 11" × 13". $1,200.

Society Dog Show (1939)

Production drawing of Mickey Mouse. Unframed. 11" × 13" (image size 5" × 3"). $795.

The Practical Pig (1939)

Production drawing of the Big Bad Wolf. Unframed. 10" × 12" (image size 6.5" × 5.5"). $250.

The Practical Pig (1939)

Production drawing. Storyboard concept drawing by Ferinand Horvath and initialed by the artist. Unframed. 7" × 5" mounted to 11" × 14". $1,200.

The Practical Pig (1939)

Production drawing of one of the pigs. Unframed. 10" × 12" (image size 3" × 2"). $125.

The Ugly Duckling (1939)

Production drawing of the Ugly Duckling. Unframed. 11" × 13" (image size 3.25" × 1.25"). $6,500.

Fantasia (1940)

Production drawing of Yensid ("Disney" spelled backwards is how this character got his name). Unframed. 11" × 13" (image size 10" h × 9" w). $2,500.

Fantasia (1940)

Production drawing of Mickey Mouse in his most famous pose drawn by Freddie Moore. Unframed. 11" × 13". $2,400.

Fantasia (1940)

Production drawing of some dinosaurs in mortal combat from the "Rite of Spring" sequence. Unframed. $2,200.

Fantasia (1940)

Production drawing of a dinosaur in graphite and colored pencil. Unframed. 11" × 13". $1,250.

Fantasia (1940)

Layout drawing of a dinosaur from the "Rite of Spring." Unframed. 11" × 13" (image size 8" h × 12" w). $650.

Fantasia (1940)

Production drawing of Hyacinth Hippo. Signed by Preston Blair. Unframed. 11" × 13". $800.

Fantasia (1940)

Production drawing of a Hippo and Alligator from the "Dance of the Hours" sequence on 10" × 12" animation paper with a stamp on the back. Unframed. Image size 8" × 9.5". $600.

Fantasia (1940)

Production drawing. Graphite and colored pencil drawing of the Chernabog as he shields his eye from the rising sun. Unframed. 12.5" × 15.5" (image size 6" × 11"). $800.

Fantasia (1940)

Production drawing. Freddie Moore rough animation drawing of a Centaurette. Unframed. 12.5" × 15.5" (image size 9.5" × 5.5"). $800.

Fantasia (1940)

Production drawing; model drawing of three fairies. Unframed. 12.5" × 15.5" (image size 8.5" × 1.5"). $600.

Fantasia (1940)

Production drawing of an Autumn Fairy. Unframed. 12.5" × 15.5" (image size 4" × 2"). $600.

Fantasia (1940)

Production drawing of Bacchus. Unframed. 12.5" × 15.5" (image size 7" × 7"). December 2001 (Est. $440–$730). $180.

Fantasia (1940)

Production drawing of the Milkweeds performing "The Waltz of the Flowers." Unframed. 12.5" × 15.5". $500.

Fantasia (1940)

Production drawing of the centaurette nicknamed "Sunflower" from the "Pastoral Symphony." Unframed. 12.5" × 15.5" (image size 4.5" × 3.5"). $800.

Fantasia (1940)

Production drawing of the Pilgrims marching from the "Ave Maria" sequence (the finale of the film). Unframed. 22.5" × 12.5" (image size 10.5" × 1"). $800.

Mr. Duck Steps Out (1940)

Four production drawings of Donald Duck and his three nephews. Unframed and trimmed and mounted to 11" × 13" board. Image size 5.5" × 4". $400.

Pinocchio (1940)

Production drawing of the Blue Fairy. Colorful image in graphite, purple and green pencil. Unframed. 11" × 13". $1,900.

Pinocchio (1940)

Production drawing of Pinocchio as a boy. Unframed. 11" × 13" (image size 5" h × 3" w). $1,250.

Pincochio (1940)

Three production drawings matted and framed together: the Blue Fairy (9" × 12"), Jiminy Cricket (8" × 9"), and Pinocchio (9" × 12"). May 2002. $1,391.

Pinocchio (1940)

Production drawing of Figaro. Unframed. 11" × 13" (image size 2" h × 3" w). $350.

Pinocchio (1940)
Production drawing of Monstro; 16-field animation paper. Unframed. Image size 12.5" × 9". $2,000.

Pinocchio (1940)
Production drawing of Pinocchio and Gepetto on their raft. Unframed. Image size 4" × 9". $200.

Pinocchio (1940)
Production drawing of Stromboli. Unframed. Image size 4" × 6". $250.

The Riveter (1940)
Production drawing of Peg Leg Pete. Unframed. 11" × 13". $695.

Tugboat Mickey (1940)
Production drawing of Mickey Mouse. Unframed. 11" × 13". $950.

Canine Caddy (1941)
Production drawing of Mickey Mouse and Pluto playing golf. Framed. 11" × 13". $2,200.

Dumbo (1941)
Production drawing of Dumbo. Unframed. 11" × 13" (image size 5" h × 6" w). $700.

Dumbo (1941)
Production drawing of Dumbo. Unframed. Image size 5" h × 6" w. $1,400.

Dumbo (1941)
Production drawing of one of the Crows. Unframed. 10" × 12" (image size 5" × 7"). $300.

Fishin' Around (1941)
Production drawing. Full-figure of Mickey Mouse. Unframed. 9.5" × 12" (image size 5.5" × 2.5"). $500.

How to Ride a Horse (1941)
Production drawing of Percy with lots of color. Unframed. 11" × 13". $495.

Lonesome Ghost (1941)
Production drawing of Donald Duck. Unframed. 10" × 12" (image size 3" × 3.75"). $400.

Nifty Nineties (1941)
Production drawing; Freddie Moore drawing of Mickey Mouse. Unframed. 10" × 12" (image size 5" × 3"). $450.

Donald's Garden (1942)
Production drawing of Pluto. Unframed. 11" × 13". $475.

Saludos Amigos (1943)

Production drawing. Concept drawing of Donald Duck by Mary Blair. Unframed. $1,750.

Duck Pimples (1946)

Production drawing of Donald Duck. Unframed. 11" × 13" (image size 7" × 4.75"). $550.

Dumb Bell of the Yukon (1946)

Production drawing of Donald Duck. Unframed. Image size 4.5" × 2.5". $80.

Make Mine Music (1946)

Production drawing. Freddie Moore production drawing of the Teenage Girl from the "All the Cats Join In" sequence. Unframed. 10" × 12" (image size 4.5" × 2"). $200.

Make Mine Music (1946)

Production drawing of the little girl from the "All the Cats Join In" sequence. Unframed. 10" × 12" (image size 3" × 2.5"). $200.

Song of the South (1946)

Production drawing of Brer Fox. Unframed. 12.5" × 15.5" (image size 3" × 7"). $750.

Song of the South (1946)

Original title artwork for the Portuguese release of the feature. Unframed. 15" × 20". $800.

Mickey and the Beanstalk (1947)

Three production drawings of the Giant plus photostat. Unframed. Image size 8" × 10.5". $1,750.

Melody Time (1948)

Production drawing of Pecos Bill and Widowmaker. Unframed. 10" × 12" (image size 6" × 8"). $300.

Ichabod and Mr. Toad (1949)

Production drawing. Graphite and colored pencil production drawing of Mr. Toad hand-signed by animator Frank Thomas. Unframed. 10" × 12.5" (image size 4.5" × 3.5"). $650.

Squatters Rights (1949)

Production drawing. Freddie Moore drawing of Mickey Mouse. Unframed. 10" × 12" (image size 5" × 5"). $400.

Cinderella (1950)

Production drawing of Cinderella's Fairy Godmother. Unframed. Image size 6.5" × 4.5". $550.

Cinderella (1950)

Production drawing of Cinderella as she holds the invitation to the ball. Unframed. 11" × 13". $975.

Cinderella (1950)
Production drawing of Cinderella and the Prince dancing, from the ballroom sequence. Framed. Image size 12" × 9". May 2002. $400.

Hold That Pose (1950)
Production drawing of Goofy. Unframed. 10" × 12" (image size 3.5" × 3.5"). $200.

Peter Pan (1953)
Production drawing of Tinkerbell with key notations. Unframed. 13" × 16" (image size 8" h × 4" w). $2,000.

Peter Pan (1953)
Production drawing of Tinkerbell with her hands over her head. Unframed. 13" × 16" (image size 8" h × 4" w). $1,800.

Peter Pan (1953)
Production drawing of Tinkerbell in a full-figured pose. Unframed. 13" × 16" (image size 8" h × 6" w). $1,700.

Peter Pan (1953)
Production drawing of John Darling. Signed by Marc Davis. Unframed. 11" × 13". $400.

Peter Pan (1953)
Production drawing of Michael with his sword. Unframed. Image size 7.5" × 3.5". $400.

Peter Pan (1953)
Production drawing of Michael as an Indian. Unframed. Image size 4" × 2.5". $375.

Peter Pan (1953)
Production drawing; concept drawings of the Darling children. Unframed. 16-field. $550.

Peter Pan (1953)
Production drawing; concept drawings of the Lost Boys. Unframed. 16-field. $550.

The Social Lion (1954)
Production drawing of the Lion by Jack Kinney. Unframed. Image size 4" × 5.5". $200.

Lady and the Tramp (1955)
Poster art of Lady and Tramp with many of the characters from the film. Unframed. 11" × 13". $2,500.

Lady and the Tramp (1955)
Production drawing of Tramp carrying a stick in his mouth. Unframed. 11" × 13". $550.

Lady and the Tramp (1955)
Production drawing of Tramp. Unframed. 11" × 13". $750.

Lady and the Tramp (1955)
Production drawing of Lady. Discoloration and a crease on the page. Unframed. 11" × 13". $495.

Lady and the Tramp (1955)
Production drawing of Tony as he exclaims "He's a Talkin' to Me!" Unframed. 12.5" × 15.5" (image size 8.5" × 8"). $500.

Sleeping Beauty (1959)
Production drawing; rough animation drawing of Maleficent. Unframed. 12.5" × 15.5" (image size 10.5" × 7.5"). $500.

Sleeping Beauty (1959)
Production drawing of Briar Rose. Unframed. 12.5" × 15.5" (image size 5" × 5"). $200.

Sleeping Beauty (1959)
Production drawing of Princess Aurora as she looks at her reflection in the mirror. Unframed. 12.5" × 15.5" (image size 6" × 3.5"). $250.

Sleeping Beauty (1959)
Production drawing of Fauna. Unframed. 12.5" × 15.5" (image size 8" × 8"). $250.

Sleeping Beauty (1959)
Production drawing of Maleficent; includes the original drawing for the overlay of her gown. Unframed. 13" × 16". $1,900.

Sleeping Beauty (1959)
Production drawing of Maleficent making a dramatic exit. Unframed. 13" × 16". $1,100.

Sleeping Beauty (1959)
Production cel of Merryweather. Unframed. 13" × 16". $950.

Sleeping Beauty (1959)
Production drawing of Briar Rose and Prince Philip. Unframed. 11" × 13". $695.

Sleeping Beauty (1959)
Production drawing of Maleficent's goons. Unframed. 11" × 13". $495.

The Sword in the Stone (1963)
Production drawing of Sir Ector. Unframed. 12.5" × 15.5" (image size 8" × 7"). $200.

The Aristocats (1970)
Production drawing of Scat Cat. Hand-signed by animators Frank Thomas and Ollie Johnston. Unframed. 12.5" × 15.5" (image size 4.5" × 3.25"). $200.

The Rescuers (1973)

Production drawing; concept featuring Nero, Brutus, and Snoops. Unframed. 12.5" × 15.5" (image size 8" × 12"). $1,000.

The Rescuers (1973)

Production drawing; concept of Bernard. Unframed and trimmed to 8" × 5.5" and mounted to board (image size 5.75" × 4.75"). $250.

The Rescuers (1973)

Production drawing; concept of Bianca. Unframed and trimmed to 8" × 5.5" and mounted to board (image size 5.5" × 3.5"). $250.

The Fox and the Hound (1981)

Production drawing of Amos. Unframed. 12.5" × 15.5" (image size 5" × 6"). $40.

The Fox and the Hound (1981)

Production drawing of Copper. Unframed. 12.5" × 15.5" (image size 3" × 4"). $40.

The Fox and the Hound (1981)

Production drawing; Glen Keane production drawing of the Bear and Tod. Unframed. 12.5" × 15.5" (image size 7.5" × 11"). $475.

The Black Cauldron (1985)

Production drawing of Doli. Unframed. Image size 4.5" × 3.5". $45.

The Black Cauldron (1985)

Production drawing of a skeleton. "Cauldron born minion of the horned king." Unframed. 11" × 13". $150.

The Black Cauldron (1985)

Production drawing of Fflam. Unframed. Image size 8" × 10". $50.

The Black Cauldron (1985)

Production drawing of Gurgi in blue pencil. Unframed. Image size 5.5" × 5.5". $90.

The Great Mouse Detective (1986)

Production drawing of Ratigan and Basil. Unframed. Image size 4.5" × 4.5". $75.

Warner Brothers Studios: Original Production Cels

Baby Plucky

Original production cel. Unframed. 11" × 13". $350.

Bugs Bunny

Original production cel. Unframed. 11" × 13". $675.

Daffy Duck

Original production cel of Daffy Duck looking a bit puzzled in his space costume. Unframed. 11" × 13". $450.

Elmer Fudd

Original production cel of Elmer Fudd from a 1960s short. Unframed. Image size 5" × 2.5". $400.

Foghorn Leghorn

Original production cel. Unframed. 11" × 13". $400.

Hippity Hopper

Original production cel of Hippity Hopper (rare character) from a 1950s Sylvester short. Unframed. 10" × 12.5" (image size 4.5" × 3.25"). $1,200.

Minerva and Dot

Original production cel. Unframed. 11" × 13". $375.

Miss Prissy

Original production cel of Miss Prissy from a 1950s short placed on color hand-painted reproduction background. Unframed. 10.5" × 15" (image size 4.5" × 2"). $600.

Pinky and the Brain

Original production cel. Unframed. 11" × 13". $375.

Plucky and Hampton

Original production cel. Unframed. 11" × 13". $350.

Porky Pig

Original production cel of Porky from a 1960s short placed on color copy background. Unframed. Image size 4" × 6". $300.

Speedy Gonzalez

Original production cel. Framed. 13" × 16". $200.

Sylvester

Original production cel of Sylvester the cat from a 1950s short. Unframed and trimmed. 10" × 10.5" (image size 5" × 6"). $650.

Tweety

Original production cel of Tweety from a 1940s short. Unframed. Image size 2.5" × 1.5". $600.

Yosemite Sam

Original production cel of Yosemite Sam. Unframed. Image size 5" × 3.5". $500.

Malibu Beach Party (1940)
Original production cel of full figure of Mary Livingston. Unframed. Image size 7" × 2". $500.

Malibu Beach Party (1940)
Original production cel of Ned Sparks buried in the sand. Unframed. Image size 11.5" × 6". $500.

Ink and the Lion (1941)
Original production cel of the Lion about to catch a steak. Unframed. Image size 6.5" × 7". $350.

Swallow the Leader (1949)
Original production cel of the main character. Unframed. 10.5" × 12.5" (image size 4" × 5"). $250.

Bully for Bugs (1953)
Original production cel of Bugs Bunny. Trimmed to image and applied to new cel. Unframed. Image size 5.5" × 4". $3,800.

Who Scent You (1960)
Original production background from the Pepe Le Pew short. Unframed. $1,700.

What's My Lion (1961)
Original production cel of Rocky the Mountain Lion. Unframed. 10.5" × 12.5" (image size 4.5" × 7.5"). $200.

Bill of Hare (1962)
Original production cel of the Tazmanian Devil placed on color copy background. Unframed. Image size 4" × 5.5". $1,200.

Louvre Come back to Me (1962)
Original production background featuring the Mona Lisa right before Pepe Le Pew wipes the smile off her face. Unframed. $1,500.

Sheep in the Deep (1962)
Original production background. Unframed. $1,500.

The Spy Swatter (1967)
Original production cel of Daffy Duck with original matching production drawing. Unframed. 10.5" × 12.5" (image size 3.25" × 2"). $150.

The Spy Swatter (1967)
Original production cel of Speedy Gonzalez and matching production drawing. Unframed. 10.5" × 12.5" (image size 1" × 3"). $150.

A Connecticut Rabbit in King Arthur's Court (1978)

Original production cel of Elmer Fudd. Unframed. Image size 5" × 4". $150.

Bugs Bunny in King Arthur's Court (1978)

Production drawing of Yosemite Sam in graphite and blue pencil. Signed by Chuck Jones. Unframed. 11" × 13". $600.

Bugs Bunny's Bustin' out All Over (1980)

Production cel of Bugs Bunny with Chuck Jones seal. Unframed. 11" × 13". $395.

Carrotblanca (1995)

Original production cel of Daffy Duck and Kitty; two cels placed on color copy background. Unframed. 10.5" × 12.5" (image size 5" × 8"). $600.

Warner Brothers Studios: Original Production Drawings

Bugs Bunny and Daffy Duck

Original production drawing. Unframed. 11" × 13". $225.

Daffy Duck

Original production drawing. Unframed. 11" × 13". $295.

Daffy Duck and Bugs Bunny

Original production drawing. Unframed. 11" × 13". $250.

Daffy Duck and Porky Pig

Original production drawing of Daffy Duck and Porky Pig cheek to cheek. Unframed. 11" × 13". $125.

Metro-Goldwyn-Mayer: Original Production Cels

Tom & Jerry

Production cel of Jerry the mouse. Unframed. 11" × 13". $295.

Tom & Jerry

Production cel of Tom the cat and Jerry the mouse. Unframed. 11" × 13". $350.

Tom & Jerry

Production cel of Tom the cat. Unframed. 13" × 16". $150.

Tom & Jerry

Master setup of Jerry the mouse. Framed. $2,500.

Tom & Jerry

Master setup of Tom the cat from *Fine Feathered Friend*. The background is a master ground from *Barney's Victory Garden* (1942). Framed. $2,200.

Zoot Cat (1944)

Production drawing of Tom the cat. Unframed. 11" × 13". $395.

Mouse Cleaning (1948)

Production drawing of Jerry the mouse. Unframed. 11" × 13". $450.

Love Me, Love My Mouse (1966)

Production cel of Jerry the mouse and a female cat. Framed. 11" × 13". $100.

Chuck Jones: Original Production Cels
How the Grinch Stole Christmas (1966)

Original production cel of the Grinch matted with the autographs of Dr. Seuss and Chuck Jones. Unframed. 9" × 9". May 2002. $3,909.

How the Grinch Stole Christmas (1966)

Production cel of the Grinch. Signed by Chuck Jones. Unframed. 11" × 13". $2,200. *See illustration #239.*

How the Grinch Stole Christmas (1966)

Production cel of the Grinch (feet on a re-created cel by the studio). Signed by Chuck Jones. Unframed. 11" × 13". $2,200.

How the Grinch Stole Christmas (1966)

Original production cel of the Grinch and Max with a color laser background. Unframed. 10.5" × 12.5". $2,500.

How the Grinch Stole Christmas (1966)

Original production cel of Max and the sleigh with a color laser background. Unframed. 10.5" × 12.5" (image size 5.5" × 7"). $1,000.

How the Grinch Stole Christmas (1966)

Original production cel of the Grinch with a color laser background. Unframed. 10.5" × 12.5" (image size 8" × 2.5"). $1,500.

How the Grinch Stole Christmas (1966)

Production cel of Max. Signed by Chuck Jones. Unframed. 11" × 13". $2,100.

How the Grinch Stole Christmas (1966)

Production cel of Max over a photo background. Signed by Chuck Jones. Unframed. 11" x 13". $2,000.

Chuck Jones: Original Production Drawings
How the Grinch Stole Christmas (1966)

Production drawing of Max signed by Chuck Jones using Autopen. Unframed. 11" × 13". $900.

217 Production cel of the Grinch
© Chuck Jones

How the Grinch Stole Christmas (1966)

Production drawing of the Grinch. Nice large image of this fabulous villain. Signed by Chuck Jones. Unframed. 11" × 13". $900.

How the Grinch Stole Christmas (1966)

Production drawing of the Grinch. Signed by Chuck Jones. Unframed. 11" × 13". $750.

The Dot and the Line (1966)

Production drawing of Dot and the Line. Signed by Chuck Jones. Unframed. 11" × 13". $650.

The Dot and the Line (1966)

Production drawing of the Line. Signed by Chuck Jones using Autopen. Unframed. 11" × 13". $650.

Horton Hears a Who (1970)

Production cel of Horton. Unframed. 12.5" × 10". $900.

Horton Hears a Who (1970)

Production drawing of Horton. Signed by Chuck Jones. Unframed. 11" × 13". $400.

Yankee Doodle Cricket (1975)

Production cel of Tucker the mouse with Chuck Jones seal. Unframed. 11" × 13". $395.

Other Studios: Original Production Cels

Winnie the Pooh

Production cel of Eeyore from *Winnie the Pooh and a Day for Eeyore* (1983). Unframed. 10.5" × 12.5" (image size 2.5" × 3.25"). $400.

Winnie the Pooh

Production cel of Kanga. Unframed. 12.5" × 16" (image size 3" × 5"). $150.

Winnie the Pooh

Production two-cel setup of Piglet from *Winnie the Pooh and the Blustery Day* (1968). Unframed and trimmed to 5.5" × 9". Image size 3" × 3". $350.

Animal Farm (1954)

Production multicel setup of two cels featuring Snowball and Boxer applied to a studio key production background. Unframed. 7.5" × 9.25". December 2001. (Est. $440–$730) $225.

Yellow Submarine (1968)

Production cel of Ringo Starr and a Blue Meanie. Unframed. 13" × 16". $1,400.

Yellow Submarine (1968)

Production cel of Ringo Starr with color laser background. Unframed. $1,400.

Yellow Submarine (1968)

Production cel of Paul McCartney and Ringo Starr with the Yellow Sub and a funky object with confetti-like dots. Unframed. 11" × 13". $1,200.

Yellow Submarine (1968)

Production cel of the Blue Meanie. Unframed. 13" × 16". $750.

Yellow Submarine (1968)

Production cel of Jeremy Hilary Boob / Nowhere Man. Unframed. 13" × 16". $650.

Yellow Submarine (1968)

Production cel of the Blue Meanie and Paul McCartney with color laser background. Unframed. 13" × 16". $950.

Other Studios: Original Production Drawings

Yellow Submarine (1968)

Production drawing of John Lennon. Unframed. 11" × 13". $350.

Yellow Submarine (1968)

Production drawing of Ringo Starr (excessive handling to page). Unframed. 13" × 16". $150.

Yellow Submarine (1968)

Production drawing of Old Fred. Unframed. 13" × 16". $150.

5 Movie Scripts

COLLECTING MOVIE SCRIPTS

Looking through a production-used movie script can give a film fan a unique insight into the creative process of filmmaking.

The adaptation of the original writers' vision into what eventually becomes the finished product—the film—is a process involving continual input and countless revisions from the directors, producers, cinematographers, script rewriters (or script doctors), and the actors themselves. *See illustration #218.*

A film script will have many variations and versions known as drafts or revisions, that vary in terms of dialogue or additional characters and revised and deleted scenes. Most of the time revised drafts of a film script do not make it out of the studio's hands until a final draft or *screenplay* is reproduced and sold as a published book to accompany the release of a film. Sometimes a photocopied script-like version of the screenplay will be sold as an acting school guide. It is very important to note that these mass-produced items are not considered collectible but consumable goods.

Collectible Movie Scripts

The items that are classified as collectible movie scripts are the *production-used* scripts that are printed in very limited quantities and actually used during the production of the film. These were *not* intended to be sold outside the production circle and are many times sequentially numbered and inscribed to a specific crew or cast member.

The following lists the key indicators that a script is a production-used collectible:

Studio Stamp on Cover

Many production-used scripts have a cover page with specific studio contact information listing the producer and the production company.

Production Code

A number assigned to the film by the studio is stamped on the front cover page.

Sequential Number

A number (001–1,000 or however large the script runs require) used to allow the studio to allocate each numbered copy to a specific cast or crew member on the project is stamped on the front cover page.

Crew Name

A script may be labeled with a specific cast or crew name and is printed by the studio or handwritten by the production office.

Leather-Bound Cover

Scripts belonging to key cast members and the director and producer may have leather-bound covers with the owner's name etched in gold lettering on the front. Many times this was done by the producers for the key players as a sign of appreciation for their participation in the project. *See illustration #219.*

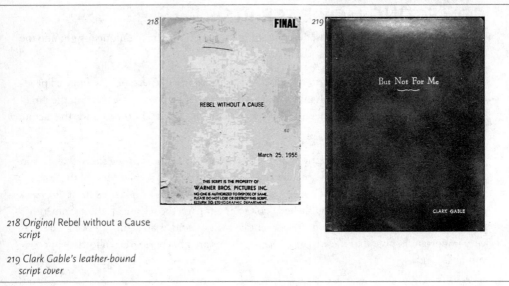

218 *Original* Rebel without a Cause
script

219 *Clark Gable's leather-bound
script cover*

Colored Insert Pages

During the course of production on a film, various scene and dialogue changes are made from the final draft script. When these scenes have been retyped, they are usually reproduced on different colored pages to distinguish them from the tan-colored pages in the regular script. Many times, these pages are found inserted loosely into the script before or after the original pages, but sometimes they are actually bound into the script, with the original pages removed.

Shooting Schedules/Production Notes

A producer distributes shooting notices or schedules regarding the film during different stages of production. In some cases, these production notes and schedules are inserted inside the script, and this is a very good indication that the script is production-used.

Handwritten Notations

Handwritten notations by a crew or cast member can vary from key dialogue and motivational notations to camera instructions to a phone number or grocery list. Many times, these notations can provide the most interesting insights into the creative process from the perspective of that particular artist.

The following pages offer examples of Paul Newman's personal shooting script from *Buffalo Bill and the Indians* (1976), the Robert Altman–directed film starring Newman in the title role of Buffalo Bill. *See illustrations # 220, 221, 222, 223, and 224.*

Factors That Determine Value
Provenance and Authenticity

All production-used scripts should be considered scarce. At the conclusion of production on a film, most studios require cast and crew to return the scripts to the studio offices where they

220

221

222

220 The script is bound in full leather with "Paul Newman of First Artists" (Newman's production company) stamped in gold on the cover.

221 Newman has boldly signed the title page, as has Robert Altman. Note: The random handwritten notes include Robert Redford's phone number at the time!

222 Included is a 1976 letter on Newman's stationery to actress Jane Fonda presenting the script to her for a charity auction that she conducted.

223

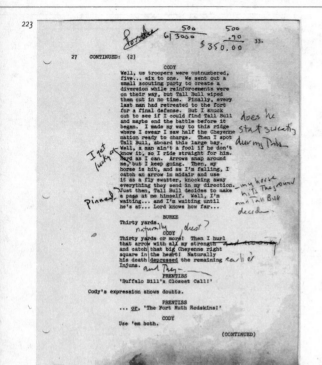

224

223 and 224 The script is heavily annotated throughout by the actor with his notes and changes to the dialogue, with many sentences written in his hand.

are locked away. The studios own the copyright to the material contained in the scripts and are very interested in keeping their expensive properties a secret until the film is released (which could be anywhere from six months to two years from the end of filming).

The few scripts that are personally kept are in most cases the leather-bound examples from the key players, and these are usually stored in the owners' private libraries. When an original script is offered to the collecting marketplace, studios attempt (sometimes successfully) to stop the sale, citing their copyright ownership of the work. Usually the only time that a sale cannot be prevented is if there is a *letter of provenance* from the original owner accompanying the script. Sometimes a celebrity will donate his or her copy of the script to a charity auction or sale, and this letter is key for this specific reason. Without this letter of provenance it is very difficult to authenticate a script as production-used.

In a collectible world that is rife with forgeries and reproductions, movie scripts are also a popular choice for those looking to deceive. The most frequent fake examples are cheaply reproduced photocopies of mass-produced screenplays that have been forged with signatures and notations from a star or stars of a film. One should always purchase from reputable dealers and look for the above-listed features of production-used scripts as a guide to authenticity.

Condition
The condition of the script can also play a role in the overall value. Collectors look for scripts that are complete, meaning all pages intact, and in the best condition possible. Stains, age toning, and water damage can also affect the value.

Content
The content of the script refers to the importance of the film or owner of the script. For example, a production-used script from *The Godfather* used by the makeup artist on the film will have a substantial value based on the importance of the film itself. A copy of the same script from the same film belonging to Marlon Brando with his personal dialogue notations would have a value probably ten to twenty times greater, based on the combination of the film and the owner. This would also mean that Brando's personal notated script from a less-known film like *Don Juan DeMarco* would have more value than a makeup artist's script from the same film, but substantially less than Brando's *Godfather* example.

MOVIE SCRIPT PRICE LISTINGS
There have been some incredible prices paid for original production-used scripts in recent years. Here are some highlights:

Bonnie and Clyde
A 129-page draft script belonging to Warren Beatty and filled with his personal handwritten notations throughout sold at auction in March 2000 for $4,500 (including buyer's premium).

Bonnie and Clyde
A 134-page final draft script dated September 6, 1966, sold at auction in March 2000 for $2,000 (including buyer's premium).

Bus Stop

A 123-page script that was Marilyn Monroe's personal copy with her initials "MM" in red ink on first page with numerous handwritten notations by Monroe throughout sold at auction in October 1999 for $40,250 (including buyer's premium).

Citizen Kane

A 156-page third revised final script dated July 16, 1940, sold at auction in March 2000 for $3,000 (including buyer's premium).

Giant

A 178-page final draft script bound with three binder clips and original chipboard cover sold at auction in March 2000 for $1,900 (including buyer's premium).

Gone with the Wind

In December 1996, Steven Spielberg paid $244,500 (including buyer's premium) for Clark Gable's leather-bound personal shooting script from the 1939 classic. It is interesting to note that Christie's auction house estimated the script would fetch between $30,000 and $50,000.

Gone with the Wind

In June 1999, another rare version of the script, dubbed a Rainbow script (due to the multi-colored pages) sold for $46,000 (including buyer's premium) in a Sotheby's auction. The script featured alternate takes, including Rhett Butler's famous line "Frankly, my dear, I don't give a damn" prepared for censorship protection to read "Frankly, my dear, I just don't care." This lot was estimated in the $40,000–$60,000 range.

Gone with the Wind

A final version of the shooting script, but without the fanfare of Gable's ownership or the rainbow-colored alternate scenes, sold for just over $8,200 in a June 2002 auction of *GWTW* memorabilia collected for over forty years by famed collector Herb Bridges.

Let's Make Love

A 139-page second revised shooting final script belonging to Marilyn Monroe sold at auction in October 1999 for $11,500 (including buyer's premium).

Philadelphia Story

A 131-page working copy script from second unit director Jack Greegwood with numerous hand notations and over fifty black-and-white production snapshots sold at auction in November of 2001 for $588 (including buyer's premium).

Rebel without a Cause

An original Warner Brothers script, 8.5" × 11", 122 pages, and five original 8.5" × 15" photo-copied screen test call sheets (listing Jayne Mansfield as a hopeful contender) issued to Beverly Long, who played the part of Helen, accompanied by Long's letter of provenance, sold at auction in June of 2000 for $3,450 (including buyer's premium).

Some Like It Hot

A 122-page script belonging to Marilyn Monroe with "MMM" (Marilyn Monroe Miller) written in red crayon on the front cover sold at auction in October 1999 for $51,750 (including buyer's premium).

Some Like It Hot

A 156-page version of the script belonging to Marilyn Monroe with her numerous handwritten notations written throughout sold at auction in October 1999 for $63,000 (including buyer's premium).

Something's Got to Give

Marilyn Monroe's personal annotated shooting script for her final, unfinished motion picture, with five cover sheets and 126 pages of script (99 pages on blue sheets, representing late revisions), dated April 17–May 22, 1962. Studio secretaries attached a typed note informing Monroe that the revised script from writer Nunnally Johnson will be sent the following day, "as it is not ready tonight," and a penciled list of her 9:00 A.M. set call for Stage 8, with scenes A133–A137 to be shot. Monroe had added her own notes and markings in pencil or crayon scattered throughout the script. This example sold in June of 2000 for $23,000 (including buyer's premium).

Star Wars

An original shooting script, fourth draft, dated 1/1/76 with original blue binder and decal labeled "The Star Wars," sold for $4,000 in an on-line auction in April 2001. This was a rare example, as very few of these original scripts have ever been offered to the collecting marketplace.

The Misfits

A 146-page script belonging to Marilyn Monroe with numerous handwritten notes throughout sold at auction in October 1999 for $43,700 (including buyer's premium).

The Seven Year Itch

Marilyn Monroe's personal 113-page working script with numerous pencil notations in her hand sold at auction in March 2000 for $100,000 (including buyer's premium).

The Wolf Man

An original Universal Studios File Copy script for *The Wolf Man* with Lon Chaney, dated December 5, 1941, sold at auction in April 1998 for $3,857 (including buyer's premium).

6 Collecting Oscar Statuettes

COLLECTING OSCAR STATUETTES

The Academy Award and its Oscar statuette signify an achievement of unparalleled excellence in filmmaking.

For the film artisan, there is no higher honor than to be awarded an Oscar by the Academy of Motion Picture Arts and Sciences (AMPAS).

For the collector of unique and one-of-a-kind movie memorabilia, there is no more appealing item than an original Oscar statuette. *See illustration #225.*

The Oscar statuette was designed by MGM art director Cedric Gibbons and sculpted by George Stanley in 1927. It is 13.5 inches high and weighs 8.5 pounds and depicts a knight holding a crusader's sword. The knight strands on a reel of film with five spokes symbolizing the original five branches of the Academy: Actors, Writers, Directors, Producers, and Technicians. Since the first Award ceremonies in 1928, the statuette itself has seen little change in overall design:

- In the 1930s, child performers received miniature replicas of the statuette.

- Walt Disney was presented one full-size and seven miniature statuettes for *Snow White and the Seven Dwarfs* (1937).

- In support of the war effort during World War II, statuettes presented between 1942 and 1944 were made of plaster. After the war, the temporary statuettes were replaced by the Academy with golden versions.

- In early 1945, the base of the statuette was changed from marble to metal.

- Starting in 1949, all Academy Award statuettes were numbered (starting with No. 501).

Oscar statuettes first began to make their way into private hands in the 1940s, when down-on-their-luck past Oscar winners began to sell their statuettes to cover their financial debts. The statuettes sometimes made their way into the display windows of Hollywood pawnshops. To protect the image and stature of the Academy Award and Oscar symbols, the Academy introduced a contract in 1950 that is still in place to this day. The contract must be signed by all Oscar winners and stipulates that an Oscar statuette may be passed down to a family member or heir, but if the recipient or heir wishes to sell the Oscar, they must offer the Academy first right of refusal in exchange for ten dollars. In the 1980s, the amount was lowered to one dollar to suggest that the money was a token figure and not an expression of the value of the statuette.

From 1950 until the early 1990s, the buying and selling of pre-1950 Oscar statuettes (not covered by the agreement) took place between dealers and collectors for a few hundred dollars. Most examples were for less-known films and less-prestigious award categories such as Best Wardrobe or Best Sound. These items were not really considered collectibles but were viewed as interesting objects to place on a fireplace mantel.

This all changed in 1993, when Vivien Leigh's Oscar statuette for her Best Actress performance as Scarlett O'Hara in *Gone with the Wind* sold for $563,000 in a Sotheby's auction. This

225

225 *Oscar statuette*

© A.M.P.A.S.

incredible price was a record for an Oscar statuette and declared the Oscar statuette a viable investment-grade commodity. The current world record price for an Oscar statuette was set in a June 1999 Sotheby's auction when $1,542,500 was paid for David O. Selznick's 1939 Best Picture Oscar from *Gone with the Wind*. The presale estimate was $300,000, and the winning bidder was Michael Jackson.

The incredible realized prices and insatiable publicity of auctions for Oscar statuettes incensed the Academy, which had pledged since the 1950 agreement to keep the Oscar a sacred award earned by achievement and not by purchase. One of the most dramatic battles between the Academy and the marketplace has been the almost ten-year legal saga of Judy Garland's 1940 Oscar for *The Wizard of Oz*. Garland was awarded a miniature Oscar statuette for her role as Dorothy Gale in the 1939 MGM classic. In 1993, Sid Luft (Garland's former husband and apparent heir to the statuette) consigned the statuette to Christie's auction house in what was expected to be the most heated and record-breaking sale in movie memorabilia history. The Academy was resigned to the fact that there was nothing it could do about the sale, as the Oscar predated the 1950 agreement by ten years. This all changed after officials watched a *Today* show program promoting the sale. The program displayed some of the sale articles, including the statuette, which appeared to look different from the statuette that was presented to Garland, as depicted in the 1940 file photos the Academy owned.

In searching its files, the Academy found a 1958 letter from Garland's publicity firm stating that the original statuette had been lost and asking for a replacement statuette at Garland's expense. The Academy replaced the Oscar after having Garland sign a first right-of-refusal contract covering the duplicate Oscar and any others that might be in her possession. The Christie's sale was stopped, and a two-year legal battle ended with Luft being ordered to return the statuette to the Academy. Luft countered that he had given the statuette to Garland's daughter Lorna Luft, and the Academy was satisfied that the statuette was now in an heir's possession and not available for sale.

In May 2000, Sid Luft consigned what he declared to be Garland's original Oscar to an on-line autograph dealer with a $3 million price tag. The Academy, still reeling from its previous battle with Luft, hired a private investigator to pose as a memorabilia dealer of Oscar statuettes. The investigator met with Luft and arranged an appraisal of the statuette by none other than the Academy's own appraiser. The appraiser authenticated the statuette as indeed being the original 1940 Garland Oscar. The Academy pressed on with another lawsuit, with Luft declaring in court that this statuette was in fact a fake that was created by a friend to raise his spirits when he was in the hospital in the mid-1980s. The Academy won its battle on two counts, as the court ruled that the signed agreement covered any and all Garland Oscar statuettes, and Luft was ordered to surrender to the Academy not only the original Oscar, but all known copies including the 1958 replacement.

Another problem for the Academy was that it did not have the budget to purchase and remove from publicly traded markets the pre-1950 Oscars it viewed as important relics of Hollywood and Academy history. In December 1996 the Academy took legal action to stop the sale of Clark Gable's 1934 Best Actor Oscar for *It Happened One Night,* which John Gable, the actor's son, had consigned to Christie's auction house. The Academy claimed that Gable had signed a first right-of-refusal agreement for his Oscar in 1960 (two years before his death). Christie's claimed the signature was a fake. The case was disallowed by the judge, who ruled that the Academy had not given proper notice to Christie's and that it did not notify John Gable (also named as a defendant) of the hearing.

On December 15, 1996, the Gable Oscar was auctioned and realized a new record price at that time of $607,500. The winning bidder was Steven Spielberg, and acting as a guardian angel for the Academy, Spielberg donated the Oscar statuette to the Academy. The Academy claimed that it had no advance knowledge of his plan. In a letter to the Academy, Spielberg stated, "The Oscar statuette is the most personal recognition of good work our industry can ever bestow, and it strikes me as a sad sign of our times that this icon could be confused with a commercial treasure." In another Christie's auction in July 2001, Spielberg anonymously bid $578,000 to win Bette Davis's 1938 Best Actress Oscar for *Jezebel* and once again donated the statuette to the Academy. In September of 2001, actor Kevin Spacey anonymously bid $156,875 to win composer George Stoll's 1945 Oscar for *Anchors Aweigh* (paying over seven times the auction house estimate) and donated the Oscar statuette to the Academy.

Currently, the marketplace for Oscar statuettes is almost nonexistent. The Academy has begun to take action against the sale of statuettes of lesser-known Oscar winners predating their 1950 agreements. In August of 2002, a collector auctioned Leonard M. Smith's 1946 Best Cinematography Oscar statuette for *The Yearling* on eBay. During the auction, the Academy publicly announced its intent to block the sale, even though it may not have had the legal right to do so. The statuette was obtained originally from the heir of the estate in April 2000 and predates the 1950 Academy agreement. The threat of costly legal action by the Academy was enough to scare off potential bidders, and the auction was unsuccessful. In October 2000, William Doyle Galleries auctioned property from the estate of James Cagney and his wife, Frances Vernon. The featured lot in the auction was Cagney's 1942 Best Actor Oscar statuette for *Yankee Doodle Dandy.* The Oscar was estimated in the $300,000–$500,000 range, but failed to reach the undisclosed reserve price.

Academy personnel welcomed the lackluster results of the Cagney sale as an indication that the marketplace no longer looks at the Oscar statuette as viable for private collectors. If auction houses and their consignors face costly legal action when they attempt to sell an Oscar statuette (even if they are legally entitled to sell it), and when private collectors know they will be vastly outbid by wealthy guardian angel celebrities, the end of the publicly traded Oscar statuette marketplace may be close to becoming a reality.

It should also be noted that there is actually a marketplace that deals in illegal sales of post-1950 Oscar statuettes. These sales are handled very privately and are never publicly reported. Hollywood stars still have the same roller-coaster career highs and lows, and their Oscar statuettes have value to a certain type of collector because of their forbidden fruit nature. It is against the law to sell or purchase a post-1950 Oscar statuette, and a collector who purchases a post-1950 Oscar will have to display the statue privately. If the statue is ever discovered and reported to the Academy, the collector will lose the purchase (and the sizable amount of money spent on it), and they, the seller, and the Oscar winner may face embarrassing criminal proceedings.

RESOURCE GUIDE

Magazines and On-Line References

Animation World Magazine
6525 Sunset Blvd., Garden Suite 10
Hollywood, CA 90028
http://mag.awn.com
(Animation Art)

Autograph Collector Magazine
Odyssey Publications
510-A S. Corona Mall
Corona, CA 91719-1420
(800) 996–3977
http://www.autographcollector.com
(Autographs)

Big Reel
Krause Publications, Inc.
700 E. State St.
Iola, WI 54990
(715) 445–4612
http://www.collect.com/interest/periodical.asp?Pub=BI
(Autographs, Posters)

Classic Images
301 East 3rd St.
Muscatine, IA 52761
(563) 263–2331
http://www.classicimages.com
(Movie Collectibles)

Internet Movie Database
http://www.imdb.com
(Ultimate movie reference database)

Movie Collector's World
Box 309
Fraser, MI 48026
(586) 774–4311
http://www.mcwonline.com
(Posters, Memorabilia)

Paper Collectors' Marketplace
Box 128W
Scandinavia, WI 54977-0128
(715) 467–2379
http://www.tias.com/mags/pcm/
(Paper Collectibles)

Posterprice.com
(845) 452–1998
http://www.posterprice.com
(Movie Poster Reference and Directory)

Collector Clubs and Organizations

International Animated Film Society: ASIFA HOLLYWOOD
725 S. Victory Blvd.
Burbank, CA 91502
(818) 842–8330
http://www.asifa-hollywood.org

International Auotgraph Collectors Club (IACC/DA)
Box 848486
Hollywood, FL 33084
http://www.iacc-da.org/

Professional Autograph Dealers Association (P.A.D.A.)
Box 1729-W
Murray Hill Station
New York, NY 10156
(888) 338–4338
http://www.padaweb.org

Universal Autograph Collectors Club (UACC)
Box 6181
Washington, DC 20044-6181
http://www.uacc.org

Auction Houses and Retailers

Bruce Hershenson
Box 874
West Plains, MO 65775
(417) 256–9616
http://www.brucehershenson.com
(Movie Posters)

Butterfields
220 San Bruno Ave.
San Francisco, CA 94103
(415) 861–7500
http://www.butterfields.com
(Autographs, Props, Wardrobe, Posters)

Christie's
360 North Camden Dr.
Beverly Hills, CA 90210
(310) 385–2600
http://www.christies.com
(Autographs, Props, Wardrobe, Animation Art, Posters)

Christie's
20 Rockefeller Plaza
New York, NY 10020
(212) 636–2000
http://www.christies.com
(Autographs, Props, Wardrobe, Animation Art, Posters)

Christie's
8 King St., St. James's
London   SW1Y 6QT
United Kingdom
44 14 7839 9060
http://www.christies.com
(Autographs, Props, Wardrobe, Animation Art, Posters)

Christie's
85 Old Brompton Rd.
London   SW7 3LD
United Kingdom
44 14 7752 7611
http://www.christies.com
(Autographs, Props, Wardrobe, Animation Art, Posters)

Daniel Cohen Autographs & Memorabilia
Box 515
Kleinburg, Ontario L0J 1C0
Canada
(905) 893–2328
http://www.danielcohen.com
(Autographs)

eBay Inc.
2145 Hamilton Ave.
San Jose, CA 95125
http://www.ebay.com
(Autographs, Props, Wardrobe, Animation Art, Posters)

Mastronet, Inc.
1515 W. 22nd St.
Oak Brook, IL 60523
(630) 472–1200
http://www.mastronet.com
(Autographs, Props, Wardrobe, Animation Art, Posters)

Profiles in History
110 North Doheny Dr.
Beverly Hills, CA 90211
(310) 859–7701
http://www.profilesinhistory.com
(Autographs, Props, Wardrobe, Scripts)

Prop Store of London
Great House Farm
Chenies, Rickmansworth
Hertfordshire, WD3 6EP
United Kingdom
44 14 9476 6485
http://www.propstore.co.uk
(Props, Wardrobe)

R & R Enterprises Autograph Auctions
3 Chestnut Dr.
Bedford, NH 03110
(603) 471–0808
http://www.rrauction.com
(Autographs, Animation Art, Props, Wardrobe, Scripts)

Reelclothes
5525 Cahuenga Blvd.
North Hollywood, CA 91601
(818) 508–7762
www.reelclothes.com
(Props, Wardrobe)

Sotheby's
1334 York Ave.
New York, NY 10021
(212) 606–7000
http://sothebys.ebay.com/
(Autographs, Props, Wardrobe, Animation Art, Posters)

Sotheby's
34-35 New Bond St.
London W1A 2AA
United Kingdom
44 20 7293 5000
http://sothebys.ebay.com/
(Autographs, Props, Wardrobe, Animation Art, Posters)

Sotheby's
Hammersmith Rd.
London W148UX
United Kingdom
44 20 7293 5555
http://sothebys.ebay.com/
(Autographs, Props, Wardrobe, Animation Art, Posters)

Startifacts
3101 East Hennepin Ave.
Minneapolis, MN 55413
(612) 331–6454
www.startifacts.com
(Props, Wardrobe)

Starwares
2817 Main St.
Santa Monica, CA 90405
(310) 399–0224
http://www.starwares.com
(Props, Wardrobe)

Wonderful World of Animation Art Gallery
218 South Robertson Blvd.
Beverly Hills, CA 90211
(310) 623–1833
http://www.animationartgallery.com
(Animation Art)

INDEX

HOUSE OF COLLECTIBLES
COMPLETE TITLE LIST

THE OFFICIAL PRICE GUIDES TO

American Arts and Crafts, 3rd ed.	0-609-80989-X	$21.95	David Rago
American Patriotic Memorabilia	0-609-81014-6	$16.95	Michael Polak
America's State Quarters	0-609-80770-6	$6.99	David L. Ganz
Collecting Books, 4th ed.	0-609-80769-2	$18.00	Marie Tedford
Collecting Clocks	0-609-80973-3	$19.95	Frederick W. Korz
Collector Knives, 14th ed.	1-4000-4834-6	$17.95	C. Houston Price
Collector Plates	0-676-60154-5	$19.95	Harry L. Rinker
Costume Jewelry, 3rd ed.	0-609-80668-8	$17.95	Harrice Simmons Miller
Dinnerware of the 20th Century	0-676-60085-9	$29.95	Harry L. Rinker
Flea Market Prices, 2nd ed.	1-4000-4889-3	$14.95	Harry L. Rinker
Glassware, 3rd ed.	0-676-60188-X	$17.00	Mark Pickvet
Hake's Character Toys, 4th ed.	0-609-80822-2	$35.00	Ted Hake
Hislop's International Guide to Fine Art	0-609-80874-5	$20.00	Duncan Hislop
Military Collectibles, 7th ed.	1-4000-4941-5	$20.00	Richard Austin
Mint Errors, 6th ed.	0-609-80855-9	$15.00	Alan Herbert
Movie Autographs and Memorabilia	1-4000-4731-5	$20.00	Daniel Cohen
Native American Art	0-609-80966-0	$24.00	Dawn E. Reno
Overstreet Comic Book Companion, 8th ed.	0-375-72065-0	$7.99	Robert M. Overstreet
Overstreet Comic Book Grading	0-609-81052-9	$24.00	Robert M. Overstreet
Overstreet Comic Book Price Guide, 33rd ed.	1-4000-4668-8	$25.00	Robert M. Overstreet
Overstreet Indian Arrowheads Price Guide, 8th ed.	0-609-81053-7	$26.00	Robert M. Overstreet
Pottery and Porcelain	0-87637-893-9	$18.00	Harvey Duke
Quilts, 2nd ed.	1-4000-4797-8	$16.00	Aleshire/Barach
Records, 16th ed.	0-609-80908-3	$25.95	Jerry Osborne

THE OFFICIAL GUIDES TO

Coin Grading and Counterfeit Detection	0-375-72050-2	$19.95	P. C. G. S.
How to Make Money in Coins Right Now	0-609-80746-3	$14.95	Scott A. Travers
The Official Directory to U.S. Flea Markets	0-609-80922-9	$14.00	Kitty Werner
The One-Minute Coin Expert, 4th ed.	0-609-80747-1	$7.99	Scott A. Travers
The Official Stamp Collector's Bible	0-609-80884-2	$22.00	Stephen Datz

THE OFFICIAL BECKETT SPORTS CARDS PRICE GUIDES TO

Baseball Cards 2004, 24th ed.	0-375-72055-3	$7.99	Dr. James Beckett
Basketball Cards 2004, 13th ed.	1-4000-4863-X	$7.99	Dr. James Beckett
Football Cards 2004, 23rd ed.	1-4000-4864-8	$7.99	Dr. James Beckett

THE OFFICIAL BLACKBOOK PRICE GUIDES TO

U.S. Coins, 42nd ed.	1-4000-4805-2	$7.99	Marc & Tom Hudgeons
U.S. Paper Money, 36th ed.	1-4000-4806-0	$6.99	Marc & Tom Hudgeons
U.S. Postage Stamps, 26th ed.	1-4000-4807-9	$8.99	Marc & Tom Hudgeons
World Coins, 7th ed.	1-4000-4808-7	$7.99	Marc & Tom Hudgeons

AVAILABLE AT BOOKSTORES EVERYWHERE!